T0321801

Applying Integration Techniques and Methods in Distributed Systems and Technologies

Gabor Kecskemeti
Liverpool John Moores University, UK

A volume in the Advances in Computer and Electrical Engineering (ACEE) Book Series

Published in the United States of America by
IGI Global
Engineering Science Reference (an imprint of IGI Global)
701 E. Chocolate Avenue
Hershey PA, USA 17033
Tel: 717-533-8845
Fax: 717-533-8661
E-mail: cust@igi-global.com
Web site: http://www.igi-global.com

Library of Congress Cataloging-in-Publication Data

Names: Kecskemeti, Gabor, 1981- editor.
Title: Applying integration techniques and methods in distributed systems and technologies / Gabor Kecskemeti, editor.
Description: Hershey, PA : Engineering Science Reference, [2019] | Includes bibliographic references.
Identifiers: LCCN 2018050687| ISBN 9781522582953 (hardcover) | ISBN 9781522582960 (ebook)
Subjects: LCSH: Electronic data processing--Distributed processing. | Computer architecture. | Cloud computing. | Distributed databases.
Classification: LCC QA76.9.D5 A68 2019 | DDC 005.75/8--dc23 LC record available at https://lccn.loc.gov/2018050687

This book is published in the IGI Global book series Advances in Computer and Electrical Engineering (ACEE) (ISSN: 2327-039X; eISSN: 2327-0403)

British Cataloguing in Publication Data
A Cataloguing in Publication record for this book is available from the British Library.

All work contributed to this book is new, previously-unpublished material.
The views expressed in this book are those of the authors, but not necessarily of the publisher.

For electronic access to this publication, please contact: eresources@igi-global.com.

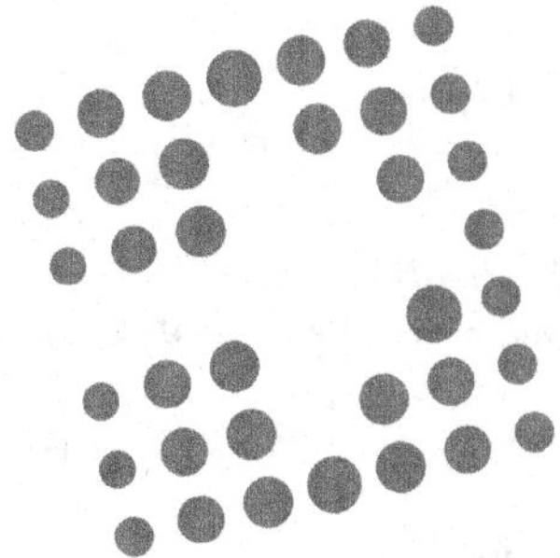

Advances in Computer and Electrical Engineering (ACEE) Book Series

ISSN:2327-039X
EISSN:2327-0403

Editor-in-Chief: Srikanta Patnaik, SOA University, India

MISSION

The fields of computer engineering and electrical engineering encompass a broad range of interdisciplinary topics allowing for expansive research developments across multiple fields. Research in these areas continues to develop and become increasingly important as computer and electrical systems have become an integral part of everyday life.

The **Advances in Computer and Electrical Engineering (ACEE) Book Series** aims to publish research on diverse topics pertaining to computer engineering and electrical engineering. **ACEE** encourages scholarly discourse on the latest applications, tools, and methodologies being implemented in the field for the design and development of computer and electrical systems.

COVERAGE

- VLSI Design
- Computer Architecture
- VLSI Fabrication
- Digital Electronics
- Algorithms
- Optical Electronics
- Sensor Technologies
- Chip Design
- Electrical Power Conversion
- Applied Electromagnetics

IGI Global is currently accepting manuscripts for publication within this series. To submit a proposal for a volume in this series, please contact our Acquisition Editors at Acquisitions@igi-global.com or visit: http://www.igi-global.com/publish/.

The Advances in Computer and Electrical Engineering (ACEE) Book Series (ISSN 2327-039X) is published by IGI Global, 701 E. Chocolate Avenue, Hershey, PA 17033-1240, USA, www.igi-global.com. This series is composed of titles available for purchase individually; each title is edited to be contextually exclusive from any other title within the series. For pricing and ordering information please visit http://www.igi-global.com/book-series/advances-computer-electrical-engineering/73675. Postmaster: Send all address changes to above address.

Titles in this Series

For a list of additional titles in this series, please visit:
https://www.igi-global.com/book-series/advances-computer-electrical-engineering/73675]

Handbook of Research on Cloud Computing and Big Data Applications in IoT
B. B. Gupta (National Institute of Technology Kurukshetra, India) and Dharma P. Agrawal (University of Cincinnati, USA)
Engineering Science Reference • ©2019 • 609pp • H/C (ISBN: 9781522584070) • US $295.00

Multi-Objective Stochastic Programming in Fuzzy Environments
Animesh Biswas (University of Kalyani, India) and Arnab Kumar De (Government College of Engineering and Textile Technology Serampore, India)
Engineering Science Reference • ©2019 • 420pp • H/C (ISBN: 9781522583011) • US $215.00

Renewable Energy and Power Supply Challenges for Rural Regions
Valeriy Kharchenko (Federal Scientific Agroengineering Center VIM, Russia) and Pandian Vasant (Universiti Teknologi PETRONAS, Malaysia)
Engineering Science Reference • ©2019 • 432pp • H/C (ISBN: 9781522591795) • US $205.00

Secure Cyber-Physical Systems for Smart Cities
Riaz Ahmed Shaikh (King Abdulaziz University, Saudi Arabia)
Engineering Science Reference • ©2019 • 280pp • H/C (ISBN: 9781522571896) • US $225.00

Handbook of Research on Smart Power System Operation and Control
Hassan Haes Alhelou (Tishreen University, Syria) and Ghassan Hayek (Tishreen University, Syria)
Engineering Science Reference • ©2019 • 489pp • H/C (ISBN: 9781522580300) • US $265.00

Cases on Modern Computer Systems in Aviation
Tetiana Shmelova (National Aviation University, Ukraine) Yuliya Sikirda (National Aviation University, Ukraine) Nina Rizun (Gdansk University of Technology, Poland) and Dmytro Kucherov (National Aviation University, Ukraine)
Engineering Science Reference • ©2019 • 488pp • H/C (ISBN: 9781522575887) • US $225.00

For an entire list of titles in this series, please visit:
https://www.igi-global.com/book-series/advances-computer-electrical-engineering/73675]

701 East Chocolate Avenue, Hershey, PA 17033, USA
Tel: 717-533-8845 x100 • Fax: 717-533-8661
E-Mail: cust@igi-global.com • www.igi-global.com

Table of Contents

Detailed Table of Contents

Cloud computing ignited many innovations and disruptions in the traditional way of doing business. The innovations in cloud computing are countable, and innovations due to cloud computing are endless, as there are several applications where cloud computing has proven its usefulness. The discussion starts with innovation records by software companies that happened due to cloud computing. This chapter illuminates an amalgamation of advanced concepts, products, and services in cloud computing. The chapter further discusses the conceptual innovations of API management, serverless computing, content delivery network, storage services, data center technologies, all-flash arrays, and digital twin due to cloud computing.

Fog computing is an encouraging computational model that extends distributed cloud computing to the edge of systems. It varies to cloud computing with some of the attributes. Fog computing has new challenges while building and maintaining the trust among the fog nodes and with edge devices. The solutions applied for the various cloud challenges cannot be directly applied for fog computing. This chapter gives an overview of these difficulties and relates solutions in a concise way. It also highlights the open challenges that still exist in fog computing.

Chapter 3
Convergence of Manufacturing Cloud and Industrial IoT 49
Manoj Himmatrao Devare, Amity University Mumbai, India

The manufacturing cloud (CMfg) covers the use of three key technologies including cloud computing, the industrial internet of things (IIoT), and collaborative engineering for achieving the productivity and quality challenges in the big manufacturing, which is enabled due to the communication, mobile, and broadcasting network. It is necessary to establish a flexible and adaptive infrastructure for manufacturing industry to share and use various manufacturing resources and services on-demand under the dynamic, complicated, and large-scale business environment. The CMfg makes the industry more agile, responsive, and reconfigurable for exposure to the industry as a global manufacturing enterprise. The chapter considers the CMfg facets and IIoT, use cases in the manufacturing industry, and explains IIoT and CMfg as a complementary technology.

Chapter 4
Security Challenges and Resolution in Cloud Computing and Cloud of Things 79
Mamata Rath, Birla Global University, India

Cloud computing is a developing zone of computing innovation that shapes the handling power and the computing assets of many associated, topographically separated PCs associated by means of internet. Cloud computing wipes out the need of having a total framework of equipment and programming to meet clients' prerequisites and applications. It very well may be thought of as a total or an incomplete outsourcing of equipment and programming assets. To get to cloud applications, a great internet association and a standard internet program are required. Cloud computing has its own particular downside from the security perspective; this chapter addresses the vast majority of these dangers and their conceivable arrangements. Cloud computing gives its client numerous abilities like getting to an expansive number of utilizations without the requirement for having a permit, acquiring, introducing, or downloading any of these applications.

The Internet of Things (IoT) paradigm is foreseeing the development of our environment towards new enriched spaces in most areas of modern living, such as digital health, smart cities, and smart agriculture. Several IoT applications also have real-time and low-latency requirements and must rely on specific architectures. The authors refer to the paradigm that best fits the selected IoT scenario as "Big Stream" because it considers real-time constraints. Moreover, the blockchain concept has drawn attention as the next-generation technology through the authentication of peers that share encryption and the generation of hash values. In addition, the blockchain can be applied in conjunction with Cloud Computing and the IoT paradigms, since it avoids the involvement of third parties in a broker-free way. In this chapter, an analysis on mechanisms that can be adopted to secure Big Stream data in a graph-based platform, thus delivering them to consumers in an efficient and secure way, and with low latency, is shown, describing all refinements required employing federation-based and blockchain paradigms.

Since the deployment of IP multicast remains restricted due to many practical and political issues, researchers have shifted focus to exploiting application-layer multicast for multicast data delivery. Recently there has been considerable interest in applying DHT routing algorithms to application-level multicast. However, early DHT-based multicast protocols are insufficient in addressing a number of technical issues such as heterogeneous capacity of nodes or node churn. In this chapter, the author describes a solution called BAM-Chord (i.e., Bandwidth Adaptive Multicast over Chord) that optimizes the topology of a multicast tree based on node bandwidth. In the proposed solution, node position (i.e., node identifier) on a BAM-Chord ring will be decided based on node bandwidth capacity such that it can build a wide and balanced multicast tree rooted at the source node. As a result, BAM-Chord protocol can utilize network resources of every node to reduce the depth of the multicast tree and take advantages of DHTs in maintaining the multicast tree.

Storage elasticity on the cloud is a crucial feature in the age of data-intensive computing, especially when considering fluctuations of I/O throughput. In this chapter, the authors explore how to transparently boost the I/O bandwidth during peak utilization to deliver high performance without over-provisioning storage resources. The proposal relies on the idea of leveraging short-lived virtual disks of better performance characteristics (and more expensive) to act during peaks as a caching layer for the persistent virtual disks where the application data is stored during runtime. They show how this idea can be achieved efficiently at the block-device level, using a caching mechanism that leverages iterative behavior and learns from past experience. Second, they introduce a corresponding performance and cost prediction methodology. They demonstrate the benefits of our proposal both for micro-benchmarks and for two real-life applications using large-scale experiments. They conclude with a discussion on how these techniques can be generalized for increasingly complex landscape of modern cloud storage.

This chapter describes the method to retrieve data from multiple heterogeneous distributed relational database management systems such as MySQL, PostgreSQL, MS SQL Server, MS Access, etc. into Oracle RDBMS using Oracle's Heterogeneous Gateway Services. The complete process starting from downloading and installation of required software, creation of data source names using open database connectivity, modification of system parameter files, checking connections, creation of synonyms for tables of remote databases into oracle, creation of database links and accessing data from non-oracle databases using database links is explained in great detail. Apart from this, data manipulation in remote databases from Oracle and execution of PL/SQL procedures to manipulate data residing on remote databases is discussed with examples. Troubleshooting common errors during this process is also discussed.

Social networking systems are usually huge centralized systems owned by a single company. However, this solution has many drawbacks (e.g., lack of privacy, lack of anonymity, risks of censorship, and operating costs). This chapter proposes a novel P2P system that leverages existing, widespread, and stable technologies such as DHTs and BitTorrent. In particular, it introduces a key-based identity system and a model of social relations for distributing content efficiently among interested readers. The proposed system, called Blogracy, is a micro-blogging social networking system focused on (1) anonymity and resilience to censorship, (2) authenticatable content, and (3) semantic interoperability using activity streams. This chapter presents the model and the implementation of the Blogracy system, discusses the experimentations to study its behavior, and presents their results regarding (1) communication delays for some simulations of node churn, (2) delays measured in test operations over PlanetLab in direct communication, and (3) through the I2P anonymizing network.

Present failure detection algorithms for distributed systems are designed to work in asynchronous or partially synchronous environments on mesh (all-to-all) connected systems and maintain status of every other process. Several real-time systems are hierarchically connected and require working in strict synchronous environments. Use of existing failure detectors for such systems would generate excess computation and communication overhead. The chapter describes two suspicion-based failure detectors of Strong S and Perfect P classes for hierarchical distributed systems working in time synchronous environments. The algorithm of Strong S class is capable of detecting permanent crash failures, omission failures, link failures, and timing failures. Strong completeness and weak accuracy properties of the algorithm are evaluated. The failure detector of Perfect P class is capable of detecting crash failures, crash-recovery failures, omission failures, link failures, and timing failures. Strong completeness and strong accuracy properties of the failure detector are evaluated.

Preface

BACKGROUND

Distributed systems intertwine our everyday life, the benefits and current shortcomings of the underpinning technologies are experienced by a wide range of people and their smart devices. The mash-up of cloud, IoT, fog and edge computing often leads to integration issues. So, the book should be well suited to the practitioners who utilize these kind of distributed systems and they would like to enable their synergistic exploitation. On the other hand, with the raise of large scale IoT and similar distributed systems cloud bursting technologies and partial outsourcing solutions planned to be offered in the book will aid the private entities to increase their efficiency and offer unparalleled availability and reliability towards their users.

WHOM IS THIS BOOK INTENDED FOR?

This book, *Applying Integration Techniques and Methods in Distributed Systems and Technologies*, is aimed at people involved in any aspects of distributed systems such as system administrators, integrators, designers, as well as developers, users for such systems. Furthermore, this book's specific focus to bring together a strong selection of updated research from the *International Journal of Distributed Systems and Technologies* (IJDST) targets at readers with specific interest in topics that might not be comprehensively addressed elsewhere.

OVERVIEW OF THE SUBMISSIONS AND THE ACCEPTED CHAPTERS

This book is an amalgamation of two kind of contributions. The first pillar of the book contains the updated versions of several articles from the International Journal of Distributed Systems and Technologies. Out of the 70 articles published by the journal, the editor only invited a few which were meeting the following criteria: the articles were expected to have relatively high citation counts and they should fall relatively close to each other in terms of their target audience and research areas. In total, slightly over 30 invitations were made in two rounds. Out of these invitations, six chapters were pushed forward for the book and five got accepted (namely, Chapters 5-7, and 9-10).

The book's second pillar was laid down by the authors who submitted proposals to our call (which was circulated late summer/early autumn of 2018). There were five proposed chapters, which were all strongly related to the scope of the book as a result they all progressed to their full chapter phases. In this phase each chapter received three to four individual peer reviews mostly contributed by the invited chapter authors. Depending on the seriousness of the problems indicated by the reviewers, the chapters received review requests with a revision duration ranging between a week and three months. All chapters received significant revisions and before they were accepted.

The book had an acceptance rate of 90%. The book is structured so it starts with more generic topics in the field of distributed computing (literature reviews on several hot topics) then it progresses towards more and more specialised topics. In the following, we provide an overview for each chapter:

Chapter 1, "Cloud Computing and Innovations," discusses the disruptive nature of cloud computing and its impact on business innovation. The chapter tries to recite the most important innovations that drive cloud computing forward and allow its unprecedented adoption. Finally the chapter reviews several important technologies that materialised in software products in the recent years. These include among others serverless computing, content delivery networks, data centre innovations, etc.

Chapter 2, "Trust Management in Fog Computing: A Survey," focuses on how the technologies discussed in the previous chapter can be extended towards edge systems for a more distributed cloud concept: fog computing. The chapter then discusses the new issues such edge focused systems face, especially if one wants to incorporate personal equipment. Trust in locally available resources & equipment is essential in fog computing and these trust issues cannot be handled with techniques already applied for clouds operating from warehouse scale data centres. Fog computing has new challenges while building and maintaining the trust among the fog nodes and with edge devices. To help advancing towards fog computing's more distributed vision the chapter then reveals the pitfalls and the still to be solved challenges.

Chapter 3, "Convergence of Manufacturing Cloud and Industrial IoT," discusses how localised, manufacturing oriented cloud systems can cope with the increasing amount of automation and sensor generated data to achieve Industry 4.0. The issues in these manufacturing oriented systems stem from the same roots as the previous chapter reveal, but extend towards large scale business critical systems which often involve communication on specialised networks or even mobile & broadcasting networks. This requires a computing infrastructure with unprecedented flexibility and reliability that can cope with the dynamic nature and complexity of industrial applications.

Chapter 4, "Security Challenges and Resolution in Cloud Computing and Cloud of Things," continues on discussing the security implications of the fusion of clouds and things. This chapter approaches the topic from a more personal perspective and addresses challenges related to people's perceptions about easy outsourcing to clouds. The chapter discusses such dangers like unauthorized access to cloud backed data or applications. This chapter closes the general overview section of the book and paves the way for the more specialised research contributed by mostly the invited authors.

Chapter 5, "Enhancing Security in a Big Stream Cloud Architecture for the Internet of Things Through Blockchain," revisits the topic of the Internet of Things (IoT) with special focus on applications that require real-time, low-latency communications. Such applications could greatly benefit from localised authentication techniques that blockchain technologies have successfully offered in the past for other contexts. In this chapter, the authors discuss how to avoid the involvement of third parties while still maintain trusted and real-time communications amongst participants of the IoT systems. As a result, the chapter fosters the creation of blockchain based real-time applications hosted on the combination of several computing paradigms such as IoT, fog or cloud computing.

Chapter 6, "Topology Optimization for Heterogeneous DHT-Based Multicast," discusses problems on multicast messaging over the internet. The author focuses our attention to application-layer scenarios where DHT-based routing could offer efficient multicast data-delivery. The past solutions for DHT based multicas were suffering from several problems (like heterogeneous nodes). To resolve these problems the chapter discusses BAM-Chord that considers the node capacity when constructing a better performing multicast topology. The proposed solution aims at balancing the topology with several approaches that could likely offer significant benefits to often used technologies (e.g., ones following the publish-subscribe pattern) in relation to clouds, fog computing and IoT systems discussed in the previous chapters.

Chapter 7, "Transparent Throughput Elasticity for Modern Cloud Storage: An Adaptive Block-Level Caching Proposal," then focuses on how elastic storage, a quintessential feature for today's big-data focused applications, can be boosted during peak utilization of virtualized I/O components. The authors introduce a two layered virtual storage component to I/O heavy applications which introduces intermittent virtual disks to tackle the application's I/O performance bottlenecks. This new storage component is accompanied with performance and cost prediction to allow its better integration with real-life workloads. As a result, these techniques can be generalized to support the increasingly complex landscape of modern cloud storage.

Chapter 8, "Accessing Data From Multiple Heterogeneous Distributed Database Systems: Heterogeneous Distributed Database, Data Sources, Database Links, Heterogeneous Gateway Service," discusses the other end of data management in clouds and distributed systems and offers a practical insight into reaching out to several database management systems (e.g., MySQL, Oracle RDBMS) in parallel. The chapter reveals the complete process ranging from the installation & configuration procedures to data management and trouble shooting techniques.

Chapter 9, "A P2P Architecture for Social Networking," proposes to break the ties with traditional cloud and single company backed social networks as they have numerous flaws e.g., lack of privacy, lack of anonymity, risks of censorship and operating costs. This chapter proposes a novel P2P system that leverages existing, widespread and stable technologies such as DHTs and BitTorrent. In particular, it introduces a key-based identity system and a model of social relations for distributing content efficiently among interested readers. The proposed system, called Blogracy, is a micro-blogging social networking system focused on (1) anonymity and resilience to censorship, (2) authenticatable content, (3) semantic interoperability using activity streams. This chapter presents the model and the implementation of the Blogracy system, discusses the experimentations to study its behaviour and presents their results regarding (1) communication delays for some simulations of node churn; (2) delays measured in test operations over PlanetLab, in direct communication; and (3) through the I2P anonymizing network.

Finally, Chapter 10, "Failure Detectors of Strong S and Perfect P Classes for Time Synchronous Hierarchical Distributed Systems," concludes the book by discussing an alternative failure detection algorithm that aims at reducing the excess computation and communication overheads of its state-of-the art alternatives. The chapter describes two suspicion-based failure detectors of Strong S and Perfect P classes for hierarchical distributed systems working in time synchronous environments. The algorithm of Strong S class is capable of detecting permanent crash failures, omission failures, link failures, and timing failures. Strong completeness and weak accuracy properties of the algorithm are evaluated. The failure detector of Perfect P class is capable of detecting crash failures, crash-recovery failures, omission failures, link failures, and timing failures. Strong completeness and strong accuracy properties of the failure detector are evaluated.

Section 1
Background

Chapter 1
Cloud Computing and Innovations

Manoj Himmatrao Devare
https://orcid.org/0000-0002-9530-3914
Amity University Mumbai, India

ABSTRACT

Cloud computing ignited many innovations and disruptions in the traditional way of doing business. The innovations in cloud computing are countable, and innovations due to cloud computing are endless, as there are several applications where cloud computing has proven its usefulness. The discussion starts with innovation records by software companies that happened due to cloud computing. This chapter illuminates an amalgamation of advanced concepts, products, and services in cloud computing. The chapter further discusses the conceptual innovations of API management, serverless computing, content delivery network, storage services, data center technologies, all-flash arrays, and digital twin due to cloud computing.

DOI: 10.4018/978-1-5225-8295-3.ch001

INTRODUCTION

The innovation, in general, can be defined as a novel, non-obvious new idea, device or method, that can be converted as an application for the better solution that meets new requirements, unarticulated needs, or existing market needs. The growth in the products, processes, services, technologies or business models effects the Gross Domestic Product (GDP) of the nation. Innovation is the successful conversion of new ideas, into products or services. Generally, innovation is protected by filing a patent in each country and territory of the interest. The innovation provides the new market to the company, beyond the borders all over the world, and offers new employment opportunities. Innovations are important because it creates a new cherished life to the citizen and increases the revenue of the companies. Sometimes, innovation triggers the partnership among the companies in the cosmopolitan areas. The innovation should not be frivolous and contrary to the well-established natural laws.

Product innovation consist of changes in the product attributes so that consumers notice it. A Car with Automatic transmission is an example of product innovation. Process innovation consists of changes regarding the product or the production process. It produces benefits in the production process, generally increasing productivity and reducing costs. For example, an automobile manufactured by robots compared to manual intervention by human workers. Innovation in the business model makes the changes in the way of offering the product or service to the market, without any change in the product. However, the method of providing products to the consumer is innovative. The consumer rents a car, or ask for the home delivery of the food, and many more changing the business process.

Every business needs to innovate the business processes such as to communicate with the Customer, collaborate for sharing knowledge, and collaborate for development in a team. Consequently, it leads to innovation in the business through the use of Cloud platforms, which provides elasticity, flexibility, cost reduction, optimal resource utilization. This chapter discusses the innovations in Cloud Computing technology in the current decade and that perhaps promote the innovations in the next decade that will have the basis of the Cloud. The innovations in Information Technology (IT) and inter-mingled technologies such as mobile devices, sensor-based devices, industrial automation, and other sectors are a rising source of innovations. Disruptors are innovators produces something new which is more efficient and more adorable to the consumer.

Innovation Impacts can be incremental, continuous improvements that represent small improvements in benefits noticed by the consumer. The innovation impact can be radical, i.e., a drastic change in the way that the product or service consumption. Generally, it brings a new paradigm to the market segment that modifies the existing business model. The emergence of the Compact Disk over the magnetic tapes and USB storage is the best example. The Android Operating System (OS) for mobile devices made the shift of the mobile users for accessing the data at the figure tips, moving away from Personal Computers, and the existing mobile OS.

The innovation factor positively affected due to Cloud Computing considered as digital disruption. At the beginning of the year 2017, as per the record of the World Intellectual Property Organization (WIPO) (WIP, 2019), the patent filing companies observed are as shown in figure 1. The innovations done by the leading Cloud vendors as well as the small innovators may produce disruptive changes.

As shown in figure 2, the observations from top 5 patents offices the highest application growth rates the patent filing overall in China. There is total Industrial Design (872800), China (569059), Europe (98162), Korea (72458), Germany (56499), and Turkey (45852).

As per the analysis was done by IBM during 2013, regarding the patents filed based on "Cloud Computing" as a keyword in the US patent document, using Thompson Innovation analysis tool, following analysis has been observed. The number of patents filed by the Cloud Computing vendors IBM (42), Microsoft (29), Sharp Lab of America (19), Google (17), Novell (11), SAP AG (11), Amazon Tech (10), Honeywell (10), Verizon Patent & Licensing (9), EMC (9). Cloud Computing will likely be an essential growth industry in the US economy.

Figure 1. The WIPO patent filing data at the beginning of the year 2017

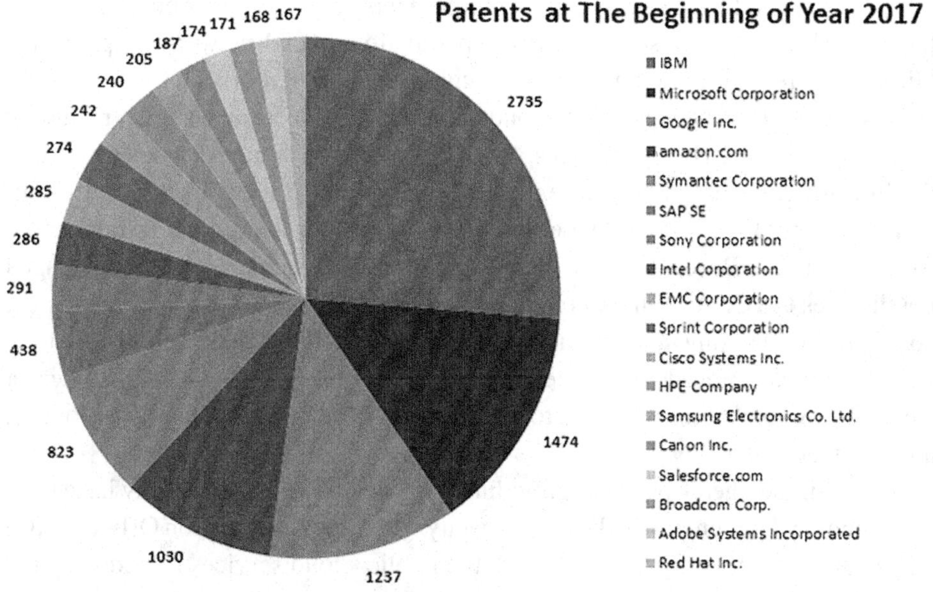

**For a more accurate representation see the electronic version.*

Figure 2. Top 5 patent office data for patent applications

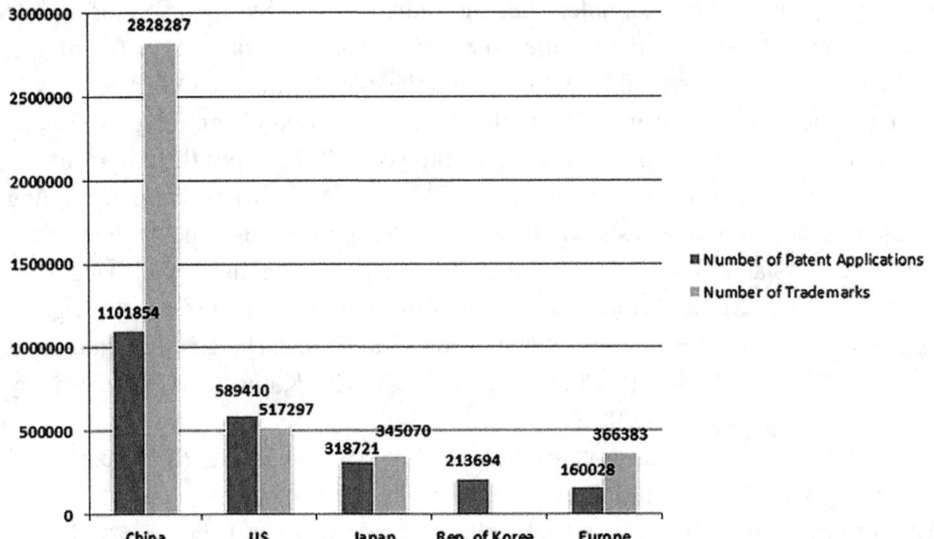

The Cloud Computing has proven its importance in the innovation of the new products and services as it has a characteristic feature to trigger new ideas for innovation not only in the field of Computer Science and Information Technology (IT) but also in the multiple disciplines. The Innovations have been observed for utilizing the dynamically scalable Cloud infrastructure, which is a hybrid of the public and private Cloud in the IaaS Cloud environments. The consumer buying pattern, targeting the particular segment of the population, social networking platforms utilization, are providing innovation through the Cloud platforms.

The customer may choose the Cloud computing products or services, including private, public or hybrid platforms. Sometimes, the customer decides to occupy the infrastructure based on the rental basis and manage it by appointing the in-house experts. The Cloud providers offer an option to maintain the infrastructure from their team. Based on the different types of Cloud, managed or unmanaged possibilities the Cloud vendors provides various products and services, which get converted into exciting innovation for the Cloud Service Providers (CSP). Although, Cloud services options look simpler to choose as per the business need, the Internet technology complications and customer demands have produced the new products and services in the Cloud.

For example, the IT business providing the SaaS to the customer may have their well-running data center with limited capacity. The Chief Information Officer (CIO) may choose to integrate the Cloud with the public Cloud services provided by the well-established vendors. The Cloud providers offer the products and services in the field of security, compatibility, compliance, high availability, application migration and many untold requirements, which can be applied in the other applications. (Atchison, 2016)

As per the data from ourworldindata.org, the latest development in Internet technology is the use of Cloud services (Murphy & Roser, 2017). The Cloud refers to data stored remotely and accessed by the user through the Internet, allowing users access to the data from any computer connected to the Internet. As per one of the estimation, there is over 1 exabyte (1 billion gigabytes) of data stored in the Cloud. There are three layers to the Cloud. Infrastructure-as-a-Service (IaaS) allows for renting and accessing storage space from the Cloud datacenter.

This chapter discusses one of the important innovations like Creation of the virtual industrial asset using the Computer Aided Design, Product Life Cycle Management, Machine Learning, and Artificial Intelligence called as the Digital Twin (DT). The DT enables the predictive maintenance of the asset and the digital image for better monitoring, analysis, and observation to improve the manufacturing plant operations. The Content Delivery Network (CDN) creates replicated and faster data and content resources accessible through the Cloud platform. The alternative, faster Cloud data storage access such as the All Flash Array (AFA), API life Cycle Management, Serverless Computing through the Cloud and related other innovations are discussed in the context of the Cloud Computing. Moreover this chapter also discusses about the security challenges, data center challenges, and interesting emerging area of research Quantum Cloud Computing. The next section discusses the important Cloud terminologies like Cloud Bursting, Cloud Washing, True Cloud, Cloud Native Applications, Managed and Unmanaged Clouds.

CLOUD TERMINOLOGIES

The Cloud has provided the virtual medium to the unlimited computing power, on the pay as per the utilization with fewer capital investments. The start-ups can bring new competitive ideas to the market due to the availability of the computational and another kind of services through the Cloud platforms. This approach is disrupting the traditional industries and bringing new possibilities in the market. The important terminologies based on the essential feature of the Cloud brought the new vocabularies which have substantially added the new enthusiasm in the market demand. This section discusses the innovative Cloud terminologies. This section excules the discussion on the basic terminologies such as virtual machine, hypervisor, IaaS, PaaS and SaaS as the it is avialble in the existing literature.

Cloud Bursting

Cloud bursting is the terminology related to the hybrid Cloud. When an existing private Cloud-based applications need to extend the capability for storage, application and computation facility, they can occupy the public Cloud services provided by the other provider. In the natural phenomenon, the rainy Cloud burst may cause a natural disaster. However, Cloud Computing adds flexibility and cost saving for the Customer. The bursting can be from the private to the public Cloud or public to public Cloud. There could be more cases like the burst from the Public to Public Cloud. In each case, the security and compatibility of the data exchange considered as the challenge in innovative product development. There are few mentioned use cases where the e-commerce websites experience an inevitable rise in the customer footfall online on the weekends and festivals. The prediction of the arrivals of legitimate visitors to the e-commerce website can be predictable at a particular level. However, the unsaid demands can be flexibly occupied by Cloud bursting.

There are operational, communication challenges, fault tolerance, high availability are few of the addressing difficulties in addition to the speed of the Internet, security layer, restrictions at the entry points of the network can make some obstacles in the initial customization of the products and the infrastructure in preparation for the Cloud burst. The applications are having requirement of the reading data from the data storage, and Content Delivery System such as database applications, high node-to-node communication applications are best suitable for the Cloud bursting. As the Cloud provides the more parallel access to the storage than the Storage Area Network (SAN), are ideal for the Cloud Bursting. It is said that the Cloud bursting suffers from the delay. It is the practice of the Cloud Burst adopters that they keep the master server in the data center and the back-up and replicas in the Cloud. The load balancer at the private and public premises are required in case of the bursting scenario.

The deployment of the high-speed link in the Wide Area Network (WAN) behind the Local Area Network (LAN) can cause the delay in case of the Cloud burst. In the initial phase of the Cloud Burst implementation, while the set-up of the hypervisors creates much of the traffic. The data replication, and synchronization, and use of the containers instead of the full-fledged hypervisors can improve the latency caused in case of the Cloud-Burst. The real world data changes rapidly in the business and in case of the Cloud Burst the data is duplicated, hence it adds the overhead of the synchronization of the replicas. Although the implementation of the Cloud Bursting is having a high amount of the technical challenges, it is more suitable for the well-established businesses where the infrastructure and the consumer base is strong. The application developers for the Cloud burst to face the challenge of state management. The state management means there should be one to one mapping between the user and the application residing on the burst Cloud.

True Cloud

True Cloud is SaaS which is version-less, multitenant software developed exclusively for the Cloud and in the Cloud. The true Cloud provides the self-provisioning, Pay-per-use billing, multitenant, virtualized and linearly scalability. The data storage in the true Cloud can be extended from the petabytes to the exabytes, and the objects stored in the Cloud are the location independent. They are not precisely similar to the well-established SAN and Networked Attached Storage (NAS). The true Cloud SaaS, PaaS and IaaS are directly accessible through the internet via Application Programming Interfaces (APIs) such as Representational State Transfer (REST) for compatibility and interoperability in the heterogeneity and the Simple Object Access Protocol (SOAP) for the client applications to access the remote procedures through the HTTP and platform and language independent Extensible Markup Language (XML).

Cloud Washing

It is an activity of purposeful and sometimes misleading but innovative attempt by a vendor in which a hosting and implementation of legacy and existing packaged software and maintaining it in a virtualized data center, to attack the new customers. The enterprises accept the kind of service because it reduces the cost of maintaining the software and hardware on which it runs. This implementation provides automatic, continuous upgrades, multi-tenancy, self-service, auto-scaling, and usage-metering capabilities. There are several Enterprise Resource Planning (ERP) Software, and some other software vendors pretend to provide the non-Cloud based products based as a True Cloud. Whereas, they are trying to access the networked resources in the complexed configuration requirements those are not in Cloud. The multitenancy, infrequent updates of the software, complex pricing structure, inconsistent user interfaces, mechanism for quickly adding and removal of users are few of the signs of the Cloud washing.

Cloud Native Applications

The development and operations (DevOps) and the light-weight container services like Kubernates isolated from the OS dependency are the critical elements of the Cloud native applications. The Kubernates can scale faster than the Virtual Machines (VMs) in the Cloud. The Cloud native applications are polyglot that is program and script written in the valid form of the variety of multiple languages such as WebSockets, Node.js, Python, and Flask. It also supports the REST, and Remote Procedure Calls (RPCs).

Cloud-native applications are purpose-built and deployed to exploit the advantages of the Cloud Computing in a rapid tunning by a small, dedicated team to a platform that offers easy scale-out and hardware decoupling that provides the organizations greater agility, resilience, and portability across the Clouds. The Cloud native applications provide the competitive market environment, flexibility in building the applications that will run on any Cloud without modification, migrate and distribute applications on across multiple Cloud vendors. Due to Cloud native developer can do their work with flexibility, and align operations with business. The organizations require a platform for building and operating Cloud-native applications and services that automate and integrates the concepts of DevOps, continuous delivery, micro-services, and containers.

The Cloud-native applications differ from traditional enterprise applications where they are highly automated, container-driven infrastructure used in Cloud platforms. The traditional applications cannot realize all of the benefits of running on a Cloud-native platform due to specific misleading techniques of development. This type of application often takes more time to build, released in big batches, can only scale gradually, and has a single point of failure. The traditional applications are demanding in case of the migration and scaling, as the applications, as dependent on the OS, hardware, storage, and backup services. Whereas, the Cloud native applications are abstracted and independent from this kind of services.

Cloud-native applications are right-sized in capacity, and traditional applications are over-sized in capacity. The A Cloud-native application platform provides adaptive automation, on-demand infrastructure provisioning, configuration, reallocating resources, and minimizing the downtime during the failures. The Cloud-native provides a collaborative environment as compared to traditional. The DevOps performs the smooth application deployment due to combining the people, process, and tools for the collaboration between development and operations functions, and automating the process of software delivery and infrastructure changes. Traditional IT operates to handover the application code from developers to operations. The DevOps brings culture and environment for building, testing and releasing software can happen in rapid, frequent, and more reliable way. The traditional organizational procedures although adapted to the agile models even working in the pair programming, but bounding with the organizational priorities and missing in the empathy about the customer needs. This could cause internal conflict, slow delivery, and compromised staff morale.

The Native Cloud applications provide continuous delivery, and the individual software updates available for release, on an immediate basis. Organizations that release software can get customer feedback and action by the IT Team. The traditional applications provide waterfall development. IT teams to release software periodically, typically weeks or months. Although the components and code are ready to release, it has to wait until the release. Due to the prolonged delivery, the customers wait to get the functional requirements into actual products and company defer to get the revenue earning.

The micro-services provide the independently decomposed, loosely coupled smaller components of the applications. The independent teams make the frequent updates, scaling and restart without affecting the other components in the Cloud ecosystem. The micro-services facility integrated with the Cloud-native applications makes it independent, and traditional applications are monolithic bundles, dependent and provide the resistance to the agility.

The Native Cloud applications provide the automation for the scalability avoids the human error decreases the downtime and easy manageability. Continuous Delivery makes an individual application change ready for release as soon as it is prepared, without waiting for bundling with other turns into a release or an event such as a maintenance window. Micro-services is an architectural approach to developing an application as a collection of small services. The Hypertext Transfer Protocol (HTTP) APIs makes the pathways between the microservices. Each micro-service can be deployed, upgraded, scaled, and restarted independently of other services in the application.

Managed Cloud Services

The Cloud as infrastructure has to be managed by either by the provider or by the customer. The Customer can do everything itself, or hire the expert, or appoint in-house personnel to perform the various tasks on the tools and application stacks. In case, there is the possibility of the single or multi-tenant combination of servers, and co-location facility.

In managed Cloud business can employ a trusted partner to handle all or most of its Cloud. It is a service that allows businesses to tap the power of Cloud Computing without the pain of becoming an expert in everything. The companies that use managed Cloud can focus on their core business, developing innovative applications and products and joins the new customers. They can stay fast, rather than having to increase expenses on the payroll with large teams of operational engineers, system administrators and other experts to manage IT that doesn't differentiate their company. The engineers from the Cloud provider can handle the customer's computing, storage, networks, and OS, but also the sophisticated tools and application stacks that run on top of that infrastructure. The latest tools include databases, e-commerce platforms, and DevOps automation tools. In the Managed Cloud environment, each customer can choose IT functions to manage in-house and remaining by the managed by the Cloud provider.

Managed Cloud services include, at the infrastructure level the skills like Architecture guidance, system administration, and operations, System monitoring, alerting, reporting, performance testing and tuning. The managed Cloud services include DevOps automation tools and additionally, specialized database management MySQL, MongoDB, Redis, and Hadoop.

Unmanaged Cloud Services

The Unmanaged Cloud, the customer, rents access to infrastructure often from a Cloud provider and wish to manage that infrastructure, as well as all the tools and apps that run on it. Customers who choose this option get lower infrastructure prices than they would get from a managed Cloud provider along and additional costs for either hiring IT experts and supervising those engineers. Some customers choose cheap rent infrastructure from one and managing service from others. This can balance either small infrastructure cost and higher cost for the hired manpower and support cost.

Cloud Models

Cloud Vendors provides the Public, Private, Multi-Cloud and hybrid Cloud platforms and services. In the Multi-Cloud environment, the customer relies on multiple Cloud providers for numerous applications. Hybrid Cloud can connect multiple deployment platforms such as public Cloud, private Cloud, and dedicated servers and on-premises servers within a single application. In the public Cloud, user's get quick access to compute, storage, app hosting and more as per the user's need. The hardware is located outside of a private data center and is shared with other customers, which keeps prices low. The servers can scale up within a minute and shrink it when the need is finished. Since public Cloud infrastructure is shared with many customers, so the customer pays only for the utilized server resources. Most public Clouds allow adding networking, storage, and databases.

SERVERLESS COMPUTING

The anonymous classes in Java provide the mechanism for anonymous functions. The lambda expression is trying to pass functionality as an argument to another method. Sometimes the action which user wants to run on the click of the User Interface (UI) component such as a Button, CheckBox or simple touch gestures in the mobile applications, Lambda expressions enables pass functionality as a method argument or code as data which internally needs the Central Processing Unit (CPU) cycles.

Table 1 shows the android app development use-case where the Graphical User Interface (GUI) Developer is calling the lambda expression on the button click and trying to access the string resources stored in the strings.xml and images from the image resource. The lambda function can be anything like a search of some person record from the database, or searcher of some items sold on the e-commerce website.

The Serverless Cloud Computing which does not care about the server and it is based on the event programming with micro-billing. Figure 3 shows the evolution of Serverless computing in the Cloud. In Serverless computing, the Functions as a Service (FaaS) are provided. Lambda functions create anonymous functions that can consume and create other functions. Here the user does not mention how many servers or units are required for usage, but want to get charged for the resources. The billing model is based on the programming model, event-based and trigger-based computing, as no need to run the VM for longer times. The Cloud innovations with Serverless computing made the lesser amount of billing cycles, with the flexibility of maintaining the provisioning and scaling automatically. Server management and capacity planning decisions are entirely hidden from the developer or operator (Fowler, 2017).

The trigger and rules defined can decide when to run the functions in Serverless code. It runs application logic in response to events or direct invocations from the web

Figure 3. Evolution of serverless computing as innovation in cloud computing

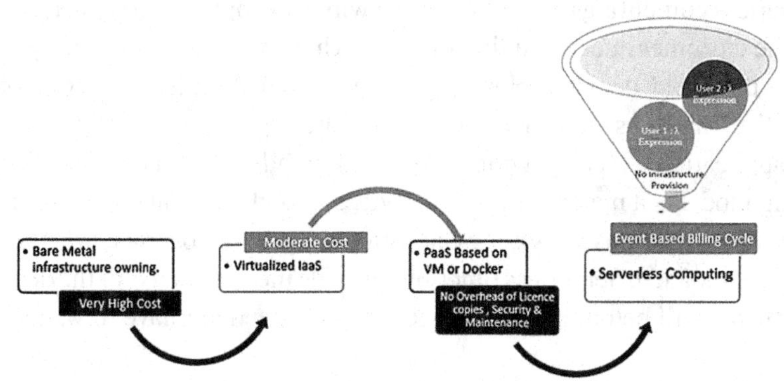

Table 1. Java-based Android app code for the Lambda expression passed on the button click

Anonymous Lambda Function Passed to the Button onClickListener()

public class MainActivity extends AppCompatActivity {
Button b1;
TextView tv1;
String s1,s2;
ImageView imv1;
int counter;
@Override
protected void onCreate(Bundle savedInstanceState) {
super.onCreate(savedInstanceState);
setContentView(R.layout.activity_main);
b1=findViewById(R.id.button);
imv1=findViewById(R.id.imageView);
s1=getResources().getString(R.string.str1);
s2=getResources().getString(R.string.str2);
b1.setOnClickListener(new View.OnClickListener() {
@Override
public void onClick(View v) {
tv1=findViewById(R.id.tv1);
counter++;
if(counter %2==0)
{
tv1.setText(s1);
imv1.setImageResource(R.drawable.abc);
}
else
{
tv1.setText(s2);
imv1.setImageResource(R.drawable.ios);
}
}
});
}

or mobile apps over HTTP. The trigger such as the customer complaint registered in the customer care software, or some changes happened in the system of sensitive data. The Serverless computing can be integrated with any application such as automatic reply to the customer query, sending the alert when an industrial furnace is heating above the threshold decided. Nowadays, the Virtual Agents (VAs) or assistance based on the Chat-bots, conversational agents are replying to the various domain-specific applications. It can get connected with mobile Cloud apps. The Serverless computing model is a match for micro-services, mobile, IoT, and many other apps. The Serverless functions are gluing the different systems together, whether that is pulling files uploaded. Serverless functions provide the simplicity for the developers, and their focus will be on the business logic. They need not have to write code for

Figure 4. Use case of the serverless computing where the event-based GUI dynamically calls the lambda expression for the Android story app

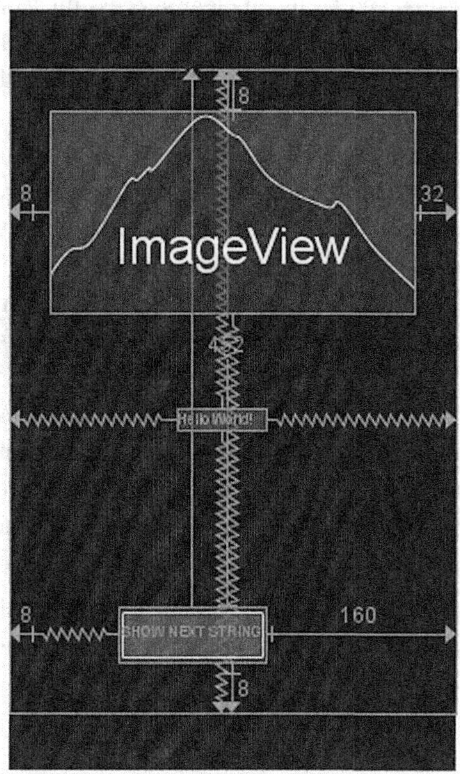

the PaaS or SaaS. Serverless is not fully featured but good for smaller services that run for a few milliseconds. If micro-services need to run for long periods, then use VM for that. The for asynchronous events that someone needs to process that come in one after another.

API LIFE CYCLE MANAGEMENT AS PRODUCT OR SERVICE IN CLOUD

As the business needs the different APIs for the agility of the business, the Cloud is a perfect vehicle and provide the Service Access Point (SAP) for the evolving APIs in the particular field or domain, which can be maintained and delivered to the specific customers. The APIs are considered as products or services, and building blocks of digital ecosystems. Business platforms enable third-party developers to consume APIs and build applications quickly. Leading platforms offer open APIs, strong developer programs, and focus on clear success measures. The services are provided through Cloud platforms. There are many APIs like Maps API, Geocoding API, Places API, Autocomplete API, Commerce APIx, Healthcare APIx, Identity APIx, Open Banking APIx, and Telecom API Exchange.

The API lifecycle is generally consisting of the creation, controlling, and consuming of the API. In details the API Lifecycle includes the model, orchestrate, transform, document, deploy, manage, secure, scale, publish, discover, invoke, and monetize. The APIs in the Cloud can be treated as a product, and hence having product lifecycle. Successful platforms clearly define and measure a combination of business metrics like direct or indirect revenue and API consumption metrics like API traffic, the number of apps, and the number of active developers (Gong, Zhang, Fang, & Sun, 2016; Nijim & Pagano, 2017; Nadareishvili, Mitra, McLarty, & Amundsen, 2016).

An API is used to connect business processes, services, content, and data to channel partners, internal teams, and independent developers. APIs are used by companies to exchange data and build consistent cross-channel customer experiences. API works as a digital glue that powering mobile and web apps, connecting disparate systems, and enabling innovation. Using APIs to power websites, mobile apps, allow partner integrations, create seamless omnichannel Experiences. APIs boost employee productivity. External APIs improve connectivity to the world, while internal APIs allow the company to operate more efficiently.

CLOUD ENABLED IOT AND DIGITAL TWIN

The use of the on-demand Cloud for various activities in the business not only for the storage but including computation, machine learning, data analytics and Artificial Intelligence (AI) based techniques for the better involvement of the all stakeholders in the project. The services through the Cloud such as NoSQL database, the Natural Language Processing, Text to Voice and Voice to Text conversion adds more exciting facilities for the user through the chatbots. The Digital Twin (DT) is one of the interesting technological innovation due to the support of the Cloud-enabled integration of all tools, techniques, and methodologies in the Product Lifecycle Management (PLM). One can see the product in the virtual image format using Augmented Reality (AR) and can talk with the twin like a human being is an excellent experience through the DT.

Most recent technological innovation happening in the industry is the Internet of Things (IoT) and furthermore extension to DT. DT creates a virtual presentation of a product that includes IoT and requires Cloud Computing as an essential part of data storage and massive computing infrastructure. As far as DT is considered, the Industrial IoT (IIoT) also called as Industry 4.0, i.e. fourth industrial revolution which combines the sensor data analysis, data processing using machine learning algorithms, pushing the data like sensor readings in the form of semi-structured messages in the form of XML or JavaScript Object Notation (JSON) data to the Cloud which automates the process of the joining two parts of the IoT ecosystem.

Mentioned about the DT in the PLM requires three elements: the physical product in real space, its DT in virtual space and the information that links the two. As an essential concept of IIoT, the DT is used in product prototyping, design, simulation, monitoring, optimization, and servicing. The designers and engineers can create the DTs in the same Computer Aided Design (CAD) and modeling software, in the initial stages of the product development. The difference with a DT is that the model is retained for later stages of the product's lifecycle, such as inspection and maintenance. While maintaining the lifecycle of the product or system the digital and virtual equivalent can be maintained through the DT (Overton & Brigham, 2017).

A DT offers context with past data, Key Performance Indicators (KPI) as present data, and insights to the future data about an asset or system, providing a holistic view, from design and build to operation and maintenance. DTs continuously update and learn with an asset's performance, allowing for better predictions and simulations of future operations. Asset operators can leverage a digital replica to capture the history of each machine, combined with intelligence, to provide unique knowledge and insights. Sensors connected to the physical product & software model can collect data and send it back to the DT, and their data processing and interaction helps in the optimization of the product's performance. For example, sensors might detect when a car's engine oil needs changing, and the car's DT will have an interactive image indicating the new information, can appear on the smartphone or the manufacturer's monitoring PLM system.

For the creation of DT, Cloud Computing, storage, hyper-scale computing, commoditization of sensor equipment, AR & VR, data science, visual analytics, digital platforms, digital toolsets & services are required. The PLM, CAD and panorama images overlaid with real-time sensor data used in AR applications for product maintenance and field service. In AR, the DT must be able to follow the product's location and movement. Some manufacturers, including power tool maker, extended the DT concept to encompass assembly lines and other factory systems. The DT is implemented where the turbine speaks with the human operator like a conversational bot. (Paris, Laflen, Grabb, & Kalitan, 2017).

The DT integrates data from many different software products. Data supported and DT enabled assets and solutions are reducing operational costs. The DT is a concept that enhances information management and collaboration, where the experts can work together, preventing costly mistakes and rework. To understand the importance of the DT, consider the example of an atomic electricity generation station, where Single unscheduled downtime of the nuclear power station results in a loss of millions of dollars per day. To avoid costly mistakes and rework, DTs are essential. The data is updated throughout the lifecycle of real-time information, a collaboration platform that prevents working in silos. The DT gives insight, where the engineers will work cost-effectively on a collaboration platform to avoid last moment actions improve the coordination, fewer mistakes and rework. Sensor data, remote monitoring, and analytics made possible by the DT enable more profitable, safe and sustainable operations.

The concept of DT is a dynamic digital representation that enables companies to predict, optimize, and analyze the performance of their machinery and business. DTs exist at the nexus of engineering, data science, machine learning, and their value translates directly to measurable business outcomes reduced asset downtime and maintenance costs, improved plant and factory efficiency, reduced cycle times, and increased market agility (Volkmann, 2018). DT sits in the continuum of the IoT, and the foundation of IoT consists of connectivity with power efficiency, accurate sensors, Business intelligence, and analytics. It enables predictive maintenance in case-based reasoning as an established IoT usage. The DT approach handles this by incorporating product data, maintenance history, from design to operation and in the latter stages.

Although the DT is in the early stages but provides the endless possibilities for the costly businesses and products like oil refineries, Virgin Hyperloop One, Airplanes, defense instruments, machinery and many more applications including the expensive cars and autonomous trucks, the ability to control, drive, design, emulate, maintain, scale, produce and repair products with the guiding intelligence and greater efficiency and innovation. Figure 5 shows, the DT creation steps applicable to the manufacturing industry (Overton & Brigham, 2017).

CLOUD-BASED CONTENT DELIVERY NETWORK

The various Web Content Management Systems (WCMS) such as Joomla, Drupal, Wordpress are useful to manage the contents efficiently. The Cloud is helpful to store and access the data of the enterprise. Nowadays, the Content Delivery Network (CDN)which is a parallel and replicated system maintained by the various vendors

Figure 5. Digital twin creation steps

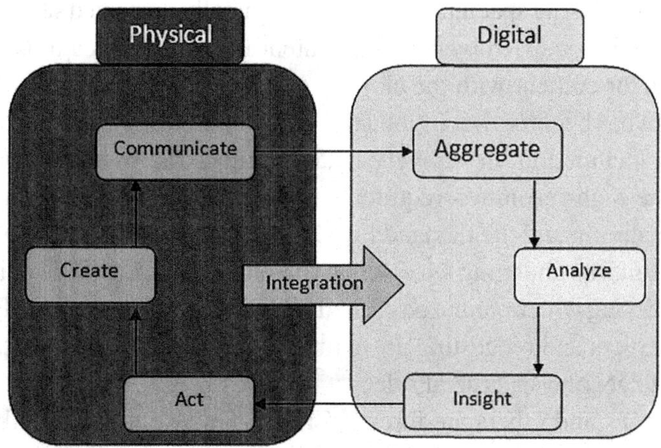

for the faster access to the web-pages and contents. The Cloud-based cached data near to the location of the user makes the quicker experience to the user. The Cloud-based CDN, and it's related activates another innovation in the CDN based online presence of the business.

A highly distributed system of servers deployed in multiple data centers across the Internet that respond directly to end-user request for web content, and useful for improving the delivery of Internet traffic worldwide. The CDN sits intermediary between a content origin server and its end users. The objective of CDN is to serve content to end-users with high availability and high performance. CDNs provide seamless web experience to their end users, and pervasive, i.e., small, medium, and massive content provider corporation rely on it.

The delivery of web applications and streaming media either through the YouTube channels, video on demand, or the live finale matches played for the Soccer or the Cricket in a fast and secure way. The speed of the delivery of the contents including video, text, images, other files matters a lot. The quicker delivery of the online contents of the websites improves the business of e-commerce vendors like Amazon and Walmart. Half of the Internet traffic is based on the CDNs including web objects, i.e., text, graphics and scripts, downloadable objects, media files, software, documents, e-commerce applications, portals, live streaming media, on-demand streaming media, and social networks.

To achieve the target of higher performance, a CDN involves layers of complexity, and CDN providers work every moment daily for dealing with the complex technical challenges of doing business online. The challenges met by deploying a global CDN include delivery of enterprise web applications, media, software delivery, and Cloud security solutions. Using specialized and geographically dispersed servers, the CDN enhances the delivery speed by caching content in multiple locations and serving to the requests for content with the closest server.

The content has become more sophisticated, and the CDN is new challenges, due to rich media included in the delivery material either the websites, materials and streaming. The high-resolution requirements of images, high definition delivery, live media streaming and the demand for video add the additional time in the page loading. The runtime changing sites with dynamic content use more complex logic to display rendering which cannot be cached. The hand-held devices are farther away from origin servers and requesting un-optimized content which is not targetted for them. Hence CDN plays a crucial role.

These changes and others are forcing CDNs to evolve to include dynamic site speed improvement for non-cacheable content, as well as front-end optimization of the code and code delivery. Content and systems are migrating from data centers to the Cloud, creating new challenges for speed improvement. CDN security is required for the retail and financial services. Moreover, more CDN providers are seeking analytics and monitoring capabilities to get comprehensive analytics to the customer's feedback to remediate issues and maintain speed and performance. The Cloud-based CDNs handles the complex operations efficiently, with less cost. Digital performance is based on video, web performance, and security. When the first CDNs were born, connections were wired, content was static, displays were uniform, and all logic and control could be maintained behind the firewall. The Cloud vendors (provides Aura Managed CDN that runs on the Commercial-off-the-Shelf (COTS) hardware or VM environment.

With increasing demand from global audiences for media streaming, CDN providers need high performance streaming media solutions to stay competitive. User's expectations are increasingly high. They want media streaming to be fast and video quality to be high, and they want their media streaming services to be available on any device, anytime, anywhere. Providers require solutions that enable them to reach audiences reliably where they are, to scale as needed, and to intelligently adjust to dynamic network environments and deliver the highest viewing quality possible. Any misstep in an online video strategy can have lasting adverse effects on a provider's brand reputation and customer loyalty.

Adaptive media delivery provides the CDN must have reliability to deliver adaptive media in extraordinary capacity and scale. The content providers who stream the world's most significant online events. It is not possible to predict the content may go viral. The CDN must have adaptive bit-rate technologies for the smooth, high-quality viewing experience. Proximity for adaptive media delivery reduces the inevitable latency, congestion and packet loss.

The content requested from the end user is first looked into the CDN servers located near to the demanding customer. As the CDN having the pre-saved cached version, it delivers the same. If the version is not available, then the request further sent to the original server with the help of the DNS resolvers, and in this case, the CDN acts as the proxy. This overall process saves the turnaround time for delivery of the content to the end-user.

There are several use-cases such as delivery of website content, 4K and HD-quality video, live matches of the favorite games such as world cup, audio streams through the government authorities such as Priminister and President of the Country, software downloads such as apps, games playing and download, and OS updates, data records that contain medical, financial, defence and space-craft information. The CDN, content providers can deliver fast, quality web experiences to all their end users irrespective of location, browser, device, or network. The CDNs delivers the web pages' faster, video buffering time is reduced, users stay more engaged, and content providers get more business. Availability means that content remains accessible to end users under high-stress situations such as excessive user traffic, occasional spikes, and potential server outages. When traffic loads peak at millions of requests per second, even the most powerful origin servers would be put to the test. Without a CDN, all this traffic has to be absorbed by a content provider's origin infrastructure and can cause the origin to fail, resulting in terrible experience to the end-user experience results in the lost business.

There are several online video and audio based entertainment apps, movie portals, e-commerce websites which launch the sale for the limited amount of the time. All the interested customers are visiting the website at the same time. The user connectivity data, device types, browsing experiences, real-time user monitoring, and media analytics are also important parameters. By providing solutions for performance, availability, security, and intelligence, CDNs help the world's top companies, and organizations do business successfully online.

Lin et. al (2011) developed cost-effective and web-based and elastic Cloud platform to manage data for web content developers, and accelerate the speed for users to access websites. This system uses the Hadoop Distributed File System (HDFS) as a Cloud infrastructure service and creates many data clusters around the world including Japan, Taiwan, Singapore, & US. Therefore, content providers could place content to the closest node from end users. The result shows high performance and flexible solution to build a personal CDN over Cloud. The cache-based mechanism is developed for proximity near to the customer's location using AWS Amazon. The different files with varying file sizes like 100KB to 8 MB transferred and the maximum, minimum and average response time is tested.

(Chen, Guo, Lin, & Porta, 2012) Investigated the problem of placing Web server replicas in storage Cloud-based CDNs along with building distribution paths among them to minimize the cost incurred by the CDN providers while satisfying QoS requirements for user requests. The storage Cloud-based CDNs have the advantage of cost over web content providers. They formulated an Integer Program and presented various offline and online Greedy heuristics. This work evaluates the performance against the optimal via Web trace-based simulations.

(Li, Shen, & Liu, 2012) Shows the Akamai CDN technology and conducted an experiment in Microsoft public Cloud, Windows Azure, to demonstrate the benefits of CDN integration with the Cloud, which shows the significant gain in large data download by utilizing CDN in Cloud Computing using Microsoft's has six data centers located in Chicago, San Antonio, Hong Kong, Singapore, Amsterdam, & Dublin.

The role of CDN is significant in reliable, scalable and quality of video streaming in the global Internet. The design of the Cloud-based control plane as a Resource Allocation Controller (RAC) is satisfying the expected peak demands of video streaming. The feedback techniques are used which is decreasing the distribution cost, without the loss of quality of the video, and throttles the number of VMs in Cloud-based CDN (Cicco, Mascolo, & Calamita, 2013).

(Hu, Luo, Wang, & Veeravalli, 2014) Cloud-based CDNs have the benefit of cost-efficient hosting services without owning infrastructure. The dynamic demand patterns need resource provisioning and replica placement in Cloud CDNs. The greedy and iterative heuristics framework called Differential Provisioning and Caching (DPC) having maximization of total demands supported for unexpired resources, and minimization of the total rental cost for new resources in demands. The dynamic placement of the contents and route maps along of cache and request balancing algorithms is developed.

(Rego, Bonfim, Ortiz, & Bezerra, 2015) The load balancer with horizontal elastic strategy management for adding or removing the virtual media servers concerning the increase and decreasing active video streaming servers is developed. The OpenFlow, which is Software Definition Network (SDN) based technology used a private Cloud infrastructure.

(Hu, Wen, Chua, & Huang, 2016) & (Hu et al, 2014) have developed an Online Social Networks (OSNs) community classification, and then replica creation of the videos in Cloud-centric CDN infrastructure, that can provide the better smoothing in optimality up to 30% over the traditional method, with same latency, satisfying the averaged time delay. The Sina Wibo data set is used for social video distribution.

CLOUD STORAGE DEVICE LEVELS

The Cloud has not only provided storage to the users for the back-up and regular storage but provided the different levels of the storage. The elasticity regarding the Cloud storage makes the IT infrastructure managers more sensitive to the underlying storage system, as they have to provide the recovery mechanism in case of the failures. The storage organization in the Cloud where the storage device mechanisms provide common logical units of data storage. Collections of data are grouped and saved into files, and collection of files located in folders. A block is the smallest and lowest level of storage and the closest to the hardware, and data that is still individually accessible. The block using either the Logical Unit Number (LUN) or virtual volume block-level storage will typically have better performance than file-level storage. The sets of data are organized into a table-based, delimited, or record formats. Data and its associated information such as indexing called as metadata are organized as web-based resources known as objects. Each of these storage levels is facilitated through the exposed APIs. File storage is having the individual data in separate files that can be in different formats organized into folders and subfolders. The newer versions of the files are replaced by the new files that are created when data has been modified, in the frequent updates by the customers.

The different type of data can be referenced and stored as Web resources, called as object storage accessible via REST or Web service-based Cloud services using HTTP as the original protocol. The storage is either Relational database management system or NoSQL storage. The storage requirements of the individuals and the businesses are now increasing and reaching toward the Big-Data regarding the volume, variety, and velocity. The needs are extended from the online transaction processing(OLTP) to the Online Analytical Processing (OLAP), for the various schemas like star, snow-flake and fact constellation to consisting of the facts and dimensions. Perhaps the data accessed by some business intelligence tools for some graphical representation, and decision support system.

The managed Cloud providers provide services like Direct Attached Storage (DAS), SAN, & NAS. The DAS is single storage dedicated, scalable up to 100s of TBs. The network storage interfaces include storage devices in compliance with industry-standard protocols, such as Small Computer System Interface (SCSI) for storage blocks and the Server Message Block (SMB), Common Internet File System (CIFS), and Network File System (NFS) for file and network storage. The SAN is the low latency, high bandwidth, either shared or dedicated storage service.

ALL FLASH ARRAY STORAGE

The fast access to the memory in the Cloud needs not only the efficient computer architecture at the micro level but also at the stack and memory access. The traditional memory organization consumes the more CPU clock cycles, and in combination with the CPU micro-operations consumes more time. Whereas, the new type of memory significantly improves the speed of data access called the All-Flash Arrays (AFA). Access to these type of memory units is possible due to the use of Cloud innovations. This section discusses the AFA.

An AFA is a non-volatile, semiconductor technology with memory that is not having moving parts. It is Solid State Storage Disk (SSD) system that contains multiple flash memory as a variation of the erasable programmed read-only memory and reprogrammed in units of memory called blocks. It is called all-flash because the blocks can be erased in a single action or "flash." The transfer of data and is much faster than electromechanical disk drives. Flash cells wear out a little every time they are erased or programmed. For enterprise applications where input-output is intense, the reliability becomes a challenge for the AFA. The expected life of a flash device is expressed in Program-Erase (PE) cycles, similar to the same spot erasing on the paper many times, tear through the paper. There are ways to minimize and even set the PE limits like over provisioning and write optimization; both are covered in greater depth in a bit (Lowe, 2017).

There are different types of the AFAs like Single-Level Cell (SLC), Enterprise Multi-Level Cell (EMLC), Consumer Multi-Level Cell (CMLC), and Triple-Level Cell (TLC). The SLC once considered the only form of flash appropriate for enterprise storage, this format of flash stores one bit in each cell. The Flash cell PE cycles are 100000, having the highest performance, BER is low, and price per GB is highest.

EMLC having high performance, Flash cell PE Cycles are 10000, price per GB is high, BER is low. MLC increases storage density and reduces cost per GB by storing two bits per cell. eMLC is a form of MLC that increases the PE cycles by reserving a significant portion of their total flash address space for Over-Provisioning (OP), a percentage of the total physical memory reserved (commonly 28% to 50%) to replace cells as they wear out. eMLC flash often includes advanced controller firmware to provide device-level optimizations like Garbage Collection (GC).

The CMLC having Flash Cell PE Cycles are 3000, having high performance, low Bit Error Rate (BER), its price per GB is moderate. MLC increases the storage density and reduces cost per GB by storing two bits per cell. CMLC is the form of MLC used in the vast majority of consumer devices and of late, enterprise storage arrays. CMLC is the highest volume form of flash being fabricated today. CMLC includes a low amount of over-provisioned flash (7% of address space) and a limited set of capabilities in controller firmware. TLC supports hundreds of write cycles. TLC allows for three bits being stored in each cell, providing a means for flash to better address capacity centric storage needs. The architecture is more susceptible to bit errors than MLC due to the narrow band in which the bit's value can be read.

QUANTUM CLOUD COMPUTING

Sometimes, the tiny particles like atoms and electrons behave differently, due to the mysteries of the tiny world of size as 10^{-10}. Quantum Physics deals with the particles of these dimensions. The Quantum theory establishes the relationship between the particles, and it had made the revolution in Physics and Chemistry. The information processing using these principles is also applicable to computing and communications. The quantum computer works on the law of the superposition and entanglement. It consists of Qubit instead of transistors, as opposed to the traditional classical computers. The electrons are either in the upward direction with high energy or the downward trend with low energy. Similar to the ordinary computer the way to manipulate its bits, the Quantum Computer can manipulate quantum states in a controlled fashion.

Chess Game to Understand Quantum Computing

Quantum Chess is a variant of Traditional Chess that throws quantum Physics into the mix. With the addition of the Quantum-Move players can move their pieces, so they exist in more than one position on the board at once. The players can get hands-on with various quantum phenomena, like superposition and entanglement, and leads to some new strategies. Along with the standard rules, with a few exceptions, the quantum move adds a whole new dimension to the game. The Chess game based on the quantum theory where the probability of having a pawn in a particular position. In this typical game, two moves in one chance are possible with the complex input. Where, as per theory the cat can be alive or dead in the box due to the availability of radioactive element.

The quantum moves give players access to the power of superposition. Pieces can exist in multiple places on the board at once. With practice, players can learn to leverage this ability for new strategies and discover the emergence of other resources like entanglement. Pawns cannot perform quantum moves. A piece has a 50% chance to reach any space up to two standard moves away, and a 50% chance not to move at all. After performing a quantum move, the board exists in a superposition. Essentially, there are two possible boards, corresponding to each of the outcomes. Pieces can achieve a quantum move more than once, further dividing probabilities and providing more board presence. (Chris Cantwell, 2018) One of the quantum chess game developed by Chris Cantwell. The other games are quantum counterfeit coin finding, battleships with partial not gates, quantum pseudo-telepathy for the magic square game. Figure 6 shows the chess game working based on the principle of superposition, and probability (Quantumrealmgames, 2018).

Accessing Quantum Computer Using Cloud

Figure 7 shows an overview of how a user interacts with the system to access the quantum computers. The traditional programmers have to unlearn the programming concepts and learn the new quantum logic gates to solve the problem in the question successfully. The Cloud-based services are the method for providing access to quantum processing. For the parallelization, as per the Amdahl's Law, adding more processors can only get so far. In the field of High-Performance Computing (HPC),

Figure 6. The chess based on the Quantum Physics, entanglement, Superposition and principles of Probability

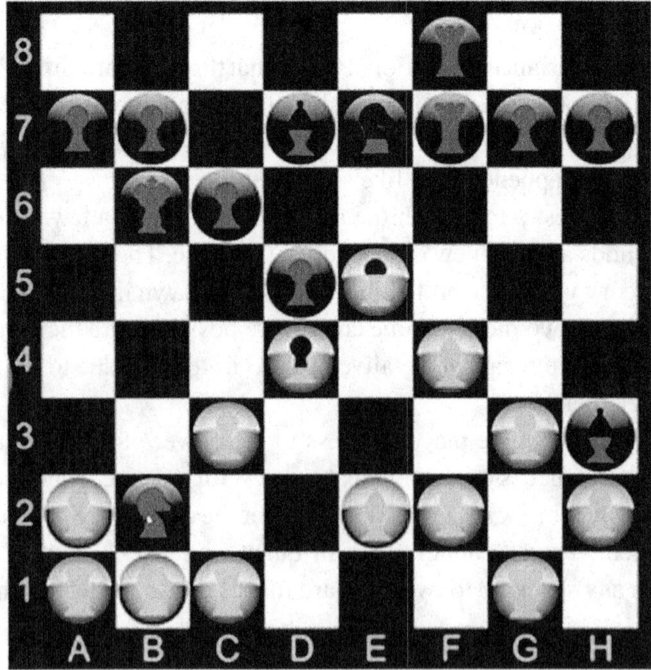

Figure 7. The quantum units accessible through cloud

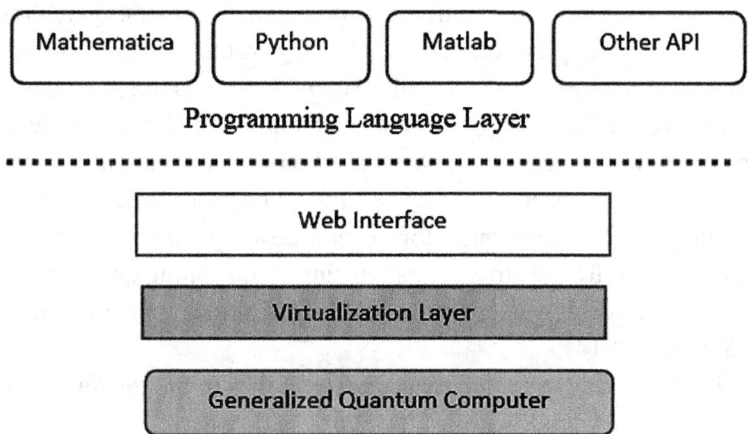

energy consumption and supercomputers are increasingly power hungry, with no end in sight (Devare, 2019). Quantum computing is providing much faster speed to solve the high calculations based on Quantum Physics. The people from universities, schools, hackers, kids, and interested people from the different fields can use the quantum computing provided by the web interface provided through Cloud for different purposes. There are two ways to offer this facility like an experimental mode, and other is simulation mode. The simulation mode offers insights about the working of quantum computers. The web interface offers which draws the chip layout and graphs data, and access to the real physical chip for real entanglement, real superposition, real lasers through the Cloud. Any programming languages can be used to access the quantum computing facility, based on the availability of the APIs.

There are some parameters to be observed in the case of Quantum computers. The Quantum computer maintains in the delicate temperature conditions to get the consistent output as a superposition of the atoms. Accessing the quantum computers through classical computers having web-based portals seems easy. However, the virtualization layers provided by the hypervisors are more architecture dependent, such as Virtualization Technology (VT) enabled microprocessors. Accessing the computing cycles of the Quantum computer through Cloud-based environment leads to new challenges. Such as passing parameters or values through the APIs, converted into the quantum understandable formats. The similar process applies to the processing of reaching to the outputs generated by QC and sent back to the web interfaces or front ends. Although, various vendors provide the APIs though programming languages like Python, C or C++ languages.

Intel announced a 49-qubit processor and chip, code-named "Tangle Lake." The processor design developed in conjunction with its Dutch partners, QuTech and Delft University of Technology. The competitive advantage in the field alongside the efforts of IBM and Google. Rigetti Forest is full-stack APIs for quantum computing in the Cloud, which gives access to 26 Qbits in the quantum VMs (Smith et al.,2016). Quil is an open quantum instruction language based on a shared classical and quantum memory model. Quil has been explicitly designed for near-term quantum computers while remaining expressive enough for general development. pyQuil is a Python library based on Quil for constructing, analyzing, and running quantum programs. The Rigetti's Forest APIs are useful to access the quantum computation in the Cloud (Singh & Sachdev, 2014).

IBM Q is an industry initiative makes accessibility to the quantum computing system, via the IBM Cloud, to run algorithms and experiments, and to explore what might be possible with Quantum Computing collaboratively. One can run algorithms on real Quantum computing hardware, using the Quantum Composer and QISKit software developer kit. IBM Quantum Computers consisting of Qbits and Radiators. The QISKIT thin Python APIs are HTTP API, enables to connect and execute OPENQASM code.

The Cloud-based platforms to access the Quantum Computer through Python-based APIs for simulations or execution on real machines is required as real-machine are costly and under experimentation for better results. The Quantum VMs are available to simulate the working mechanism. The logic gates provided by the Quantum Computers can be considered as one of the different working mechanism, as compared to the classical one. In the initial stage, the classical-quantum hybrid is the best solution. Accessing the services of the quantum computer serves the enormous amount of opportunities to everyone either the Big-Data processing scientist or the engineers testing their simulated environments. The storage services provided through the traditional storage services, or through the flash arrays in the Cloud are well suited. However, the more and more research in the stable quantum computers will give the rising opportunities of computation and storage in the quantum computers. It will be the opportunity for the machine learning and scalable data science researchers which is the task of automating the automation to solve their problems in the scientific applications as the huge amount of computational power will be offered by the quantum computers. The input data and corresponding output labels provided in case of the supervised learning needs the vast data sets.

CLOUD DATA CENTERS INNOVATIONS

The data center maintenance due to the Cloud-enabled technologies and support for the sustainable provisions for the reeducation in the Carbon footprints due to the energy consumptions for cooling the data center and server racks is a kind of innovation. The Cloud vendors also use the robotic arms to arrange, repair and dispose of the hard-disks is an innovation in the Cloud data centers. Due to the shift of consumer-side computing to the SaaS and Cloud Computing, the scale of increase in the data center is increased. The consumers are using Cloud services with collocation or multi-tenant. The virtualization is allowing utilizing the power of the servers with more cost and space effectiveness. Hence the traditional server providers are stabilizing and not increasing their business. Because server virtualization allows the higher server utilization, and therefore no further requirements of the bare metal hardware. The servers in the data center are virtualized and significantly contributing to the cost reduction and carbon footprint reduction (Stansberry, 2017; Gao, 2014).

Some Cloud service providers are moving to use renewable energy sources for running their data centers. Data centers consist of the mechanical, electrical and control systems. To keep the user data safe, the few Cloud data center owners, crush the failed hard disk drives. The people working in the data center are using a bicycle to move from one place to another. They use the highly-pressured water in the pipes in case of a fire. This water, in particular, is cleaned and filtered so that they can use it. Google also use the barcode based robotic arms to load and unload the stacked tapes kept in the data centers. Google optimize servers and racks to use minimal fan power, and the fans are controlled to spin only as fast as necessary to keep the server temperature below a certain threshold.

SECURITY OF CLOUD SERVERS AND ECO-SYSTEM

In case of the use of VMs in the Cloud, the attack vector has to crack the kernel of VM, hypervisor and then the host ok kernel. In the case of the multiple containers inside the Cloud, can compete for the resources and there is a possibility of the Denial of Service (DoS) attack. Another attack vector starts with the APIs used, and the API keys, simple passwords to the user accounts can cause the attacks. There are possibilities of the malware attacks on the Cloud system such as; hypervisor entry points through the shared folder between the host and guest OS, options in VMWare. The hypervisors suffer from the attackers such as VM sprawl, VM escape, DoS, incorrect VM isolation, and Unsecured VM migration. The Hyperjacking is the malicious attack control that creates the virtual environment of VM. The point of the attack is to target the OSthat is below that of the VM so that the attacker's program can run and the applications on the VMs above it will be completely oblivious to its presence (Perez, Szefer, & Lee, 2013).

The administrators generally keep the shared folders as read-only, to avoid the attacks on the host as well as on the guest file system. Botnets are used to spread spam. The malware, worms, trojan horses, or other back-door channels can affect the Cloud system. The VM traffic monitoring, Administrative control, Customer security, and VM segregation are few of the security countermeasures to avoid the security attacks on the VM.

Usually, the Privacy of data in the Cloud is maintained using the transport layer encryption technology, such as Secure Socket Layer (SSL) and Virtual Private Network (VPN). Intrusion Detection Systems (IDS) can detect botnets, malware, and spams. The hypervisors are the essential elements in the Cloud which store the important data. (Diego, Jakub & Lee, 2013). The hypervisors such as Xen, KVM, OpenVZ, Hyper-V, and VMWare may suffer from the security attack vectors. There is the likelihood of attacks such as code Vulnerabilities and cross-site scripting attacks.

Meng & Gong (2013) has improved the crucial traditional distribution system and Public Key Infrastructure(PKI) in the Cloud security key distribution scheme to adapt in the library applications. The PKI-based Cloud computing communication, privacy, authentication, homomorphic encryption protection mechanisms for the library are introduced. (Jia, & Tian, 2013) The enterprise file encryption system (eCryptfs) implemented a secure private Cloud encryption system combined with the overall architecture of the private Cloud system within the Ubuntu10.04 of the enterprise private Cloud file storage server. (Saad, Jalil, & Manaf, 2013) The data provenance is a tool to achieve transparency and accountability between the Cloud provider and users. The idea is behind the data provenance is to provide historical data from its original resources and can facilitate trust using the logging system.

(Poonguzhali, Priyadarsini, Magnifique, & Asvini, 2015) Discusses the mitigation of the timing attack on the Cloud servers and implemented the modified RSA algorithm engine. In Modified RSA algorithm, the techniques are introduced where the random delay is added by multiplying the secret random number before decryption. (Thamizhselvan, Raghuraman, Manoj, & Paul, 2015) introduced the third party encryption approach in the Cloud for confidentiality, authentical and integrity with the help of the hash function. The security algorithms such as Rivest, Shamir, and Adleman (RSA), Data Encryption Standard (DES), RC4, 3DES, Advanced Encryption Standard (AES), & Blowfish are used for encryption and decryption purpose are generally used by many researchers for the Cloud security mechanism. Rath (2017) suggests the Resource provision and QoS support with added security for client side applications in Cloud Computing.

(Kundan & Malik, 2015). Discussed the Trusted Tenant System (TTS). The TTS introduced Cloud trust to the data security where the AES encryption algorithm and Tunneled transport layer security (TTLS) is used. (Quang et al., 2015) Has discussed Secure Cloud Storage (SCS), a framework for Data Protection as a Service (DPaaS) to Cloud computing users. The DPaaS is compared over the existing Data encryption as a Service (DEaaS) used by Amazon and Google. The DPaas separates data management from security management. (Tao & Lee, 2015) Presented the development of the multi-tiered Cloud security (MTCS) standards to certify the Cloud services and serve as the SaaS. Vinodhini & Ayyasamy (2017) discussed the Minutiae Map (MM) algorithm implemented for the processing of fingerprint-based authentication, to access the location of the personal file on the multi-Cloud environment. The Cross-site request forgery (CSRF) and Cross-site scripting (XSS) prevention are possible through the proposed MM algorithm. The authors have compared the Orientation Map, Gabor Filter and core point detection techniques.

CHALLENGES IN DISTRIBUTED CLOUD COMPUTING

There are many challenges where Cloud preparation includes distributed Distributed Systems. Thea tasks such as Monitoring, Automatic Management, Relocation, Efficiency, and Optimization. These problems are addressed in the several works in the form of the HPC provided through the Cloud. As running the compute-intensive HPC tasks involves huge complications to set up the Cloud environment Devare et al., (2019) developed the systematic analysis and solutions to these which includes the heterogeneous types of architectures consisting of the different processor architectures, inter-connectivity techniques, the problems of the shared memory, distributed memory, and hybrid architectures in distributed computing like resilience, scalability, check-pointing, and fault tolerance.

SUMMARY

The measurable amount of disruption is happening due to the adoption of innovations in Cloud Computing as part of the different businesses. It changes the life of the employees of the organization, as they can focus on the core business activities. The HPC unit producing companies are also observing the stability plateau in their sales, instead of a rising graph. The reason is apparent that the businesses are deploying the hypervisors on the bare-metal hardware and creating the multiple virtualized infrastructure. This results in a massive amount of cost-cutting. The maintenance of the Cloud infrastructure, hiring expenses, and expenditure on the skilled manpower is shifted to the Cloud vendors. The companies having their existing private infrastructure are elastically extending the capabilities to the public Cloud providers.

The Cloud-based innovations adopted by CDN owners are using the Cloud services for better speed, performance, and the needs of the times when the popular events like football, nation-wide elections campaigning need the secure and consolidated infrastructures. The different web-based application is developing vendors, security service providers, mobile-based application developers highly reliable on Cloud-based services. Such as when the website traffic is increasing on the peak times like new-year event, festivals and mega-sales by the e-commerce portals, the elastically extending services provided by the Cloud vendors are holistically suitable for the technical requirements of resource provisioning.

To avoid the overheads, there is the introduction of the Serverless computing called FaaS is highly acceptable at the lowest level of granularity. The manufacturing, logistics, oil and gas, shipping, applying the Cloud Computing in the product life cycle management and monitoring of the vital assets and equipment using Digital Twins. For example, industrial robots, turbines, engines, boilers and many more are monitoring, controlled, and maintained very well due to the DT which is the extended application of IIoT.

The recent advancement in the development of Quantum computers by the leading vendors has invested enormous resources and created a faster computer. To access quantum computers similar to the classical computers the APIs and VM based Cloud access is enabling the several research opportunities in this new innovative field, to find the unsolved mysteries of the science such as in the biological, chemical and teleportation problems.

REFERENCES

Chen, F., Guo, K., Lin, J., & Porta, T. L. (2012). Intra-Cloud Lightning: Building CDNs in the Cloud. *Proceedings - IEEE INFOCOM*, 433–444.

ChrisC. (2018). Retrieved from https://www.youtube.com/watch?v=LikdmXfWO2A&t=2312s

Cicco, L. D., Mascolo, S., & Calamita, D. (2013). A Resource Allocation Controller for Cloud-based Adaptive Video Streaming. *IEEE International Conference on Communications: IEEE ICC'13 - 1st International Workshop on Mobile Cloud Computing and Services*, 723-727.

Devare, M. H. (2019). Challenges and Opportunities in High Performance Cloud Computing. In S. Singh & R. Mohan Sharma (Eds.), *Handbook of Research on the IoT, Cloud Computing, and Wireless Network Optimization* (pp. 85–114). Hershey, PA: IGI Global. doi:10.4018/978-1-5225-7335-7.ch005

FowlerM. (2017). Retrieved from https://martinfowler.com/articles/serverless.html

Gao, J. (2014). *Machine Learning Applications for Data Center Optimization*. Google.

Gong, Y., Zhang, C., Fang, Y., & Sun, J. (2012). Protecting Location Privacy for Task Allocation in Ad Hoc Mobile Cloud Computing. *IEEE Transactions on Emerging Topics in Computing*, 1–12.

Hu, H., Wen, Y., Chua, T. S., Huang, J., Zhu, W., & Li, X. (2016). Joint Content Replication and Request Routing for Social Video Distribution Over Cloud CDN: A Community Clustering Method. *IEEE Transactions on Circuits and Systems for Video Technology*, *26*(7), 1320–1333. doi:10.1109/TCSVT.2015.2455712

Hu, H., Wen, Y., Chua, T. S., Huang, J., Zhu, W., & Wu, D. (2014). Community-Based Effective Social Video Contents Placement in Cloud Centric CDN Network. *Proceedings of IEEE ICME*. 10.1109/ICME.2014.6890134

Hu, M., Luo, J., Wang, Y., & Veeravalli, B. (2014). Practical Resource Provisioning and Caching with Dynamic Resilience for Cloud-Based Content Distribution Networks. *IEEE Transactions on Parallel and Distributed Systems*, *25*(8), 2169–2179. doi:10.1109/TPDS.2013.287

Jia, Z., & Tian, X. (2013). A Novel Security Private Cloud Solution Based on ECryptfs. *6th International Conference on Information Management, Innovation Management and Industrial Engineering*, 38- 41. 10.1109/ICIII.2013.6703598

Kundan, K., & Malik, L. G. (2015). TTS: A Study of Trusted Tenant System in Cloud Computing Environment. *IEEE Sponsored 2nd International Conference on Innovations in Information Embedded and Communication Systems*, 1-5.

Li, Y., Shen, Y., & Liu, Y. (2012). Utilizing Content Delivery Network in Cloud Computing. *Proceedings of, ICCP2012*, 137–143.

Lin, C. F., Leu, M. C., Chang, C. W., & Yuan, S. M. (2011). The Study and Methods for Cloud-based CDN. *International Conference on Cyber-Enabled Distributed Computing and Knowledge Discovery*, 470-475. 10.1109/CyberC.2011.82

Lowe, S. D. (2017). *All-Flash Data Centers for Dummies, Pure Storage Edition, Published by*. John Wiley & Sons, Inc.

Meng, Q., & Gong, C. (2013). Research of Cloud Computing Security in Digital Library. *6th IEEE International Conference on Information Management, Innovation Management and Industrial Engineering*, 41-44. 10.1109/ICIII.2013.6703173

Murphy, J., & Roser, M. (2017). *Internet*. Retrieved from https://ourworldindata.org/internet/

Nadareishvili, I., Mitra, R., McLarty, M., & Amundsen, M. (2016). *Micro-Service Architecture Aligning Principles, Practices, and Culture*. O'Reilly Media.

Nijim, S., & Pagano, B. (2017). APIs for Dummies. John Wiley & Sons, Inc.

Overton, J., & Brigham, J. C. (2017). *The Digital Twin, Data-Driven Simulations Innovate the Manufacturing Process*. DXC Technology White Paper.

Paris, C. J., Laflen, J. B., Grabb, M. L., & Kalitan, D. M. (2017). *The Future for The Industrial Services: The Digital Twin, Infosys Insight*. General Electric, White Paper.

Perez, B. D., Szefer, J., & Lee, R. B. (2013). Characterizing Hypervisor Vulnerabilities in Cloud Computing Servers. *Proceedings of the Workshop on Security in Cloud Computing (SCC)*.

Poonguzhali, E., Priyadarsini, A., Magnifique, P., & Asvini, S. (2015). A Security Model For Timing Attack in Cloud Environment. *IEEE Sponsored 2nd International Conference on Innovations in Information Embedded and Communication Systems ICIIECS'15*, 1-5.

Quang, H. V., Maurizio, C., Rasool, A., Ali, S., Fadi, A. E., & Theo, D. (2015). Secure Cloud Storage: A framework for Data Protection as a Service in the multi-Cloud environment. *1st Workshop on Security and Privacy in the Cloud*, 638-642.

Quantumrealmgames. (2018). Retrieved from http://quantumrealmgames.com/#qcrules

Rath, M. (2017). Resource Provision and Qos Support with Added Security for Client Side Applications in Cloud Computing. *International Journal of Information Technology*, *9*(3), 1–8.

Rego, P. A. L., Bonfim, M. S., Ortiz, M. D., & Bezerra, J. M. (2015). *An OpenFlow-based Elastic Solution for Cloud-CDN Video Streaming Service*. IEEE. doi:10.1109/GLOCOM.2015.7417789

Saad, M. I. M., Jalil, K. A., & Manaf, M. (2013). Data Provenance Trusted Model in Cloud Computing. *3rd International Conference on Research and Innovation in Information Systems (ICRIIS'13)*, 257-262. 10.1109/ICRIIS.2013.6716719

Singh, H., & Sachdev, A. (2014). The Quantum Way of Cloud Computing. *International Conference on Reliability, Optimization and Information Technology – ICROIT*, 397-400.

Smith, R., Curtis, M. J., & Zeng, W. J. (2016). *A Practical Quantum Instruction Set Architecture*. Retrieved from https://arxiv.org/abs/1608.03355

Stansberry, M. (2016). *Data Center Industry Survey. Making Your Asset Smarter with the Digital Twin*. DNVGL.

Tao, Y. S., & Lee, H. Y. (2015). Certifying SaaS in the MTCS Framework. *2015 International Conference on Cloud Computing Research and Innovation*, 15-18.

Thamizhselvan, M., Raghuraman, R., Manoj, S. G., & Paul, P. V. (2015). A Novel Security Model For Cloud Using Trusted Third-Party Encryption. *IEEE Sponsored 2nd International Conference on Innovations in Information Embedded and Communication Systems ICIIECS'15*, 1-5.

Vinodhini, A. N., & Ayyasamy, S. (2017). Prevention of Personal Data in Cloud Computing Using Bio-Metric. *IEEE International Conference on Innovations in Green Energy and Healthcare Technologies*, 1-6. 10.1109/IGEHT.2017.8094085

Volkmann, D. (2016). *The Rise of Digital Twins*. Retrieved from https://www.ge.com/digital/blog/rise-digital-twins

WIP. (2019). *World Intellectual Property Indicators, Economics and Statistics Series by WIPO, Info-graphics, Comparison 2015-16*. WIP.

Chapter 2
Trust Management in Fog Computing:
A Survey

Sunilkumar S. Manvi
REVA University, India

Naveen Chandra Gowda
REVA University, India

ABSTRACT

Fog computing is an encouraging computational model that extends distributed cloud computing to the edge of systems. It varies to cloud computing with some of the attributes. Fog computing has new challenges while building and maintaining the trust among the fog nodes and with edge devices. The solutions applied for the various cloud challenges cannot be directly applied for fog computing. This chapter gives an overview of these difficulties and relates solutions in a concise way. It also highlights the open challenges that still exist in fog computing.

DOI: 10.4018/978-1-5225-8295-3.ch002

INTRODUCTION

Distributed Cloud Computing has definitely changed the scene of data/information technology by giving some real advantages to IT clients, including dispensing with forthright IT venture, scalability, relative expenses and so on (Ghahramani, 2017; Zheng, 2017). In Wojciech Burakowski (2018), the idea of distributed cloud computing frameworks reaching out to Cloud Federation (CF) by combining various clouds into one framework is presented. Cloud service providers work in geologically distributed fashion where different servers take on client requests like calamity recuperation and multi-site reinforcements which ended up across the board. Figure 1 depicts the CF where 5 clouds are connected to it.

Processing resources in a cloud based framework can be effortlessly worked out and can discharge with negligible administration association. Along these lines, the cloud foundation develops a two layer stage, where fundamental information gathering undertakings are done in the edge gadgets, and after that the examination related tasks are performed in the cloud.

Distributed cloud computing has numerous favorable circumstances including on-request self-benefit, interminable scaling, putting away of expansive measure of information and so forth. The computation in a cloud has its own issues while performing administration, for example, vast reaction time for exchanging the crude information to the cloud and afterward preparing it there, disturbance in the basic correspondence organization, issues identified with information security and

Figure 1. Ideal CF with of 5 clouds connected by network

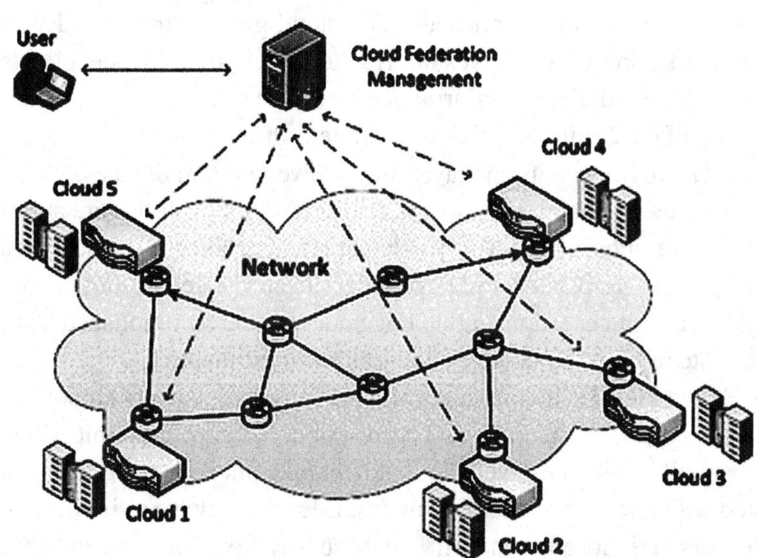

protection. Keeping in mind the end goal to conquer these issues, the idea of fog computing (Bonomi, 2012) has been risen as of late, which discusses doing the play between the edge gadgets and the cloud servers.

The rest of the paper is organized as follows. Section 2 introduces the fog computing with its working architecture and characteristics. Section 3 summarizes the different security and privacy issues in fog computing. Section 4 discusses the trust issues and the works carried out by the researchers. Section 5 presents the open challenges so that better solutions can be worked out. Finally, section 6 concludes the paper.

FOG COMPUTING

Fog computing is a platform where the edge gadgets, i.e. switches, routers, sensor hubs and nodes with gateways, interchange with the cloud servers keeping in mind the end goal to give administrations. Fog computing was first started by Cisco to stretch out the distributed computing to the edge of a system (Cisco, 2017). Cloudlet (Satyanarayanan, 2014) was worked before the proposition of fog, yet intrinsically agrees fog computing idea. Figure 2 represents the three-tier engineering (Sarkar, 2018), which is one of the fundamental and broadly utilized models in fog computing. Correspondences between Fog-Fog, Fog-Cloud, and Fog-Edge are all bi-directional.

The tiers are discussed as follows:

- **The Cloud (Tier 1):** It incorporates superior servers and capacity sectors for broadcasting, information warehousing and enormous information examination (Hua, 2017). The information is forwarded to the cloud using fast remote or wired correspondences. The cloud gives extreme and worldwide scope. As a storehouse, it gives information stockpiling to meet clients' long-haul needs and intelligent information examination.
- **The Fog (Tier 2):** It comprises of a system of interrelated Fog nodes (Hua, 2017). The fog nodes in this layer are involved system devices, for example, switch, gateway, router, and Access Points (APs). Fog nodes are autonomous and can be interrelated for participation. Organization and community technique are associated on Fog nodes to complete the organization and control. The joint exertion among Fog nodes can be accomplished by methods for remote or close-by correspondences amongst them.
- **The Edge (Tier 3):** It comprises of a few physical gadgets empowered with their universal ID, detecting, and correspondence capacity limit (Hua, 2017), for example, machines, vehicles and mobile phones. Every edge node is related with one of the other Fog nodes. Edge nodes have a significant variety of sensors and close-by data. It is particularly luxurious and dreary to send

Figure 2. Fog computing architecture

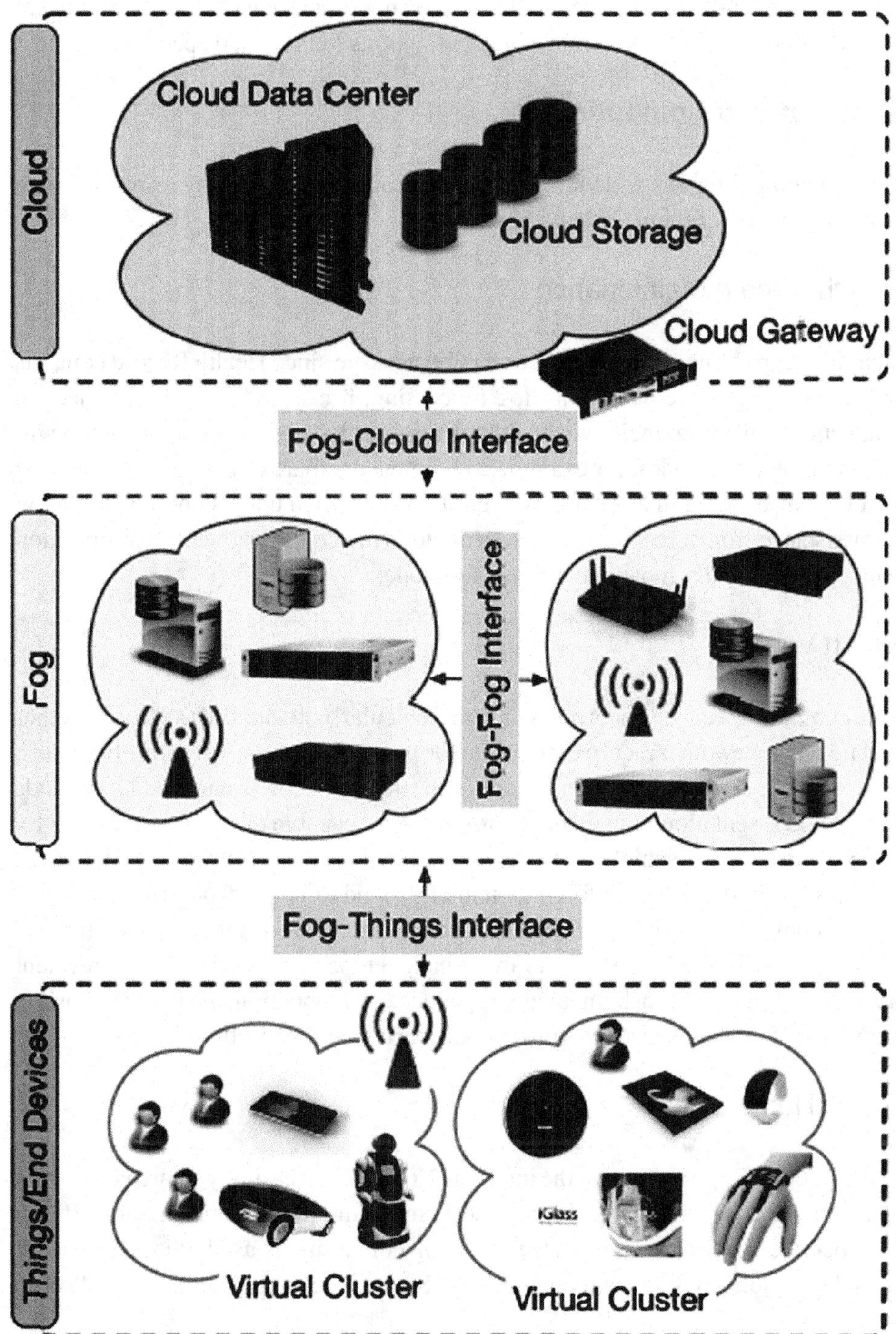

all of the data from terminal edge contraptions to the cloud over a framework. Consequently, by interfacing them to Fog nodes, one can deal with the sincere data anyway not trade from edge contraptions to the cloud speedily.

Scope of Fog Computing

The fog computing has wide range of applications on which many researchers are working on, few of them are stated below.

Health Record Maintenance

Health Record Maintenance has been a delicate issue since Health Record contains profitable and private data. With fog processing, it can understand the objective that patient will claim their own health information locally. Those information will be put away in fog nodes, for example, cell phone or smart vehicle. The processing will be redistributed in a private-safeguarding way when understanding is looking for assistance from a restorative lab or a doctor's office. Adjustment of information happens specifically inpatient-claimed fog node.

Smart Vehicle

Fog computing can be incorporated into vehicular networks. Based on whether additional framework is required, vehicular fog processing can be sorted into two kinds, infrastructure based and self-sufficient. The first is VTube (Luan, 2011), depends on fog nodes sent along the roadside; fog hubs are capable to send/recover data to/from the driving-by vehicles. The second is referenced in (Eltoweissy 2010) uses vehicles on-the-fly to shape fog or potentially cloud to help adhoc occasions; each fog can convey its customer inside and other fogs. There are different applications for vehicular fog computing, no matter the principal type or the second sort. Prevalent applications are: traffic light planning, blockage alleviation, insurance sharing, stopping office the executives, traffic data sharing, and so forth.

Smart Home

With the quick improvement of the Internet of Things, increasingly smart gadgets and sensors are associated at home. In any case, items from various merchants are difficult to cooperate. To take care of these issues, fog computing is used to incorporate all trash into a solitary stage and enable those SmartHome applications with flexible resources. To utilize home security application for instance, widely deployed secure sensors comprise of shrewd lock, video/audio recorder, different sensor screens (for example light sensor, occupancy sensor, and movement sensor and so forth). If not results of same vendor, those secure gadgets are difficult to consolidate.

Fog computing is a profoundly virtualized stage (M. Aazam, 2016) that expert computing, stockpiling, and systems administration benefits between End User and Data Center of the conventional distributed computing. Fog Computing has the attributes (M. Aazam, 2016): low inactivity and location awareness, geographic appropriation, mobility, high number of node computation, wireless access, real-time applications and heterogeneity.

SECURITY AND PRIVACY ISSUES IN FOG COMPUTING

Security and Privacy issues of current researches are classified into four types: 1) Attacks, 2) Authentication, 3) Trust and 4) Privacy.

Attacks

Since the fog nodes are deployed in few spots with generally less protected, may experience different malicious assaults (P. Hua, 2017), like Man in the middle attack. DoS attack, etc. The Lee et al, in (K. Lee, 2015) endeavor to discover the answers for the assaults from the malignant nodes. In their examination, the overwhelming workload in the fog nodes are separated into a few employments and handled by every individual fog node. So regardless of whether a portion of these hubs are assaulted by pernicious clients, it is difficult to guarantee the security of information. And still, at the end of the day they neglect to give the precise arrangement. Be that as it may, in the meantime assaults may happen from the malignant edge nodes of clients, in which distinguishing the malignant edge is vital in information security. Sohal et al proposed (A. S. Sohal, 2014) a system by utilizing Markov model and virtual honey pot device to take care of the issue.

Authentication

The authentication among the devices of organized fog network is must to get the administrations. A gadget needs to end up being a piece of the framework by verifying itself to the haze plans. This is principal to keep the area of unapproved nodes. It transforms into a commanding troubles as the gadgets related with the framework are constrained in various ways including power, storage and processing. Ordinary confirmation using declarations and Public-Key Infrastructure (PKI) are not proper due to the asset imperatives of gadgets. Numerous scientists proposed the arrangements including an open key system using multicast confirmation for secure correspondences (Y.W. Law, 2013). Verification ought to be offered as an organization administration to a gadget that requires to get approved to the haze hub with the help of the representative, may be the Certifying Authority (CA).

Trust

The network systems are required to give solid and secure administrations to the end users. This requires all devices that are part of the fog system to have a specific level of trust on one another. Authentication assumes to be a noteworthy part in building up beginning arrangement of relations between edge devices and fog nodes in the system. However, this isn't sufficient as devices can simply breakdown for any malfunction activities. So, maintaining trust is a huge challenge in encouraging relations in light of past cooperation. Trust should play a two way in a fog system: the fog nodes that offer administration services to edge devices and the edge devices that send information to the fog nodes. It needs a hearty trust model set up to guarantee dependability and security in fog infrastructure.

Privacy

The Fog nodes are scattered in extensive zones, unified control is getting to be difficult. Once an intruder enters inside the system can mine and take clients security information that is traded among substances. Expanded correspondence among the three tiers that constitute the fog engineering can likewise prompt protection leakage. Area security, as examined in (K. Lee, 2015), is a standout amongst the most critical models for security, since the place of gear can be connected to the proprietors. As appeared in (Y. Hong, 2017) smart meters' readings can unveil data about the time that the house is vacant or even the TV programs that the End User wants to watch.

As new frameworks that depend on fog computing are expert postured, new protection challenges likewise emerge. In (D. Koo, 2018), author represent Fog-based Vehicular Crowd Sensing (FVCS). In this framework vehicular fog nodes can incidentally store and break down all sensing information that is transferred by vehicles all together to give nearby administrations, playing the part of focal cloud servers. By trading information about nearby circumstance.

Regardless of whether frameworks are all around structured and safely actualized, they can uncover basic data through their side channels. Potential outcomes of data spillage through side diverts are called attention to in the writing and incorporate electromagnetic radiation, discernibly timing of specific exercises, control utilization of specific gadgets and even light acoustic or warmth spreads from hardware (D. Koo, 2018). All these protection issues emerge the requirement for increasingly modern arrangements and countermeasures.

TRUST RELATED ISSUES IN FOG COMPUTING

Trust assumes a noteworthy part in encouraging relations in light of past communications among Fog nodes and edge devices. The most basic part of Fog computing is the fog node as it is responsible for guaranteeing protection and secrecy for end-clients (A. M. Elmisery, 2014).. In addition, this segment must be trusted for appointment, as they should be guaranteed that the Fog node actualizes the worldwide disguising process on their discharged information and triggers non-malignant exercises as it were. The Fog system must have a specific level of trust on each other. Some of the trust related issue are: Middleware trust model, Service trust, Location based trust and Trust based attacks.

Middle Wear Trust Model

A trust model is the one which is considered for two purposes. Firstly, identifying the parameters required for measuring the trust in a fog service. Second, build a model which can verify and monitor the parameters set for measuring the trust level. (A. M. Elmisery, 2014). Introduced a Fog-based middleware system, where trust specialists ascertain the approximated relational trust between a Fog node and the Cloud. The trust computation can also be done in a decentralized manner by utilizing the entropy definition of fog nodes. (Soleymani, 2017). Bring up that trust foundation among vehicles is essential to integrity and reliability of uses, which uses a fuzzy based trust model. The work (T. Wang, 2017) presents a Trusted Third Party (TTP) for its protection. Since malignant assaults can make sensor correspondences be problematic, a trust assessment technique is expected to guarantee the unwavering quality relationship among sensors to oppose noxious attacks.

Service Trust

A safe and reliable way for clients is required in fog computing (A. M. Elmisery, 2014). In any case, the Service Level Agreement (SLA) is regularly influenced by numerous components, for example, cost, utilization, kind of applications, network usage. Subsequently, given a specific situation, it is very hard to determine a service trust, which merits top to bottom investigation. Trust assessment instruments in the cloud can be changed to build the security of Fog administrations (Y. Xia, 2017).

Location Based Trust

There are various devices at various areas and with different correspondence types and associations structures in the Fog computing. In any case, Fog nodes can give nearby and territorial computation to clients for quicker reaction. In this manner, how to achieve these objectives is one of future examinations suitable to the Fog's characteristics. (T. D. Dang, 2018) Propose an area based trust model for trust correspondences among Fog nodes at distinctive districts. One Fog node is chosen as head node per region which can perform administration and task execution in a district. Head nodes are utilized to process trust esteems for nodes in a similar district.

Trust Related Attacks

Fog computing can be subjected to a malicious attacks and without legitimate safety efforts set up may seriously undermine the abilities of the system. Some of the attacks are: Denial of Service, Man in the middle and Collusion attacks.

1. **Denial of Service (DoS)**: Since dominant part of the devices associated to the systems are not mutually authenticated, propelling a DoS attacks turns out to be straight forward (Rashmi V Deshmukh, 2015). The attack might be propelled when devices that are associated, request for communication. That is a traded off or breaking down node prepare requests to a fog node in this way slowing down demands made by authentic nodes.
2. **Man in the Middle Attack:** The transmissions can be made secured between the fog node and edge devices, even then it can be eavesdropped or modified by the attackers before it can be authorized by the fog node (A. M. Elmisery, 2014). Since all the controller signals are sent over this channel, once assaulted,

the framework is completely constrained by an aggressor. It is a catastrophe for both the framework associations and their customers. A countermeasure using the Bloom channels to tackle the assaults is proposed (C. Li, Z. Qin, 2017). One can likewise take care of the issue by receiving encryption and decoding (P. Hua, 2017).

3. **Collusion Attacks:** The trust plan of a Publish-Subscribe system (PSS) in the Fog computing is proposed to achieve trust against collusion attacks (Q. Wang, 2017). A dealer based PSS is given in (E. Onica, 2016). The part of a dealer is an imperative piece of a PSS. Dealers speak with various substances and coordinate the reasonable client prerequisite and transmit client's information (E. Onica, 2016). They are also used to decouple clients' connection and give asynchronous interchanges. A malicious node (might be publisher or subscriber) who should keep the mystery of other nodes would purposely release the key to the threatening specialists. To diminish the security dangers and vulnerabilities, the investigation (Q. Wang, 2017) proposes content-based PSS with differential protection in a Fog system.

OPEN TRUST CHALLENGES IN THE FOG COMPUTING.

Tending to issues identified with trust in a fog computing is marginally trickier contrasted with distributed cloud computing condition. The transparency of fog computing condition and the two-way necessity of trust are significant difficulties in outlining a trust maintenance in fog system. At the end of the day, distributed cloud computing condition have a set up security framework adhering to standards in security, so there is a huge necessity of setting such bench marking trust model in fog computing too. Among which few of the much needed challenges are as follows,

Trusted Node Identification

As the Fog computing is with very constrained resources, it is very challenging task to identify the crucial fog node opted for the user task in a better way. Since Fog nodes have a tendency to be resource constrained, a light-weight algorithm is to be designed for trust calculation in view of a locale Fog might be planned for meeting certain obliged resource prerequisites. On the off chance that the computation undertaking is huge, it might be executed in the cloud. Apply any probabilistic methods to analyze the trust values based on which the trust node can be selected.

Building Trust Model

Many researchers have adopted the trusted third party in their research (A. M. Elmisery, 2014) but it could not solve the location based trust problems. The author in (T. D. Dang, 2018) considers the location based trust management by considering the cluster of locale nodes with the head node. But the main risk is what if the head node itself is a malicious node? Facing a major challenge. Fog nodes may not be provided with better monitor and protection while deployment in the trust model, which leads to security threats, so once a node is malicious it spreads over the model and damages and whole system. It is again a challenging task to keep the model to be trusted by avoiding such spreading of malicious activities.

Orchestration

Large scale Fog Infrastructures can be adopted in different applications such as healthcare, smart cities and so on. It is challenging task to produce a trust network which can suite any applications. An agent based trust model might be utilized for organization. A multi-agent coordination technique might be received to screen the applications and arrange them safely, progressively in the Fog. It is also important to look in to the fog nodes architecture, as in a cluster of fog nodes if any one of the node is attacked it should be repaired or removed from the cluster by moving the task and data of removed node to other node by orchestrating/reorganizing the clusters. A complex decision making protocol is to be designed for analyzing the propagation of malicious nodes in fog network.

Collusion Trust

A new techniques are to be developed to maintain the trust against the collusion attacks. The collusion attacks need to be addressed are: firstly, if providers becomes malicious it affects brokers. Brokers spread the malicious fake information to the fog device causing them to become malicious. Secondly, the attack may also happen from user and spreading across the edge devices and fog nodes. Both has the major security threat for maintaining the trust, need to be addressed.

CONCLUSION

The fog computing extends the cloud computing but irreplaceable. Like the cloud computing, fog computing too has many issues related to security and trust maintenance. The well-developed solutions in cloud computing cannot be applied directly on fog computing due to various reasons like attribute and functionality variations. This paper presented the outline of trust related issues in the fog computing. The aim of this survey is to summarize the research contributions towards the trust and outline the future challenges to maintain the trust among fog nodes and with edge devices.

REFERENCES

Aazam, M., & Huh, E. N. (2016). Fog computing: The cloud-IoT/IoE middle- ware paradigm. *IEEE Potentials*, *35*(3), 40–44. doi:10.1109/MPOT.2015.2456213

Bonomi, F., Milito, R., Zhu, J., & Addepalli, S. (2012). *Fog computing and its role in the internet of things. In Mobile cloud computing* (pp. 13–16). ACM.

Burakowski, W., Beben, A., van den Berg, H., Bosman, J. W., Hasslinger, G., Kertesz, A., ... Stiller, B. (2018). Traffic Management for Cloud Federation. *Springer, LNCS*, *10768*, 269–312.

Cisco. (2017). *Cisco Delivers Vision of Fog Computing to Accelerate Value from Billions of Connected Devices*. Press Release. Available: https://newsroom.cisco.com/press-release-content?type=webcontent&articleId=1334100

Dang, T. D., & Hoang, D. (2018). A Data Protection Model for Fog Computing. *Second International Conference on Fog and Mobile Edge computing (FMEC)*, 32-38.

Elmisery, A. M., Rho, S., & Botvich, D. (2014). A Fog Based Middleware for Automated Compliance with OECD Privacy Principles in Internet of Healthcare Things. *IEEE Access: Practical Innovations, Open Solutions*, *4*, 8418–8841. doi:10.1109/ACCESS.2016.2631546

Eltoweissy, M., Olariu, S., & Younis, M. (2010). Towards autonomous vehic-ular clouds. Ad hoc Networks, 49, 1-16.

Ghahramani, Zhou, & Hon. (2017). Toward Cloud Computing QoS Architecture: Analysis of Cloud Systems and Cloud Services. *IEEE/CAA Journal of Automatica Sinica, 4*, 5-17.

Hong, Y., Liu, W. M., & Wang, L. (2017). Privacy preserving smart meter streaming against information leakage of appliance status. *IEEE Transactions on Information Forensics and Security*, *12*(9), 2227–2241. doi:10.1109/TIFS.2017.2704904

Hua, P., Dhelima, S., Ning, H., & Qiu, T. (2017). Survey on fog computing: Architecture, key technologies, applications and open issues. *Journal of Network and Computer Applications*, *98*, 27–42. doi:10.1016/j.jnca.2017.09.002

Koo, D., & Hur, J. (2018). Privacy-preserving deduplication of encrypted data with dynamic ownership management in fog computing. *Future Generation Computer Systems*, *78*, 739–752. doi:10.1016/j.future.2017.01.024

Law, Palaniswami, Kounga, & Lo. (2013). WAKE: Key management scheme for wide area measurement systems in smart grid. *IEEE Communication Managements, l51*, 34-41.

Lee, K., Kim, D., Ha, D., Rajput, U., & Oh, H. (2015). On Security and Privacy Issues of Fog Computing Supported Internet of Things environment. *6th International Conference on the Network of the Future (NOF)*, 1-3. 10.1109/NOF.2015.7333287

Li, C., Qin, Z., Novak, E., & Li, Q. (2017). *Securing SDN Infrastructure of IoT-Fog Network from MitM Attacks. IEEE Internet of Things Journal.*

Luan, H., Cai, L. X., Chen, J., Shen, X., & Bai, F. (2011). Vtube: Towardsthe media rich city life with autonomous vehicular content distribution. *IEEE Communications Society Conference on Sensor, Mesh and AdHoc Communications and Networks (SECON)*. 10.1109/SAHCN.2011.5984918

Onica, E., Felber, P., Mercier, H., & Riviére, E. (2016). Confidentiality-preserving publish/subscribe: A survey. *ACM Computing Surveys*, *49*(2), 1–41. doi:10.1145/2940296

Rashmi, V. (2015). Understanding DDoS attack & its effects in cloud environment. *Procedia of Computer Science, Elsevier*, *49*, 202–210. doi:10.1016/j.procs.2015.04.245

Sarkar, S., Chatterjee, S., & Misra, S. (2018). Assessment of the suitability of fog computing in the context of Internet of things. *IEEE Transaction on Cloud Computing*, *6*(1), 46–59. doi:10.1109/TCC.2015.2485206

Satyanarayanan, M., Chen, Z., Ha, K., Hu, W., Richter, W., & Pil-lai, P. (2014). Cloudlets: at the leading edge of mobile-cloud convergence. *IEEE International Conference on Mobile Computing, Applications and Services (MobiCASE)*, 1-9. 10.4108/icst.mobicase.2014.257757

Sohal, A. S., Sandhu, R., Sood, S. K., & Chang, V. (2017). *A cybersecurity framework to identify malicious edge device in fog computing and cloud-of-things environments. In Computers & Security* (pp. 1–15). Elsevier.

Soleymani, S. A., Abdullah, A. H., Zareei, M., Anisi, M. H., Vargas-Rosales, C., Khan, M. K., & Goudarzi, S. (2017). A Secure Trust Model based on Fuzzy Logic in Vehicular Ad Hoc Networks with Fog computing. *IEEE Access: Practical Innovations, Open Solutions*, *99*, 1–10.

Wang, Q., Chen, D., Zhang, N., Ding, Z., & Qin, Z. (2017). PCP: A Privacy-Preserving Content-Based Publish-Subscribe Scheme with Differential Privacy in Fog computing. *IEEE Access: Practical Innovations, Open Solutions*, *5*, 17962–17986. doi:10.1109/ACCESS.2017.2748956

Wang, T., Li, Y., Chen, Y., Tian, H., Cai, Y., Jia, W., & Wang, B. (2017). Fog-Based Evaluation Approach for Trustworthy Communication in Sensor-Cloud System. *IEEE Communications Letters*, *14*, 1–4.

Xia, Y., Hong, H., Lin, G., & Sun, Z. (2017). A Secure and Efficient Cloud Resource Allocation Scheme with Trust Evaluation Mechanism Based on Combinatorial Double Auction. KSII. *Transactions on Internet and Information Systems (Seoul)*, *9*, 4197–4219.

Zheng, W. B., Zhou, M. C., Xia, Y. N., Wu, L., Luo, X., Pang, S. C., & Zhu, Q. S. (2017). Percentile performance estimation of unreliable IaaS clouds and their cost-optimal capacity decision. *IEEE Access: Practical Innovations, Open Solutions*, *5*, 2808–2818. doi:10.1109/ACCESS.2017.2666793

Chapter 3
Convergence of Manufacturing Cloud and Industrial IoT

Manoj Himmatrao Devare
https://orcid.org/0000-0002-9530-3914
Amity University Mumbai, India

ABSTRACT

The manufacturing cloud (CMfg) covers the use of three key technologies including cloud computing, the industrial internet of things (IIoT), and collaborative engineering for achieving the productivity and quality challenges in the big manufacturing, which is enabled due to the communication, mobile, and broadcasting network. It is necessary to establish a flexible and adaptive infrastructure for manufacturing industry to share and use various manufacturing resources and services on-demand under the dynamic, complicated, and large-scale business environment. The CMfg makes the industry more agile, responsive, and reconfigurable for exposure to the industry as a global manufacturing enterprise. The chapter considers the CMfg facets and IIoT, use cases in the manufacturing industry, and explains IIoT and CMfg as a complementary technology.

DOI: 10.4018/978-1-5225-8295-3.ch003

INTRODUCTION

Cloud Models and Its Relevance in the Context

The Cloud Computing services provide the flexible, on-demand, and hosted resources pool delivered on the Internet. The Cloud offers the ready to use services with minimal intervention either in the private or secured public and hybrid models. The broad network access to more comprehensive services, resource pooling on demand like computing, memory, storage, networking, and access to the Application Programming Interfaces (APIs) through the Cloud makes it more suitable to adopt in the Manufacturing industry and Industrial Automation enabled with the sensor based Industrial Internet of Things (IIoT). The Cloud provides the rapid elasticity feature which scales up and down with an inevitable rise and fall of the demand of the resources in the Manufacturing industry. It has measured service, i.e., metered usage and billing that provides the pay-as-you-go and only for actual utilization, i.e., to reduce the operational expenditure (OPEX) and capital expenditure (CAPEX).

The basic Cloud models like Infrastructure-as-a-Service (IaaS), Platform-as-a-Service (PaaS) & Software-as-a-Service (SaaS) are entirely useful in the manufacturing industry at the various stages in the manufacturing process. The taxonomy of the Cloud-based services listed as in figure 1. The Manufacturing Cloud (CMfg) addresses the challenges and integrates the various software on the Cloud which reduces the overall cost in terms of OPEX and CAPEX. The Cloud-based services provided for simplifying the manufacturing processes through the information technology supported infrastructure in the Cloud-based services either through the public, private or hybrid type of methodologies.

The Cloud provides scalable and flexible support, in the various stages of the manufacturing processes and resource sharing. One can look towards the CMfg as the various software services provided in the Cloud environment, related to the manufacturing process. Whereas, it is a broad area to ensure the manufacturing services and shared resources not only in the form of software but also the integration of the various resources, availability, efficiency, affordability securely and systematically. The involvement of the data transfer techniques, tools and protocols play a crucial role such as in the IIoT. The economics of providing all these services through the Cloud platform is very much pragmatic and mostly does not add any cost in the finished product and reduces the overall cost of the manufacturing. The under-utilized capacity of the manufacturing assets can available on a rental basis, through the Cloud-based integration. The scalability issue of the CMfg can be easily solved due to the various scalability, elasticity and Cloud Bursting features of the Cloud. (Lartigau, Nie, Xu, Zhan & Mou, 2012) & (Rath, 2018).

Figure 1. Cloud taxonomy

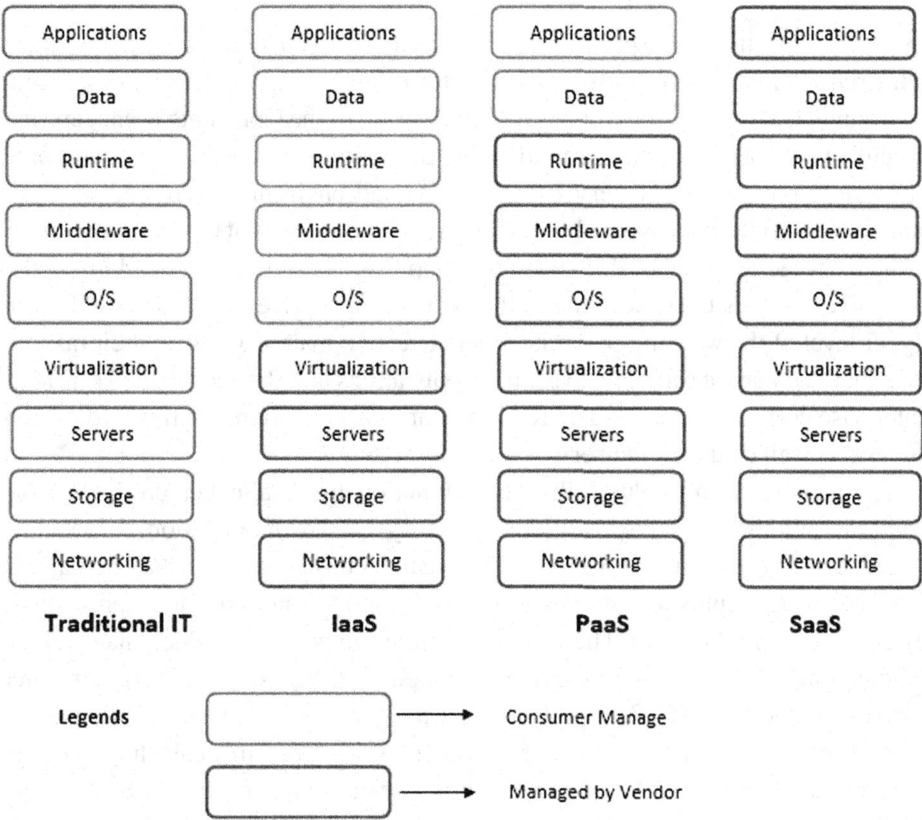

**For a more accurate representation see the electronic version.*

The Virtualization Technology (VT) enables the use of costly product simulation, design and modeling software on a rental basis in the Cloud environment. Due to the pay-as-you-go model of the Cloud, the manufacturer does not have to pay a lot, as compared with buying the license copy of the software and bare-metal hardware to run the simulation software. Like running simulation of the products on the HPC enabled Cloud infrastructure. The IT team of the manufacturer and engineers can create the private Cloud in their premises and can extend it to the public Cloud services to utilize the compute cycles from the virtual cluster with lambda services like Function-as-a-Service (FaaS) also known as serverless computing (AWS, 2019). Cloud adoption gives immense flexibility for various tasks in the automation of the manufacturing industry.

Manufacturing Industry Scope and Software Requirements

The industries like aerospace, defense, automotive, on demand constructions, industrial machinery and industrial manufacturing are having similar type of working environment, and need from the level of the worker to the Corporate Managers and Executives on the top of the pyramid where the centralized hassle-free operational software is required to be served from the Cloud environment. Better the tools available, better the decision making through the data analysis of the various sections of the manufacturing plant right from the shop floor, purchase, and working of the expensive assets is possible through the centralized services of the Cloud, for the higher level of the working pyramid, where decision makers perform their task. In general, the database services, Systems, Applications and Products (SAP) services, Enterprise Resource Planning (ERP) software can be offered through the Web servers, as well as the Cloud services.

The manufacturing industry has daily functionality challenges on the various fronts as per the scope, spread, and diversity of the organization. Especially, considering the medium and large scale manufacturing industry has demanded the cost saving, sophisticated operational tools, and technologies to improve their efficiency and productivity. There are manufacturing processes which may include product concept, research & development, Computer Aided Design (CAD), Computer Aided Manufacturing (CAM), 3D Printing, Prototype testing, and production as per the demand or in escalated manner. Manufacturers either from small shops to large manufacturing plants, work in various sectors, and they fond of using the SaaS model of Cloud for their need in inventory management, product lifecycle management (PLM), business process management (BPM). The SaaS Cloud model is also successfully used in mission-critical manufacturing technology such as warehouse management systems (WMS) and transportation management systems (TMS). It is even finding a place in the analytics side of manufacturing, from demand data in SaaS point of sale (POS) systems to SaaS Business Intelligence (BI). Cloud computing services are particularly attractive to manufacturers running global supply chains because they provide visibility into multiple facilities and aid in business process management (BPM) boosted by vendor mergers. The flow of inventory as per the status of the production, the predictions of failure, and prescriptive analytics are demands of the modern manufacturing industry where the IIoT in combination with Machine Learning provides the services through the Cloud platforms.

There is a vast need of combining the PLM, CAD, Cloud Services, Sensor data analytics, and Machine Learning capabilities for the visualization of the present status and the predictions about the various assets of the manufacturing industry.

The Augmented Reality (AR) based product visibility, such as a Digital Twin (DT) at smaller or the larger scales in the manufacturing plant is a demand from the industry. It needs the utilization of the daily operational data source either generated and accumulated through the Online Transaction Processing (OLTP) & Sensor data generated through the IIoT, and accessibility of the Computational Infrastructure and facilities available through the Cloud-based services. The use of the AR is the most common service, i.e., maintenance of the machine in the CMfg, is promising. The shop-floor monitoring service and an AR application, such as use of CAD parts like geometry position, assembly sequence, and assembly direction (Wright, 2017). The WSN is used which will support text instructions, human-computer interaction, part positioning, and animation of parts and tools. The maintenance can be performed from the remote location, with the help of fast speed Internet services.

Predicting the asset failure, reducing the scrap, reducing the downtime, improving the productivity of the manufacturing assets are few of the use cases which radially need the involvement of the Artificial Intelligence (AI), ML, and services based on the process and industrial automation. The IIoT provide an essential role in the agility and faster development of the products and services in the manufacturing industry. The statistical analysis and ML techniques can be applied to the data (Shitole & Devare, 2018). The data collection usually happens either at the web server and co-located databases. However, the IIoT sensor data and daily operational data from the CMfg meaningfully used for the improvement and value addition in the manufacturing companies. This is the point where the CMfg and IIoT converge to improve the happiness index of the manufacturing industry.

Manufacturing Cloud (CMfg)

The CMfg became modern terminology in China, probably due to the Chinese policy of spreading their goods all over the world. In 2009, the CMfg concept initially proposed by the research group led by Prof. Bo Hu Li and Prof. Lin Zhang. However, the same idea is highly applicable to the vast manufacturing sector all over the world. The CMfg express the future, where manufacturing assets are accessible anywhere and traceable in real-time, allowing adaptive decision making based on parallel simulation and forecasting. The Service Oriented Architecture (SOA) plays a vital role in the configuration and setup of the CMfg. The Cloud Computing acts as the interoperability platform for the information exchange, due to its flexible and dynamic nature. The CMfg provides on-demand manufacturing where a cooperative work environment for the enterprises and individuals, among the entire manufacturing ecosystem is involved in the engineering processes. It includes resource pool virtualization and aims to orchestrate and allocate such distributed resources and render production services for clients. As the CMfg mostly focuses on the virtualization of resources, the IIoT provides the metadata about the co-relation between dependent and independent variables. The convergence of the IIoT is CMfg is the need of the modern manufacturing industry, where the engineer can use the research and development software served through the Cloud, and the CEO of the company can use the better visibility reports and status of the overall working of the company.

The CMfg is also looked as the distributed resources network consisting of the manufacturing instruments and capabilities working in parallel. All the users involved in the manufacturing process are part of the CMfg. The Cloud-based design and manufacturing can be considered as the subset of the CMfg, where the infrastructure, software, hardware, the platform can be used as a service. The CMfg perhaps covers all production activities (Oracle, 2017) & (GE, 2017), production scheduling, management related issues, and solutions, product design considerations and engineering abilities in the manufacturing industry. It is not just only involving the computing and data storage, but also covers physical equipment, monitors, materials, and supply chain related activities. It is a feasible approach to share the precious resources using the Internet and even local network. This improves the utilization rate of rarely used equipment, and due to sharing it reduces the cost of the expensive instruments, indirectly. This condition is a win-win situation for the owner of the equipment as well as the manufacturer who needs that equipment for the short duration of the time.

In the broader perspective, the CMfg & IIoT is not just involved in the manufacturing industry but also supply-chain and management related issues. The industrial process automation and the Sensor data exchange in IoT called as the IIoT creates sophisticated tools, those are useful at the various stages of the manufacturing. The data collected from the industrial sensors is not helpful in isolation. Hence, usually processed with the data analysis techniques to find useful business information out of it, such as Python-based or R based libraries to create the models and use it in the production environments by creating the RESTful APIs using the frameworks such as Flask.

In addition to the advanced services, the primary manufacturing process and related activities in the industry need the ERP, SAP, Research & Developments tool techniques accessible through the affordable prices to reduce the overall manufacturing cost. The significant amount of the cost can be reduced if the services shifted to the Cloud-based infrastructure. Not for all but the manufacturing industry with IT related products may follow the smiling curve in the whole process of production to the market delivery, to which the CMfg adds the value.

The Cloud Computing can be adopted in conjunction with already existing IIoT mechanisms in a modern company, where the optimization of the inventory in the supply chain can improve the business processes. Such as there are Make to Order (MTO), Stock to Order (STO), Engineering to Order (ETO), Configure to Order (CTO), or Build to Order (BTO) style of the inventory management through the Cloud-based services and software improves working of the modern Manufacturing company. Every Manufacturing company tries to maintain the balance between the push or pull (Sometimes also known as elevator or escalator) type of the inventory and stock to avoid the dead investments.

The data is generated from the IIoT and Supervisory Control and Data Acquisition (SCADA) based systems improved with the prescriptive and predictive analytics for the various parts of the machinery of the industrial plants. The prescriptive and predictive analytics and ML services can be provided through the Cloud. The IIoT combined with the sensor data analysis using the statistical and ML techniques offered through the Cloud-based services with prediction such as the Machine parts replacement alerts well before time, or failure prediction well before time avoids the downtime.

This chapter address the convergence of the Manufacturing Cloud and IIoT where integration techniques and Methods are applied in distributed systems and technologies. Such as the protocols which may support the convergence of the CMfg and IIoT. This work provides the tools and techniques helpful to make it more supportive of each other.

BACKGROUND

Table 1 here summarizes the various contributions done by the researchers in the CMfg and IIoT convergence and separation.

CLOUD-BASED APPROACH IN IIOT-ORIENTED COMPANIES

The measurable parameters such as feed, vibration, amplitude, frequency, machine health value, health stages, and failure modes are necessarily record in the IIoT. The primary intention of the CMfg and IIoT convergence is to transform manufacturing resources such as equipment, workforce, industrial robots, sensors, and production capabilities, etc. into manufacturing services. The sensor data could be smaller, and abstracted data can be sent to the Cloud. However, in the manufacturing activities may refer to the existing data which perhaps in terabytes called the Bigdata. The

Table 1. Review of the efforts in the CMfg and IIoT

Author	Key Contribution	Summary
(N. Liu, X. Li & Q. Wang, 2011)	Manufacturing Resource virtualization using XML	The resource virtualization is necessary for cooperative manufacturing and the mapping of the different manufacturing resources to the varied Cloud resources, and the combination of services. The resource virtualization process transforms manufacturing resources into Cloud services in two phases, i.e., virtual description and service encapsulation. The Extensible Markup Language (XML) schema is used for the virtual description. Attributes, states, and capabilities of resources keep on changing throughout the whole resource life cycle. The representation of the attributes is required for the data exchange between the web servers, Cloud Servers, and applications.
(M. Wang, J. Zhoul & S. Jing, 2012)	The model for the CMfg i.e. GetCM	The dynamic networked manufacturing environment is necessary for collaborations. The GetCM is the proposed model for Cloud Computing in Manufacturing.
(C. Esposito, A. Castiglione, B. Martini & K.K.R. Choo, 2016), & (Rath M. (2017)	CMfg for MRP	Production Engineering to create accurate lists of items and instructions needed to build each product, Inventory Management to tune Material Requirements Planning (MRP) to reflect actual vendor performance and actual production, Lot & Serial Control to trace the source of supply or production for any item. The Cloud Material Requirements Planning automatically plans what should buy or make in time to build products.
(W. Xu, J. Yu, Z. Zhou, Y. Xie, D.T. Pham & C. Ji, 2015)	Ontology Creation	The changing condition and capabilities of the manufacturing machines and equipment on a real-time basis is necessary. The knowledge description of manufacturing equipment and their capabilities helps for the Cloud-based services management. For this ontology need to be built, fundamental information ontology, functional ontology, and manufacturing process ontology.
(F. Tao, L.Zhang, Y. Liu, Y. Cheng, L.Wang & X. Xu, 2015)	The IoT, Big Data, and Cloud Computing.	CMfg needs attention for improvement in the quality of service (QoS) and the manufacturing service management (MSM). The CMfg aims to realize the full-scale sharing, free circulation and transaction, and on-demand The advances in MSM technology from various aspects are searching, matching, evaluation, selection & composition, scheduling, operation, execution, monitoring, fault-tolerance, logistics services, release, disaggregation, aggregations, investigation, and summarization. The MSM in CMfg is closely related to the IoT, Big Data, and Cloud Computing. The Cloud environment consisting of the manufacturing services lifecycle with various important aspects.
(H. Zheng, Y. Feng & J. Tan,2017)	Genetic and Fuzzy based energy model for CMfg.	The CMfg is utilized for the energy consumption and monitoring the of manufacturing resources. The hybrid energy-aware resource allocation approach to help requestors to acquire energy-efficient and satisfied manufacturing services. Then a local selection strategy based on fuzzy similarity degree is to put forward to obtain appropriate candidate services. A multi-objective mathematical model for energy-aware service composition is established, and the non-dominated sorting genetic algorithm (NSGA-II) is adapted to conduct the combinatorial optimization process. Furthermore, a technique for order preference by similarity to an ideal solution (TOPSIS) is used to determine the optimal composite services. Finally, a case study is illustrated to validate the effectiveness of the proposed approach.
(U. Rauscheckerl & M. Stohrl, 2012)	CMfg for the Inventory and Supply Chain Management.	The Manufacturing service providers' parties are those who own manufacturing facilities and would like to deliver products to a CMfg. The Manufacturing service consumers are the users who want to purchase a product or subproduct in case they are not able to manufacture the products by themselves due to reasons like cost-effectiveness or know-how leakages. Especially when making services provide the ability to be configured by their consumers, the adaption of products to customer requirements would be supported the Manufacturing service integrators of a supply chain or production network who combine manufacturing services in order to build up an aggregated and inter-linked manufacturing service structure which represents the structure of the respective production network.

data storage tool is Hadoop Database (HBase) based on the key and value pair, which is different from the Relational Database Management Systems (RDBMS). The Hadoop tools like parallel programming supporting Map-Reduce provide the linear scaling, low integrity, dynamic schema, petabyte-scale data size, write once and read many times characteristics. It also provides data storage with structured, semi-structured, and temporal data writing. (Bao, Ren, Zhang, Zhang & Luo, 2012).

The hardware resources can be described, with its capabilities and characteristics, etc. Such as an industrial robot that shares among the collaborating manufacturing units of the same company for further workload completion. The weighing capacity, manufacturing dates, number of hours of usage, the life of the different parts, their wear and tear are few of the characteristics that can be considered as the resource description. The use of sensor-based resources monitoring is highly expected, like speed, pressure, temperatures, humidity, RPM measurement, oil level indicators, power and energy monitoring are few of them.

The manufacturing capabilities such operated in an intelligent and unified way to enable the full sharing and circulation of manufacturing resources and manufacturing capabilities, with efficient technique. The big manufacturing lifecycle covers product design, simulation, production, test, and maintenance. At the smaller scale, the CMfg can be viewed as deploying manufacturing software on the Cloud, such as CAD and CAM software can be supplied as a service on the CMfg. The on-demand leasing and releasing manufacturing assets in a utility-like fashion. The rapid elasticity through scaling leased assets up and down if necessary and pay-per-use through metered service.

The Cloud-based SaaS and PaaS is an excellent combination with the container-based services. The different software services are offered by the different Cloud vendors useful for the IIoT-Oriented Companies. The considerable cost can be saved if the IIoT Oriented companies adopt the advantages of the various models of the Cloud. For example, if the public Cloud is the choice, then the cost of the ownership is zero and pay-as-you-go gives more flexibility. There are furthermore options like private Cloud adoption, where in-house administrator should be appointed to monitor the local infrastructure and network components. One can also choose the hybrid approach such as continuing with the in-house private Cloud and extending the service from the public Cloud provider for various purposes such as storage, or serverless computing. The facilities such as Notification services by the Cloud vendor is useful from the public Cloud provider.

Furthermore, the Cloud can be co-located hardware for the various purposes in the managed or unmanaged style. In any case, the adoption of the Cloud in the IIoT oriented companies is beneficial. During the design of the new product, the simulation and analysis need the high-performance computing infrastructure either virtualization enabled Clusters or the Graphics Processing Units (GPUs) for running the parallel computing applications. The advantages of Cloud Computing, the IIoT, and SOA are supporting technologies to achieve the CMfg.

To improve productivity, product quality, and safety, the manufacturers use the IoT devices to capture higher-fidelity production process data that is, more detailed data about each activity and sub-activity, instead of obtaining only the data needed for existing KPIs. The IoT devices can similarly monitor plant machines to determine their operation versus idle time, the quality of the parts they produce, and the reliability. The manufacturers could take corrective actions to achieve these improvements include breaking down plant processes to more exceptional activities, for example, by considering not only how many people and machines are on the job and how many products they produce, but also how much time they spend in less productive activities that could be eliminated, reduced, or replaced. Another direction is to electronically detect and monitor activities and sub-activities in the production process, including their input, output and the resources they use.

The IoT is ideal for this purpose because it can use existing Radio Frequency Identification (RFID), Near Field Communication (NFC), Beacons, new low-cost sensors, "bring your own" smartphones, put this data on the Internet for KPI computation and alerts. Manufacturers might also compute higher-fidelity productivity, quality, and safety KPIs from monitoring such activities and resources in real time. Other possible directions are improving the production process to include more productive, fewer unproductive activities and periodically repeating IoT-based production process improvement steps (Georgakopoulos, Jayaraman, Fazia, Villari, & Ranjan, 2016).

The data acquisition from the various sources, and pushing it to the Cloud requires real skill, where the security plays essential role and handshaking of the web-based protocols, news protocols in the IoT (Such as MQTT) and industrial automation protocols are required. The IoT protocols MQTT is useful on the publish and subscribe type of model called a pub-sub model. The Cloud Kubernates and the pipelined data acquisition are the significant challenges to plug and play these two systems. The edge devices send the data to the Cloud in the IIoT scenario such as the ARM, Raspberry Pi or other Single Board Computers (SBCs). It has been said that the organization spends more of the money in maintaining the equipment as compared to the cost of the machine. Hence, the instruments health-related data analysis in the manufacturing industry is essential, and amalgamation of CMfg and IIoT gives a valuable improvement in the people and process part of the manufacturing operations.

The Digital Twin (DT) is the final product outcomes from the CMfg, IIoT, and AR. The DT gives meaningful insight into the health and status of the manufacturing instruments as well as inventory tracking. The techniques like Kanban and Just-in-Time (JIT) needs the visual information about the raw material utilized in the manufacturing company. Here, the co-partners involved in the process of kanban to provide the right quantity of the raw material and parts of the more significant assembly at the right time. As the manufacturing industry works on the principal of the "Investment in the raw material inventory is wastage." Hence, the Cloud-based manufacturing and ERP updates in the Cloud and the IIoT based updates about the manufacturing machinery in the real-time gives the sophisticated environment which improves the processes and reduces the cost. Beyond a single factory or company, suppliers, sister factories, downstream plants, warehouses, and logistics centers, and distribution channels can all be coordinated through the Cloud, leading to economic benefits in terms of resource utilization, time to market, inventory holding costs, and customer satisfaction. Product sales can be facilitated through Cloud-based customer relationship management software. Distribution and logistics companies can coordinate via the Cloud. Similar, ocean carriers (shipping companies) and terminal operators (ports) to coordinate ship arrivals, unloading, loading, and departures by optimizing across geographic locations based on ship locations, weather forecasts, and container stacking.

ROLE OF IT MANAGEMENT IN CONVERGENCE OF CMFG AND IIOT

The Information Technology (IT) Management team has several essential roles in the manufacturing company right from maintaining the computer systems, networking devices, and physical wirings such as cabling and connectors. Moreover, the selection of open source software over the licensing software to reduce the overall cost of the company. During the establishment of the networking among the operating devices such as computers, switches and routers decisions on the logical and physical cabling in the organization's physical premises is necessary. Maintaining the Local Area Network (LAN), bounding routers, switches, and troubleshooting wired and wireless networks and interfaces, communicating with the Internet Service Providers (ISPs) are the few of the tasks of the IT team.

There is several Computer Numerical Control (CNC) machine in the manufacturing plant they are either connected by wired or wireless networking for the serval functionalities. The IT Management team mainly solves the maintenance and rectifications of the errors in the daily working. If the database servers are maintained in-house, then they have to take care of the tuning and maintenance for the better operations. However, if it is made from the Cloud premises, then it has to be coordinated with the Managed or un-managed Cloud Services. The IT team is helpful in the various phases of the manufacturing including design, simulation, production, test, and maintenance.

When the industrial automation is done in the manufacturing company, then third-party expert vendors play their role by identifying the functional requirements. However, during the implementation phase, the IT team has to play its part to utilize the in-house resources and services. Here, the IIoT and CMfg come together to serve the purpose of deploying the industrial sensors and connecting them with wired or wireless data transfer technologies.

The manufacturing industry can be considered as the client for the IT organizations. The manufacturing industry in any country can be either divided by the turnover in terms of the financial transactions, the products they produce, and the number of labors and engineers working in the industry. Based on their capability to invest in the automation of the daily manufacturing operations, and various software-based transactions make they enable to use either Cloud-based or non-Cloud based service. In addition to all of these traditional and emerging applications for the Cloud in manufacturing and supply chain processes, product companies can use some innovative mechanisms to exploit the Cloud to create value (Oracle, 2017).

VIRTUALIZATION OF THE MANUFACTURING RESOURCES

The process of manufacturing covers various resources. To simplify those can be divided as soft, hard and another type of resources. The soft resources include software, knowledge, skill, personnel, experience, and business network. The hard resources cover manufacturing equipment, monitoring and control resources like RFID, Wireless Sensor Network (WSN), virtual managers and remote controllers. The hard resources also include the computational resources, materials, storage, machine tools, CNC Machines, testing equipment, transportation machine tools, cutters, milling machines, monitoring equipment, fabrication tools, furnace, lathe machines, and industrial robots. Due to the emergence of Industry 4.0, the monitoring and controlling resources like WSN, NFC, and RFID are also part of the CMfg system. The computational resources like storage media, servers, computers, handheld devices are also part of the CMfg. There are resources like raw materials, finished products, power, water, and lubricants. There are many transportation modes like air, rail, road, water, and pipelines which are also important aspects of the resource virtualization.

The properties of the resources are either static or dynamic. The design of the aware device system, it is necessary to know the identification methods, data collection methods and data transfer protocol for each of the equipment. For example, the CNC machine provides the RS232 interface or some other type of interface to transfer the data. The industrial robots have some data transfer interfaces, wireless tools and techniques for use to get the real-time, off-line data and status of the devices. It is frequently required to monitor the small vehicles used on the shop floor to find its performance, such as the distance it traveled, the materials shipped from one place to another place, the fuel consumption in a particular shift, the efficient operator and driver to consume the less fuel, etc. Also, these parameters are used to avoid accidents and downtime of the work (Wikipedia, 2017) & (Jiming, Zhiping & Rongbo, 2012).

The virtualization of the manufacturing resources either soft or hard resources for CMfg is essential to phase in the implementation. There are three types of resources in manufacturing, i.e., equipment, implements, and auxiliaries. There are functional and non-functional features of the manufacturing resources. The task information, the process information, and the production information provide the functional elements of the resource. The task information strictly depends on the design, geometry, and processes of products. The process information describes the processing routine to convert the raw material into final products. The production information shows the manufacturing resource status during producing. The ontology, description and the capability of the resources can be represented in the form of Extensible Mark-up Language (XML) files as the media independent, vendor-independent way to transport the data from one point of the network to another (Liu, Li & Wang, 2011). The CMfg is distributed network of the resources it is necessary to virtualize the resources and its capabilities in terms of the XML attributes either can be read through the Document Type Definition (DTD) or schemas.

The attributes in the CMfg purpose virtualized resources capability and features descriptions available in the form of the XML files, and also in the way of the semantic web. When the IIoT comes in the picture, the existing XML files need additional attributes in the form of the sensor based readings. Both files, i.e. the XML file describing the manufacturing resource for the CMfg as well as the other XML for IIoT is an essential part of the system, to provide better insights to the system. As shown in Table 2, the XML for the description of the resource in case of the manufacturing Cloud and in addition to the IIoT is explained with the example.

CMFG ARCHITECTURE

The CMfg is defined by the researchers from China, as a network, intelligence, and SOA with the use of IoT, and elaborated the layered architecture. As shown in figure 2, the architecture considered here is consisting of six layers from top to bottom as Physical Layer, a Resource-oriented interface layer, virtual resource layer, core

Table 2. Manufacturing resource description in CMfg and when converge with IIoT

XML of Resource Description in CMFg	Additional XML When CMfg Converges With IIoT
<?xml version="1.0" encoding="UTF-8"?> <RDescription> <Attributes> <UniqueNUM>EqMac001</ UniqueNUM> <Name>PathRepeaterRobot</Name> <Specification>Programmable</Specification > <Width>2</Width> <Height>6</Height> <Trip>6</Trip> <Time>1</Time> <Distance>Meter </Distance> <TimeUnit> Minute </TimeUnit> </Attributes> <VendorInfo> <Vendor>Fanuc Corporation</Vendor> <CurrentOperator>30</CurrentOperator> <Location>Plant2</Location> </ VendorInfo > <Capacity> <MaxWeightLift> 35 </MaxWeightLift> <WeightUnit> kg </WeightUnit> <MaxHourWork>6</MaxHourWork> </ Capacity> <RepairingInfo> <LastDateOfRepairing> 03/03/2019 </ LastDateOfRepairing> <DateFormat>DD/MM/YYYY</DateFormat> </RepairingInfo> </RDescription>	<?xml version="1.0" encoding="UTF-8"?> <PeripheralInfo> <TimeofReading> 11.10 am </TimeofReading> <Sensor1Description> <Name> Heat </Name> <MaxAllowedTemp> 50 </MaxAllowedTemp> <MinAllowedTemp> 2 </MinAllowedTemp> <CurrnetValue> </Sensor1Description> <Sensor2Description> <Name> Pressure </Name> <MaxPressure>30 </MaxPressure> <MinPressure> 10</MinPressure> </Sensor2Description> <ValveDescription> <Name> Globe Valve </Name> <LastOffDate>05/03/2019 </LastOffDate> </ValveDescription> </PeripheralInfo>

service layer, a service-oriented interface layer, and application layer. If someone looks it as the three-dimensional layered model then the user management, system management, and the security will be considered as the vital operational points in the CMfg. The manufacturing equipment and capacity are considered as resources. There are various aspects to the Manufacturing Industry.

The CMfg gives five layered structures, namely the physical resource layer, virtual resources layer, core services layer, application interface layer and application layer. The physical resources layer divided into four classes respectively is computational resources, hard manufacturing resources, soft manufacturing resources, and manufacturing ability. Manufacturing tasks can be classified into six big categories, such as manufacturing and processing tasks (MPT), research and design tasks (RDT), management and maintenance tasks (MMT), logistics and inventory tasks

Figure 2. Layers in CMfg

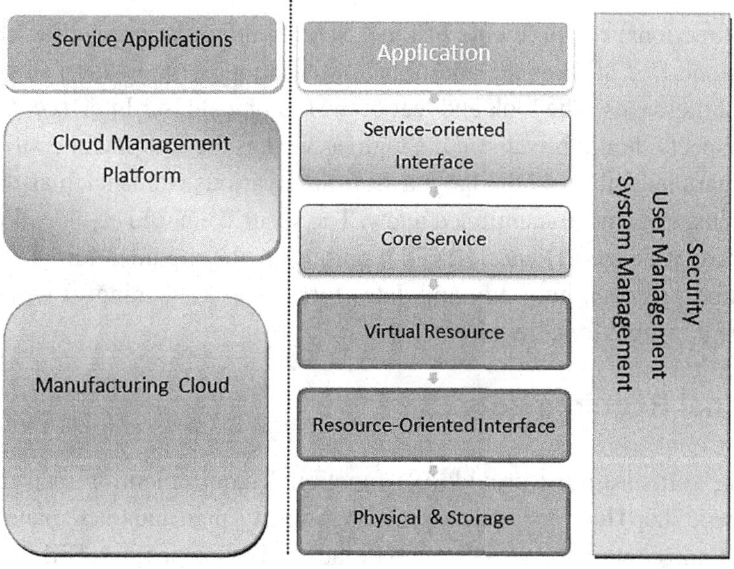

(LIT), transaction tasks (TT) and other tasks (OT). There is an essential task in the CMfg like resource description, classification, modeling, discovery, resource capability modeling, service matching, service composition, and optimal selection. Interestingly, the customer establishes and asks for the on-demand service through the task completion request called ontology. The manufacturing resources features and their capabilities should be matched through the manufacturing ontology mapping (Xinjuan & Quan, 2016).

FUNCTIONAL REQUIREMENTS FOR THE CMFG AND IIOT

As a part of the Software Requirement Specification (SRS), there is a need for writing the meaningful, clear and unambiguous functional requirements document. The system offerings can be represented in the form of use case diagram from the Unified Modelling Language (UML) specification. The common resources descriptions can be placed in the Object-Oriented System in the general class, and the special features can be placed in the specialized classes. In a similar manner, the features and functionalities of the manufacturing resource available for the different actors or users can be generalized in the use cases. Furthermore, the extended use cases can be developed as the convergence of the system either to the CMfg or IIoT would be more comfortable.

Non-Functional Requirements

The non-functional requirements of the systems in convergence in the context of the CMfg and IIoT such as the additional notification in the form of Email, SMS, or Chatbot messages. The look and feel of the Graphical User Interface (GUI), and security aspects should be satisfied in login as well as the equipment configuration. The internationalization of the languages on the various fronts such as the report, notifications, etc. can be mentioned a few. The security should be extended in case of the Bring your own Device (BYOD) culture of the organization. The units of temperature, pressure, humidity and dates formats in a meaningful way can be a part of the non-functional requirements.

Functional Requirements

The CMfg software must provide the functional requirement as manage master data, manage shop floor operations, provide visibility, plan and track manufacturing costs. It should contain the visualization of the production process, Bill of Materials (BOM), and route. The master data is about production assets, process standards, calendars, work center resources, and standard operations. Engineers can define plant hierarchy and process standards including working calendars, work areas, work center resources, and standard operations and use them repeatedly. Production supervisors use a control center to get a quick look at how work areas or work centers are running. Figure 3 shows the use case diagram for the functional requirements of the CMfg and IIoT. There are two possibilities in industrial automation.

1. Adding the CMfg to the existing IIoT
2. Adding the IIoT to the existing CMfg.

If the industrial automation with the systems like SCADA is already done and the data is collected at the one machine, or on the Cloud, then adding the CMfg to will move all the production, ERP and other inventory related data to the Cloud. In case of the existing CMfg running ERP and other manufacturing software, where the data and software available on the Cloud. The new functionalities of the IIoT system and the data generated from it can be combined all together in the one system, for the optimization of the results.

To manage the production, it should provide the quick view to status and take action, create and manage work orders, print the production documents, such as travelers & parts lists, view history and collaborate with co-workers. To execute the production, it should provide the shop floor execution, enforce and manage serialized work orders with integrated barcoding capabilities, report order-less completions

Figure 3. Use case diagram for the Functional Requirements of the CMfg & IIoT.

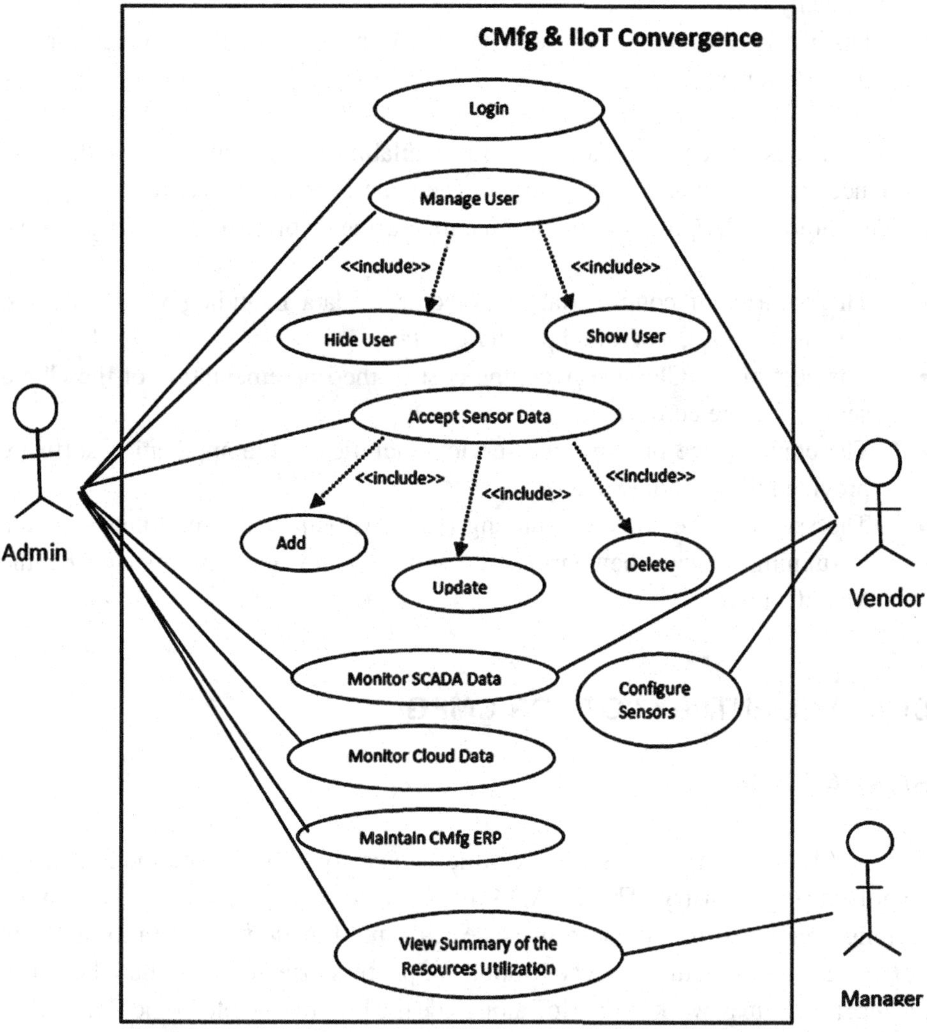

to support lean manufacturing. To review work order and operation performance, access all production tasks, provide transaction history of material and resource usage, offer detailed reporting and summarized view and status with plant-level insight.

Lartigau et al. discuss the stepwise approach for the Scheduling Methodology for Production Services in CMfg as:

1. Initialize the orders to be treated and their requested deadline.
2. Identify the set and sequence of the tasks to perform before the delivery.
3. Identify the batches targeting the required functions.

4. Define the batch parameters and constraints from the request proposal form filled by RSP.
5. Distinguish the renewable resources from the non-renewable resources implied in the batches.

Also, necessary checking to ensure the availability of the time ranges, this task sequence, batch sequence, and quantity of the non-renewable resources.

The choice of the Cloud vendor for manufacturing involves the following factors.

- The security of confidential manufacturing data including vendor names, customer names, sales, and purchase data.
- The cost of the Cloud service, the cost of the implementation of the Cloud services in the company.
- The convenience of using the service, facilities in the application software provided through the SaaS.
- The speed of the software running on the Cloud if the important software is running slowly, then virtualized infrastructure perhaps rejected by the Manufacturers.

COMPLEMENTARY IIOT FOR CMFG

SCADA System

The SCADA system is most of the time choice for process automation in the manufacturing industry. The SCADA provides gathering, analyzing, alarming, logging, trending, and operator interface real-time functionality data in the form of the sensors and actuators. The supporting process oriented Distributed Control System (DCS) may work in the IIoT alongside the Programmable Logic Controllers (PLC), Sensors and Actuator. The SCADA is more event-driven whereas the DCS is state driven systems. In any case, the data on the Cloud can be processed through the Machine Learning and Data Analysis techniques in the Cloud which is nowadays available as the essential parts of the Cloud.

The data storage is a SQL database for storing the data logs from SCADA systems grows fast and requires maintenance. The maintenance of the SCADA systems is time consuming and tedious task. The SCADA software requires upgrades and patches to keep up with the latest OS patches and virus updates. Due to the obsolete nature of the OS, the new SCADA versions need to be installed in a few years. When integrated the IIoT with the CMfg, the Remote Monitoring systems use a local edge node device to communicate with the local control system and push data securely to the Cloud hosted server. The server stores the data and provides custom web dashboards, email and text notifications, historical trends, custom reports, branded smartphone apps, and connectivity to other enterprise software systems. Figure 5 shows the data acquisition stages and various techniques in industrial automation.

Data Acquisition and IoT Protocols

The IIoT adds essential facet in the process automation as the captured environmental attributes; sensor values provide the important decision-making attributes in the manufacturing stages. The IIoT with the energy efficient protocols like Low Range (LORA), Zigbee, Sigfox, Neul, Ingenu, Low-Power Wide-Area Network (LOW-WAN), Low-Power Wide-Area Network (LOWPAN), Muti-Queue Telemetry Transport (MQTT), and Constrained Application Protocol (COAP) etc. (Devare, 2018) can save the energy. The physical location monitoring system enables with the ML, and the statistical analysis such as for the shop floor, industrial premises, inventory management, and logistics provide essential inputs to the manufacturing related software provided through the Cloud platforms.

While converting the manufacturing into the CMfg, the data availability should be checked. If the sufficient data is not available, then the Cloud-based real-time system should collect the data by externalization processes such as finding out machines, employees, and Radio Frequency Identification (RFID) tags, etc. Most of the manufacturing units are now come with the interfaces to be used for the automation. Another important aspect is the design the logical architecture, including data collection, data analysis, and data intelligence. The choice of technology is the most extended process includes the Cloud providers and subsystems, security and governance (Linthicum, 2016).

Kanban is a Japanese term for "visual signal" or "card" used alongside with the JIT is sometimes a manual system. However, the CMfg and IIoT can make JIT & Kanban more effective by showing it in the form of the digital display in the company premises. The Toyota line-workers used a Kanban (i.e., an actual card) to signal steps in their manufacturing process. The system's highly visual nature allowed teams to communicate more efficiently on what work needed to be done and when. It also standardized cues and refined processes, which helped to reduce waste and maximize value. The Kanban, Poka-Yoke, Heijunka (demand leveling) systems are required in the CMfg convergence with the IIoT.

Figure 4 shows the CMfg as a layered architecture, where the foundation layer as a resource layer is indicating the machinery, equipment, etc. Next layer on the top of the physical resources is the Cloud-based virtual resources layer provides the virtualization layer. The Cloud-enabled services layer provides the facility to the applications. The layered architecture represents the one manufacturing factory unit for CMfg. Whereas, the network of the connected sites is necessary for the virtual organizations sharing the resources.

Figure 4. CMfg and IIoT in layered approach

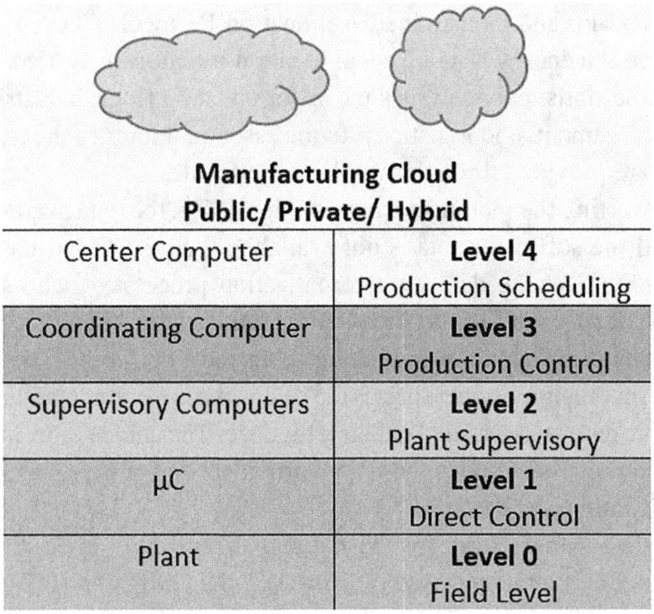

Manufacturing Cloud
Public/ Private/ Hybrid

Center Computer	**Level 4** Production Scheduling
Coordinating Computer	**Level 3** Production Control
Supervisory Computers	**Level 2** Plant Supervisory
μC	**Level 1** Direct Control
Plant	**Level 0** Field Level

Figure 5. Data acquisition from the various techniques to the IIoT

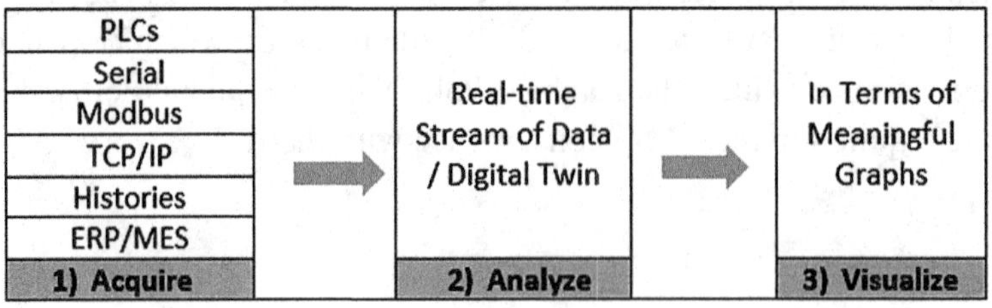

PLCs
Serial
Modbus
TCP/IP
Histories
ERP/MES
1) Acquire

Real-time Stream of Data / Digital Twin
2) Analyze

In Terms of Meaningful Graphs
3) Visualize

SECURITY ISSUES IN IIOT AND CMFG

The SCADA is the dominating Industrial Control Systems (ICSs) used in the industrial process automation. These systems were not designed to be exposed to the traditional TCP/IP based networks. However, it connects to the Local Area Network as usual. The data transfer happens through the Fieldbus network which uses its own, proprietary communication protocol, such as Modbus or Profibus, and further extended to the Ethernet-based networks. When the system connected to through the IP based network, then huge possibilities of the vulnerabilities arises.

There are records found such as Stuxnet malware, Slammer worm, Duqu, Printer Spooler vulnerability, Trojan-Spy.0485, Malware-Cryptor.Win32.Inject.gen.2, a rootkit that targets PLCs and few more have caused the damage to the SCADA systems. The propagation of the malware is possible through the use of the USB and Peer-to-Peer communication updates. The necessary countermeasures such as network segregation, risk management, and analysis can avoid these attacks. (D¨unhaupt, 2012). Catastrophic and non-catastrophic attacks can be a few preventive measures to the system. The heavily interconnected networks, lack of logging mechanisms, unpatched operating systems, lack of authentication and encryption, open connections with notebooks, SQL injections, and lacking in the password management are the key security concerns.

Along with the flexibility the Cloud brings the problem of entry point through the Containers and Dockers services. The OLTP data collected in the location of the database in the Cloud manufacturing services and the IIoT data collected gets shifted into the heterogeneous type of the data storages. As the Cloud supports the NoSQL databases, provides faster data storage and retrieval. The IIoT is having its security challenges such as malware attack, physical devices protection from the theft and un-necessary damages. When the convergence of these two systems happens then the privacy, authentication, non-repudiation, and integrity need to be addressed.

If the existing system already has the authentication, then whether to adopt the same or additional authentication will create the login fatigue to the users. The nexus of the vendor trust between the Cloud and the IIoT needs to be addressed. The overemphasis on the security perhaps adds the overhead and speed of the processing can be compromised. The matrix of the security cases in the two system convergence shown in Table 3.

In the context of the CMfg and IIoT combination, there are many parties involved the system such as the Cloud vendors in the public scenario, the data mart users from the different departments of the manufacturing company, the local administrators, the process automation experts, engineers and the workers on the individual machineries,

Table 3. Security matrix when combined as CMfg and IIoT

CMfg / IIoT	Integrity	Non-Repudiation	Authentication	Privacy
Integrity	Overhead of Repetition			
Non-Repudiation		Overhead of Repetition		
Authentication			Overhead of Repetition	
Privacy				Overhead of Repetition

operators of the milling, lathe, CNC machines, and robots. The security and safety of the instruments in the diverse field of the manufacturing industry heterogeneous. Such as the security protocols of the privacy maintenance in case of the public and private keys generated through the RSA and DSA mechanism when the data exchange is happening can work in the one part of the system either from the machine to the cloud or from the sensor to the cloud. The non-repudiation in the form of the digital signatures can happen in the form of the Message Digest (MD) mechanisms. The eavesdropper's issues should be maintained through the use of the Virtual Private Network (VPN) through the use of the IP Security protocol either in the transport or the tunneling mode.

Most of the attacks on the system can happen from the insider entities rather than from the outsiders. Hence the multi-factor authentication inside the organization can work for the anomaly detection. As the context of the system is distributed in nature, to coordinate the information exchange from the ERP, machinery data, and analytics data needs to happen the trusted environment. The SSH, SCP and other security tools can be used for further data exchange. The preventive measures for the Denial of Service (DoS) attacks in the distributed natures have to happen such as to avoid the port scanning. The TCP port attacks should be avoided through the captcha and similar mechanism. The cross-site scripting mechanism should be used in the systematic mechanism and to treat the SQL injection.

There is interesting security, key management, Privacy, and Forensic Concerns in CMfg. It has been observed that the Public Cloud service providers have introduced the IoT supported services to push the data on the Cloud in the various data storage systems. The IIoT devices can be configured in a secure way with the public and private key exchange between the Cloud services. The flexible and elastic nature

Figure 6. The CMfg as the Network of Network

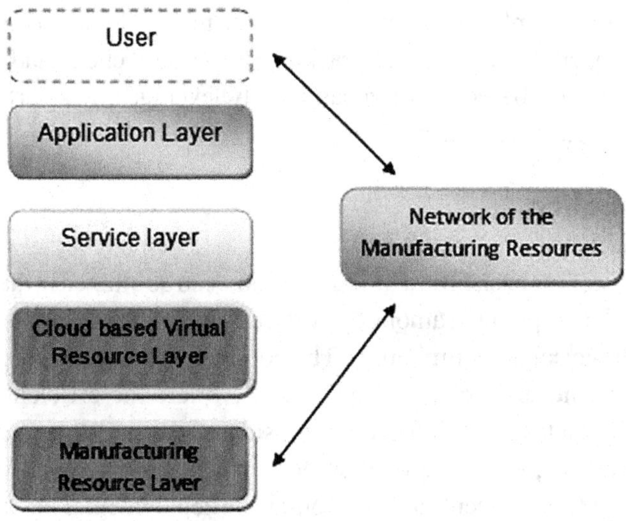

of the Cloud services provides the plug-configure-and-play approach which makes the synergy between the CMfg and IIoT integration. Figure 6 shows the CMfg as the network of the network where the multiple stakeholders can play their role in the different networks.

CMFG AND IIOT USE CASES

Case 1: Inventory Management Using IIoT

Optimizing Inventory Management Manufacturers could use smartphones or the IoT wearable devices to collect information from manual inventory management operations, and use this information to maximize and automatically guide workers' picking and packing activities based on product weight, age, and quality. In particular, the IoT-based solutions that dynamically track, optimize, and guide picking and packing activities could improve plants' productivity by reducing labor costs and the time involved in moving and finding the appropriate products stored in the warehouses. This solution allows plants to minimize product inventory, storage, heating and chilling capacity to the minimal level needed to fill customer orders.

The IoT-based solutions could also improve a manufacturer's ability to track, find, and store products based on quality and weight, and enhance production line agility to accommodate multiple customer orders concurrently. Smart mobile devices are widely available, and ubiquitous IoT tracking devices are cheap and easy to install and maintain. An IoT-based solution can readily leverage any smart mobile or the IoT tracking device (Warehouse, 2016).

Case 2: Robotics

The multiple sides are consisting of industrial robots can be utilized in the collaboration environment. The cooperation among the different manufacturing units can overcome the problem of the capacity limitation. The complex tasks solving using the robots are explained in the research done by Li et al., where the efficient utilization of distributed manufacturing is done. They considered the performance of four robot deployment methods, including random deployment, robot-balanced deployment, function-balanced deployment, and location-aware deployment. They also introduced a genetic algorithm for the three subtask-scheduling strategies derived from three optimization objectives, including load-balance of robots, minimizing overall cost, and minimizing total processing time.

Moreover, these strategies are implemented by the genetic algorithm. They show that the physical distance between two enterprises can influence the overall cost, and location-aware deployment leads to smaller transportation cost. Location-aware implementation and function-balanced deployment lead to the shorter overall processing time for the low-workload state and high-workload state of the system, respectively. (Jiming, Zhiping & Rongbo, 2012) & (Li, Zhu, Yang, Shu, Ngai & Ma, 2017). The multiple site robot data integrated into the Cloud Services is the best example of utilizing the Robot working capabilities in the convergence services.

Case 3: 3D Printing

3D printing is an additive process of creating rapid prototyping and customized production. It is the process of making a physical object from a 3D digital model, typically by laying down many thin layers of material. In this method, the thinly sliced successive layering is created until the object is not formed. The 3D printing needs the virtual design of the object using a CAD file. 3D modeling application (e.g., Blender) or with a 3D scanner can be useful to a 3D digital copy of an existing object. Like future smartphones will be probably have integrated 3D scanners. Microsoft Kinect and Google enabled their hardware to perform 3D scanning.

The production integration and product customization of 3D printing are designed and proposed by (Yinan, Wu, Peng, Chen, & Zhang, 2016) for 3D printing Cloud-integrated platform architecture based on Cloud manufacturing. They have solved the problem of selecting the services of different distributed 3D printing terminals in a Cloud platform. The fuzzy set theory is used for effectively quantifying quality and accuracy. The sensor-based data of the expensive 3D printer can be integrated with the Cloud services.

Case 4: Energy Aware CMfg

The architecture of green CMfg architecture is suggested divided into six significant levels, i.e., physical resource layer, a virtualization layer, core middle-ware layer, service layer, a user interface layer, and the user layer. The multi-objective optimal selection model of energy consumption and QoS aware service combination module include a description of the service combination, the basic structure model of service composition, the construction, energy assessment and QoS assessment of service composition execution path, the CMfg energy-saving incentives for service composition. This module mainly aims to establish an execution path of service composition and offer support for the optimal selection of service composition. (Xiang, Xu & Jiang, 2016). Energy saving is one of the use cases of Cloud computing. Carbon footprints can be reduced due to Cloud computing. As the actual physical machines can reduce the power requirements for running and the cooling, through the use of the IIoT and the CMfg.

Case 5: SketchPart

The manufacturing industry is having diverse roles of users and various requirements, which reflects the domain-specific user experiences. The user interface issues play a significant role in pushing this new area forward — the intelligent user interface (IUI) for CMfg, i.e., neutrality, smart mobility, self-configuration, and flexible customization. The SketchPart is a sketch-based pad system for searching part drawings in the Cloud, to show the advantages of the proposed Cloud-plus-IUI solution, is developed. The engineers and other manufacturing industry people often use the drawings of the parts, for various troubleshooting of the machinery. They have the database of parts of drawings. During the several work practices, the need for the searching facilities is required like based on the sketch-based user interface. (Xu, Yu, Zhou, Xie, Pham & Ji, 2015)

Case 6: Oracle Manufacturing Cloud

Oracle Manufacturing Cloud (OMC) and Supply chain solution provide cost controlling with streamline manufacturing processes through visualization, back-flushed transactions, and social collaboration. The OMC defines and manages master data, manage shop floor operations, provide visibility, plan and track manufacturing costs. The production process visualization combines BOM and routing into an integrated, tablet-friendly, graphical view that goes where the engineer does. Manufacturing engineers can quickly define the necessary master data for their production assets, process standards, calendars, work center resources, and standard operations. Production supervisors use a control center to get a quick look at how work areas or work centers are running. One-click access lets them drill into the details and take action, print travelers, generate a parts list and view production history. (Oracle, 2017)

Case 7: Cloud Storage for Factory Automation

The efficient management of the data storage for the CMfg is required. The system managers and engineers work in the main office or at the remote location far from the factory also need to monitor, check, the production rate, and share data of the manufacturing system in the factory. The cloud storage for the manufacturing system in global factory automation consists of four types of databases and one management server. The interfaces of the data exchange process between the manufacturing systems and each database are developed. (Jeong, Park & Lee, 2014)

Case 8: Data Mining Use in CMfg

The manufacturing data are obtained from the database of the production lines in the food industry. The correlation analysis and the decision tree algorithm are applied. The workflow computing block can be tailored made to fit the food manufacturing data. The RapidMiner, a GUI based tool for data mining, and statistical analysis modules are then built as plugged-in. To construct a workflow, plant engineers can use the necessary data mining modules. The RapidAnalytics is customized to allow the computing blocks to be scheduled onto the private Cloud. (Kitcharoen, Kamolsantisuk, Angsomboon & Achalakul, 2013)

Case 9: Oil and Gas Businesses

The oil and gas businesses with powerful processing capabilities in the Cloud. It is required to facilitating the links between multiple offices across the world and enhancing the security of sensitive information by storing it in a virtual hub rather than on local servers all at an appealingly low cost of entry. The Cloud hybrid version of the technology that combines software as a service (public Cloud) and software infrastructure as a service (private Cloud) could not only bring IT costs down, but could also improve the way the business is managed. Along with the IoT, drones, capable rigs, and leak-detection software, Cloud computing is one of the critical technology. The speed requirement for the oil and gas sector is essential and not allow the downtime. Hence the Cloud is one of the better options. The forecasting the oil and gas prices are one of the use cases of Cloud usage. There are remote teams, suppliers, investors, and especially joint venture partners, in this business (Rodd & Carlton, 2013).

CONCLUSION

The CMfg provides huge scope to of the software services through the Cloud platform. The Cloud Manufacturing leverages all the benefits of Cloud computing and inevitably reduces the overall cost of the final product to deliver to the consumer. However, the supportive use of the Industrial IoT, Digital Twin (DT) can provide the rich monitoring and visualization effect of the product, in support of edge and Cloud computing. The monitoring, controlling, utilizing, maintaining and sharing of the manufacturing resources through the Cloud in the big manufacturing reduces the cost of the product. The processes in the manufacturing industry either at the high-level decisions by the managers, the operations at the assembly line needs, and routine work by the other stakeholders working in the different departments of the manufacturing unit can efficiently utilize the resources and software if the IT infrastructure provided through the Cloud-based system. The rich experiences to the customer can be provided through the access of the high performance IT infrastructure on the sharing basis through the Cloud Manufacturing. There is a need of the skilled man-power in the field of the IIoT and CMfg, as it includes the complex operations and protocols. The adoption of the Cloud in manufacturing and IIoT is the need of the time. Both technologies can complement each other for the betterment of the manufacturing industry.

REFERENCES

AWS. (2019). Retrieved from https://aws.amazon.com/serverless/?nc2=h_m2

Bao, Y., Ren, L., Zhang, L., Zhang, X., & Luo, Y. (2012). Massive Sensor Data Management Framework in Cloud Manufacturing Based on Hadoop. *IEEE10th International Conference on Industrial Informatics*, 397-401. doi: 10.1109/INDIN.2012.6301192

Cloud Manufacturing. (2017). In *Wikipedia*. Retrieved from https://en.wikipedia.org/wiki/Cloud_manufacturing

Devare, M. (2018). Low Power Communication Protocols for IoT Enabled Applications. In *Protocols and Applications for the Industrial Internet of Things*. IGI Global.

Ding, T., Yan, G., Lei, Y., & Xu, X. (2016). Research on Critical Technologies of Manufacturing Execution Based on Cloud-Service. *3rd International Conference on Information Science and Control Engineering*, 538-542.

D¨unhaupt, S. (2012). *Vulnerabilities of Industrial Automation Systems*. RUHR-University Bochum, Seminar Thesis report.

Esposito, C., Castiglione, A., Martini, B., & Choo, K. K. R. (2016). Cloud Manufacturing: Security, Privacy, and Forensic Concerns. *Computers & Society*, 16–22.

Georgakopoulos, D., Jayaraman, P. P., Fazia, M., Villari, M., & Ranjan, R. (2016). Internet of Things and Edge Cloud Computing Roadmap for Manufacturing. *Computers & Society*, 66–73.

Ian Wright. (2017). *What Can Augmented Reality Do for Manufacturing?* Retrieved from https://www.engineering.com/AdvancedManufacturing/ArticleID/14904/What-Can-Augmented-Reality-Do-for-Manufacturing.aspx

Jeong, H. Y., Park, J. H., & Lee, J. D. (2014). The Cloud Storage Model for Manufacturing System in Global Factory Automation. *28th International Conference on Advanced Information Networking and Applications Workshops*, 895- 899. 10.1109/WAINA.2014.138

Jiming, Y., Zhiping, G., & Rongbo, S. (2012). Perception of Manufacturing Resources In Cloud-Manufacturing System. *International Conference on Computer Science and Service System, IEEE Computer Society*, 1993-1996. 10.1109/CSSS.2012.497

Kitcharoen, N., Kamolsantisuk, S., Angsomboon, R., & Achalakul, T. (2013). RapidMiner Framework for Manufacturing Data Analysis on the Cloud. *10th International Joint Conference on Computer Science and Software Engineering*. 10.1109/JCSSE.2013.6567336

Lartigau, J., Nie, L., Xu, X., Zhan, D., & Mou, T. (2012). Scheduling Methodology for Production Services in Cloud Manufacturing. *International Joint Conference on Service Sciences, IEEE Computer Society*, 34-39. 10.1109/IJCSS.2012.19

Li, W., Zhu, C., Yang, L. T., Shu, L., Ngai, E. C. H., & Ma, Y. (2017). Subtask Scheduling for Distributed Robots in Cloud Manufacturing. *IEEE Systems Journal*, *11*(2), 941–950. doi:10.1109/JSYST.2015.2438054

Linthicum, D. S. (2016). The Technical Case for Mixing Cloud Computing and Manufacturing. *IEEE Cloud Computing*, 12-15.

Liu, N., Li, X., & Wang, Q. (2011). A resource & capability virtualization method for Cloud Manufacturing Systems. IEEE.

Oracle Executive. (2017). *Why End-to-End Visibility Is Key to a Modern Manufacturing Process*. Oracle Executive Paper.

Rauscheckerl, U., & Stohrl, M. (2012). Using Manufacturing Service Descriptions for flexible Integration of Production Facilities to Manufacturing Clouds. *Proceedings of the 18th International Conference on Engineering, Technology, and Innovation*.

Rodd, S., & Carlton, B. (2013). *Exclusive Story- Cloud Technology Boosts Oil and Gas Operations*. Available at https://www.aogr.com/web-exclusives/exclusive-story/cloud-technology-boosts-oil-and-gas-operations

Ruth, M. (2017). Resource provision and QoS support with added security for client-side applications in cloud computing. *Springer International Journal of Information Technology*, *9*(3), 1–8.

Ruth, M. (2018). A Methodical Analysis of Application of Emerging Ubiquitous Computing Technology with Fog Computing and IoT in Diversified Fields and Challenges of Cloud Computing. *International Journal of Information Communication Technologies and Human Development, 10*(2). DOI: doi:10.4018/978-1-5225-4100-4.ch002

Shitole, A., & Devare, M. (2018). Machine Learning Supported Statistical Analysis of IoT Enabled Physical Location Monitoring Data. *International Conference On Computational Vision and Bio-Inspired Computing, Springer Lecture Notes in Computational Science and Engineering*.

Tao, F., Zhang, L., Liu, Y., Cheng, Y., Wang, L., & Xu, X. (2015). Manufacturing Service Management in Cloud Manufacturing: Overview and Future Research Directions. *Journal of Manufacturing Science and Engineering*, *137*(4), 040912. doi:10.1115/1.4030510

Wang, W., & Liu, F. (2012). *The Research of Cloud Manufacturing Resource Discovery Mechanism.* The 7th International Conference on Computer Science & Education, Melbourne, Australia.

Warehouse. (2016). *Wearable Technology in the Warehouse*. Retrieved from https://www.supplychain247.com/ article/wearable_technology_in_the_warehouse

Wu, Y., Peng, G., Chen, L., & Zhang, H. (2016). Service Architecture and evaluation model of distributed 3D printing based on Cloud manufacturing. *IEEE International Conference on Systems, Man, and Cybernetics*, 2762-2767.

Xiang, F., Xu, L., & Jiang, G. Z. (2016). Green Manufacturing Service Composition in Cloud Manufacturing System: An Introduction. *Proceedings of IEEE 11th Conference on Industrial Electronics and Applications*, 1988-1993. 10.1109/ICIEA.2016.7603915

Xinjuan, J., & Quan, L. (2016). Research on the On-Demand Service Mode in Cloud Manufacturing. IEEE.

Xu, W., Yu, J., Zhou, Z., Xie, Y., Pham, D. T., & Ji, C. (2015). Dynamic Modeling of Manufacturing Equipment Capability Using Condition Information in Cloud Manufacturing. *Journal of Manufacturing Science and Engineering*, *137*(4), 1–14. doi:10.1115/1.4030079

Zheng, H., Feng, Y., & Tan, J. (2017). A Hybrid Energy-aware Resource Allocation Approach in Cloud Manufacturing Environment. IEEE.

Chapter 4
Security Challenges and Resolution in Cloud Computing and Cloud of Things

Mamata Rath
https://orcid.org/0000-0002-2277-1012
Birla Global University, India

ABSTRACT

Cloud computing is a developing zone of computing innovation that shapes the handling power and the computing assets of many associated, topographically separated PCs associated by means of internet. Cloud computing wipes out the need of having a total framework of equipment and programming to meet clients' prerequisites and applications. It very well may be thought of as a total or an incomplete outsourcing of equipment and programming assets. To get to cloud applications, a great internet association and a standard internet program are required. Cloud computing has its own particular downside from the security perspective; this chapter addresses the vast majority of these dangers and their conceivable arrangements. Cloud computing gives its client numerous abilities like getting to an expansive number of utilizations without the requirement for having a permit, acquiring, introducing, or downloading any of these applications.

DOI: 10.4018/978-1-5225-8295-3.ch004

INTRODUCTION

Privacy and security issues of IoT devices and the communication information has been focussed in research works that gives bits of knowledge into the most essential existing issues of security and protection of the Cloud Computing (CC), Internet of Things (IoT) and Cloud of Things (CoT) ideas particularly classification issue. With the advancement of omnipresent computing, everything is associated all over the place, along these lines these ideas have been broadly contemplated in the writing. In any case, interruptions and vulnerabilities will be more repetitive because of the frameworks multifaceted nature and the trouble to control each entrance endeavour. To handle this issue, analysts have been focussing on different methodologies upholding security and protection. Change elements and arrangements in regard to these advances are assessed then present and future patterns are examined.

A plan for Cloud-of-Things and Edge Computing (CoTEC) movement administration in multi- domain systems has been projected to coordinate the activity course through the administration nodes, a basic departure point has been characterized for each movement stream in the CoTEC arrange utilizing numerous departure switches to improve the movement stream; this is known as Egress-Topology (ET). Along these lines, the proposed ET consolidates customary multi-topology directing in the CoTEC system to address the irregularities between benefit overlay steering and the fringe portal convention strategies. Moreover, the proposed ET presents various programmable nodes that can be designed to facilitate the continuous activity on the system and re-adjust administrations among alternate nodes in multi-area systems. The outcomes demonstrate that the said calculation has a lower execution time and better nature of administration.

Figure 1 describes different cloud services offered by Cloud Computing. It also provides organizations an expanded stockpiling than conventional capacity frameworks. Programming updates and groups are exceptionally mechanized with diminished number of contracted exceedingly talented IT staff. Following are different types of cloud deployment models.

1. Private cloud: The cloud is overseen by an association and serve it exclusively; it can exist inside or outside the association's edge .
2. Community cloud: The cloud is overseen by a few associations and backings a particular community that has a similar intrigue.
3. Public cloud: The cloud framework is possessed and overseen by an extensive Cloud Service Provider (CSP).
4. Hybrid cloud – The cloud foundation is made out of at least two of the above models (e.g. Private and public, private and community)

Figure 1. Cloud computing services

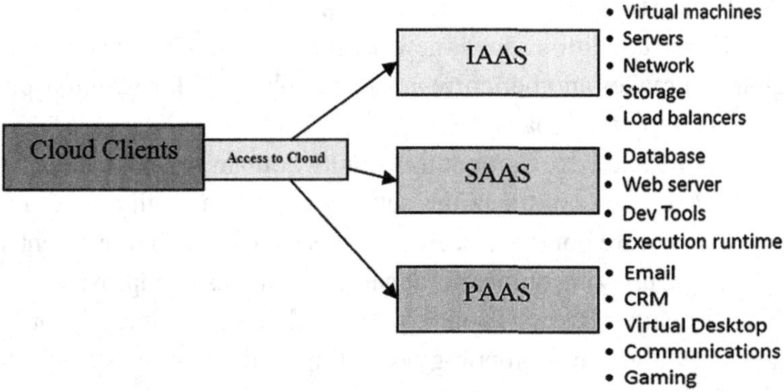

Cloud computing includes three components. Cloud Customer or client, Cloud Service Provider CSP and Cloud organize (more often than not the Internet that can be considered as the transmission media of the cloud) as outlined in figure 2.

2. LITERATURE REVIEW

Numerous research works have overviewed Cloud and IoT independently and, all the more absolutely, their fundamental properties, highlights, basic innovations, and open issues, yet these works do not have an itemized investigation of the new Cloud IoT worldview, which includes totally new applications, difficulties, and research issues. To address the issue, a detailed review on the incorporation of Cloud and IoT has been done .Standard highlights of OS and also hardware IoT platforms (Afzal et al., 2017) and OS-to-hardware structures highlights mapping while at the same time investigating the special necessities of SIoT applications. In doing as such, asset obliged IoT devices are especially accentuated because of their memory imperatives and power constraints. Further, a model OS design is proposed for devices in SIoT applications and related open research challenges are distinguished. This examination

Figure 2. Cloud computing levels

will profit designers to best use IoT platform assets and to conceive a productive OS for cutting edge SIoT applications. uniting of MANET with WSN utilized as a part of universal shrewd conditions opens new prospect in checking the substantial scale urban region and makes another correspondence platform for various applications in Internet of Things (IoT) space.

Cloud-of-Things and Edge Computing in multi- domain systems has been projected in (Jian et al., 2018) to coordinate the activity course through the administration nodes, a basic departure point has been characterized for each movement stream in the CoTEC arrange utilizing numerous departure switches to improve the movement stream; this is known as Egress-Topology (ET). Along these lines, the proposed ET consolidates customary multi-topology directing in the CoTEC system to address the irregularities between benefit overlay steering and the fringe portal convention strategies. Article (wu et al., 2018) proposes a proficient and secure accessible encryption convention utilizing the trapdoor stage work (TPF). The convention is intended for cloud-based IoT (additionally alluded to as Cloud of Things – CoT) sending, for example, Cloud of Battlefield Things and Cloud of Military Things.

The proposed arrangement depicted in was seen to be more vitality proficient. Similarly potential dangers of individual administrators and markets of unified MaaS (Metal as a service) that has been developed to help and facilitate the deployment of hyper scale computing environment and cloud services, suppliers have been ordered in (Franco et al., 2018) and it proposes fitting countermeasures to alleviate the issues. Also, it thinks about the developing instance of Cloud-of-Things (CoT) for mobility, i.e., systems of universal, unavoidable devices that give continuous information on items and individuals. Mechanization and inescapability of CoT make an extra assault surface for insiders. With an end goal to utmost such wonder, it introduces an overlay organizing engineering, in light of talk conventions, that gives clients a chance to impart data on mobility to each other. Privacy and security issues of IoT devices (Rath et al., 2018) and the communication information has been focussed in research work (Syrine et al., 2017) that gives bits of knowledge into the most essential existing issues of security and protection of the Cloud Computing (CC), Internet of Things (IoT) and Cloud of Things (CoT) ideas particularly classification issue(Rath et al., 2018).

Sensors utilized for IoT applications, sense the earth and send the information to the portal hub, which thus send the gathered information to the MANET hub, particularly utilized for information reaping. the creators considered two IoT applications (Mukherjee et al., 2017) which are checked by remote sensor hubs. The testing some portion of this work is to influence a platform by uniting sensor to coordinate with the MANET organize on the grounds that hubs have diverse power levels, heterogeneous conventions and have odds of co-channel obstructions.

Mobile devices are quickly turning into the significant administration members these days. Be that as it may, conventional client-server based mobile administration models are not ready to meet the expanding requests from mobile clients as far as administrations decent variety, client experience, security and protection (Rath et al., 2016), et cetera. Cloud computing empowers mobile devices to offload complex tasks of mobile applications, which are infeasible on mobile devices alone. Huang et al. (2013) show an exhaustive report to spread out existing mobile cloud computing administration models and key accomplishments, and present another client driven mobile cloud computing administration model to progress existing mobile cloud computing research.

Cloud Computing has been imagined as the cutting-edge design of IT Enterprise. It moves the application programming and databases to the brought together vast server farms, where the administration of the information and administrations may not be completely reliable.

Specifically, to accomplish productive information elements, we enhance the current verification of capacity models by controlling the great Merkle Hash Tree development for square label validation. To help productive treatment of different inspecting errands, advance strategy of bilinear total mark are investigated to expand fundamental outcome into a multiuser setting, where TPA can play out numerous reviewing assignments all the while. Broad security and execution investigation demonstrate that the proposed plans are very proficient and provably secure (Rath et al., 2019).

The most pertinent Fog-empowered CoT framework models are proposed by Mukhtar M.E et. al, in (2018) who proposes a vitality mindful designation system for putting application modules (assignments) on Fog devices. At last, the execution of the proposed system is assessed in correlation with the default allotment and Cloud-just strategies, utilizing the "iFogSim" test system. The proposed arrangement in was seen to be more vitality proficient. Franco Callegati, et. al, (2018) orders the potential dangers of individual administrators and markets of unified MaaS suppliers and proposes fitting countermeasures to alleviate the issues. Also, it thinks about the developing instance of Cloud-of-Things (CoT) for mobility, i.e., systems of universal, unavoidable devices that give continuous information on items and individuals.

Mechanization and inescapability of CoT make an extra assault surface for insiders. With an end goal to utmost such wonder, it introduces an overlay organizing engineering, in light of talk conventions, that gives clients a chance to impart data on mobility to each other. Privacy and security issues of IoT devices and the communication information has been focussed in research work that gives bits of knowledge into the most essential existing issues of security and protection of the Cloud Computing (CC), Internet of Things (IoT) and Cloud of Things (CoT) ideas particularly classification issue. Cloud-of-Things and Edge Computing (CoTEC) movement administration in multi- domain systems has been projected in to coordinate the activity course through the administration nodes, a basic departure point has been characterized for each movement stream in the CoTEC arrange utilizing numerous departure switches to improve the movement stream; this is known as Egress-Topology (ET).

3. CLOUD FRAMEWORKS AND SECURITY CONCERN IN COT

The data in a private association permits just the verified clients to get to the data. The entrance benefit must be given just to the concerned clients and examiners with a specific end goal to limit such risks. At the point when there is an access from an inward to outside source, the likelihood of risk is more if there should arise an occurrence of touchy data. Isolation of the data is vital in cloud computing as the data is disseminated over a system of physical gadgets. Data defilement emerges if suitable isolation isn't kept up. Right now, there are no government arrangements tending to how government data is gotten to. Accessibility assumes a noteworthy part in cloud computing since the necessities of the clients ought to be gone to on time.

Authorized cloud appropriation and shadow IT generated by the simple accessibility of snap to-figure cloud applications and services like Box or AWS, and additionally quickly moving administrative prerequisites like those rising in the European Union are likewise making worries around cloud data security, data residency and consistence. The Cloud Generation Gateway enables clients to survey and control the danger of unsanctioned cloud use, while adding basic security controls to kill data spillage, hold data residency through tokenisation, and keep up consistence for endorsed cloud applications. Web Security Service (Cloud Service, figure 3) Offers on-demand web security, providing customisable reporting and actionable intelligence that enables (https://www.cstl.com) to improve the effectiveness of your web application and operation controls. The Blue Coat Cloud Service identifies and categories new web content in real-time, so you have up-to-date protection against web-based threats.

Cloud Computing is also a quick rising business standard. Business enterprise think that it is useful in few different ways. Cloud Computing improves openness, gives virtual storage room, addresses reinforcement issues, it gives security against

Figure 3. Symantec web security service

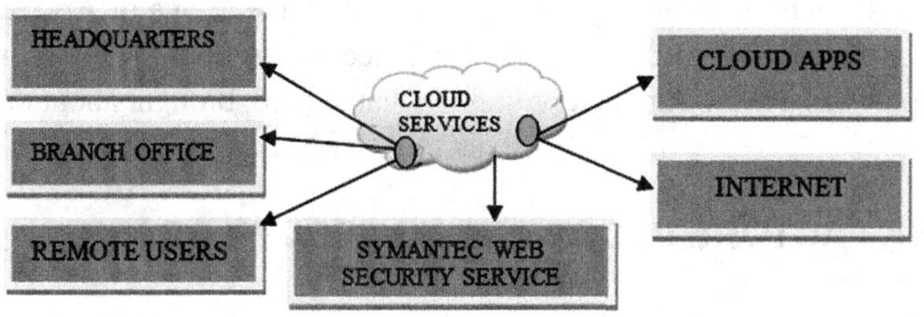

unapproved access and loss of data. Key favourable position is that clients can pay just for the assets they have utilized on 'the cloud' and get rid of the real speculations for data stockpiling, programming licenses, servers and hardware. According to an IBM measurement around 85% of new applications are being developed around Cloud Computing. The business is relied upon to develop immensely, determined predominantly by the services that enable clients to reinforcement their records including photographs and music, while guaranteeing simple accessibility of documents in instances of hard drive crash. Concentrates by NASDAQ show that interests in cloud technology is probably going to grow over US$ 40 million constantly 2018.Candidates trying to seek after a vocation in Cloud Computing need to have excellent IT and programming aptitudes. Required specialized aptitudes include a solid hang on programming dialects, perception innovations and HTML. Professionals trying to prevail in the administrative stream need to pick up a comprehension of issues related with approach, assentions, hazard analytics, web based promoting systems and in addition the capacity to manage clients. Cloud Technologies are for the most part virtualization conditions. Wannabes looking to make great in the Cloud should be proficient in systems administration and virtualization and pick up hands-on presentation with live organizations. Analysts can likewise explore different avenues regarding their Cloud Technology Skills on couple of sites that offer lab framework, for example, Azure, AWS and Google Cloud among others.

An explore from the University of California had followed the accessibility and blackouts of four noteworthy cloud sellers. It was based on Cloud infrastructure, Cloud Platform, Cloud Application, Computational assets and Capacity of Communications. It was discovered that over-burden on the framework caused programming mistakes bringing about framework accidents and disappointments. Due to the absence of reinforcement recuperation Apple, MobileMe, Google Gmail, Citrix and Amazon s3 detailed times of inaccessibility going from 2 to 14hrs of every a range of only 60 days. This brought about lost certainty among the clients and the sellers. Cataclysmic events can likewise exhibit huge risks. A helping strike at one of Amazon.com's offices caused the administration to go disconnected for around 4 hours. This part of the cloud was hard to supplant promptly what's more, brought about deferrals.

3.1 RISK FACTORS IN COT DUE TO SERVER CRASH

Cloud organize load can likewise end up being negative to execution of the cloud computing framework. In the event that the limit of the cloud is more prominent than 80%, at that point the PCs can end up lethargic because of high volumes .The PCs what's more, the servers crash because of high volume movement of data between the circle and the PC memory. The rate of limit edge likewise represents a risk to the cloud clients. At the point when the edge surpasses 80%, the merchants secure their administrations and pass the corruption on to clients. It has been shown that in specific cases the blackout of the framework to the clients are still not got to . Adaptability and versatility ought to be viewed as urgent when planning and actualizing a cloud framework. Cash what's more, time additionally assumes an essential part in the outline of the framework. Clients will dependably have desires on the toughness and the productivity of the framework. Going forward the clients will likewise request the need of interoperability, capacity to switch suppliers and movement alternatives. Another risk factor of cloud computing is the execution of the application programming interfaces (Programming interface).

Data uprightness influences the exactness of data kept up in the framework. In a cloud computing model data legitimacy, quality and security influence's the framework's activities and wanted results. The program proficiency and execution are tended to by the respectability. An adept case for this would be that of a cell phone specialist co-op who put away all the client's data including messages, contact records and so on in a Microsoft backup. The Provider lost the data and the cloud was inaccessible. The clients needed to hold up until they got the essential data from the cloud and the data was re-established.

Another key standard in a cloud is the data security. Data has to be suitably anchored from the outside world. This is important to guarantee that data is secured and is less inclined to debasement. With cloud computing turning into an up and coming incline, various vulnerabilities could emerge when the data is as a rule unpredictably shared among the fluctuated frameworks in cloud computing. Trust is an imperative factor which is missing in the present models as the specialist co-ops utilize broadened components which don't have legitimate security measures. The accompanying sub area depicts the risks factors in cloud conditions.

Data Location is another angle in cloud computing where specialist organizations are not gathered in a solitary area be that as it may, are circulated all through the globe. It makes ignorance among the clients about the correct area of the cloud. This could block examinations inside the cloud and is hard to get to the movement of the cloud, where the data isn't put away in a specific data focus however in a disseminated design. The clients may not be comfortable with the basic situations of the shifted segments in the cloud.

3.2 Data Segregation and Security

Data Segregation isn't effortlessly encouraged in all cloud situations as every one of the data can't be isolated agreeing to the client needs. A few clients don't scramble the data as there are chances for the encryption itself to demolish the data. To put it plainly, cloud computing isn't a situation which works in a toolbox. The traded off servers are closed down at whatever point a data is should have been recuperated. The accessible data isn't effectively sent to the client consistently of need. While recouping the data there could be examples of replication of data in different destinations. The rebuilding of data must be snappy and finish to evade additionally risks. We look at how cloud computing is evaluated in a biomedical research facility which encounters risks due to programmers .In a biomedical research facility, data is dependably presented to dangers both inner and outer. Less partition is given by the cloud if there should arise an occurrence of a different server in a research center. The risks incorporate the hacking of the hypervisor, where a mutual CPU can be effortlessly attacked. The data can be controlled, erased or devastated because of the attack. Such attacks on biomedical data can have genuine suggestions to the end clients. Along these lines the Data Base Manage Framework (DBMS) and web servers confront defenselessness if the framework of the cloud isn't appropriately composed. There are sure non specialized risks which emerge because of outsourcing of data. Scrambling the data from the specialized perspective is essential to guarantee that the data isn't hacked or attacked. Solid encryption is required for touchy data and this would mean expanded expenses

3.3 Client-Side Cloud Security With Secret Key

Key-introduction conflict has dependably been a critical issue for top to bottom digital guard in numerous security applications. As of late, how to manage the key presentation issue in the settings of cloud stockpiling examining has been proposed and considered. In the current technological cloud based battle for inviting more number of customers, Amazon Web service (AWS) has proved itself to be the leading one by incorporating customer satisfaction to its upcoming IoT cloud on top of AWS. Figure 4. describes cloud applications in context of CoT.

To address the test, existing arrangements all require the client to refresh his mystery enters in each day and age, which may definitely get new nearby weights to the client, particularly those with constrained calculation assets, for example, mobile telephones. Yu et al., (2016) center around how to make the key updates as straightforward as workable for the client and propose another worldview called cloud stockpiling inspecting with unquestionable outsourcing of key updates. In this worldview, key updates can be securely outsourced to some approved gathering, and along these lines the key-refresh trouble on the client will be kept negligible. Specifically, the outsider inspector (TPA) is used in many existing open examining outlines, let it assume the job of approved gathering for our situation, and make it accountable for both the capacity reviewing and the safe key updates for key-introduction opposition. In this plan, TPA just needs to hold an encoded rendition of the client's mystery key while doing all these troublesome undertakings for the benefit of the client. The client just needs to download the encoded mystery key from the TPA while transferring new documents to cloud. Moreover, this plan additionally outfits the client with ability to additionally confirm the legitimacy of the scrambled mystery keys given by the TPA. All these notable highlights are precisely intended to make the entire examining methodology with key presentation opposition as straightforward as workable for the client. It formalizes the definition and the security model of this worldview.

Figure 5 describes Cloud as a Service to IoT connected devices as and when customized applications require various customer services from Cloud.The security evidence and the execution recreation demonstrate that our itemized plan instantiations are secure and proficient. With the advent of big data era, clients lack of computational and storage resources tends to outsource data mining tasks to

Figure 4. Cloud applications

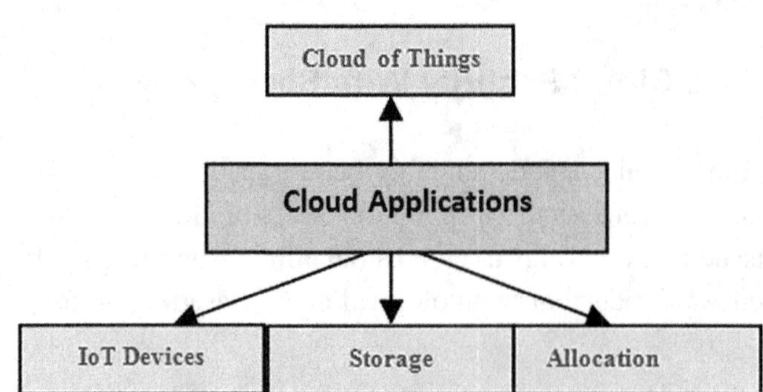

Figure 5. Cloud as a service to IoT devices

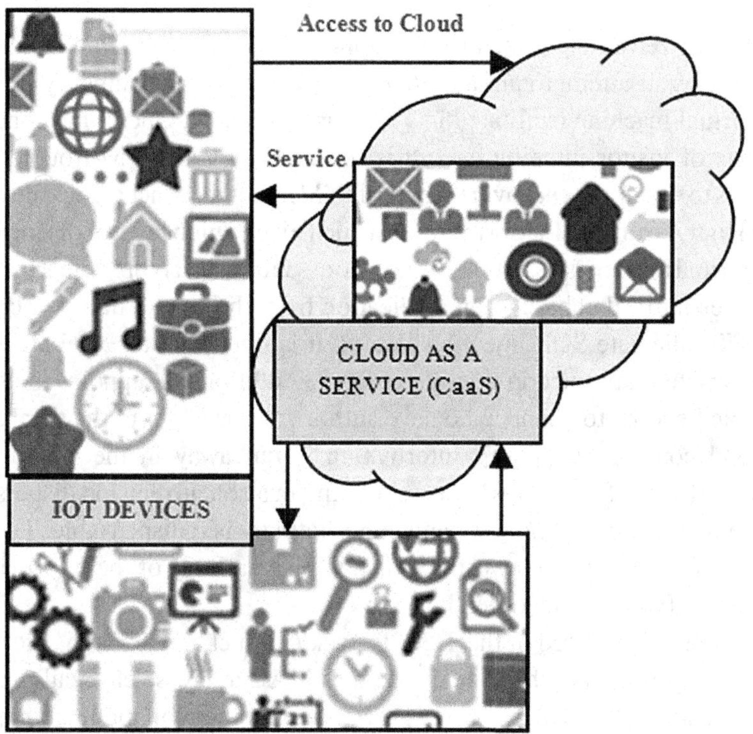

cloud computing providers in order to improve efficiency and save costs. Generally, different clients choose different cloud companies for the sake of security, business cooperation, location, and so on. However, due to the rise of privacy leakage issues, the data contributed by clients should be encrypted under their own keys. Rong et al. (2016) focuses on privacy-preserving k-nearest neighbor (kNN) computation over the databases distributed among multiple cloud environments. Unfortunately, existing secure outsourcing protocols (Rath et al., 2015)are either restricted to a single key setting or quite inefficient because of frequent client-to-server interactions (Rath et al., 2016), making it impractical for wide application. To address these issues, a set of secure building blocks and outsourced collaborative kNN protocol has been proposed. Theoretical analysis shows that our scheme not only preserves the privacy of distributed databases and kNN query but also hides access patterns in the semi-honest model. Experimental evaluation demonstrates its significant efficiency improvements compared with existing methods.

3.4 Guest-Hopping Attack and SQL Injection

It is s characterized as any detachment disappointment between shared foundations. An aggressor will attempt gain admittance to one virtual machine by infiltrating another virtual machine facilitated in a similar equipment. One of the conceivable alleviations of visitor jumping assault is the Forensics and VM troubleshooting apparatuses to watch any endeavor to trade off VM. Another conceivable alleviation is utilizing High Assurance Platform (HAP) which gives a high level of disengagement between virtual machines. Is frequently used to assault sites. It is proficient by infusing SQL charges into a database of an application from the web to dump or crash that database. To alleviate SQL injection assault; it is important to expel all put away methodology that are once in a while utilized. Additionally, appoint the slightest conceivable benefits to clients who have authorizations to get to the database.

In cloud computing, client's information is put away in the Cloud Service Provider (CSP) set of servers, which are running in a concurrent and dispersed way. Guaranteeing information honesty and unhesitatingly is indispensable. There are a few intends to guarantee trustworthiness and unhesitatingly of the information put away at the CSP that are recorded beneath.

This protocol is utilized in the TCP/IP stack (Rath et al., 2017) to determine an IP address (legitimate) at the sender side into MAC address (physical) address at the recipient side. The ARP reserve stores a table that maps all the IP address of the arranged gadgets and their relating MAC addresses. An assailant can abuse some shortcoming in the ARP convention to delineate IP deliver of the system to one malignant MAC (Rath et al., 2018), and after that refresh the ARP reserve with this noxious MAC address. To moderate this assault it is conceivable to utilize static ARP passages, this system can work for little systems like private clouds; however on huge scale clouds it is smarter to utilize different strategies, for example, port security includes that bolts a particular port on the switch (or organize gadget) to a particular IP address.It ought to be seen that CSP must have the most recent system security improvement strategies, for example, Firewalls, Intrusion Detection/ Prevention procedures, Centralized antivirus and hostile to malware methods that runs multi antivirus arrangements all the while to guarantee best infection and malware assurance. Another imperative issue is to utilize IPSEC/VPN strategies between the CSP and cloud clients at whatever point it is conceivable. Likewise, high physical security at the CSP server farm/s is indispensable, physical information security incorporates: Access control just for approved faculty, unique fire frameworks, quite certain information stockpiling and reinforcement strategists, and so forth. Figure 6 depicts Dependency of cloud applications on storage, database, server and mobility.

Figure 6. Dependency of cloud applications

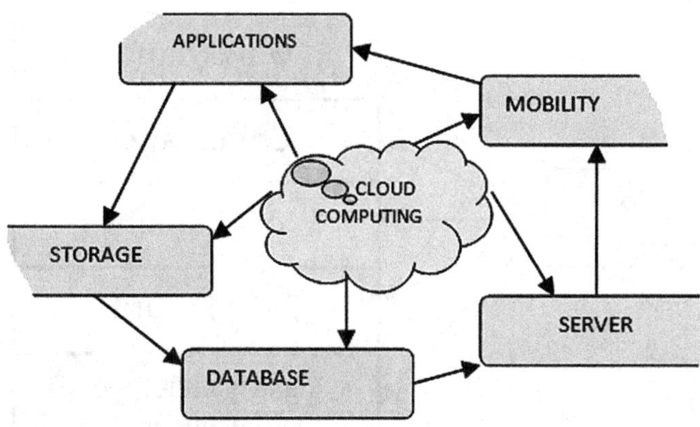

3.5 DNS-Related Security Issues

In the Internet, computers are characterized by names that are anything but difficult to recollect by people, while PCs manage numbers. Each associated PC to the Internet has a comprehensively interesting Internet Protocol (IP) (Rath et.al, 2019). The Domain Name System (DNS) changes over host names into relating Internet Protocol (IP) addresses utilizing a dispersed database plot. Web DNS servers are liable to various kinds of assaults, for example, ARP reserve harming area capturing, and man-in-the-center assaults. A talk of these assaults can be found underneath.Domain hijacking involves changing the name of a domain exclusive of the knowledge or consent from the domain's proprietor or creator. Domain hijacking allows intruders right of entry to sensitive corporate information and carry out illegal activity such as phishing.IP spoofing is the place the attacker increases unapproved access to a PC by imagining that the activity has begun shape a honest to goodness PC. IP caricaturing is used to make different attacks, for example, Denial of Service attack and Man in The Middle attack.

Figure 7 describes the cloud security service for IoT Devices using Cloud of Things. In Current IoT technology, Advanced Persistent Threats (APTs) are increasing at an extraordinary rate. The predicted cyber threat scenery is drastically different than just a few years back (Elizabeth et. al, 2018) . Attacks are much more planned and complicated. They are difficult to detect and even harder to foresee. In the foreseeable future it's going to get a whole lot difficult scenario to manage security in technology. Knowledge till now will drastically get changed and it will be very challenging to keep up with changing technology (Rath et.al, 2019). Organisations

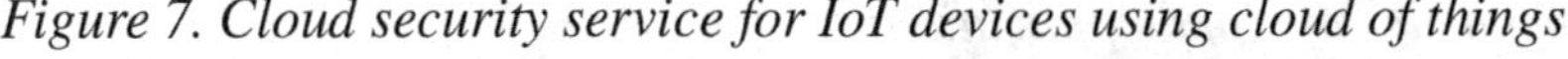

Figure 7. Cloud security service for IoT devices using cloud of things

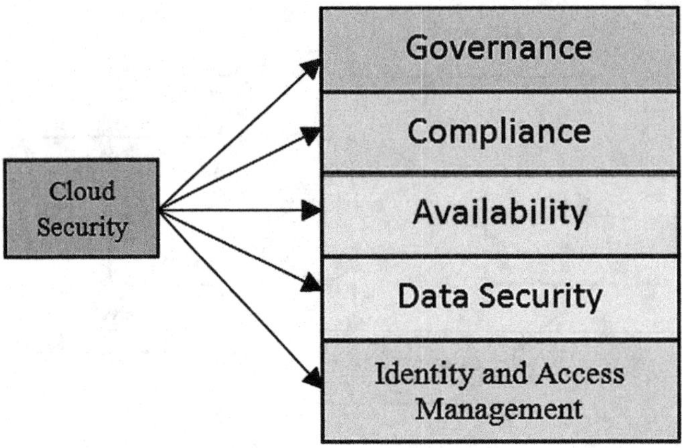

will have to frequently switch over to new technology with respect to higher cost. Latest tools, methods and enough expertise to control threats and vulnerability.

5. CYBER SECURITY CHALLENGES IN CLOUD COMPUTING

The reason for these attacks is influencing the objective to organize/PC assets inaccessible. In DoS attack the attacker surges the casualty have with a colossal number of parcels in a short measure of time, DoS is concerned just with devouring data transfer capacity and assets of the objective system/PC. The attacker utilizes a ridiculed IP address as the source IP deliver to make following and halting of Dos exceptionally troublesome (Rath et.al, 2019). Besides, it is conceivable to the attacker to utilize various bargained machines which he has just seized to attack the casualty machine in the meantime (this attack is known as Distributed DoS) and it is exceptionally hard to track and stop. TCP SYN flooding - Is a case of DoS attack; the attacker surges the casualty machine with a flood of mock TCP SYN parcels. This attack misuses the constraints of the three route handshake in keeping up half-open associations. Man In The Middle Attack (MITM)-An attacker accesses the system activity utilizing system bundle sniffer, steering and transport conventions defects, these attacks could be utilized for robbery of classified data. IP ridiculing can be lessened utilizing bundle separating by firewall, solid encryption and root confirmation methods., the following table 1 depicts all the studied challenges and issues.

The majority of the cloud clients' attacks are phishing, extortion, and misuse of programming vulnerabilities still work and can debilitate the cloud service framework. Phishing and extortion: are endeavors to take the personality of a true blue client, for example, usernames, passwords, and Mastercard subtle elements. Phishing is commonly completed by sending the client an email that contains a connection to a misrepresentation site that resembles a true blue one, when the client goes to that phony site, his client name and watchword will be sent to the attacker who can utilize them to attack the cloud. Another type of phishing and extortion is to send the client an email that claims to end up from the cloud service supplier and requesting that the client supply his username and secret key for upkeep purposes for instance; yet without a doubt that ridiculed email originated from an attacker to pick up the client certifications at that point utilizing them to attack the cloud. Countermeasures of phishing are the utilization of Spam-channels, utilizing module spam blocker in the Internet programs lastly prepare the clients not to react to any mock email and not to give their qualifications to any site.

Figure 8. Challenges in cloud computing

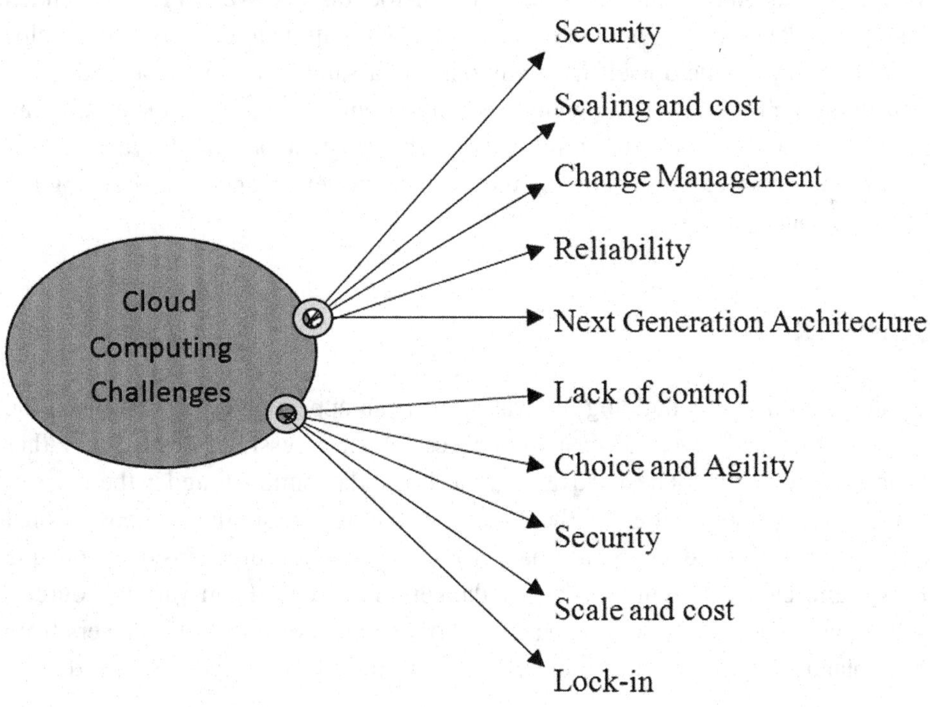

Cloud computing is a technology that utilizations remote servers and the web to deal with the applications and keep up the data. For example BCNI(The Business Computer Network (Rath et.al, 2014)Inc) cloud stockpiling services are enabling organizations to utilize their applications without access or establishment if their documents at any PC with web get to. Figure 8 depicts various Challenges in Cloud Computing. Device security is one of the significant difficulties for fruitful usage of Internet of Things and haze computing condition in current IT space. Specialists and Information Technology (IT) associations have investigated numerous answers for shield frameworks from unauthenticated device assaults (known as outside device assaults). Mist computing utilizes arrange devices (e.g. switch, switch and hub) for dormancy mindful preparing of gathered information utilizing IoT. At that point, recognizable proof of pernicious edge device is one of the basic exercises in information security of haze computing condition. Keeping assaults from pernicious edge devices in mist computing condition is more troublesome in light of the fact that they have certain conceded benefits to utilize and process the information. Many cyber security structure utilizes three advances which are Markov display, Intrusion Detection System (IDS) and Virtual Honeypot Device (VHD) to distinguish malignant edge device in haze computing condition. A two-arrange shrouded Markov display is utilized to adequately classify edge devices in four unique levels. VHD is intended to store and keep up log archive of all recognized malignant devices which helps the framework to shield itself from any obscure assaults later on. Proposed cyber security system is tried with genuine assaults in virtual condition made utilizing Open Stack and Microsoft Azure. Results showed that proposed cybersecurity structure is effective in recognizing the malevolent device and also lessening the false IDS caution rate.

CONCLUSION

Cloud computing is a budding innovation. It is an appealing collection when the framework or the IT work force are not accessible or excessively costly; but rather it has its disadvantage. The disadvantage can be fundamentally found in the security dangers and vulnerabilities of the cloud computing. Dissimilar to conventional arrangements where dangers originate from two known sources inside or outside the system; cloud computing security dangers may begin from various sources. In this paper we talked about the vast majority of the cloud security dangers from three planned levels: application, system and client levels. Likewise we deliver some conceivable approaches to decrease security as could be expected under the circumstances. The rapid improvement of Internet-based computing enables various technologies to be produced to fulfill an expanding service and security request. In any case, the significance of security and protection is as yet rising. In this present chapter, an exhaustive inspection of Internet-based cloud computing has been exhibited. Especially, the connections and contrasts between Internet based cloud security and CoT have been cleared up, alongside their designs and empowering advancements to secure computing, potential protection and security issues that could influence the viability of the framework.

REFERENCES

Akatyev, N., & James, J. I. (2017). Evidence identification in IoT networks based on threat assessment. *Future Generation Computer Systems.*

Al-Ali, A. R., Zualkernan, I. A., Rashid, M., Gupta, R., & Alikarar, M. (2017). A smart home energy management system using IoT and big data analytics approach. *IEEE Transactions on Consumer Electronics, 63*(4), 426–434. doi:10.1109/TCE.2017.015014

Alaba, F. A., Othman, M., Ibrahim, A. T. H., & Alotaibi, F. (2017). Internet of Things security: A survey. *Journal of Network and Computer Applications, 88*, 10-28.

Botta, A., de Donato, W., Persico, V., & Pescapé, A. (2016). Integration of Cloud computing and Internet of Things: A survey. *Future Generation Computer Systems, 56*, 684-700. doi:10.1016/j.future.2015.09.021

Callegati, F., Giallorenzo, S., Melis, A., & Prandini, M. (2018). Cloud-of-Things meets Mobility-as-a-Service: An insider threat perspective. *Computers & Security, 74*, 277-295. doi:10.1016/j.cose.2017.10.006

Cerullo, G., Mazzeo, G., Papale, G., Ragucci, B., & Sgaglione, L. (2018). IoT and Sensor Networks Security. In Intelligent Data-Centric Systems (pp. 77-101). Academic Press. doi:10.1016/B978-0-12-811373-8.00004-5

Chibelushi, Eardley, & Arabo. (2013). Identity Management in the Internet of Things: the Role of MANETs for Healthcare Applications. *Computer Science and Information Technology, 1*(2), 73-81.

Chifor, B.-C., Bica, I., Patriciu, V.-V., & Pop, F. (2017). A security authorization scheme for smart home Internet of Things devices. *Future Generation Computer Systems.*

Choo, K.-K. R., Bishop, M., Glisson, W., & Nance, K. (2018). Internet- and cloud-of-things cybersecurity research challenges and advances. *Computers & Security, 74*, 275-276. doi:10.1016/j.cose.2018.02.008

Farahani, B., Firouzi, F., Chang, V., Badaroglu, M., Constant, N., & Mankodiya, K. (2018). Towards fog-driven IoT eHealth: Promises and challenges of IoT in medicine and healthcare. *Future Generation Computer Systems, 78*(2), 659-676.

Farahzadi, A., Shams, P., Rezazadeh, J., & Farahbakhsh, R. (2017). Middleware technologies for cloud of things-a survey. *Digital Communications and Networks.* doi:10.1016/j.dcan.2017.04.005

Farris, I., Orsino, A., Militano, L., Iera, A., & Araniti, G. (2018). Federated IoT services leveraging 5G technologies at the edge. *Ad Hoc Networks, 68*, 58-69.

Khan & Salah. (2017). IoT security: Review, blockchain solutions, and open challenges. *Future Generation Computer Systems*. doi:10.1016/j.future.2017.11.022

Khanna, A., & Anand, R. (n.d.). IoT based smart parking system. *International Conference on Internet of Things and Applications (IOTA)*, 266-270.

Li, S. (2017). Security Requirements in IoT Architecture. In *Securing the Internet of Things* (pp. 97–108). Boston: Syngress. doi:10.1016/B978-0-12-804458-2.00005-6

Lv, Z., Song, H., Basanta-Val, P., Steed, A., & Jo, M. (2017). Next-Generation Big Data Analytics: State of the Art, Challenges, and Future Research Topics. *IEEE Transactions on Industrial Informatics, 13*(4), 1891–1899. doi:10.1109/TII.2017.2650204

Mahmoud, Rodrigues, Saleem, Al-Muhtadi, Kumar, & Korotaev. (2018). Towards energy-aware fog-enabled cloud of things for healthcare. *Computers & Electrical Engineering, 67*, 58-69. .2018.02.047 doi:10.1016/ j.compeleceng

Mamata, R. B. P. (2018). Communication Improvement and Traffic Control Based on V2I in Smart City Framework. *International Journal of Vehicular Telematics and Infotainment Systems*, *2*(1).

Mukherjee & Biswas. (2017). Networking for IoT and applications using existing communication technology. *Egyptian Informatics Journal*. doi:10.1016/j.eij.2017.11.002

Nan, Li, Bao, Delicato, Pires, & Zomaya. (2018). A dynamic tradeoff data processing framework for delay-sensitive applications in Cloud of Things systems. *Journal of Parallel and Distributed Computing, 112*(1), 53-66. doi:10.1016/j.jpdc.2017.09.009

Numms, J. (n.d.). *Salesforce turns to Amazon Web Services for Internet of Things Cloud*. Retrieved from https://www.cbronline.com/emerging-technology/

Pattanayak, B., & Rath, M. (2014). A Mobile Agent Based Intrusion Detection System Architecture For Mobile Ad Hoc Networks. *Journal of Computational Science, 10*(6), 970–975. doi:10.3844/jcssp.2014.970.975

Rath & Oreku. (2018). Security Issues in Mobile Devices and Mobile Adhoc Networks. In Mobile Technologies and Socio-Economic Development in Emerging Nations. IGI Global. doi:10.4018/978-1-5225-4029-8.ch009

Rath. (2019). Information Security Problem and Solution Approaches in Social Applications. In Cyber-Physical Systems for Social Applications (pp. 207-220). IGI Global.

Rath & Pattanayak. (2019). Security Protocol with IDS Framework Using Mobile Agent in Robotic MANET. *International Journal of Information Security and Privacy, 3*(1), 46-58.

Rath, M. (2017). Resource provision and QoS support with added security for client side applications in cloud computing. *International Journal of Information Technology*, *9*(3), 1–8.

Rath, M. (2018a). An Exhaustive Study and Analysis of Assorted Application and Challenges in Fog Computing and Emerging Ubiquitous Computing Technology. *International Journal of Applied Evolutionary Computation, 9*(2), 17-32. Retrieved from www.igi-global.com/ijaec

Rath, M. (2018b). A Methodical Analysis of Application of Emerging Ubiquitous Computing Technology With Fog Computing and IoT in Diversified Fields and Challenges of Cloud Computing. *International Journal of Information Communication Technologies and Human Development, 10*(2). Doi:10.4018/978-1-5225-4100-4.ch002

Rath, M., & Panda, M. R. (2017). MAQ system development in mobile ad-hoc networks using mobile agents. *IEEE 2nd International Conference on Contemporary Computing and Informatics (IC3I)*, 794-798.

Rath, M., & Panigrahi, C. (2016). Prioritization of Security Measures at the Junction of MANET and IoT. In *Second International Conference on Information and Communication Technology for Competitive Strategies*. ACM Publication. 10.1145/2905055.2905187

Rath, M., & Pati, B. (2017). *Load balanced routing scheme for MANETs with power and delay optimisation. International Journal of Communication Network and Distributed Systems,* 19.

Rath, M., Pati, B., & Pattanayak, B. (2015). Energy Competent Routing Protocol Design in MANET with Real time Application Provision. *International Journal of Business Data Communications and Networking*, *11*(1), 50–60. doi:10.4018/IJBDCN.2015010105

Rath, M., Pati, B., & Pattanayak, B. (2015). Delay and power based network assessment of network layer protocols in MANET. *2015 International Conference on Control, Instrumentation, Communication and Computational Technologies (IEEE ICCICCT)*, 682-686. 10.1109/ICCICCT.2015.7475365

Rath, M., Pati, B., & Pattanayak, B. (2016). Energy Efficient MANET Protocol Using Cross Layer Design for Military Applications. *Defence Science Journal*, *66*(2), 146. doi:10.14429/dsj.66.9705

Rath, M., Pati, B., & Pattanayak, B. (2016). Comparative analysis of AODV routing protocols based on network performance parameters in Mobile Adhoc Networks. In Foundations and Frontiers in Computer, Communication and Electrical Engineering (pp. 461-466). CRC Press, Taylor & Francis.

Rath, M., Pati, B., & Pattanayak, B. (2016). Resource Reservation and Improved QoS for Real Time Applications in MANET. *Indian Journal of Science and Technology*, *9*(36). doi:10.17485/ijst/2016/v9i36/100910

Rath, M., Pati, B., & Pattanayak, B. (2016). QoS Satisfaction in MANET Based Real Time Applications. *International Journal of Control Theory and Applications*, *9*(7), 3069-3083.

Rath, M., Pati, B., & Pattanayak, B. K. (2016). Inter-Layer Communication Based QoS Platform for Real Time Multimedia Applications in MANET. Wireless Communications, Signal Processing and Networking (IEEE WiSPNET), 613-617. doi:10.1109/WiSPNET.2016.7566203

Rath, M., Pati, B., & Pattanayak, B. K. (2017). Cross layer based QoS platform for multimedia transmission in MANET. *11th International Conference on Intelligent Systems and Control (ISCO)*, 402-407. 10.1109/ISCO.2017.7856026

Rath, M., Pati, B., & Pattanayak, B. K. (2018). Relevance of Soft Computing Techniques in the Significant Management of Wireless Sensor Networks. In Soft Computing in Wireless Sensor Networks (pp. 86-106). Chapman and Hall/CRC, Taylor & Francis Group. doi:10.1201/9780429438639-4

Rath, M., Pati, B., & Pattanayak, B. K. (2019). Design and Development of Secured Framework for Efficient Routing in Vehicular Ad-hoc Network. Int'l Journal of Business and Data Communication Network, 15(2).

Rath, M., Pati, B., & Pattanayak, B. K. (2019). Mobile Agent-Based Improved Traffic Control System in VANET. In A. Krishna, K. Srikantaiah, & C. Naveena (Eds.), *Integrated Intelligent Computing, Communication and Security. Studies in Computational Intelligence* (Vol. 771). Singapore: Springer. doi:10.1007/978-981-10-8797-4_28

Rath, M., & Pattanayak, B. (2016). A Contemporary Survey and Analysis of Delay and Power Based Routing Protocols in MANET. *Journal of Engineering and Applied Sciences (Asian Research Publishing Network), 11*(1), 536–540.

Rath, M., & Pattanayak, B. (2017). MAQ:A Mobile Agent Based QoS Platform for MANETs. *International Journal of Business Data Communications and Networking, IGI Global, 13*(1), 1–8. doi:10.4018/IJBDCN.2017010101

Rath, M., & Pattanayak, B. K. (2014). A methodical survey on real time applications in MANETS: Focussing On Key Issues. *International Conference on, High Performance Computing and Applications (IEEE ICHPCA)*. 10.1109/ICHPCA.2014.7045301

Rath, M., & Pattanayak, B. K. (2018). Monitoring of QoS in MANET Based Real Time Applications. In Information and Communication Technology for Intelligent Systems (ICTIS 2017) (vol. 84, pp. 579-586). Springer. doi:10.1007/978-3-319-63645-0_64

Rath, M., & Pattanayak, B. K. (2018). SCICS: A Soft Computing Based Intelligent Communication System in VANET. Smart Secure Systems – IoT and Analytics Perspective. *Communications in Computer and Information Science, 808*, 255–261. doi:10.1007/978-981-10-7635-0_19

Rath, M., & Pattanayak, B. K. (2019). Performance Evaluation of Optimized Protocol in MANET. International Journal of Information and Computer Security.

Rath, M., Pattanayak, B. K., & Pati, B. (2017). *Energetic Routing Protocol Design for Real-time Transmission in Mobile Ad hoc Network. In Computing and Network Sustainability, Lecture Notes in Networks and Systems* (Vol. 12). Singapore: Springer.

Rath, M., Rout, U. P., & Pujari, N. (2017). *Congestion Control Mechanism for Real Time Traffic in Mobile Adhoc Networks, Computer Communication, Networking and Internet Security. In Lecture Notes in Networks and Systems* (Vol. 5, pp. 149–156). Singapore: Springer.

Rath, M., Swain, J., Pati, B., & Pattanayak, B. K. (2018). *Attacks and Control in MANET. In Handbook of Research on Network Forensics and Analysis Techniques* (pp. 19–37). IGI Global.

Rath, M. (2018). Smart Traffic Management System for Traffic Control using Automated Mechanical and Electronic Devices. *I Mater. Sci. Eng., 377*. doi:/377/1/01220110.1088/1757-899X

Rath, M. (2018c). Effective Routing in Mobile Ad-hoc Networks With Power and End-to-End Delay Optimization: Well Matched With Modern Digital IoT Technology Attacks and Control in MANET. In *Advances in Data Communications and Networking for Digital Business Transformation*. IGI Global. Doi:10.4018/978-1-5225-5323-6.ch007

Rath, M. (2018d). An Analytical Study of Security and Challenging Issues in Social Networking as an Emerging Connected Technology. In *Proceedings of 3rd International Conference on Internet of Things and Connected Technologies*. Malaviya National Institute of Technology. Retrieved from https://ssrn.com/abstract=3166509

Romdhani, I. (2017). Existing Security Scheme for IoT. In *Securing the Internet of Things* (pp. 119–130). Boston: Syngress. doi:10.1016/B978-0-12-804458-2.00007-X

Romdhani, I. (2017). Confidentiality and Security for IoT Based Healthcare. In *Securing the Internet of Things* (pp. 133–139). Boston: Syngress. doi:10.1016/B978-0-12-804458-2.00009-3

Sahmim & Gharsellaoui. (2017). Privacy and Security in Internet-based Computing: Cloud Computing, Internet of Things, Cloud of Things: A Review. *Procedia Computer Science, 112*, 1516-1522. doi:10.1016/j.procs.2017.08.050

Sahoo, J., & Rath, M. (2017). Study and Analysis of Smart Applications in Smart City Context. *2017 International Conference on Information Technology (ICIT)*, 225-228. 10.1109/ICIT.2017.38

Saravanan, K. (2017). Cloud Robotics: Robot Rides on the Cloud – Architecture, Applications, and Challenges. In R. Kumar, P. Pattnaik, & P. Pandey (Eds.), *Detecting and Mitigating Robotic Cyber Security Risks* (pp. 261–274). Hershey, PA: IGI Global. doi:10.4018/978-1-5225-2154-9.ch017

Saravanan, K., & Radhakrishnan, A. (2018). *Energy Aware Resource Allocation Model for IaaS Optimization. In Cloud Computing for Optimization: Foundations, Applications, Challenges, Studies in Big data*. Springer. doi:10.1007/978-3-319-73676-1_3

Saravanan, K., & Saraniya, S. (2018). Cloud IOT based novel livestock monitoring and identification system using UID. *Sensor Review, 38*(1), 21–33. doi:10.1108/SR-08-2017-0152

Saravanan, K., & Srinivasan, P. (2017). Examining IoT's Applications Using Cloud Services. In P. Tomar & G. Kaur (Eds.), *Examining Cloud Computing Technologies Through the Internet of Things* (pp. 147–163). Hershey, PA: IGI Global. doi:10.4018/978-1-5225-3445-7.ch008

Scarfò, A. (2018). The Cyber Security Challenges in the IoT Era. In Intelligent Data-Centric Systems. Academic Press.

Sohal, A. S., Sandhu, R., Sood, S. K., & Chang, V. (2018). A cybersecurity framework to identify malicious edge device in fog computing and cloud-of-things environments. *Computers & Security, 74*, 340-354. .2017.08.016 doi:10.1016/j.cose

Stergiou, C., Psannis, K. E., Kim, B.-G., & Gupta, B. (2018). Secure integration of IoT and Cloud Computing. *Future Generation Computer Systems*, *78*(3), 964–975. doi:10.1016/j.future.2016.11.031

Sun, E., Zhang, X., & Li, Z. (2012). The internet of things (IOT) and cloud computing (CC) based tailings dam monitoring and pre-alarm system in mines. *Safety Science*, *50*(4), 811–815. doi:10.1016/j.ssci.2011.08.028

Sun, J., Sun, S., Li, K., Dan, L., Sangaiah, A. K., & Chang, V. (2018). Efficient algorithm for traffic engineering in Cloud-of-Things and edge computing. *Computers & Electrical Engineering*. doi:10.1016/j.compeleceng.2018.02.016

White, E. (n.d.). Retrieved from http://hp.sys-con.com/node/3250225/CloudandInternetofThings

Wu, Chen, Choo, & He. (2018). Efficient and secure searchable encryption protocol for cloud-based Internet of Things. *Journal of Parallel and Distributed Computing, 111*, 152-161. .2017.08.007 doi:10.1016/j.jpdc

Yang, J., Wang, C., Zhao, Q., Jiang, B., Zhihan, L., & Sangaiah, A. K. (2018). Marine surveying and mapping system based on Cloud Computing and Internet of Things. *Future Generation Computer Systems, 85*, 39-50. .future.2018.02.032 doi:10.1016/j

Section 2

Integration Techniques

Chapter 5
Enhancing Security in a Big Stream Cloud Architecture for the Internet of Things Through Blockchain

Luca Davoli
University of Parma, Italy

Laura Belli
University of Parma, Italy

Gianluigi Ferrari
University of Parma, Italy

ABSTRACT

The Internet of Things (IoT) paradigm is foreseeing the development of our environment towards new enriched spaces in most areas of modern living, such as digital health, smart cities, and smart agriculture. Several IoT applications also have real-time and low-latency requirements and must rely on specific architectures. The authors refer to the paradigm that best fits the selected IoT scenario as "Big Stream" because it considers real-time constraints. Moreover, the blockchain concept has drawn attention as the next-generation technology through the authentication of peers that share encryption and the generation of hash values. In addition, the blockchain can be applied in conjunction with Cloud Computing and the IoT paradigms, since it avoids the involvement of third parties in a broker-free way. In this chapter, an analysis on mechanisms that can be adopted to secure Big Stream data in a graph-based platform, thus delivering them to consumers in an efficient and secure way, and with low latency, is shown, describing all refinements required employing federation-based and blockchain paradigms.

DOI: 10.4018/978-1-5225-8295-3.ch005

INTRODUCTION

Considering the last 15 years, the forecast of a worldwide network of pervasively deployed and connected heterogeneous networks is now a reality. The Internet of Things (IoT) is now involving billions of different devices, connected in an Internet-like structure, and has definitely changed the way in which people and things interact, in several aspects of our modern living. The actors involved in IoT scenarios have extremely heterogeneous characteristics, in terms of energy supply and consumption, processing and communication features, and availability and mobility, spanning from Smart Objects (SOs) - i.e., constrained devices equipped with actuators or sensors, smartphones, wearable devices and other personal ones - to Internet hosts and the Cloud.

In order to allow heterogeneous nodes to efficiently communicate with each other and with existing Internet actors, shared and interoperable communication mechanisms and protocols are currently being defined and standardized. The most prominent driver for interoperability in the IoT is the Internet Protocol (IP), namely its 128-bit version called IPv6. An IP-based IoT can extend and operate with all existing Internet nodes, without any additional efforts. Standardization institutions, such as the Internet Engineering Task Force (IETF) and several research projects, are contributing to the definition of mechanisms able to bring IP to SOs (e.g., the 6LoWPAN (Kim, Kaspar, & Vasseur, 2012) adaptation layer). This is motivated by the need to adapt higher-layer protocols (e.g., application-layer protocols) to constrained environments. As a result, IoT networks are expected to generate huge amounts of traffic, whose transmitted data can be subsequently processed and used to build several useful services for end users. In this way, the Cloud has become the natural collection environment for sensed data retrieved by IoT nodes, due to its cost-effectiveness, scalability, and robustness. In Figure 1, the hierarchy of different levels involved in data collection, processing and distribution in a typical IoT scenario is shown.

Sensed data are collected by SOs composing the IoT networks and sent uplink to the Cloud, which operates as a collection entity and service provider. In some cases, intermediate processing entities, identified as Local Network Collectors (LNCs), can perform some preliminary tasks on the traffic before sending data uplink, such as protocol translation, data aggregation, and temporary data storage. This layered model is extremely general and can be applied to several IoT scenarios, in which, as an example, the LNCs functionalities can be impersonated by proxies or border routers.

Figure 1. Actors involved in an IoT and Cloud platform: data generated by IoT networks are sent to the Cloud, where services are provided to consumers. An intermediate level, performs local operations, such as data collection, processing, and distribution.

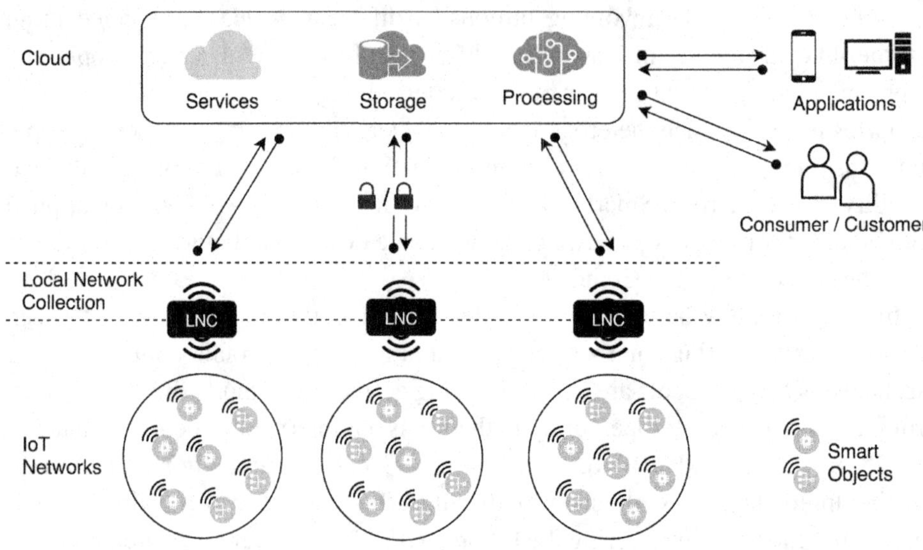

Several relevant IoT application environments (e.g., industrial monitoring, automation, and transportation) aften require real-time performance guarantees or, at least, a predictable latency. Moreover, the performance requirements (e.g., in terms of data sources) may change even abruptly. The potentially large number of IoT nodes, acting as data sources and generating a high rate of incoming data, and the low-latency constraints, call for innovative Cloud architectures able to efficiently handle such massive information amount.

A possible and suitable solution is given by Big Data approaches, developed in the last few years and become popular due to the evolution of online and social/crowd services, which can address the need to process extremely large amounts of heterogeneous data for various purposes and coming from very diverse sources. However, these techniques typically focus on the data and have an intrinsic inertia (as they are based on batch processing), rather than providing real-time processing and dispatching (Zaslavsky, Perera, & Georgakopoulos, 2013; Leavitt, 2013). For this reason, Big Data approaches might not represent the right solution to manage the dynamicity of IoT scenarios with real-time processing. In order to better fit these requirements, it is possible to shift the Big Data paradigm to the "Big Stream" paradigm.

While both paradigms deal with massive amounts of data, Big Data and Big Stream paradigms differ in the following aspects.

- Nature of data sources: the Big Data paradigm deals with a wide range of different areas composed by heterogeneous data sources (e.g., health, economy, social, industrial, natural phenomena), not necessarily related to IoT. Instead, data sources dealing with the Big Stream concept are strictly related to the IoT, where heterogeneous devices generate, as a whole, a continuous and massive information stream, even sending small amounts of data.
- The meaning of the term "Big:" in Big Data it refers to "volume of data," while in Big Stream it refers to "data generation rate."
- Low-latency and/or real-time or requirements of different consumers: typically both these concepts are not taken into account by Big Data.
- Objective: Big Data focuses on information analysis, management, and storage, following the Data-Information-Knowledge model (Aamodt & Nygard, 1995); instead, the Big Stream paradigm focuses on the data flows management, being able to perform *ad-hoc* and real-time data processing, in order to speed up the incoming data stream forwarding to consumers.

Another keypoint of Big Stream-oriented systems is that they should provide smart resource allocation, efficiently reacting to changes and, thus, implementing scalable and cost-effective Cloud services. This also affects the relevance given to the data, in different processing steps, for the final consumers. For instance, while for Big Data applications the ability to store all data is important, in order to be able to perform any successive required computation, Big Stream applications might decide to perform data filtering, aggregation or pruning, in order to minimize the information latency in conveying the final processing output to consumers, with no persistence need. Eventually, as a generalization, Big Stream data flows can be delivered to a Big Data application, which can act as a final consumer performing storage operations.

For these reasons, in previous works (Belli, Cirani, Ferrari, Melegari, & Picone, 2014; Belli, et al., 2015) we have designed and implemented a graph-oriented Cloud architecture suited for IoT scenarios, composed by applications with real-time and low-latency requirements (i.e., Big Stream applications). The proposed architecture relies on the concepts of data listener and data-oriented graph processing, in this way implementing a highly configurable, scalable, and dynamic computations chain on incoming data streams, dispatching data with a push-based approach, and providing the shortest delay between the time instant in which the information is generated and the time instant in which it is consumed.

To fulfill the IoT vision, some issues must be addressed, such as the inbound and outbound security of such IoT scenarios. Securing the IoT faces off with different aspects and, thus, entails both authorization and authentication mechanisms in order to address privacy, confidentiality, and trust. Security has been identified as one of the most critical aspects that should be dealt with in several IoT applications.

As in a previous work (Belli et al., 2015), we assume that streams generated by IoT nodes in the proposed graph-oriented architecture are "open" and potentially accessible by any interested entity, which can be seen as a subscriber for an interested topic. However, this assumption can not meet the security requirements of all developers or consumers accessing the Big Stream-oriented architecture, even more so that security management has become necessary in application scenarios that require to control or filter accesses to one or more streams by subscribers. For this reason, the architecture preliminary proposed in (Belli et al., 2015; Belli, Cirani, Ferrari, Melegari, & Picone, 2014) has to be extended also taking into account security aspects. In particular, the extension introduces additional modules useful to make the proposed graph-oriented architecture able to handle both secured and "open" data streams, focusing on solutions able to decouple security roles and management purposes (e.g., OAuth protocol, an *n*-legged authorization protocol), even adopting some central authority-free models (e.g., relying on the blockchain paradigm).

The rest of this work is organized as follows. In the following, an overview of related works is presented. Next, the new concepts and modules needed to "secure" data streams are detailed, analyzing which are the main issues in Cloud-oriented architectures and how the proposed entities can intervene against these issues, in this way increasing the platform security. Then, Big Stream architecture component are shown, highlighting the differences between the unsecured platform and describing how the blockchain technology can enhance the platform. Finally, we draw our conclusions.

RELATED WORKS

Internet of Things

In (Mineraud, Mazhelis, Su, & Tarkoma, 2016), the authors present a survey on IoT platforms in order to highlight differences in term of distribution of applications and services and to evaluate the gap between current IoT solutions and expectations of users. Finally, the authors provide a list of recommendations that should be followed by future platforms to fill the identified gaps.

The work described in (Afzal, Umair, Shah, & Ahmed, 2017) focuses on the recent paradigm of Social IoT (SIoT), an emerging subset of IoT aiming at establishing social relationships among SOs which start to interact each others and with the final users. The main concept characterizing this particular paradigm is that each device in the network cooperates to provide different kind of services, trying to achieve a common goal. After describing SIoT features, the authors analyze the Operating Systems (OSs) that better fit this scenario, also proposing an OS model architecture.

At the same time, the European Union (EU), under its 8th Framework Program Horizon 2020 (H2020, 2014-2020), is supporting a significant number of IoT related projects addressing different challenge and aspects. Among them, we recall the “Aggregate Farming in the Cloud” (AFarCloud) project (European Union, 2017), which aims at providing a new distributed platform for autonomous farming based on the real time integration and cooperation of agriculture Cyber Physical Systems (CPS). The AFarCloud platform also support monitoring and decision-making solutions and has the goal of increase efficiency, productivity, animal health, and food quality. The “Interoperability of Heterogeneous IoT Platforms” (Inter-IoT) is another European project (European Union, 2016) focusing instead on the integration problem, since, according to authors, most of existing IoT systems are isolated, and based on “closed-loop” concepts. InterIoT partners propose a multi-layered approach integrating different IoT devices, networks, platforms, services and applications allowing a global continuum of data and services creating an ecosystem of interoperable IoT platforms. With this approach, companies and developers can quickly create new IoT services and devices for the ecosystem, even in absence of global IoT standards.

Security With Blockchain Technology

The concept of blockchain technology can be presented from different perspectives and can be applied in different contexts, ranging from monetary scenarios to security ones. In (Park, & Park, 2017), this newly emerging technology is discussed in both analytical and practical ways, and thus focusing on its most relevant research trends, as well as investigating the way in which the blockchain security can be adapted to Cloud Computing. In (Gaetani, et al., 2017), the authors highlight the relevant importance of the data, together with the malicious effects that data attempts of threats may have on business decisions, especially in Cloud Computing-related scenarios. To solve these issues, it is possible to adopt a federated infrastructure that may improve data integrity and safety, rather than a trusted and decentralized blockchain-based data provenance architecture, as described in (Liang et al., 2017), in which the relevance of Cloud, secure and blockchain-based data origin, and their involvements in each specific context is discussed, thus pursuing blockchain transactions characteristics for embedding the data provenance. In (Puthal, Mohanty, Nanda, & Choppali, 2017), an overview of traditional security solutions, cyber threats, and possible security models to overcome current security drawbacks are discussed. Considering the wide variety of devices used in computer networks and the role played by cybersecurity in securing and improving the performance of these systems, traditional security solutions often target to network-based cyberspace solutions, which is well-known to be sometimes an open door to attackers. Hence, these security holes sometimes happen when the communication starts before the authentication, thereby leaving a space for entering the system before authentication by an attacker. In order to improve the strength of Cloud-based architectures, it is possible to refer also to the interconnection of Edge Datacenters (EDCs) and Cloud DataCenters (CDCs) in scenarios in which IoT-oriented sensing devices are communicating together, considering, as a key performance indicator, the impact of data analysis (in terms of data storage, fusion, and processing) and the effects of applying security measures in these scenarios (Puthal, Nepal Ranjan, & Chen, 2016). In (Biswas, & Muthukkumarasamy, 2016), the context of smart cities is analyzed, proposing a blockchain-based security framework that provide a secure communication platform with IoT-oriented smart devices, in order to protect and assure the data privacy when managing physical, social, and business infrastructures, for enhancing the direct interaction and collaboration between citizens and the local government (Kshetri, 2017). Moreover, knowing that one possible problem related to the adoption of the blockchain technology in IoT-oriented scenarios is the need of an algorithm based on Proof of Work (PoW) for defining the parties involved in the mining process, the definition of a blockchain-based IoT-oriented solution may be a turning point to eliminate the PoW in the system core; this may happen modelling the system in several tiers, in which the owner of the resource impersonates the role of a miner, in charge also of handling all communication within and external to the smart home (Dorri, Kanhere, Jurdak, & Gauravaram, 2017). Finally, another interesting scenario which can be covered by both a Cloud Computing-based data processing and blockchain-based data storage and retrieval is represented by Vehicular Networks (VNs). In these scenarios, it is possible to define secure and reliable architectures allowing a better utilization of both the infrastructure and resources of Intelligent Transport Systems (ITSs) and smart cities (Sharma, Moon, & Park, 2017).

Protocols and Communication Models for IoT

It is a common assumption that, in IoT, the most prominent driver to provide interoperability is IPv6. Referring to the IP stack, at the application layer developers find a variety of possible protocols applicable to different IoT scenarios, according to specific application requirements. Among the many options, the following are relevant.

- HyperText Transfer Protocol (HTTP) is mainly used for the communication with the consumer's devices.
- Constrained Application Protocol (CoAP), defined in (Shelby, Hartke, Bormann, & Frank, 2014), is built on the top of User Datagram Protocol (UDP), follows a request/response paradigm, and is explicitly designed to work with a large number of constrained devices operating in Low power and Lossy Networks (LLNs).
- Extensible Messaging and Presence Protocol (XMPP) is based on XML, supports decentralization, security (e.g., TLS), and flexibility.
- MQ Telemetry Transport (MQTT) is a lightweight publish/subscribe protocol running on top of TCP/IP. It is an attractive choice when a small code footprint is required and when remote sensors and control devices have to communicate through low bandwidth and unreliable/intermittent channels. It is characterized by an optimized information distribution to one or more receivers, following a multicast approach. Being based on a publish/subscribe communication paradigm, it acts through a "message broker" element, responsible for dispatching messages to all topic-linked subscribers.
- Advanced Message Queuing Protocol (AMQP) is an asynchronous protocol based on the publish/subscribe model that arose from the financial industry. It can run on top of different transport protocols but it assumes an underlying reliable transport protocol such as TCP. The main advantage of this protocol is its store-and-forward feature that ensures reliability even after network disruptions.
- Constrained Session Initiation Protocol (CoSIP), described in (Cirani, Picone, & Veltri, 2013; Cirani, Davoli Picone & Veltri, 2014), is a lightweight version of the Session Initiation Protocol (SIP) aiming at allowing constrained devices to instantiate communication sessions in a standard fashion, optionally including a negotiation phase of some parameters, which will be used for all subsequent communications.

In (Karagiannis., Chatzimisios, Vazquez-Gallego, & Alonso-Zarate, 2015), the authors provide a comprehensive description and comparison of IoT protocols employed in IoT at the application layer. the paper analyzes both communications between things and between end-users application and the internet, evaluating their reliability, security, and energy consumption characteristics.

Cloud Stream and Real-Time Management

Many researchers focus their efforts on the definition of Cloud Computing-based IoT architectures, where: the Cloud is the infrastructure for data and service management; and the final consumer/user drives the use of data and infrastructure to develop new IoT applications.

As IoT development is generally complex and extremely difficult to do it from scratch, many companies offer IoT data platforms that can be employed as a starting point, as they usually combine many of the tools needed to manage the deployment of an IoT system, spanning from the device management, till data prediction and insights into one service. In the following, some examples of these commercial platforms are provided.

The Google Cloud Platform, and in particular the Google Cloud IoT Core (Google, 2018) is a fully managed service Cloud platform to connect and manage IoT devices, from a few to millions. The service can store data from connected devices and build new applications that can also be integrated with the other Big Data services provided in the Google Cloud Platform ecosystem.

Azure IoT (Microsoft, 2018) is the Microsoft collection of services and solutions designed to help developers to create end-to-end IoT applications. Solutions can be hosted both as Software as a Service (SaaS) or specialized Platform as a Service (PaaS) and can be integrated with other technologies (e.g., SAP, Oracle databases, Microsoft Dynamics). Finally, this platform supports different protocols commonly employed in IoT, like HTTP, AMQP and MQTT.

Another relevant solution is the IBM Watson IoT platform (IBM, 2018), which propose a set of tools promising to securely connect, collect and start processing IoT data quickly and easily. Watson permits to build a growing ecosystem connecting different IoT devices using standard protocols like MQTT and HTTP. It also allows developers to aggregate and transform collected data into custom structures leveraging on machine learning and cognitive APIs.

Cloud Computing, as well as others paradigms, has to deal with different kinds of sources and data amounts. One of the most important challenges in the IoT era is to be able to collect and process massive and heterogeneous data flows generated by billions of interconnected SOs.

In the realm of Cloud-related IoT user-driven architectures, many propose the concept of Fog Computing (Bonomi, Milito, Natarajan, & Zhu, 2014) as a solution for a variety of IoT services and applications that have low-latency and location awareness requirements. Fog Computing can be described as a highly virtualized platform that provides networking, processing, and storage services, acting on the edge of the constrained network of SOs, working between endpoint IoT devices and traditional Cloud Computing platforms. Thus, it can be considered as an integration or an extension of the Cloud, providing support to the endpoints to fulfill services that could comply with low-latency and real-time consumer requirements. Another solution, besides the Big Data Paradigm, is provided by the recent Big Stream approach. The term Big Stream was first introduced in (Belli, Cirani, Ferrari, Melegari, & Picone, 2014) and has been then developed in other works. In particular, in (Belli, et al., 2016; Davoli, Belli, Veltri & Ferrari, 2018) the authors faced the problem of the introduction of security functionalities on the proposed Big Stream platform. In the last few years, the research community worked on this topic, providing other solutions. In (Dastjerdi, et al., 2016), it is remarked how most of IoT solutions based on a centralized Cloud does not scale to requirements of such environment generally requiring low latency or realtime response (e.g., health monitoring and emergency applications). The delay of these solutions is mainly caused by transferring data to the Cloud to be stored, and then back to the application needing that information. For the authors, data in IoT environment can be classified into two categories:

- **Little Data or Big Stream:** Transient data that is captured constantly from IoT smart devices.
- **Big Data**: Persistent data and knowledge stored and archived in centralized Cloud storage.

IoT environments, including smart cities and infrastructures, according to authors, need both Big Stream and Big Data to achieve effective real-time analytics and decision making. For this reason, authors in (Dastjerdi et al., 2016) propose the Fog Computing paradigm as a suitable solution, discussing a reference architecture.

In (Malek et al., 2017), authors propose an holistic platform combing tools for IoT, complex event processing, and Big Data technologies. The aim of the platform is to allow processing of large-scale sensor data and to develop context-aware applications and services. The implementation of the proposed system is based on the combination of Kaa (Kaa, 2018) and Storm (Mera et al., 2014) technologies. Kaa is an open-source middleware tool for building, managing and integrating with various

IoT devices, Apache Storm instead, is a free, open-source, distributed event stream processing system that allows the processing of streams into several processing units to reach near real-time requirements. It can be integrated with different queueing and database technologies, providing mechanisms to define custom network topologies in which nodes consume and process data streams in arbitrarily and complex ways.

Security Issues in Cloud and IoT Publish/Subscribe Scenarios

In the literature, several methods and strategies to enable confidentiality in publish/subscribe IoT infrastructures are proposed. IoT systems have to avoid security threats, providing strong security foundations built on a holistic view of security for all IoT elements at all stages: from object identification to service provision; from data acquisition to stream processing. All security mechanisms must ensure: resilience to attacks; data authentication; access control; and client privacy.

In (Collina, Corazza, & Vanelli-Coralli, 2012), IoT systems are expected to bridge the physical and the "virtual" worlds, using a novel broker that supports protocols such as HTTP and MQTT, adhering to the REST paradigm and allowing developers to easily and responsively expose fundamental entities as REST resources. This broker does not address any security issues, claiming that possibles solutions could include: plain authentication; Virtual Private Networks (VPNs); Access Control Lists (ACLs); as well as OAuth, a new type of authorization which is used to grant access to personal data by third-party applications (Hardt, 2012).

In (Lagutin, Visala, Zahemszky, Burbridge, & Marias, 2010), the authors examine the roles of different actors comprising an inter-domain publish/subscribe network, along with security requirements and minimal required trust associations between entities, introducing and analyzing an architecture that secures both data and control planes. The main security goals for a publish/subscribe architecture are: (i) integrity; (ii) scalability; (iii) availability, and (iv) prevention of underived traffic. Finally, in (Lagutin, Visala, Zahemszky, Burbridge, & Marias, 2010) different actors and security mechanisms are identified. The main used mechanism is Packet Level Authentication (PLA) which, combined with cryptographic signatures and data identifiers tied to secured identifiers, creates a strong binding between data and traffic, thus preventing Denial of Service (DoS) attacks.

In (Yang, et al., 2017), the privacy problem is faced, and authors propose an Attribute-Keyword-based data Publish-Subscribe (AKPS) scheme for Cloud platforms protecting the privacy of the published data against the Cloud server and other entities which are not subscribers of the system. To protect the subscribers' interests, a new searchable encryption is proposed, to enable the subscribers to selectively receive interested data. The AKPS supports multiple publishers and multiple subscribers, while none of two publishers/subscribers share the same secret keys. To avoid bypassing an access/subscription policy checking procedure, the AKPS ties both access policy and subscription policy by two secrets: one to bundle the ciphertext and the tags together; and the other to bundle the subscription trapdoor and the pre-decryption key together.

In (Raiciu, & Rosenblum, 2006), the authors present a study of confidentiality in Content-Based Publish/Subscribe (CBPS) systems, defined as an interaction model storing the interests of subscribers in a content-based infrastructure, to guide routing of notifications to interested subjects. In (Fremantle, Aziz, Scott, & Kopecky, 2014) the use of Federated Identity and Access Management (FIAM) in IoT is analyzed, following a consumer-oriented approach, where consumers own data collected by their devices, having a control over entities who access these data. Traditional security models, based on the concept of roles with a hierarchical structure, are not applicable to IoT scenarios (because of the billions of devices involved, the impossibility to adopt a centralized model of authentication, and the necessity to support mechanisms for delegation of authority). The authors propose OAuth2 as a possible solution to achieve access management with IoT devices which support the MQTT protocol. The overall system consists of: (i) a MQTT broker, (ii) an Authorization Server supporting OAuth2, (iii) a Web Authorization tool, and (iv) a device.

The work of (Bacon, et al., 2010) tackles the problem of application security in the Cloud, aiming at incorporating end-to-end security, so that Cloud providers not only can isolate their clients from each other, but can also isolate the data generated by multiple users which access a particular service provided by the Cloud. An approach called "application-level virtualization," which consists of (i) removing from applications all the details regarding security and flow control, (ii) placing the security management logic in the Cloud infrastructure, and (iii) allowing providers to permit only the interactions that the clients specify, is proposed.

Finally, a comprehensive state-of-the-art analysis of security solutions for Cloud publish/subscribe systems is provided in (Uzunov, 2016), where a set of solutions providing concrete security architectures are reviewed "horizontally" considering several aspects, more in detail the author analysis took into account the constituent security patterns the pertinent threats addressed, thus providing a contextualized "vertical" dimension to each solution individually.

Blockchain in a Nutshell

Blockchain has drawn attention as the next-generation technology through the authentication of peers that share encryption, the generation of hash value, and virtual money (e.g., Bitcoin, Ethereum, Ripple, EOS, IOTA, Tron, Monero (Bushmaker, 2018)). In addition, the blockchain technology can be applied in conjunction with the Cloud Computing and the IoT paradigms, due to its efficiency in sharing the stored information and availability in being shared among different parties. One of its main strength points is that it involves the communication solely between peers and without the involvement of third parties, in a broker-free way. In general, the use of the blockchain technology can provide higher security levels compared to storing all data in a centralized database, since attacks on a database can be prevented more easily. Moreover, since the blockchain has an openness connotation, it can provide data transparency when applied to contexts in which data disclosure is required. Due to such strengths, the blockchain technology can be utilized in diverse areas including the financial sector and the IoT environment, and its applications are expected to rapidly expand.

The blockchain main objective is to finalize transaction records through the work of an authentication process, such as the Proof-of-Work (PoW). The blockchain corresponds to a structured list that saves data in a form similar to a distributed database allowing all members of a community to keep a sort of ledger containing all transaction data, and to update and maintain their ledgers integrity when there is a new transaction. Since the advancement of the Internet and encryption technology has made possible for all members to verify the reliability of a transaction, the single point of failure arising from the dependency on an authorized third party has been solved. In fact, as a blockchain can be considered as a public ledger for transactions, it can prevent hacking during transactions involving different entities. The distributed database associated to transactions is a data record list that continuously grows, and it is designed to disable arbitrary tampering.

In order to authenticate a new blockchain transaction, a hash value is generated by verifying the PoW process and connecting to the previous block, in turn periodically updated and reflected on the electronic transaction details to share the latest transaction detail block. This process is a reliable mechanism to provide security since the network participants save and verify the blockchain. Since the hash values stored in each peer in the block are affected by the values of the previous blocks, it is very difficult to falsify and alter the registered data. Although data alteration is possible if at least 51% of peers are hacked at the same time (meaning that the attacker must have at least 51% of the computational power of all users), this attack scenario is realistically very difficult (especially in terms of coordination activity directly orchestrated by the attacker). This is called "51% attack" and is due to the fact that although there should be only one blockchain, being a sequential connection of generated blocks, a blockchain may be intentionally divided into two different sub-branches because the two latest blocks can be generated temporarily if two different peers succeed in mining the answer for generating the block at the same time. In this case, the block that is not chosen as the latest block by the majority of peers will become meaningless. This reflects into the fact that the transactions will follow the majority of peers who have 50% or more mining capability and, if this happens, the attacker has the control on the overall blockchain and it can include falsified transactions, and this may represent an enormous problem. To solve the problem, and prevent such tampering, an intermediate verification process must be provided. Thus, in blockchain-oriented scenarios, in order to improve the security of the parties participating in the P2P network, it is possible to adopt public key-based verification mechanisms, such as the Elliptic Curve Digital Signature Algorithm (ECDSA) (Triwinarko, 2002). In this way, although the identification of an account information with an anonymous public key enables one to know the entity who sent the information to another peer, it still ensures a certain anonymity, since there is no way of finding information pertaining to the original owner. Moreover, if an enhanced security measure is needed, it is possible to adopt a hash function to verify that the data block containing the transaction details have not been altered, as well as to guarantee the data integrity during a transaction. Hence, since the information on a transaction ownership is shared by a number of entities, this makes hacking more difficult than on other data models, transactions are automatically approved and recorded in the ledger, and the overall architecture is always ready to process data. Moreover, in modern blockchain architectures it is possible to outsource different functionalities out of the core of the ledger; this opens several possibilities, allowing the system to be easily implemented, connected, and expanded using open source libraries. Unfortunately, this latter point clearly introduces a warning point: since these open source scripts can be written using heterogeneous programming language with some flexibility, there can be the risk that an improperly configured transaction may damage the overall blockchain (e.g., a money transaction using an improperly configured locking script may be discarded since nobody can use it as the unlocking script cannot be generated).

Another measure that can be adopted in order to assure the security of a virtual information wallet is the multisig technique, which manage multiple signature and allow a new transaction only when there is more than one signature for the transaction. This approach can be used as a redundant security feature of the wallet, and can be enforced also adopting biometric or physical, offline, cold storage-type equipments, in this way adhering to a two-factor authentication mechanism. An example of hardware wallet is Trezor (Trezor, 2018), that stores the key in a tamper-proof storage unit connected to the processing unit through a USB connection only when needed. In this way, the tamper-proof storage unit is connected only when a transaction should be established, remaining in cold status the rest of the time. As can be easily understood, problems such as lack of usability and loss of tamper-proof storage unit also afflict the hardware wallet.

Among the different attacks related to the pure networking aspect of a blockchain-oriented architecture, those which can introduces several issues, and to which some countermeasures are needed in these scenarios, are the following: (i) Distributed Denial of Service (DDoS) attacks, which flood a target with superfluous requests, in order to overload the system, prevent the normal service provisioning and, in case of blockchain's users, prevent from receiving the regular service; (ii) bandwidth-consuming attacks, which exceed the bandwidth available for the overall network; (iii) Packet-per-Second (PPS)-consuming attacks, which cause the denial of service to other servers in the same network or an internal system failure; and (iv) HTTP-flooding attacks, which cause a denial of service to a targeted server transferring a large amount of HTTP packets to it.

As can be easily understood, sensitive user data leaks may provide several damages in all the fields in which they are employed and this is even more pronounced in Cloud Computing environments. With these premises, the blockchain technology can be seen as a convenient service that provides stronger security, with the agreement of following some basic rules on the user data management. Otherwise, this could backfire on security: as an example, if user anonymity is ensured using some blockchain methods, when a user decides to delete its electronic profile from the system (and, thus, from the blockchain), he/she has to be sure that all data will be promptly removed. If it is not the case, and his/her electronic profile is not properly deleted, the user information can be left behind, and this make the entire system vulnerable, as there is the possibility to exploit the remaining user information to guess the real user profile data. Hence, the blockchain has to provide solid measures for secure restoration in case of infringement by an attacker, verification of execution code for self-protection, and data and settings protection. Finally, the blockchain has to provide the following features: (i) privacy protection, standing for the protection that has to be assured to the peers' information participating in the transaction; (ii) anonymity, assuring that the entity involved in a transaction is not identifiable in any way; (iii) integrity, standing for the need to check if the information used in a transactions have been falsified or altered during the transaction itself; and (iv) confidentiality, meaning the need to check if a data has been leaked by unauthorized peers from the blockchain itself. These needs highlight the necessity of protecting a Cloud-based system against threats to data integrity, since it is of paramount relevance and due to the fact that normally data owners can not control some fundamental data aspects, such as physical data storage and its accesses. Unfortunately, this become more and more true even knowing that nowadays public and private organisations resort to the data outsourcing due to the local need of data storage and the burden of maintenance cost.

As highlighted before, the use of the blockchain technology to fulfill these security needs may represent an interesting choice, having to deal with its throughput, latency, and stability. In the light of what has been previously said, it is possible to classify different data impairments for each category, as detailed in the following.

The compromission of data availability prevents data to be retrieved only for a certain time period, thus providing full functionality once data are accessible again. Sabotaging confidentiality cannot be retrieved and discloses private data, thus leaving original ones still usable and available. Data tampering can thus be undetected for a long time and drive malicious operations, by altering or deleting specific data entries. Finally, the compromission of the data integrity involves that there is no way to restore the original data, since they are lost forever.

Focusing on on the use of the blockchain concept in Cloud Computing-oriented scenarios, one of its strengths may be the possibility to audit all the operations happening in fixed moment, thus enforcing the concept that Cloud auditing can only be effective if all operations on the data can be tracked reliably. This may be guaranteed on the data assuring that the origin of each of them along all the path that they follow, determining their history from their original sources till their arrival point. As can be easily understood, data provenance can help in detecting access violations, that need to be identified at a fine granularity, within the Cloud Computing infrastructures. However, data provenance represents a critical issue, since it may contain sensitive information about the original data and the data owners. Hence, it is required that a blockchain-based Cloud Computing-oriented architecture needs to secure data and also to ensure the trustworthiness of data origin. In detail, as can be easily understood, sometimes it is preferable to not directly store the data, but instead the list of modifications that have been applied to them. In this way, the insertion and validation time inside the blockchain by each participating peer is reduced, while the overall blockchain operativity is maintained and preserved.

As for other types of architectures, even in Cloud Computing-based ones, there exists several security issues at each level of the architecture itself, ranging from physical device level to application level.

At the *physical layer* the security issues may be related to: (i) sybil attack, in which an attacker forges multiple devices identities and inject corrupted data with multiple malicious data sources with the same identity (e.g., with the same IP address), thus compromising the data integrity; (ii) encryption leakage, in which an attacker exploit the knowledge of the identity of a device even if its traffic is encrypted; (iii) malicious data and fake device, in which an attacker can inject fake data or code through the usage of a malicious sensor node; (iv) node tampering, in which an attacker can physically tamper with different modes the node, stealing data, code and keys; and (v) malicious behaviour inference, in which the attacker tries to deduce the behaviour of a device even in presence of encrypted or anonymized traffic.

At the *perception layer* the security issues may include: (i) timing attack, in which an attacker analyzes the encryption algorithm trying to obtain the adopted secret key and, once it has collected all possible secret keys, it uses each key to decrypt the encrypted packets; (ii) jamming, in which an attacker forces a malicious device to broadcast radio signals on the same frequency of a fair device, overpowering its original signal; (iii) selective forwarding, in which an intruder commands its malicious nodes to forward, refuse or simply drop certain messages; (iv) replay attack, in which the attacker tries to destroy the certificate's validity replying with a false response on behalf of the destination device, in this way reaching in accessing to the trusted properties of the fair device itself; (v) sinkhole attack, in which an attacker exploits unfaithful routing information to attracts the fair devices, thus affecting the overall communication process; (vi) routing attack, in which an intruder creates routing loops, to block or resend the routing information and increase the overall transmission delay; (vii) spoofing, in which an intruder successfully reaches in creating routing loops, attracting or denying traffic, extending or shortening traffic routes, generating false error messages, partitioning the network, increasing end-to-end latency; (viii) wormhole attack, in which an adversary hijacks the incoming traffic to malicious destination nodes through a tunneling operation; (ix) HELLO flooding attack, in which an attacker broadcasts malicious data with enough transmission power to convince everyone in the network that its malicious node is the right neighbor for their routing tables entries; (x) exploit attack, in which an adversary profits by some existing vulnerabilities to mutate the normal behavior and to confuse the entities participating in the communication; and (xi) Man-In-The-Middle (MITM) attack, in which an attacker secretly introduces itself in the communication and becomes able to intercept and manage the traffic incoming from each side of the network communication.

At the *application layer* the security issues may be related to: (i) data availability, in which unauthorized accesses should be prevented and only authenticated users should be allowed to access the data (e.g., key agreement, maintaining confidentiality with private information protection, access control, data security protection); (ii) authentication, in which it is fundamental to apply effective mechanisms to authorize users to utilize the systems based on the specific privileges associated with their roles, preventing, unauthenticated access; (iii) software vulnerabilities, in which an attacker can exploit some known security holes at the software level, such as cross-site request forgery, SQL injection, and buffer overflow; and (iv) data protection and recovery, in which it is fundamental to prevent malicious attacks and to be able to safely and securely restore data after catastrophic events.

BIG STREAM CLOUD ARCHITECTURE

The IoT paradigm is foreseeing the development of our current environment towards new enriched spaces in the most areas of modern living, such as digital health, smart agriculture, pollution control, smart cities, smart homes, and smart grids. The research community and companies have been working on the IoT topic, from different perspectives, from more than fifteen years, providing an abundance of solutions to interconnect SOs for systems with different scales, technologies and objectives. In general, an IoT platform can be defined as an infrastructure allowing end users to interact with the SOs composing an IoT network and take advantage from personalized and custom services. IoT is already influencing common people activities and, depending on the specific applicative scenario, a lightweight platform can be deployed in a single home to manage connected objects such as the electrodomestics, lights, and the heating system. Considering a broader scale, a smart city can enhance its management with an IoT platform handling thousands of sensors. The outcome of this trend is the generation of a huge amount of data that should be handled, aggregated, analyzed, transformed and delivered to the final user of the platform in an effective and efficient way, through commodity services.

As already stated, most relevant IoT applications like alerting and monitoring systems have real-time performance or require, at least, a predictable and consistent latency. Moreover, in the IoT scenario, a large number of data sources globally generate data at a very high rate even though a single IoT service generates a limited amount of data. The low latency constraints call for an architecture able to efficiently handle such massive amount of information and to shift from the already known Big Data paradigm to the new one, denoted in literature as "Big Stream." The term "Big Stream" was first presented in (Belli, Cirani, Ferrari, Melegari, & Picone, 2014), where a Cloud-oriented graph-based architecture, explicitly designed to fit Big Stream IoT scenarios, is proposed and implemented. The architecture aims at minimizing the delay between the instant of raw data generation by deployed sensors and the instant at which properly processed information is provided to a final consumer (e.g the user of a smartphone application, a data warehouse or a server). In order to achieve a better performance and to avoid whortless wait, the proposed Big Stream architecture adheres to the publish/subscribe model and is based on the concept of "listener." More in detail, the fundamental components of the graph-based Cloud architecture are the following.

- **Nodes**: Are processing units which treat incoming data streams to generate a new one. The task performed by each unit is self contained and is not directly linked to a specific task. A graph node can be a listener of one or more input streams and a publisher of a new stream for other nodes.
- **Edges**: Are streams linking together various nodes, allowing to build a complex behavior combining different processing operations.

Nodes in the Graph are organized in concentric layers, with an increasing degree of complexity. This means that data streams, started from IoT networks, flow in the graph and are processed by nodes. Streams, generated from nodes in a generic layer of the graph, can be used by nodes in higher-degree layers, to perform more complex processing operations, generating new streams which can be used in higher layers, and so on. The graph architecture should be exploited on the Cloud to improve the system's scalability and to manage the workload with a huge quantity of data sources and processing nodes. Therefore, this architecture can be considered as a common open platform in which data streams are shared for developers interested in building applications based on data originated by IoT networks, with real-time constraints and low overhead. Developers authenticated on the platform can thus customize paths in the graph through the definition and deployment and combination of new processing nodes. It is important to observe that, by accessing the Big Stream architecture, each developer can operate on data streams coming from IoT networks which he/she does not own.

In the proposed implementation (Belli, et al., 2015), shown in Figure 2, the system is based on three main modules: (i) the Acquisition and Normalization modules; (ii) the Graph Framework module; (iii) the Application Register module. As the architecture is based on a queue-communication paradigm, the implementation adopts an instance of RabbitMQ queue server as publish/subscribe engine. The first Acquisition step handles raw data coming from external SOs through different application-layer protocols. The implementation proposed in (Belli, et al., 2015) supports different protocols, namely: (i) HTTP, through Nginx and PHP; (ii) CoAP, by means of the mjCoAP (Cirani, Picone, & Veltri, 2015) library; and (iii) MQTT, with the ActiveMQ library. Then, the Normalization block consists of a set of Java processes, which work on incoming data from the Acquisition dedicated queues and perform some preliminary optimization operations, in order to structure data into

Figure 2. Generic structure of the Big Stream architecture with detail of composing modules

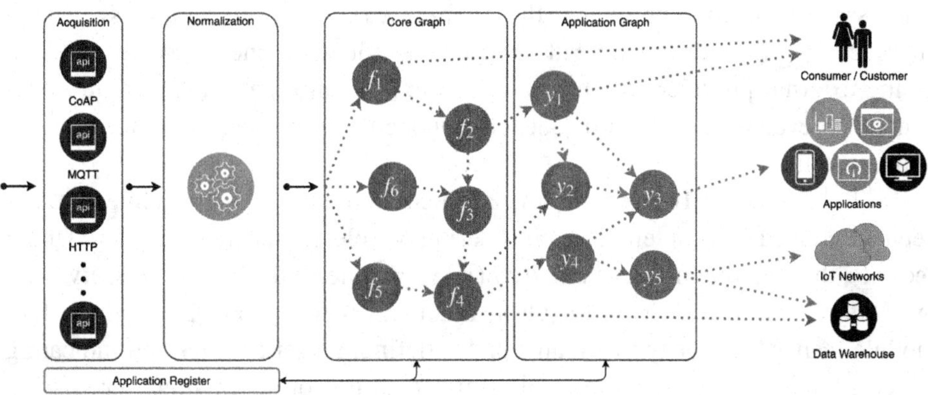

a common and easily manageable JSON format. The Graph Framework module represents the processing block, in which nodes of each level are implemented with Java processes connected through queues. To ensure proper data propagation and avoid loops, layers in the Graph Framework are implemented through dedicated RabbitMQ Exchanges, each of one connected, through one-way links, with the Exchange of the consecutive layer. The data flow starts from inner levels and goes out until it reaches the last layer's Exchange, responsible to manage notifications to external entities that are interested in final processed data. These external entities are heterogenous, and can be, in example, browsers, Data Warehouse, smart entities, or external Cloud Graph processes.

Finally, the Application Register (AR) module is the management Java process that coordinates both the interactions between Graph nodes and with external services. Moreover, the Application Register module has the fundamental responsibility to maintain all the information about the current status of the platform and the graph structure. More precisely, the Application Register module performs the following operations:

- manage the attachment of new nodes or consumers, interested in some of the streams provided by the platform;
- manage the detachment of nodes from the Graph, when they are no longer interested in receiving flows, and, possibly, re-attach them;
- handle nodes that are publishers of new streams;
- maintain information regarding topics of data, in order to correctly generate the routing keys, and to compose data flows between nodes in different Graph layers.

Security in Big Stream

Addressing the security problem in the graph-based Cloud system requires a general approach, owing to different needs of each specific component involved. In fact, giving external providers the possibility to upload into the graph custom nodes containing executable software code, clearly opens several security vulnerabilities in the system.

In (Belli, et al., 2016), security management in the Big Stream architecture has been introduced and implemented considering two clearly separated levels: (i) inner security, through the In-Graph Security (IGS) module, and (ii) outer security, with the Outdoor Front-end Security (OFS) module. As shown in Figure 3, the IGS module manages security in streams paths, defining a set of rules and indicating which actors are authorized to send/receive data to/from each single processing node. In other words, the IGS module allows developers to define paths in which some segments can be "secured" and some others can be "public" according to the kind of data treated and the specific application. To accomplish this task, the IGS module works in combination with the AR module, which is composed by the following components (shown in Figure 3):

Figure 3. Main building blocks of the proposed listener-based graph architecture with security models. Information streams between nodes can be "open" or "secured."

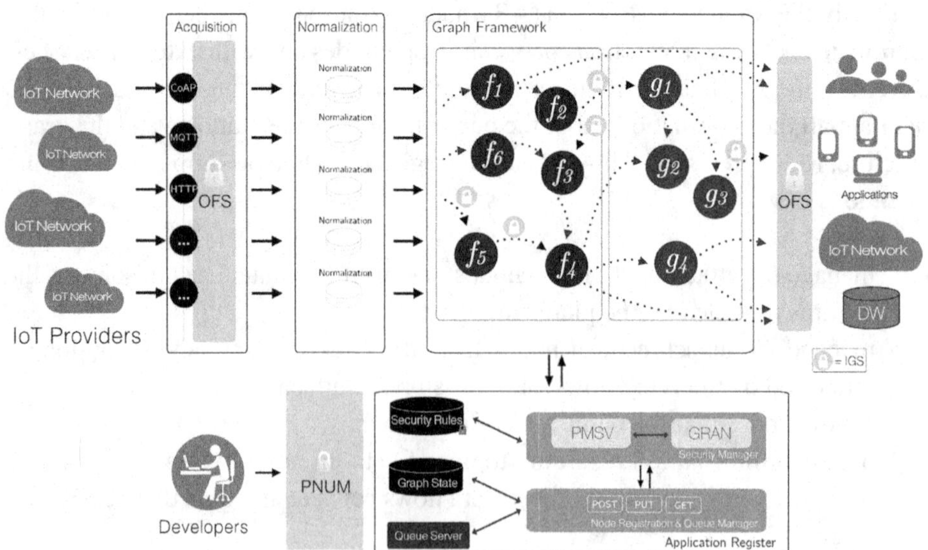

- the Graph State Database (GSDB) and the Node Registration and Queue Manager (NRQM) modules, which cooperate to manage the authorization policies adopted by the graph nodes;
- the Policy Manager and Storage Validator (PMSV) module;
- the Graph Rule Authorization Notifier (GRAN) module;
- the Persistent Security Storage Container (PSSC) module.

The other module related to security, namely, the OFS module, operates at the edge of the platform, after receiving input data from IoT networks, as well as before pushing out streams to final consumers. OFS has a crucial role, since it authorizes the interactions between the external entities and the frontier of the Cloud platform.

These basic security features in the core part of the platform have been further improved in (Davoli, Belli, Veltri, & Ferrari, 2018), where the concept of federated authentication is introduced. With this new feature, a federation of trusted entities can access to the Big Stream platform, through a federated access paradigm (namely Shibboleth) and to share their own nodes with the community. The adoption of a federation-based access paradigm allows to get rid of the need to store and maintain an account for each developer, reducing system vulnerabilities and making the architecture more scalable and accessible. Federated authentication is also adopted for the output stage of the Big Stream platform, in order to authenticate a final consumer requesting one or more streams coming from the higher layer nodes. The Big Stream architecture is thus enriched with a new module, denoted as Traffic Handler Orchestrator & Rapid Intervention (THORIN), deployed in the graph platform and connected to the AR module.

THORIN has been introduced to monitor the traffic on the overall platform, analyzing in real-time the behavior of the different components, and cooperate with the Application Register module aiming at:

- controlling the interactions between the external providers and the acquisition front-end nodes;
- analyzing the behavior of nodes in the graph to find potentially suspicious activities carried out by processing units;
- reacting to malicious activities and protecting the other active nodes, allowing them to safely continue their operations.

To reach these goals, THORIN implements a Shibboleth instance that allows different providers (linked to a wide federation) to connect and provide their processing nodes to the Big Stream platform.

Regarding its monitoring activity, THORIN operates according to the following heuristic principles, namely: (i) running an internal Java module that aggregates and performs statistics on data flows, as well as (ii) interacting with external heuristic services and (iii) analyzing behaviors and comparing URLs used by inner processing nodes with publicly available dangerous blacklists (e.g., spam URLs, malware and ransomware URLs, darknet onion-like URLs, etc.).

Alongside the security modules proposed previously, an interesting approach that can be applied to a Cloud-based architecture like the one oriented to Big Stream, is the adoption of the blockchain technology. Due to the fact that the Big Stream-based architecture has a graph structure, it can be suitable to involve the blockchain in the security management tier of the architecture itself. More in detail, as shown in Figure 4, the Big Stream architecture can be improved as follows. The Cloud-based architecture maintains a blockchain composed by blocks with different meanings.

When a new node request to join the platform, the federation to which it belongs to releases it a Universally Unique Identifier (UUID) that will be stored inside the new block, in turn added to the blockchain and verified with a PoW by the nodes pertaining to the blockchain itself. In this way, the masquerade identity information is persistently stored in the chain and shared among all the participants of the federation, and cannot be hijacked by anyone.

When an external developer produces a new processing unit and he/she decides to add it to the Big Stream architecture, the already described PNUM module collaborates with the blockchain and calculates a hash value for the newly provided processing unit; then, the PNUM module creates a new smart contract containing the UUID of the developer and the previously calculated hash value, together with a timestamp corresponding to the time instant in which the processing unit has been included in the Big Stream architecture. In this way, the architecture is furtherly secure, since the information on the uploader and the Java unit are shared and stored in several ledgers, assuring the absence of alterations and, at the same time, speeding up the operation of management of new nodes in the system.

The adoption of the blockchain also allows to improve the second uploading module, the one allowing the upload of new processing units through the FTP protocol: in this case, it is possible to furtherly secure the insertion operation requiring a confirmation of the current operation to the uploading developer. This can be done through the request of a One Time Password (OTP), as well as another random information, created through the usage of a hardware tamper-proof storage unit (e.g., Trezor). This approach enforces the system security and helps in tracing possible attackers trying to hijack the system essaying different OTP combinations in a certain time period.

Figure 4. Security modules, involving both THORIN module and a blockchain component, collaborating in order to counteract internal and external security threats in the proposed Big Stream platform.

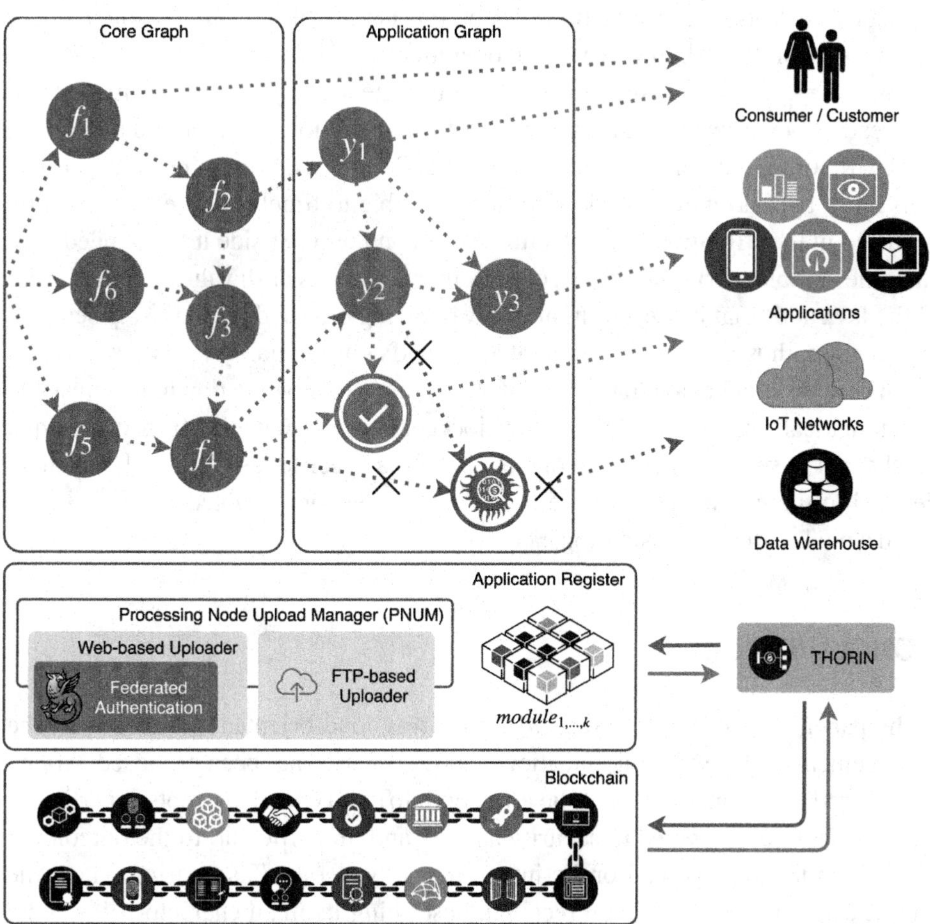

The blockchain also welcomes the blocks originated by the PMSV module, which, in turn, stores the policies defined by the owner of the processing units not only inside the PSSC module, but also inside a new block composed by a hash value representing the specific policy, and a timestamp corresponding to the time instant in which the policy has been firstly defined. Hence, this allows the Big Stream architecture to trace the modifications of these policies each time that these happen, having the PMSV module in charge of creating a new block for each modification, containing, among all the information, the current modification timestamp. In this way, the blockchain allows to maintain and extract the complete modification history, being sure that these informations have not been hijacked in any way.

The blockchain also works as a shared ledger, as previously highlighted, allowing each processing unit to verify, at each time, if a particular stream can be processed in a specific way and/or if this stream can be forwarded, once processed, to a particular next-hop processing node or not; this is possible by simply conferring to the blockchain the task to verify these operations.

Moreover, each processing node may participate in a shared community control, by creating new blocks containing a log of the operation made on a data stream, the UUID of the originator processing unit and the UUID of the destination one. This has a twofold gain: on one side, it is possible to timely trace each operation occurred in the Big Stream architecture, while on the other side it is not needed to store the complete original processed stream, but only its hash value and the UUID of the Java node that processed it, in this way saving time and not exposing sensible information, thus maintaining data integrity and confidentiality.

In case the blockchain management shows signs of slowing down, it is possible to automatically balance the load on the blockchain itself, switching from one unique blockchain to several ones, each one devoted to a specific task (e.g., a blockchain devoted to the maintenance of the processing nodes, one devoted to the policies, one devoted to the processing logs, etc.).

CONCLUSION

In this paper, an analysis of the security issues in a Cloud-oriented architecture for the management of Big Stream applications in IoT scenarios has been proposed. After a brief introduction on the state of the art of both IoT and Cloud concepts, a particular attention has been devoted to security aspects and, in particular, to the outcoming blockchain technology, and on its integration in general IoT scenarios. Then, the Big Stream paradigm has been recalled, describing its main characteristics and a recently proposed Graph-based Cloud architecture targeting IoT-based networks. The implementation of each operative module of the platform (Acquisition Module, Normalization Module, Graph Framework, Application Register) has been introduced, together with a panoramic on the weight that the adoption of security measures may have on each of them, thus describing the introduction of security-related modules, in particular the IGS module, acting inside the graph, the OFS module, operating at the boundary of the architecture, and the THORIN module. Finally, an enhancement of the architecture based on the blockchain technology, which can be employed in the proposed graph architecture to improve general security and speed up the management of new nodes, has been proposed.

REFERENCES

Aamodt, A., & Nygard, M. (1995). Different roles and mutual dependencies of data, information, and knowledge — An AI perspective on their integration. *Data & Knowledge Engineering*, *16*(3), 191–222. doi:10.1016/0169-023X(95)00017-M

Afzal, B., Umair, M., Shah, G. A., & Ahmed, E. (2017). Enabling IoT platforms for social IoT applications: Vision, feature mapping, and challenges. *Future Generation Computer Systems*.

Bacon, J., Evans, D., Eyers, D. M., Migliavacca, M., Pietzuch, P., & Shand, B. (2010). Enforcing End-to-End Application Security in the Cloud. In Middleware 2010 (pp. 293-312). Springer Berlin Heidelberg. doi:10.1007/978-3-642-16955-7_15

Belli, L., Cirani, S., Davoli, L., Ferrari, G., Melegari, L., & Picone, M. (2016). Applying Security to a Big Stream Cloud Architecture for the Internet of Things. *International Journal of Distributed Systems and Technologies*, *7*(1), 37–58. doi:10.4018/IJDST.2016010103

Belli, L., Cirani, S., Davoli, L., Melegari, L., Mònton, M., & Picone, M. (2015). An Open-Source Cloud Architecture for Big Stream IoT Applications. In I. Podnar Žarko, K. Pripužić, & M. Serrano (Eds.), *Interoperability and Open-Source Solutions for the Internet of Things* (Vol. 9001, pp. 73–88). Springer International Publishing; doi:10.1007/978-3-319-16546-2_7

Belli, L., Cirani, S., Ferrari, G., Melegari, L., & Picone, M. (2014). A Graph-Based Cloud Architecture for Big Stream Real-Time Applications in the Internet of Things. In *Advances in Service-Oriented and Cloud Computing* (Vol. 508, pp. 91–105). Springer International Publishing. doi:10.1007/978-3-319-14886-1_10

Biswas, K., & Muthukkumarasamy, V. (2016, December). Securing Smart Cities Using Blockchain Technology. In *High Performance Computing and Communications; IEEE 14th International Conference on Smart City; IEEE 2nd International Conference on Data Science and Systems (HPCC/SmartCity/DSS), 2016 IEEE 18th International Conference on* (pp. 1392-1393). IEEE. 10.1109/HPCC-SmartCity-DSS.2016.0198

Bonomi, F., Milito, R., Natarajan, P., & Zhu, J. (2014). Fog Computing: A Platform for Internet of Things and Analytics. In Big Data and Internet of Things: A Roadmap for Smart Environments (pp. 169-186). Springer International Publishing. doi:10.1007/978-3-319-05029-4_7

Bushmaker, J. (2018). *Cryptocurrencies*. Retrieved from https://www.investinblockchain.com/top-cryptocurrencies/

Cirani, S., Davoli, L., Picone, M., & Veltri, L. (2014, Jul). Performance Evaluation of a SIP-based Constrained Peer-to-Peer Overlay. In *2014 IEEE International Conference on High Performance Computing Simulation* (pp. 432-435). IEEE. 10.1109/HPCSim.2014.6903717

Cirani, S., Picone, M., & Veltri, L. (2013). CoSIP: A Constrained Session Initiation Protocol for the Internet of Things. In *Advances in Service-Oriented and Cloud Computing* (Vol. 393, pp. 13–24). Springer Berlin Heidelberg. doi:10.1007/978-3-642-45364-9_2

Cirani, S., Picone, M., & Veltri, L. (2015). mjCoAP: An Open-Source Lightweight Java CoAP Library for Internet of Things Applications. In Interoperability and Open-Source Solutions for the Internet of Things. Springer. Doi:10.1007/978-3-319-16546-2_10

Collina, M., Corazza, G. E., & Vanelli-Coralli, A. (2012). Introducing the QEST broker: Scaling the IoT by bridging MQTT and REST. In *2012 IEEE 23rd International Symposium on Personal Indoor and Mobile Radio Communications* (pp. 36-41). IEEE. DOI: 10.1109/PIMRC.2012.6362813

Dastjerdi, A. V., Gupta, H., Calheiros, R. N., Ghosh, S. K., & Buyya, R. (2016). Fog computing: Principles, architectures, and applications. In Internet of Things (pp. 61-75). Academic Press.

Davoli, L., Belli, L., Veltri, L., & Ferrari, G. (2018). THORIN: An Efficient Module for Federated Access and Threat Mitigation in Big Stream Cloud Architectures. *IEEE Cloud Computing*, *5*(1), 38–48. doi:10.1109/MCC.2018.011791713

Dorri, A., Kanhere, S. S., Jurdak, R., & Gauravaram, P. (2017, March). Blockchain for IoT Security and Privacy: The Case Study of a Smart Home. In *Pervasive Computing and Communications Workshops (PerCom Workshops), 2017 IEEE International Conference on* (pp. 618-623). IEEE.

European Union. (2016). *Interoperability of Heterogeneous IoT Platforms (INTER-IoT)*. Retrieved from https://cordis.europa.eu/project/rcn/199587_en.html

European Union. (2017). *Aggregate Farming in the Cloud (AFarCloud)*. Retrieved from https://cordis.europa.eu/project/rcn/216117_en.html

Fremantle, P., Aziz, B., Scott, P., & Kopecky, J. (2014, Sep). Federated Identity and Access Management for the Internet of Things. *3rd International Workshop on the Secure IoT*. 10.1109/SIoT.2014.8

Gaetani, E., Aniello, L., Baldoni, R., Lombardi, F., Margheri, A., & Sassone, V. (2017). *Blockchain-based database to ensure data integrity in cloud computing environments*. Academic Press.

Google. (2018). *Google Cloud IoT Core*. Retrieved from: https://cloud.google.com/iot/docs/

Hardt, D. (2012). *RFC 6749: The OAuth 2.0 Authorization Framework*. Retrieved from http://tools.ietf.org/html/rfc6749

IBM. (2018). *IBM Watson IoT*. Retrieved from https://www.ibm.com/internet-of-things

Kaa. (2018). Retrieved from https://www.kaaproject.org/

Karagiannis, V., Chatzimisios, P., Vazquez-Gallego, F., & Alonso-Zarate, J. (2015). A survey on application layer protocols for the internet of things. *Transaction on IoT and Cloud Computing*, *3*(1), 11–17.

Kim, E., Kaspar, D., & Vasseur, J. (2012, Apr). *Design and application spaces for ipv6 over low-power wireless personal area networks (6LoWPANs)* (No. 6568). RFC 6568 (Informational). IETF. Retrieved from http://www.ietf.org/rfc/rfc6568

Kshetri, N. (2017). Can blockchain strengthen the internet of things? *IT Professional*, *19*(4), 68–72. doi:10.1109/MITP.2017.3051335

Lagutin, D., Visala, K., Zahemszky, A., Burbridge, T., & Marias, G. F. Roles and security in a publish/subscribe network architecture. In *2010 IEEE Symposium on Computers and Communications* (pp. 68-74). IEEE. 10.1109/ISCC.2010.5546746

Leavitt, N. (2013). Storage challenge: Where will all that Big Data go? *Computer*, *46*(9), 22–25. doi:10.1109/MC.2013.326

Liang, X., Shetty, S., Tosh, D., Kamhoua, C., Kwiat, K., & Njilla, L. (2017, May). Provchain: A blockchain-based data provenance architecture in cloud environment with enhanced privacy and availability. In *Proceedings of the 17th IEEE/ACM International Symposium on Cluster, Cloud and Grid Computing* (pp. 468-477). IEEE Press. 10.1109/CCGRID.2017.8

Malek, Y. N., Kharbouch, A., El Khoukhi, H., Bakhouya, M., De Florio, V., El Ouadghiri, D., Latre, S., & Blondia, C. (2017). *On the use of IoT and Big Data Technologies for Real-time Monitoring and Data Processing*. Academic Press. DOI: . doi:10.1016/j.procs.2017.08.281

Mera Pérez, D., Batko, M., & Zezula, P. (2014). Towards Fast Multimedia Feature Extraction: Hadoop or Storm. *2014 IEEE International Symposium on Multimedia*, 106-109. 10.1109/ISM.2014.60

Microsoft. (2018). *Azure IoT: the Internet of Things (IoT) for every business*. Retrieved from https://azure.microsoft.com/en-us/overview/iot/

Mineraud, J., Mazhelis, O., Su, X., & Tarkoma, S. (2016). A gap analysis of Internet-of-Things platforms. *Computer Communications*, *89*, 5–16. doi:10.1016/j.comcom.2016.03.015

Park, J. H., & Park, J. H. (2017). Blockchain Security in Cloud Computing: Use Cases, Challenges, and Solutions. *Symmetry*, *9*(8), 164. doi:10.3390ym9080164

Puthal, D., Mohanty, S. P., Nanda, P., & Choppali, U. (2017). Building Security Perimeters to Protect Network Systems Against Cyber Threats. *IEEE Consumer Electronics Magazine*, *6*(4), 24–27. doi:10.1109/MCE.2017.2714744

Puthal, D., Nepal, S., Ranjan, R., & Chen, J. (2016). Threats to networking cloud and edge datacenters in the internet of things. *IEEE Cloud Computing*, *3*(3), 64–71. doi:10.1109/MCC.2016.63

Raiciu, C., & Rosenblum, D. S. (2006). *Enabling Confidentiality in Content-Based Publish/Subscribe Infrastructures*. Securecomm and Workshops. doi:10.1109/SECCOMW.2006.359552

Sharma, P. K., Moon, S. Y., & Park, J. H. (2017). Block-VN: A distributed blockchain based vehicular network architecture in smart City. *Journal of Information Processing Systems*, *13*(1), 84.

Shelby, Z., Hartke, K., Bormann, C., & Frank, B. (2014). *RFC 7252: The Constrained Application Protocol (CoAP)*. Internet Engineering Task Force.

Trezor. (2018). *Trezor: The safe place for your coins*. Retrieved from https://trezor.io/

Triwinarko, A. (2002). *Elliptic Curve Digital Signature Algorithm (ECDSA)*. Makalah TA, Departemen Teknik Informatika ITB.

Uzunov, A. V. (2016). A survey of security solutions for distributed publish/subscribe systems. *Computers & Security*, *61*, 94–129. doi:10.1016/j.cose.2016.04.008

Yang, K., Zhang, K., Jia, X., Hasan, M. A., & Shen, X. S. (2017). Privacy-preserving attribute-keyword based data publish-subscribe service on cloud platforms. *Information Sciences*, *387*, 116–131. doi:10.1016/j.ins.2016.09.020

Zaslavsky, A., Perera, C., & Georgakopoulos, D. (2013). *Sensing as a Service and Big Data*. Retrieved from http://arxiv.org/abs/1301.0159

Chapter 6
Topology Optimization for Heterogeneous DHT-Based Multicast

Hoai Son Nguyen
VNU University of Engineering and Technology, Vietnam

ABSTRACT

Since the deployment of IP multicast remains restricted due to many practical and political issues, researchers have shifted focus to exploiting application-layer multicast for multicast data delivery. Recently there has been considerable interest in applying DHT routing algorithms to application-level multicast. However, early DHT-based multicast protocols are insufficient in addressing a number of technical issues such as heterogeneous capacity of nodes or node churn. In this chapter, the author describes a solution called BAM-Chord (i.e., Bandwidth Adaptive Multicast over Chord) that optimizes the topology of a multicast tree based on node bandwidth. In the proposed solution, node position (i.e., node identifier) on a BAM-Chord ring will be decided based on node bandwidth capacity such that it can build a wide and balanced multicast tree rooted at the source node. As a result, BAM-Chord protocol can utilize network resources of every node to reduce the depth of the multicast tree and take advantages of DHTs in maintaining the multicast tree.

DOI: 10.4018/978-1-5225-8295-3.ch006

INTRODUCTION

The disadvantages of implementing multicast at the IP level (Deering, & Cheriton,1990) have led to the emergence of interesting application-level multicast approach (Banerjee, Bhattacharjee, &Kommareddy, 2002; Tran, Hua, & Do, 2004; Magharei, & Rejaie, 2010; Tsuneizumi, Aikebaier, Ikeda, Enokido, & Takizawa, 2011). Application-level multicast utilizes network capacity of end nodes that act not only as receivers but also as senders. Each end node can forward its received data to other end nodes, and therefore reduce the load at streaming servers. Since network capacities are heterogeneous between nodes and nodes can join/leave a network in anytime, a big challenge of application-level multicast protocols is how to build and maintain a multicast tree which can efficiently utilize network resources of end nodes while still guaranteeing the availability of data delivery.

In recent years, Distributed Hash Table (DHT) (Ratnasamy, Francis, Handley, & Karp, 2001; Stoica, Morris, Karger, Kaashoek, & Balakrisnan, 2001; Rowstron, & Druschel, 2001) becomes an active and ongoing area of research. Originally, DHTs were developed with applications like peer-to-peer file sharing. Recently, there has been considerable interest in applying DHTs to application-level multicast (Ratnasamy, Handley, Karp, & Shenker, 2001; Castro, Druschel, Kermarrec, & Rowstron, 2002; El-Ansary, Alima, Brand, & Haridi, 2003; Li, Sollins, & Lim, 2005; Huanga & Zhang, 2010) since DHTs have many advantages that are good for multicast applications: decentralization, scalability, fault tolerance, load balancing, and good routing performances. Generally, DHT-based application-layer multicast protocols utilize the structure of DHT-based overlay networks to send multicast messages. Thus, nodes in these systems do not need to maintain extra links to other nodes in the overlay network, except the links to neighbor nodes defined by a DHT algorithm. DHT-based multicast also gets benefits from failure recovery algorithms, which are implemented in most of DHT networks. Therefore, DHT-based application-layer multicast schemes can scale to multicast groups of thousands of nodes.

However, early DHT-based multicast designs are insufficient in addressing all of following issues:

- **Heterogeneous Bandwidths Between Nodes:** Since the number of child nodes of a node in a multicast tree is decided based on the links to neighbor nodes without consideration of node's bandwidth capacity, a node with low bandwidth may become a bottleneck if it is an internal node of a multicast tree and has a lot of child nodes;
- **Effective Bandwidth Utilization:** If a node with high bandwidth is a leaf node, the system cannot utilize the bandwidth capacity of the node to deliver multicast messages;

- **Dynamic Membership:** The optimization of multicast trees must be achieved even when member nodes join or leave at any time.

To utilize bandwidth of nodes effectively, Castro, Druschel, Kermarrec, Nandi, Rowstron, and Singh (2003) propose SplitStream, a multiple-tree solution constructing multiple multicast trees such that a node, which is an interior node of one tree will be a leaf node of all other trees. However, SplitStream require nodes to have equal out-bandwidth. In CAM-Chord design proposed by Zhang, Chen, Ling and Chow (2005), heterogeneity is tackled by allowing each node to decide its out-degree according to its out-bandwidth. However, their work did not consider the bandwidth capacity of nodes when building a multicast tree. Thus, effective bandwidth utilization issue still remains open. Huanga and Zhang (2010) tried to build a balanced tree on a Chord ring but the path length from source node to leaf nodes of the multicast tree is still long.

In this chapter, the authors propose a DHT-based bandwidth adaptive multicast scheme called BAM-Chord (i.e. Bandwidth Adaptive Multicast over Chord), which focuses on host heterogeneity, network scalability and effective bandwidth utilization. In the proposed scheme, a source node of a multicast group will create a wide and balanced virtual multicast tree on a Chord-based ring. When a node joins into the multicast group, it will find out an appropriate position (i.e. node identifier) in the virtual multicast tree based on its out-bandwidth. By the use of virtual multicast tree, the real multicast tree can be built efficiently and balanced even when there are node joins and leaves. The proposed method can make tradeoff between depth of the multicast tree and out-degree of every node and retain the advantages of a DHT network: decentralization, scalability and fault tolerance.

The authors choose Chord, a representative DHT algorithm to implement the proposed protocol but the authors believe that the proposed scheme can adapt to other DHT-based multicast algorithms. Simulation is performed to evaluate performance of proposed BAM-Chord. The simulation results show that the proposed scheme can utilize the network resources of end nodes effectively and improve the path length of multicast routing with smaller cost of control overhead comparing with the case of CAM- Chord.

The rest of this chapter is organized as follows. First, the related works in DHT-based multicast and topology optimization is given in the next section. Then, the proposed solution: Bandwidth Adaptive Multicast over DHT (BAM-Chord) is described in detail. In the next section, the effectiveness of the proposed method is evaluated and demonstrated by simulation results. The last section concludes the work.

BACKGROUND

Chord Protocol

Chord (Stoica et al., 2001) is a typical DHT- based P2P network protocol, which uses an m-bits address space. Each node is assigned a m-bit identifier from a one-dimensional circular key space (i.e. a Chord ring) that comprises 2^m keys ranging from 0 to $2^m - 1$. Further, each node is responsible for a portion of the DHT key space between its counterclockwise neighbor's identifier and its own identifier.

Using a consistent hash function, each participating node randomly chooses an identifier and then joins to a position in the ring by a joining process. A successor node of an identifier is defined as the node which identifier is nearest the identifier in the Chord ring clockwise.

In order to route a message destined to a key, each participating node maintains a set of links to its successor node and a number of neighbor nodes in a finger table, which has m entries. Assuming that the identifier of the current node is k, the *ith* entry in the table holds the information about the successor node of identifier $(k + 2^i - 1)$.

When a node receives a message destined to an identifier in the Chord ring, it will look up its finger table to find the nearest node to the identifier counter-clockwise and forward the message to that node. The forwarded node will recursively repeat the same operation. The process continues until the message reaches the successor of the destination identifier.

By the use of finger tables, Chord can route a message to a node responsible for a destination identifier in $O(logN)$ hops while each node only needs to maintain $O(logN)$ links to other nodes, where N is the number of nodes in the network. Hence, Chord can offer a promising solution for scalable and efficient message routing on P2P networks

DHT-Based Multicast

Application-layer multicast is an effective group communication method. While IP Multicast is implemented at the network layer by network nodes (i.e. routers), application-layer multicast is implemented at application layer by end nodes. Although application-layer multicast cannot avoid multiple copies of the same packet on the same link, it is easy to employ and can effectively utilize the network resource of end nodes to reduce work load for a source node.

Many application-layer multicast protocols have been proposed recently. In application-layer multicast protocols, participating nodes are eventually organized into multicast tree to disseminate multicast data. However, two major problems can

Figure 1. An example of chord-based multicast method. in this example, node 1 sends messages to all nodes in the chord ring

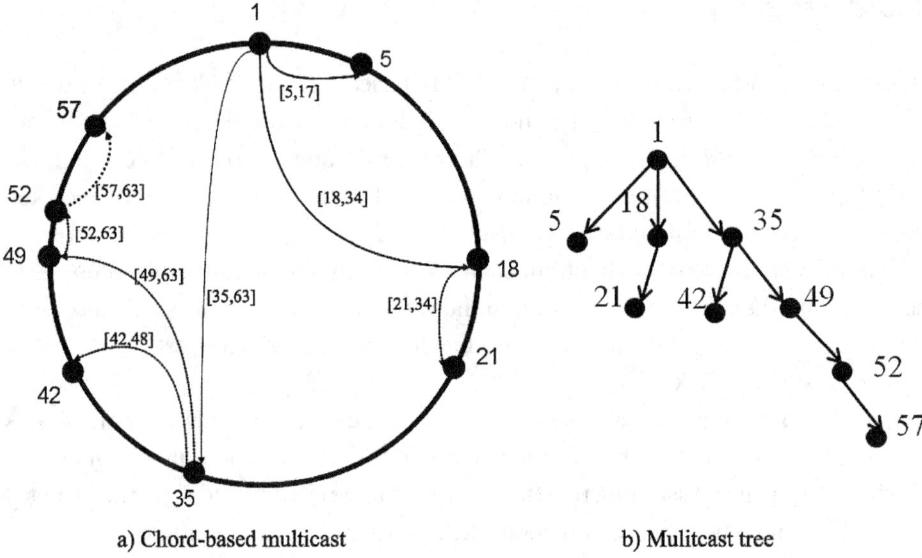

be seen for tree-based designs. Firstly, the leave/failure of any interior node may cause packet outage in all its descendant nodes.

Secondly, the network topology should be optimized to utilize the network resources of end nodes efficiently. There are a number of researches that works on DHT-based multicast as a solution for the first problem.

In Chord-based multicast (El-Ansary et al., 2003; Li et al., 2005), when a node wants to send multicast messages to a number of nodes in a continuous range (called multicast range) of a Chord ring, it will look up its finger table and determine all nodes which belong to the multicast range. It then specifies the multicast range that each node will be responsible for and sends a multicast message with each responsible multicast range to each node. Receiving nodes similarly select nodes belonging to the multicast range that they are responsible for from the list of nodes in their finger table. They then send multicast messages with new multicast ranges to these nodes. For example, in Fig. 1 when node 35 receives a multicast message with a multicast range of [35,63], it will send a multicast message to node 42 with a multicast range of [42,48] and send a multicast message to node 49 with a multicast range of [49,63].

This multicast algorithm has advantages of scalability and simplicity since it only relies on the construction of finger tables of nodes in a Chord ring to send multicast messages. Therefore, each node only needs to maintain a *O(logN)* of links to other nodes.

Several works such as Scribe proposed by Castro, Druschel, Kermarrec and Rowstron (2002) or CAN-based multicast proposed by Ratnasamy, Handley, Karp and Shenker (2001) also study the DHT-based multicast approach which builds a multicast tree on a DHT network such as Pastry (Rowstron, &Druschel, 2001), CAN (Ratnasamy, Francis, Handley, &Karp, 2001)) or Kademlia (Peris, Hern, & Huedo, 2012).

However, due to the inherent properties of DHT's routing table (i.e. finger table in the case of Chord), the size of responsible multicast ranges may be different between receiving nodes at the same level. Thus, there are nodes whose depths are much higher than other nodes and DHT-based multicast algorithms tend to construct an unbalanced multicast tree. Nodes with high depth will suffer high delay and unstable data rate. Further, as Bharambe, Rao, Padmanabhan, Seshan and Zhang (2005) indicated, in the case of node heterogeneity there are bottlenecks at nodes with low bandwidth if these nodes are required to send a large number of multicast messages to other nodes.

Topology Optimization for DHT-Based Multicast

Researches on topology optimization for application-layer multicast are done on many works such as the works of Venkataraman, Francis and Calandrino (2006), Luan, Kwong, Hei and Danny (2010) and Zhang, Wang, Li and Sun (2017). However, these works do not address for DHT-based multicast, which utilizes DHT links to deliver multicast messages.

Castro, Druschel, Kermarrec, Nandi, Rowstron and Singh (2003) proposed SplitStream as a solution for efficient utilization of network resources for DHT-based multicast. In SplitStream, nodes are structured into multiple diverse trees such that an interior node in this tree will be a leaf node of all other trees. Video streams are split into several smaller sub-streams and each sub-stream's data is delivered by one tree. However, SplitStream requires all nodes to have equal bandwidth. Otherwise, its performance will be degraded. Some researches (Bianchi, Melazzi, Bracciale, Piccolo, & Salsano, 2010; Liang, Liu, & Ross, 2009) overcome the disadvantage of Splitstream by optimizing the construction of multi trees even when nodes have different bandwidths. However, multi-tree based approach still has high cost of maintaining and recovering multicast trees when there is a node churn.

In CAM-Chord (Zhang et al., 2005), node heterogeneity is tackled by allowing nodes to vary out-degree according to the node's capacity. Multicast algorithm in CAM-Chord is similar to the algorithm proposed by El-Ansary et al. (2003) but different from making the multicast trees more balanced. CAM-Chord tries to build multicast tree as balanced as possible. Each node chooses child nodes in neighbor list to forward multicast data such that the multicast range is split into even sub regions. This makes multicast tree is tending to be balanced. Each node in CAM-Chord has a capacity of cx, which specifies the maximum number of child nodes it can forward multicast messages to. Therefore, the number of children for any internal node is always equal to the node's capacity. However, CAM-Chord cannot optimize the performance of multicast because there may exist internal nodes with low bandwidth and leaf nodes with high bandwidth.

Huanga and Zhang (2010) built a balanced multicast tree on DHT- based network by the use of a token-based broadcast algorithm and a partition-based broadcast algorithm over DHT. In the token-based algorithm, each node selects finger nodes as its children by a token value. In the partition-based algorithm, each node partitions its identifier space into subspaces and selects an agent node in each subspace as its child node. However, since each node has only two child nodes, the path length from source node to leaf nodes of the multicast tree is long and therefore the transmission delay is large.

Other works related to DHT-based multicast include the work of Disterhöft, Sandkühler, Ippisch and Graffi (2018), which proposes a protocol that enhances the robustness of existing tree-based approaches by building up multiple trees, and replicating and maintaining aggregated data. Peris, Hernández and Huedo (2016) proposed several techniques to enhance their proposed Kademlia-based broadcast method when adverse circumstances such as churn and failure rate conditions are present. The improvements include redundancy, resubmissions or flooding, and also combinations of those.

SYSTEM MODEL

Overview

Consider a multicast group of n nodes, which forms a Chord-like network. A source node whose ID is 0 will send multicast messages to all nodes in the network. The goal of the proposed system is to build a wide and balanced multicast tree based on the structure of the Chord overlay network even when nodes join or leave at any time and the bandwidth capacity of nodes is heterogeneous.

The authors consider that the relative relation between nodes in a Chord-based multicast tree depends on the positions of nodes (i.e. node IDs) in a Chord ring and the links between nodes (i.e. entries of finger tables of nodes). In the proposed method, since the structure of a Chord ring is used mainly for multicast data delivery and message routing, it is not necessary to create node IDs randomly as conventional Chord protocol. Furthermore, the links between nodes should be created such that a wide and balanced multicast tree can be built by the use of these links.

Therefore, the main ideal of BAM-Chord is to create a virtual wide and balanced multicast tree on a Chord ring. The higher level a node is, the more child nodes the node has. Each node in the virtual multicast tree is assigned with a node ID and finger table of a node must contain all child nodes of the node in the virtual multicast tree. The size (i.e. the number of nodes) of the virtual multicast tree is large enough to include all nodes in a real multicast tree.

Real nodes will be assigned to node positions in the virtual multicast tree to form a real multicast tree. Each newly joining node will select its node ID from a number of candidate IDs corresponding to nodes in the virtual multicast tree. In order to utilize effectively the bandwidth of a newly joining node while not creating a bandwidth bottleneck in the tree, candidate IDs of a newly joining node are selected based on the out bandwidth of that node. The higher bandwidth it has, the higher level its candidate IDs have. Therefore, nodes with high bandwidth will be assigned to positions of high level virtual nodes. Here, the maximum number of nodes that a node can forward is roughly estimated based on the out-bandwidth of a node, which is estimated based on some bandwidth estimation method or based on the setting of users.

By the use of a virtual multicast tree and the assignment of real nodes to the tree, the proposed multicast scheme can build a wide and balanced multicast tree on a Chord ring while using the bandwidth capacity of nodes effectively. The proposed multicast scheme is done completely decentralized to avoid a single point of failure. The detail of the proposed scheme is given in the next subsection.

Construction of Virtual Multicast Tree

In the proposed protocol, when a source node wants to send multicast data, it will create a virtual multicast tree, or a virtual tree in brief, on a Chord ring in which the root node of the virtual tree is the source node itself. Each node of the tree is assigned with an ID, which is also the ID of the node on the Chord ring. The root node of the tree has an ID of 0. Each node in the virtual tree has a node level, which is defined as the path length from the root node to the node. The root node has a node level of 0. Nodes in the same node level has the same number of child nodes, which is called the out-degree of a node in that level.

The out-degrees $l_0, l_1, ..., l_n$ of a node in each node level 0, 1, 2, …, *n* are predefined in which $l_1 \geq ... \geq l_n$. It means that in a virtual tree, the higher level a node is, the more child nodes the node has. Here, n is the height of the virtual tree and is predefined before the virtual tree is constructed. Since the number of nodes in level *i, i=1,...,n,* is, the size (i.e. the number of nodes) of the virtual tree can be calculated as

When a source node starts a new multicast group, the node will estimate the number of nodes that may receive the multicast data. It also calculates a set of out-degrees $l_0, l_1, ..., l_n$ of nodes in each node level due to bandwidth distribution of nodes in which the size of the virtual tree is over the estimation number of receiving nodes. The bandwidth distribution of nodes can be estimated based on some experiments (Huang, Li, & Ross, 2007).

Suppose that the size of the multicast group is estimated as N and the bandwidths of joining nodes are estimated as $outBw_1, ..., outBw_N$ based on some bandwidth distribution and $outBw_1 \geq outBw_2 \geq ... \geq outBw_N$. And suppose that *br* is the bit rate of the multicast data stream that the source node wants to send. The out-degree of node *i* (i.e. $outDegree_i$) is defined as an integer number equal to $[outBw_i/b_r]$. Here, $[x]$ means the nearest integer of *x*. We also have $outDegree_1 \geq outDegree_2 \geq ... \geq outDegree_N$. In fact, the out-degree of a node is the maximum number of child nodes that the node should have to avoid bandwidth bottleneck.

The values of $l_0, l_1, ..., l_n$ in each level 0, 1, …, *n* of a virtual multicast tree are calculated as follows.

- l_0 is the out-degree of the source node. $l_0 = outDegree_s$.
- l_1 is the out-degree of l_0^{th} node. $l_1 = outDegree_{x1}$, $x_1 = l_0$. It means that there are *lo* nodes at level 1, each of which have an out-degree larger than l_1
- l_2 is the out-degree of $(l_0 + l_0 l_1)^{th}$ *node.* $l2 = outDegree_{x2}$, $x_2 = l_0 + l_0 l_1$. It means that there are $l_0 l_1$ nodes at level 2, each of which have an out-degree larger than l_2
- …
- $l_n = outDegree_{xn}$, $x_n = \sum_{i=1}^{n} \prod_{j=0}^{i-1} l_j$

The authors consider that a node whose level is *t* should be responsible to send multicast messages to nodes belonging to the range beginning from its ID up to the ID of the next clockwise level-*t* node. In order to achieve a balanced tree, the multicast range of nodes in the same level should be the same. Therefore, the ID of a node at each node level of a virtual multicast tree is calculated as follows.

- ID of *level*-0 node (i.e. root node) is 0.

Figure 2. Node IDs of a virtual multicast tree on a chord ring

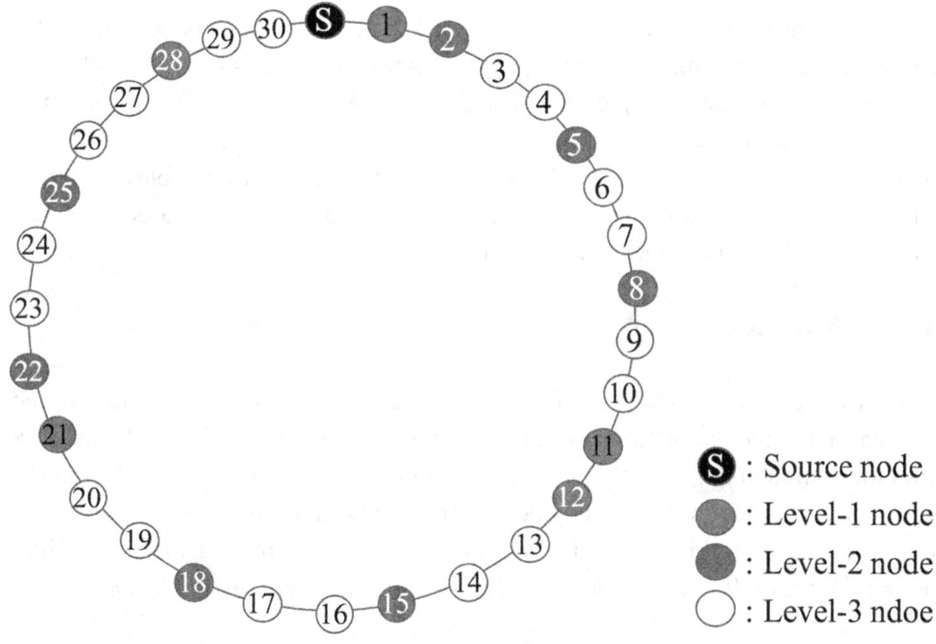

- IDs of *level*-1 nodes are $\left[1 + \frac{x_0 \cdot 2^m}{l_0} \right]$, where $x_0 \in \{0, ..., l_0 - 1\}$. There are l_0 IDs assigned to *level*-1 nodes and the distance between them is $\frac{x_0 \cdot 2^m}{l_0}$.
- ...
- IDs of *level-t* nodes are $\left[1 + \frac{x_0 \cdot 2^m}{l_0} + \frac{x_1 \cdot 2^m}{l_0 l_1} + \ldots + \frac{x_{t-1} \cdot 2^m}{l_0 l_1 \ldots l_{t-1}} \right]$ where $x_i \in \{0, ..., l_i - 1\}$, $\forall i \in \{0, ..., t - 1\}$. There are $l_0 l_{1 \ldots} l_{t-1}$ IDs assigned to *level-t* nodes and the distance between them is $\frac{x_{t-1} \cdot 2^m}{l_0 l_1 \ldots l_{t-1}}$.

Here, *m* is the bit size of ID space.

For example, in Fig. 2, there are 3 *level*-1 IDs of 1, 11, 21 and 9 *level*-2 IDs of 2, 5, 8, 12, 15, 18, 22, 25, 28. Node 1 is responsible for the multicast range of [1,10] which contains the ID of 3 *level-2* nodes (i.e. 2, 5, 8), each of which is responsible for a multicast range that include the ID of 2 level-3 nodes (i.e. (3, 4), (6,7) and (9,10)).

Figure 3 shows an example of a virtual multicast tree. In fact, not all nodes in a virtual multicast tree are associated with real nodes. However, in the proposed method real nodes will be assigned to nodes in virtual multicast tree based on their bandwidth. The next subsection shows the construction of a Chord-based multicast network based on the proposed multicast scheme.

Network Construction

When a source node wants to send multicast data, it creates a virtual multicast tree as described in the previous section. When a node x wants to receive multicast data from the source node, it firstly contacts to a bootstrap node to receive information about the source node. It then contacts to the source node to get the information related to streaming bit rate b_r and information of virtual multicast tree including the out-degrees $l_0, l_1, ..., l_n$ of nodes at each level of the tree. Suppose that the out-

Figure 3. Virtual multicast tree on BAM-chord ring

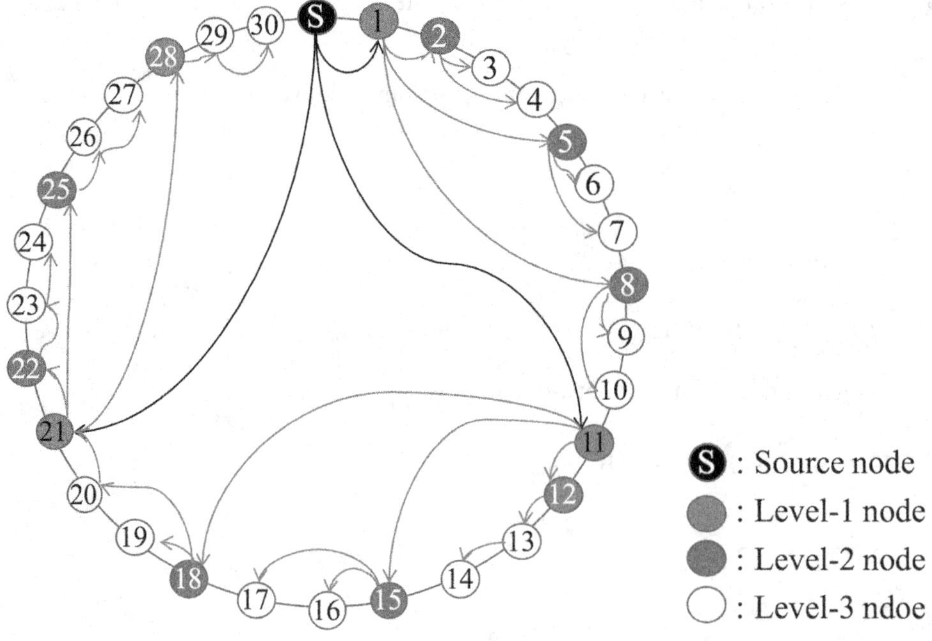

bandwidth of the node is b_w, then the node should join to a position corresponding to a node at level t of the virtual multicast tree, which has out-degree of l_t and $l_t \leq b_w/b_r$. Thus, the joining node calculates a number of candidate IDs at different levels and chooses an ID from candidate IDs.

Candidate IDs for a joining node at level t are calculated from a set of randomly values $x_0, x_1, ...x_{t-1}, x_i \in \{0, ..., l_{i-1}\} \forall i \in \{0, ..., t-1\}$ as mentioned above.

The node then contacts with a bootstrap node and sends a join probe message to each node responsible for each candidate ID by the use of conventional routing algorithm of Chord. If a candidate ID is not already used by any node, the successor node of that ID will send a reply message. In the case there are more than two available candidate IDs, the joining node will select an ID randomly among available IDs.

All candidate IDs corresponding to the level t may be hold by other nodes. In that case, the node will select candidate IDs whose level is smaller than t and probe the existence of nodes at positions corresponding to these candidate IDs again.

If a node cannot find any position in the Chord ring, it will ask the source node to increase the height of the virtual multicast tree. When the height of the virtual multicast tree increases by one from n to $n+1$, the number of nodes in the virtual multicast tree will increase by $l_0\, l_1 ...l_{n-1}$.

In Chord-based multicast, entries of a finger table of a node take two roles. Firstly, they are used to route a message to the next node, which is close to the destination node. Secondly, they are used to determine nodes belonging to the node's responsible multicast ranges, so that the node can forward multicast messages to these nodes.

BAM-Chord creates links between nodes for both message routing and multicasting. Since each node joins to a position corresponding to a node in the virtual multicast tree, it is necessary to create links from the node to nodes corresponding to child nodes in the virtual tree. However, not all of nodes in the virtual tree are associated with real nodes since node can join/leave at any time and each node joins the network in a decentralized manner. Therefore, the proposed method also adds redundant links, which can be used for failure recovery procedure, to the finger table of each node.

Concretely, a level-t node whose ID and out-degree are id_n and l_t will have four types of entries in its finger table. Here, *succ(x)* means that the successor node of the ID x since a node whose ID is x may not exist.

- l_t entries: succ($id_n + 1$), succ($\left\lceil id_n + 1 + \frac{2^m}{l_0 l_1 \cdots l_{t-1} l_t} \right\rceil$), ..., succ($\left\lceil id_n + 1 + \left(l_t - 1\right)\frac{2^m}{l_0 l_1 \cdots l_{t-1} l_t} \right\rceil$) linking to l_t child nodes in level $t+1$. These links are used for sending multicast messages to child nodes of level t+1, whose IDs belong in the multicast range of the node.

- $l_{t-1}-1$ entries: succ($\left[id_n+\frac{2^m}{l_0l_1\dots l_{t-1}}\right]$, ..., succ($\left[id_n+\left(l_{t-1}-1\right)\frac{2^m}{l_0l_1\dots l_{t-1}}\right]$) linking to $l_{t-1}-1$ nodes in level t, which are redundant links used for multicast routing. When the parent node of a level-t node leaves the network, the level-t node temporally takes the place of its parent node. The redundant links of the node will be used to send multicast messages to other level t nodes.
- l_1 -1 entries: succ ($\left[id_n+\frac{2^m}{l_0l_1}\right]$), ..., succ($\left[id_n+\left(l_1-1\right)\frac{2^m}{l_0l_1}\right]$) linking to l_1 -1 nodes, whose IDs are equally located in the range of $\left(id_n, id_n+\frac{2^m}{l_0l_1}\right)$. These links are used for Chord-based message routing with destination keys near to the node id_n.
- l_0-1 entries: succ(), ..., succ($\left[id_n+\left(l_0-1\right)\frac{2^m}{l_0}\right]\left[id_n+\left(l_0-1\right)\frac{2^m}{l_0}\right]$) linking to l_0-1 nodes, whose IDs are equally located in the whole Chord ring. These links are used for Chord-based message routing with destination keys far from the node id_n.

Source S which ID is 0 has l_0 entries: 1, succ($\left[1+\frac{2^m}{l_0}\right]$), ..., succ($\left[id_n+\left(l_0-1\right)\frac{2^m}{l_0}\right]$)

The proposed network construction method is completely decentralized. It is not required any centralized server to maintain network topology or node information. When a node leaves the network, a failure recovery mechanism of Chord with some improvement for data streaming (Rhea, Geels, Roscoe, & Kubiatowicz, 2004) can be used. Other failure detection mechanisms (Lavinia, Dobre, Pop, & Cristea, 2010) can also be used to improve service quality of the system. Therefore, BAM-Chord can scale to a network of thousands of nodes.

Multicast Method

In the proposed protocol, when a source node has multicast messages to send to all nodes in a multicast group, which forms as a Chord ring, it will send the messages to all nodes in its finger table. Each message is sent with a multicast range that the receiving node is responsible for.

Assuming that the IDs of nodes in the finger table of the source node are put in clockwise order as $ID_0, ID_1, ..., ID_k$, the multicast range that the node ID_i, $0 \leq i \leq k-1$, is responsible for will be $[ID_i, ID_{i+1} - 1]$, where ID_{i+1} is the ID of the next node in the finger table. A multicast message should be delivered to nodes whose IDs belong to the multicast range attached to the multicast message.

When a node receives a multicast message, it will select a number of nodes in the finger table to send the multicast message. These nodes are selected as follows. whose IDs belong to the responsible multicast range attached in the multicast message.

Assume that a node, whose ID and out-degree are ID_x and outDeg$_x$, receives a multicast message with a multicast range of $[ID_x, ID_y]$. It first lookups its finger table to find all nodes in the multicast range. Assume that the IDs of nodes in the multicast range are put in clockwise order as ID_0, ID_1, ..., ID_{k-1}. If the number of these nodes (i.e. k) is smaller than or equal to the out-degree $outDeg_x$ of the node ID_x, the node will select all these nodes to send the multicast message with a new responsible multicast range. If the number of these nodes (i.e. k) is bigger than the out- degree $outDeg_x$ of the node ID_x, the node will choose the node ID_0 and $outDeg_x$ - 1 nodes from the list of nodes (ID_1, ..., ID_k) to send the multicast message. The number of nodes to be sent must not be over the out-degree of the node in order not to create a bandwidth bottleneck. Furthermore, the levels of selected nodes in the virtual multicast tree must be higher than the level of unselected nodes. Since higher level nodes may have higher out-bandwidth than lower level nodes, sending a multicast message to a high level node will make the multicast message be sent to a large number of nodes in the next step.

Figure 4 shows an example of data multicast on a Chord ring. There are some nodes in the virtual multicast tree that are not associated with any real node. It is because of the decentralized mechanism of node joining and nodes may join/leave the multicast group at any time.

EVALUATION

To evaluate the effectiveness of BAM-Chord method, the authors built a simple simulation program and compared the performance of BAM-Chord method with original Chord-based multicast (Huebsch, 2003) and CAM-Chord method (Zhang et al., 2005) through some aspects:

- The path length from a source node to leaf nodes
- The number of links that each node must maintain.

Figure 4. Multicast transmission using BAM-chord method

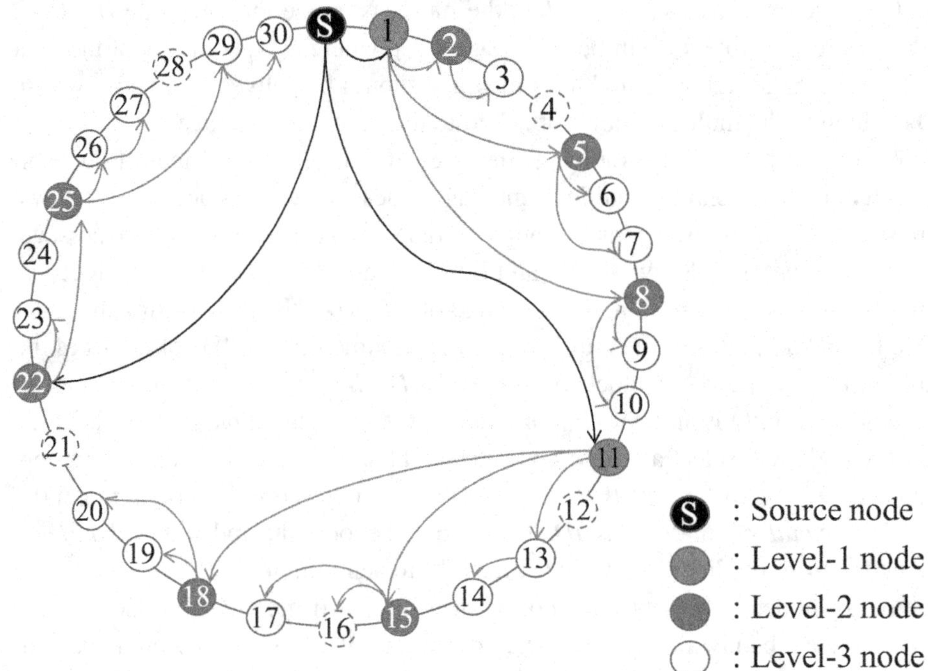

The simulation program is implemented with the following parameters:

- The bit length of the ID space is 32
- The estimated size of the multicast group is 5000 nodes
- The out degrees of nodes are taken from [2..20] randomly

Node joins and leaves randomly during simulation time based on Pareto distribution (Petersen, 1994). At each time step, there are a number of node joins and leaves. After each time step, the topology of the multicast tree is analyzed to get performance results.

The next subsections show the simulation results.

Path Length

Figure 5 shows the distribution of path lengths from a source node to leaf nodes of Chord-based multicast, CAM-Chord and BAM-Chord. Y axis indicates percentage of nodes and X axis indicates path length. As shown in the figure, BAM-Chord

Figure 5. Distribution of path lengths from a source node to leaf nodes of Chord, CAM-Chord and BAM-Chord

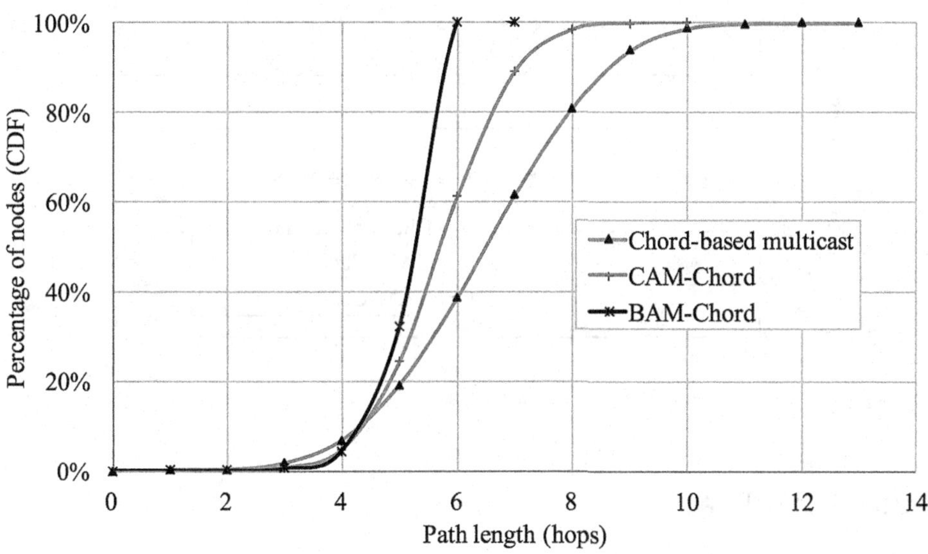

achieves the best result regarding to path length in comparison with Chord- based multicast and CAM-Chord. In Chord-based multicast, since the multicast tree is unbalanced, only 40% of leaf nodes have the path length up to 6 hops and 80% of leaf nodes have path length up to 8 hops. In CAM-Chord, the multicast tree is more balanced than Chord-based multicast. Therefore, 60% of leaf nodes have path length up 6 hops while about 95% of leaf nodes have path length up to 8 hops. In the case of BAM-Chord, 100% nodes have path length up to 6 hops. It is because the proposed method has optimized the positions of nodes such that nodes with high bandwidth will tend to be put at high level in the multicast tree and vice versa.

Moreover, the goal to build a multicast tree in BAM-Chord is to obtain a balanced, wide and bandwidth adaptive multicast tree. Figure 6 shows the change of maximum value of path length in the multicast tree during the simulation time. The smaller maximum path length means the multicast tree is wider. It is clear from Fig. 6 that the multicast tree in BAM-Chord is widest. At any simulation time step, maximum value of path length of BAM-Chord is 6 hops while in CAM-Chord it is 10 hops and in Chord-based multicast it is 13 hops.

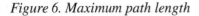

Figure 6. Maximum path length

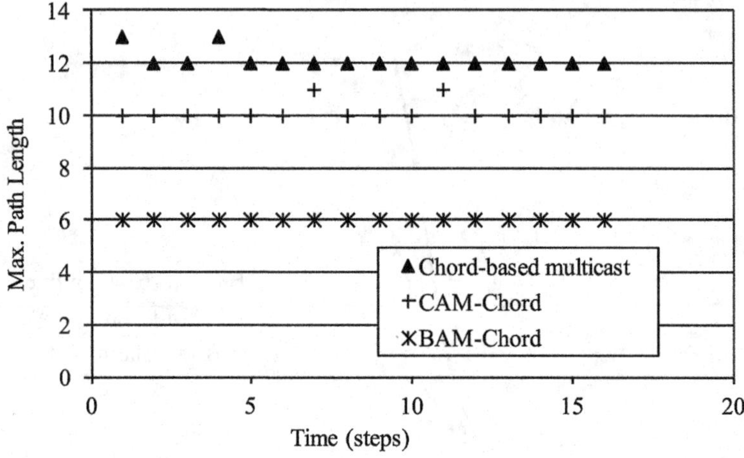

Control Overhead

The authors evaluate control overhead based on the number of links to neighbor nodes of each node. Each node must exchange information with their neighbor nodes and this message ex- change will cause control overhead. As shown in Fig. 7, in Chord-based multicast about 73% of nodes have the number of neighbor nodes up to 14 and the maximum number of neighbor nodes is 27. In the case of BAM-Chord each node must maintain links to a larger number of neighbor nodes. About 55.5% of nodes have the number of neighbor nodes up to 25 and the maximum number of neighbor

Figure 7. Average link number per node in Chord

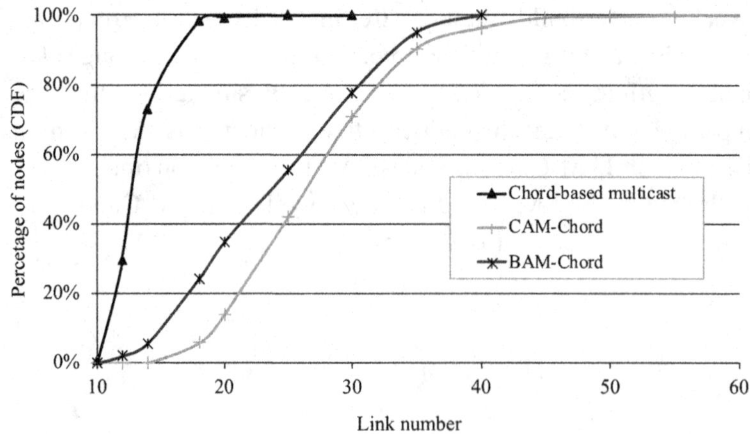

nodes per a node is 36. However, the proposed method is still more effective than CAM-Chord. In the case of CAM-Chord, about 70.7% of nodes have the number of neighbor nodes up to 30 and the maximum number of neighbor nodes per a node is 62. On average, the number of links per node is 13.6 in the case of Chord-based multicast, 24.1 in the case of BAM-Chord and 27.4 in the case of CAM- Chord.

CONCLUSION

DHT-based multicast schemes have advantages of scalability and simplicity since they only rely on the construction of routing tables of nodes to send multicast messages. Further, they also get benefits from failure recovery algorithms, which are implemented in most of DHT networks. Therefore, DHT-based multicast schemes can scale to multicast groups of thousands of nodes. However, the constructed multicast tree is unbalanced and heterogeneity of node bandwidths can create bottlenecks at internal nodes with low bandwidth. Further, the network should utilize network resources of high bandwidth nodes efficiently.

In this chapter, the authors have proposed BAM-Chord (Bandwidth Adaptive Multicast over Chord) protocol. The proposed protocol builds a virtual multicast tree on a Chord ring and let nodes join to positions corresponding to virtual nodes in a virtual multicast tree. The proposed protocol optimizes the topology of multicast tree in two novel points. Firstly, by the use of virtual multicast tree, the proposed protocol allows nodes to select appropriate positions on a BAM-Chord ring based on their output bandwidth such that a node with high output bandwidth will take a high level in the multicast tree. Secondly, each node will maintain a number of links to its neighbor nodes such that a wide and balanced multicast tree is constructed. The simulation results show the efficiency of BAM-Chord in respect of average path length, control overhead comparing with Chord-based multicast and CAM- Chord.

REFERENCES

Banerjee, S., Bhattacharjee, B., & Kommareddy, C. (2002). Scalable application layer multicast. In *Proceedings of ACM/IEEE Sigcomm 2002* (pp. 205-217). ACM/IEEE.

Bharambe, A., Rao, S., Padmanabhan, V., Seshan, S., & Zhang, H. (2005). The impact of heterogeneous bandwidth constraints on DHT-based multicast protocols. In *Proceedings of the 4th International Conference on Peer-to-Peer Systems* (pp. 115-126). Academic Press. 10.1007/11558989_11

Bianchi, G., Melazzi, N. B., Bracciale, L., Piccolo, F. L., & Salsano, S. (2010). Streamline: An optimal distribution algorithm for peer-to-peer real-time streaming. *IEEE Transactions on Parallel and Distributed Systems*, *21*(6), 857–871. doi:10.1109/TPDS.2009.114

Castro, M., Druschel, P., Kermarrec, A. M., Nandi, A., Rowstron, A., & Singh, A. (2003). SplitStream: High-bandwidth multicast in cooperative environments. In *Proceedings of 19th ACM Symposium on Operating Systems Principles* (pp. 298-313). ACM.

Castro, M., Druschel, P., Kermarrec, A. M., & Rowstron, A. (2002). Scribe: A large-scale and decentralized application-level multicast infrastructure. *IEEE Journal on Selected Areas in Communications*, *20*(8), 1489–1499. doi:10.1109/JSAC.2002.803069

Deering, S. E., & Cheriton, D. R. (1990). Multicast routing in datagram internet-works and ex- tended LANs. *International Journal ACM Transactions on Computer Systems*, *8*(2), 85–110. doi:10.1145/78952.78953

Disterhöft, A., Sandkühler, P., Ippisch, A., & Graffi, K. (2018). Mr. Tree: Multiple Realities in Tree-based Monitoring Overlays for Peer-to-Peer Networks. In *Proceedings of 2018 International Conference on Computing, Networking and Communications (ICNC)* (pp. 354-360). Academic Press. 10.1109/ICCNC.2018.8390361

El-Ansary, S., Alima, L. O., Brand, P., & Haridi, S. (2003). Efficient broadcast in structured P2P networks. *Proceedings of 2nd International Workshop on Peer-To-Peer Systems (IPTPS'03).*

Hosseini, M., Ahmed, D. T., Shirmohammadi, S., & Georganas, N. D. (2007). A survey of application-layer multicast protocols. *Journal IEEE Communications Surveys and Tutorials*, *9*(3), 58–74. doi:10.1109/COMST.2007.4317616

Huang, C., Li, J., & Ross, K. W. (2007). Can internet video-on-demand be profitable? In *Proceedings of ACM SIGCOMM'07* (pp.133-144). ACM.

Huanga, K., & Zhang, D. (2010). DHT-based lightweight broadcast algorithms in large-scale computing infrastructures. *Future Generation Computer Systems*, *26*(3), 29–310.

Huebsch, R. (2003). *Content-based multicast: Comparison of implementation options (Tech. Rep. UCB/ CSD-03-1229)*. Berkeley, CA: University of California.

Lavinia, A., Dobre, C., Pop, F., & Cristea, V. (2010). A failure detection system for large scale distributed systems. *International Journal of Distributed Systems and Technologies*, *2*(3), 64–87. doi:10.4018/jdst.2011070105

Li, J., Sollins, K., & Lim, D. Y. (2005). Implementing aggregation and broadcast over distributed hash tables. *Newsletter ACM SIGCOMM Computer Communication Review*, *35*(1), 81–92. doi:10.1145/1052812.1052813

Liang, C., Liu, Y., & Ross, K. W. (2009). Topology optimization in multi-tree based P2P streaming system. In *Proceedings of 21st International Conference on Tools with Artificial Intelligence (ICTAI '09)* (pp. 806–813). Academic Press.

Luan, H., Kwong, K. W., Hei, X., & Danny, H. K. T. (2010). Adaptive topology formation for peer-to-peer video streaming. *Journal Peer-to-Peer Networking and Applications*, *3*(3), 186–207. doi:10.100712083-009-0048-4

Magharei, N., & Rejaie, R. (2010). PRIME: Peer- to-peer receiver- driven mesh-based streaming. *Journal IEEE/ACM Transactions on Networking*, *17*(4), 1052-1065.

Mercan, S., & Yuksel, M. (2016). Virtual direction multicast: An efficient overlay tree construction algorithm. *Journal of Communications and Networks (Seoul)*, *18*(3), 446–459. doi:10.1109/JCN.2016.000060

Peris, A. D., Hern, J. M., & Huedo, E. (2012). Evaluation of the broadcast operation in Kademlia. In *2012 IEEE 14th International Conference on High Performance Computing and Communication & 2012 IEEE 9th International Conference on Embedded Software and Systems* (pp. 756-763). IEEE. 10.1109/HPCC.2012.107

Peris, A. D., Hernández, J. M., & Huedo, E. (2016). Evaluation of alternatives for the broadcast operation in Kademlia under churn. *Peer-to-Peer Networking and Applications*, *9*(2), 313–327. doi:10.100712083-015-0338-y

Petersen, J. L. (1994). *Estimating the parameters of a pareto distribution* (Master thesis). Retrieved October 16th, 2018, from http://www.math.umt.edu/gideon/pareto.pdf

Ratnasamy, S., Francis, P., Handley, M., & Karp, R. (2001). Scalable content-addressable network. In *Proceedings of ACM SIGCOMM'01* (pp. 161-172). ACM.

Ratnasamy, S., Handley, M., Karp, R., & Shenker, S. (2001). Application-level multicast using content-addressable networks. In Proceedings of Networked Group Communication (pp. 14-29). Academic Press. doi:10.1007/3-540-45546-9_2

Rhea, S., Geels, D., Roscoe, T., & Kubiatowicz, J. (2004). Handling churn in a DHT. *Proceedings of the USENIX Annual Technical Conference*.

Rowstron, A., & Druschel, P. (2001).Pastry: Scalable, distributed object location and routing for large-scale peer-to-peer systems. In *Proceedings of IFIP/ACM International Conference on Distributed Systems Platforms* (pp. 329–350). IFIP/ACM. 10.1007/3-540-45518-3_18

Stoica, I., Morris, R., Karger, D., Kaashoek, M. F., & Balakrisnan, H. (2001). Chord: A scalable peer- to-peer lookup service for Internet applications. In *Proceedings of ACM SIGCOMM'*01 (pp. 149-160). ACM. 10.1145/383059.383071

Tran, D. A., Hua, K. A., & Do, T. T. (2004). A peer- to-peer architecture for media streaming. *Journal IEEE JSAC Special Issue on Advances in Service Overlay Networks*, *22*(1), 121–133.

Tsuneizumi, I., Aikebaier, A., Ikeda, M., Enokido, T., & Takizawa, M. (2011). Design and implementation of hybrid time (HT) group communication protocol for homogeneous broadcast groups. *International Journal of Distributed Systems and Technologies*, *2*(3), 37–48. doi:10.4018/jdst.2011070103

Venkataraman, V., Francis, P., & Calandrino, J. (2006). Chunkyspread: Heterogeneous unstructured tree-based peer-to-peer multicast. In *Proceedings of the 2006 IEEE International Conference on Network Protocols* (pp. 2–11). IEEE. 10.1109/ICNP.2006.320193

Zhang, X., Wang, L., Li, Y., & Sun, M. (2017). A centralized optimization solution for application layer multicast tree. *IEEE eTransactions on Network and Service Management*, *14*(3), 771–785. doi:10.1109/TNSM.2017.2731521

Zhang, Z., Chen, S., Ling, Y., & Chow, R. (2005). Resilient capacity-aware multicasting based on overlay networks. In *Proceedings of the 25th IEEE International Conference on Distributed Computing Systems* (pp. 565–574). IEEE.

KEY TERMS AND DEFINITIONS

Application-Layer Multicast: Sending multicast data at the application layer in which multicast routing is implemented at peers instead of routers.

Chord Protocol: A typical DHT- based P2P network protocol proposed by Stoica et al. in the year 2001. In Chord, nodes and keys are assigned an m-bit identifier using from a one-dimensional circular key space and a finger table is built at each node for key-based lookup.

DHT-Based Message Routing: Route a message with a destination key to a node which is responsible for the destination key by the use of a DHT routing algorithm.

Distributed Hash Table: A class of decentralized distributed systems which support a hash table interface for storing and retrieving (key, value) pairs on P2P networks where a key is used to determine the node responsible for storing a value associated with the key.

End Node: A user computer or a server which joins a P2P network. End nodes may join/leave the network freely with or without notification.

Finger Table: A table contains a set of links between a node to its successor node and a number of neighbor nodes. A node uses its finger table to determine the next hop during key location.

Multicast-Tree: A tree rooted at the source node, which gives the paths of sending multicast data from the source node to other nodes of the tree.

Peer-to-Peer Networks: A network of computers, each of which acts as a node sharing computing resources such as file storage or network bandwidth within the network.

Chapter 7
Transparent Throughput Elasticity for Modern Cloud Storage:
An Adaptive Block-Level Caching Proposal

Bogdan Nicolae
Argonne National Laboratory, USA

Zhuo Zhen
University of Chicago, USA

Pierre Riteau
StackHPC, UK

Kate Keahey
Argonne National Laboratory, USA

ABSTRACT

Storage elasticity on the cloud is a crucial feature in the age of data-intensive computing, especially when considering fluctuations of I/O throughput. In this chapter, the authors explore how to transparently boost the I/O bandwidth during peak utilization to deliver high performance without over-provisioning storage resources. The proposal relies on the idea of leveraging short-lived virtual disks of better performance characteristics (and more expensive) to act during peaks as a caching layer for the persistent virtual disks where the application data is stored during runtime. They show how this idea can be achieved efficiently at the block-device level, using a caching mechanism that leverages iterative behavior and learns from past experience. Second, they introduce a corresponding performance and cost prediction methodology. They demonstrate the benefits of our proposal both for micro-benchmarks and for two real-life applications using large-scale experiments. They conclude with a discussion on how these techniques can be generalized for increasingly complex landscape of modern cloud storage.

DOI: 10.4018/978-1-5225-8295-3.ch007

1. INTRODUCTION

Elasticity (i.e., the ability to acquire and release resources on-demand as a response to changes of application requirements during runtime) is a fundamental feature that drives the popularity of cloud architectures. To date, much effort has been dedicated to studying the elasticity of computational resources, which mostly revolves around how to acquire/release virtualization units that provide performance isolation and multi-tenancy for computations, such as virtual machines (VMs) or containers (Tesfatsion, Klein, & Tordsson, 2018). Elasticity of storage has gained comparatively little attention, despite the fact that applications are becoming increasingly data-intensive and thus need cost-effective means to store and access data.

An important aspect of storage elasticity is the management of I/O access throughput. Traditional clouds offer little support to address this aspect: users have to manually provision raw virtual disks of predetermine capacity and performance characteristics (i.e., latency and throughput) that can be freely attached to and detached from VM instances (e.g., Amazon Elastic Block Storage (EBS) (AmazonEBS, n.d.)). Naturally, provisioning a slower virtual disk incurs lower costs when compared with using a faster disk; however, this comes at the expense of potentially degraded application performance because of slower I/O operations.

This trade-off has important consequences in the context of large-scale distributed scientific applications that exhibit an iterative behavior. Such applications often interleave computationally intensive phases with I/O intensive phases. For example, a majority of high-performance computing (HPC) numerical simulations model the evolution of physical phenomena in time by using a bulk synchronous approach. This involves a synchronization point at the end of each iteration in order to write intermediate output data about the simulation, as well as periodic checkpoints that are needed for a variety of scenarios (Nicolae & Cappello, 2013) such as migration, debugging, and fault tolerance. Since many processes share the same storage (e.g., all processes on the same node share the same local disks), this behavior translates to periods of little I/O activity that are interleaved with periods of highly intensive I/O peaks.

Since time to solution is an important concern, users often over-provision faster virtual disks to achieve the best performance during I/O peaks and under-use this expensive throughput outside the I/O peaks. However, scientific applications tend to run in configurations that include a large number of VMs/containers and virtual disks, which means the waste can quickly get multiplied by scale, prompting the need for an elastic solution.

In our previous works (Nicolae, Riteau, & Keahey, 2014b, 2015) we introduced an elastic disk throughput solution that can deliver high performance during I/O peaks while minimizing costs related to storage. Our proposal focuses on the idea of using small, short-lived, and fast virtual disks to temporarily boost the maximum achievable throughput during I/O peaks by acting as a caching layer for larger but slower virtual disks that are used as primary storage. In this context, we developed both a strategy and performance model to decide when to boost I/O throughput with temporary virtual disks and how large they need to be in order to deliver optimal performance with minimal cost. We have shown how this approach can be efficiently achieved for HPC applications in a completely transparent fashion by expos- ing a specialized block device inside the guest operating system that hides all details of virtual disk management at the lowest level, effectively casting the throughput elasticity as a block-device caching problem where performance is complemented by cost considerations.

Despite increasing complexity of the cloud landscape, the general principles of our proposal can be applied to provide transparent I/O throughput elasticity for cloud storage in a general fashion, beyond the specific context of HPC applications that use virtual disks. Therefore, in this chapter we refine our proposal with a discussion in this direction. We place the discussion in the context of modern applications, cloud infrastructures and virtualization technologies, which introduce new challenges and perspectives (e.g. new cost models).

We summarize our contributions as follows in the rest of this chapter: (1) we define the concept of throughput elasticity, as well as a series of requirements, design considerations and a cost model. Using these concepts, we propose a ephemeral cloud storage solution that enables I/O throughput elasticity in a transparent fashion at the block-device level. In particular, we describe a caching strategy that adapts to an iterative behavior and learns from the past experience in order to maximize the I/O boost during peaks, while minimizing the usage of fast virtual disks; (2) we introduce a methodology to predict the performance and cost of running large scale HPC applications that interleave computationally intensive phases with write intensive phases corresponding to checkpointing. We also show how these results can be used to optimize the cache size selection strategy in order to minimize the cost for a particular run within given performance degradation bounds; (3) we show how to apply these design considerations in practice through a series of building blocks (and their corresponding implementation as a prototype) that run inside the VM instances of the users and interact with a typical IaaS cloud architecture; (4) we evaluate our approach in a series of experiments conducted on dozens of nodes of the Shamrock experimental testbed, with results showing large reductions of storage cost at minimum performance loss. Furthermore, we validate our performance and cost prediction methodology against the real life results, showing high prediction accuracy; (5) We discuss the challenges of modern cloud storage and the opportunities to generalize our proposal beyond the original scope that targets HPC applications leveraging virtual disks for saving checkpoints at regular intervals.

2. RELATED WORK

Hybrid file systems (A.-I. A. Wang, Kuenning, Reiher, & Popek, 2006; Qiu & Reddy, 2013) and associated caching strategies (Forney, Arpaci-Dusseau, & Arpaci-Dusseau, 2002; Wu, He, & Eckart, 2012) have long been used to combine multiple devices of different types (e.g., SSDs, HDDs, nonvolatile memories). Generally, however, they are designed to use fixed storage resources available as physical hardware in order to improve access performance. Unlike our approach, such strategies are not concerned with being economical and minimizing resource usage. Furthermore, if the application needs a storage abstraction that is not file-based, then a file system introduces unnecessary overhead.

In the area of caching, Wang et. al. studied the problem of dynamically selecting the caching policy under varying workloads (Y. Wang, Shu, Zhang, Xue, & Zheng, 2010). The caching framework selects a caching policy and re-configures the storage system on the fly based on access traces gathered and analyzed during application runtime. An aspect of adaptation to access pattern is also explored by our previous work (Nicolae & Rafique, 2013; Nicolae, Karve, & Kochut, 2015), however, the focus is on scalable virtual disk on-demand image content delivery at large scale. Also with respect to caching strategies, an increasingly popular target is the newer generation of flash-based devices. For example, in (Chang, Hsu, Lu, & Kuo, 2011), special hybrid trees are proposed to organize and manipulate intervals of cached writes. Although orthogonal to our own work, such efforts provide valuable insight in terms of how caching is handled on the host that exposes the virtual disks to the VMs, which may influence how to best leverage guest-level caching if additional information is available.

Moving upward in the storage stack at the virtualization level, several approaches aim to accelerate the throughput of virtual disks at hypervisor level or below. Jo et al. (Jo et al., 2010) proposed a hybrid virtual disk based on a combination of an SSD and an HDD. Contrarily to our solution, the SSD in their approach is read-only and used only to improve read performance to the template VM image. All write operations are sent to the HDD to avoid degrading the performance of flash storage.

Using a fast device to cache both reads and writes from a read-only virtual disk snapshot is possible using copy-on-write and/or mirroring (QCOW2, n.d.; Meyer et al., 2008; Nicolae, Bresnahan, Keahey, & Antoniu, 2011). However, one of the disadvantages in this context is fragmentation, for which specialized strategies might be necessary (Nicolae & Cappello, 2013).

How to virtualize bandwidth in a cloud environment was explored at various levels. The S-CAVE developers (Luo et al., 2013) propose to leverage the unique position of the hypervisor in order to efficiently share SSD caches between multiple VMs. Similarly, vPFS (Xu et al., 2012) introduces a bandwidth virtualization layer for parallel file systems that schedules parallel I/Os from different applications based on configurable policies. Unlike our approach, the focus in this context is bandwidth isolation between multiple clients, as opposed to elasticity.

Storage elasticity on IaaS clouds was explored at coarse granularity by Lim et al. (H. C. Lim, Babu, & Chase, 2010) for multi-tier application services, with a focus on how to add and remove entire storage nodes and how to rebalance the data accordingly. Higher level service processing acceleration was described in (Chiu, Shetty, & Agrawal, 2010). This work introduces an elasticity aspect in the form of a series of algorithms to scale the cache system up during peak query times and back down afterwards to save costs. LogBase (Vo, Wang, Agrawal, Chen, & Ooi, 2012) is another elastic storage effort that employs a log-structured database system targeted at write-intensive workloads. Unlike our approach, the goal is to improve the write performance and simplify recovery. Chen et al. introduced Walnut (Chen et al., 2012), an object store that provides elasticity and high availability across Yahoo!'s data clouds and is specifically optimized for the data-intensive workloads observed in these clouds: Hadoop (White, 2009), MObStor (unstructured storage similar to (AmazonS3, n.d.)), PNUTS (Cooper et al., 2008), and so forth. The main goal is sharing of hardware resources across hitherto siloed clouds of different types, offering greater potential for intelligent load balancing and efficient elastic operation, while simplifying the operational tasks related to data storage.

Transparent caching at low level was extensively explored. FlashTier (Saxena, Swift, & Zhang, 2012) provides a cache-oriented flash device, known as solid-state cache (SSC), with memory-efficient address space management and cache consistency for data recovery. Energy efficiency is addressed by efforts such as FlashCache (Kgil & Mudge, 2006), which is based on NAND flash memory but with two level of file buffer cache to consume orders of magnitude less idle power, while preserving performance. Nitro (Li et al., 2014) focuses on improving storage performance via deduplication and compression, in order to achieve a capacity-optimized SSD cache. However, none of these efforts consider the cost-effectiveness dimension made possible by elasticity.

Cost-aware caching has received relatively little attention. Hou et al. (Hou & Chen, 2017) explore a comprehensive cache design by considering not only the access locality but also the object size, associated latency, and price, aiming at improving both access latency and monetary cost. Elastic in-memory key-value stores used as caches are proposed in (Carra, Neglia, & Michiardi, 2018), where the authors propose a dynamic algorithm for TTL caches, which is able to obtain close-to-minimal costs. Unlike our proposal, the authors focus on object caching rather than transparent caching at block-device level.

Several approaches acknowledge the importance of estimating and leveraging cost and performance prediction for clouds. Log2cloud (Perez-Palacin, Calinescu, & Merseguer, 2013) is one such effort that uses established results from queuing network theory to predict the minimum VM cost of cloud deployments starting from existing application logs. Other research focuses on modeling specific applications and workloads, such as database queries (Karampaglis, Gounaris, & Manolopoulos, 2014). Specifically in the area of storage, efforts such as ACIC (Liu et al., 2013) automatically search for optimized I/O system configurations, relying on machine learning models to perform black-box performance/cost predictions.

Our own previous work (Nicolae, Riteau, & Keahey, 2014a) focuses on storage elasticity from a different perspective: space utilization, aiming to adapt transparently to growing/shrinking data sizes by means of a POSIX-compatible file system that automatically adds and removes virtual disks accordingly. FCFS (Puttaswamy, Nandagopal, & Kodialam, 2012) is another storage solution that aims to reduce the cost of operating a file system in the cloud by adapting the storage volume sizes of each service to provide a cost-efficient solution with provable performance bounds.

With respect to throughput elasticity, we have explored in our previous work (Nicolae et al., 2014b) a generic approach that adapts to the I/O intensive phases of the application automatically, striking a good all-around trade-off between minimizing the waste caused by over-provisioning of throughput while at the same time minimizing the performance degradation. We complemented this work with a new performance and cost prediction methodology (Nicolae, Riteau, & Keahey, 2015) that can can be applied for well-define I/O access patterns both independently to estimate in advance what trade-off between performance and cost is possible, as well as a dynamic optimization technique for cache size selection.

3. SYSTEM DESIGN

In a nutshell, our proposal relies on a simple core idea: the use of small and short-lived virtual disks of high-throughput capability (with higher price per gigabyte) to *transparently* boost the I/O performance during peak utilization of slower (and cheaper per gigabyte) virtual disks that are continuously used by the application to accumulate persistent data. We use the former as a ephemeral caching device and the latter as a backing device. When the caching device is in operation, it acts as a read/write caching layer at the block level that uses an adaptive mechanism to asynchronously flush dirty blocks back to the backing device. Besides the technical challenges related to achieving transparency efficiently at the block level, the main challenge in this context is the focus on cost reduction, which brings a novel perspective to the otherwise well-studied caching domain. Several critical questions arise: How large should the virtual disk acting as a cache be? When and for how long do we need it? What caching strategy should we use?

To answer these questions, we introduce a series of design considerations formulated in response to the problem we study.

3.1 Design Principles

Our proposal relies on three key design principles:

Transparent Block-Level Caching

Storage is typically provisioned on IaaS clouds in the form of virtual disks that are created by using a predefined size and performance characteristics (i.e., throughput). Although the virtual disks can be freely attached to and detached from running VM instances, this degree of elasticity is hard to leverage directly at the application level in order to deal with fluctuating I/O throughput requirements: data would have to be constantly migrated to/from a slower/faster device, thereby generating high performance and cost overheads that are unacceptable if a large amount of data accumulates during runtime or if the fluctuations happen over short periods of time. Even if such an approach were feasible, applications often do not leverage virtual disks directly but rely on storage abstractions (e.g., a file system) that were not designed to add/remove disks on the fly. Thus, it is desirable to handle throughput elasticity in a transparent fashion at the lowest level.

In response to this need, we propose a solution that works at the block level. Specifically, we expose a block device in the guest operating system that replaces the virtual disk normally leveraged by users directly, using it as a backing device that all I/O is redirected to. When I/O throughput utilization rises above the utilization threshold (UT), a second, faster virtual disk (referred to as the caching device) is provisioned to act as a caching layer for the backing device, temporarily boosting I/O throughput until the threshold falls below UT. At this point, the data from the caching device is flushed to the backing device, and the caching device is removed, with I/O passing directly to the backing device again. Such an approach enables transparency not only from the user's perspective but also from the cloud provider's perspective: it works at the guest level and does not require changes to the virtualization infrastructure or provisioning model.

Adaptive Flushing of Dirty Blocks

A solution that alternates between a fast and a slow virtual disk to achieve elasticity suffers from poor I/O performance and is unsustainable, because an increasingly larger set of accumulated data needs to be migrated between the two devices. On the other hand, a solution based on caching dramatically reduces the amount of data movements, because only the most recently used blocks are involved (we call these blocks "hot"). Even when considering only the "hot" blocks, however, the constant movement between the backing device and the caching device naturally steals bandwidth from both devices, effectively limiting the potential to boost the I/O throughput at full capacity.

To address this issue, we propose to make the caching device act like a regular block-level read/write cache but with a custom dirty block commit strategy. More specifically, during a read operation, any requested blocks that are not already available on the caching device are first fetched from the backing device and written to the caching device by using an LRU (least recently used) eviction strategy. Then, the read operation is fully redirected to the caching device. In the case of a write operation, all dirty blocks are initially written to the cache only and are later committed to the backing device.

The strategy to commit dirty blocks works in two phases. In the first phase, we use a mechanism that closely resembles writeback and prioritizes the application I/O: it flushes dirty blocks asynchronously to the backing device only when spare bandwidth is available or when the caching device is full and needs to evict. Once the required I/O throughput drops to a level that the backing device is able to sustain on its own, a transition to the second phase is initiated, in which the priority is reversed: the flushing process proceeds at full speed at the expense of application I/O. At the same time, only reads are allowed from the caching device starting from this moment onward, with writes bypassing the caching device and being redirected to the backing device. We refer to this two-phase strategy as "dynamic writeback."

Note that finding the right moment to reverse the priority is important: if it happens too soon, the application will suffer a performance penalty because of background flushes. If it happens too late, the caching device stays up longer than necessary and thus incurs extra costs. In order to deal with this issue, the decision of when to reverse the priority is based on a configurable amount of time ID (inactivity delay), which represents how much the application's I/O throughput needs to stay below UT before we reverse the flush priority. Since the flush process is prioritized after the reverse and writes bypass the caching device, eventually all dirty blocks will be committed to backing device. At this point, one can safely detach the caching device and remove its corresponding virtual disk.

Access-Pattern-Aware Cache Sizing

Using a caching device can be expensive: while it is active, the user is charged for both the caching device and the backing device. Thus, the caching device cannot be arbitrarily large for two reasons.

First, the flushing of dirty data does not happen instantly after the decision was made to proceed to the second phase of the commit strategy, which delays the moment when the caching device can be safely removed. Second, since dirty data tends to accumulate proportionally to the cache size, a large caching device is likely to cause a long flush delay. On the other hand, if the cache size is too small, flushing may be forced prematurely, limiting the potential to boost application I/O at full capacity. Thus, it is important to automatically optimize the cache size specifically for the access pattern of the application observed during the I/O-intensive phase.

To optimize the size of the caching device, we propose to leverage the predominantly repetitive I/O behavior of large-scale scientific applications in order to learn from the experience of the previous I/O-intensive phases for which a caching device was in use. More specifically, we start with a large cache size for the first time when an I/O boost is needed and then monitor the cache utilization. If the caching device was used only partially, then we decrease its size for the next I/O-intensive phase down to the size that was actually used. Similarly, if too much flushing was forced prematurely during the first phase of the commit strategy (in which application I/O is prioritized), we increase the cache size for the next I/O-intensive phase by the amount that had to be evicted.

3.2 Cost Model

We assume a cost model that charges users for utilization at fine grain that can be as little as the order of seconds. This approach is already adopted in real-life: for instance, Google Compute Engine charges persistent disks at a granularity of seconds (Google, 2014). Since we are dealing with different types of virtual disks, we approximate a realistic cost by defining utilization as a function of both the size of the virtual disk and its throughput characteristics (i.e., reserved bandwidth).

Note that the utilization is based on reserved bandwidth, which relates to the high-end spectrum of cloud offerings such as the Object Storage offered by IBM SoftLayer (SoftLayer, n.d.) or provisioned Elastic Block Store (EBS) volumes offered by Amazon (AmazonEBS, n.d.). This is different from the more popular "classic EBS" model where users are not offered any bandwidth guarantees and are charged per IOPS instead. We justify the need to rely on reserved bandwidth because our primary target is tightly coupled HPC applications that run at large scale and are known for their susceptibility to system noise amplification (Hoefler, Schneider, & Lumsdaine, 2010) (i.e., the bulk-synchronous nature makes processes sensitive to delays that affect all other processes, which in our context means that a slow virtual disk attached to a VM instance causes slowdown of all other VM instances where the application processes are running). Thus, reasoning in terms of average throughput (as is the case of classic EBS volumes) is not feasible in our context.

To quantify the utilization in accordance with the requirements mentioned above, we introduce a metric called *adjusted storage accumulation*, which reflects the total cost that accumulates over a period of time t for a VM instance as a result of storage use. We assume that for every time unit of utilization, a virtual disk of size N and reserved bandwidth B incurs a cost of $N \cdot B$. Thus, if a single virtual disk is attached to a VM instance for the whole duration t, the total cost is $C(t)=B \cdot N \cdot t$. When using both a backing device and a caching device to implement our approach, the backing device will continuously contribute to the total cost, as in the case of a single virtual disk, whereas the caching device will contribute only while it is used and proportionally to its dynamically adjusted size. More formally, this approach can be expressed as follows:

$$C\left(t\right) = B_b \cdot N \cdot t + B_c \cdot \int_0^t M\left(x\right) \cdot dx$$

N and B_b are the size and bandwidth of the backing device, respectively; B_c is the bandwidth of the caching device; and $M(x)$ is the size of the caching device at a given moment x (0 if the caching device is not used at that moment). We express the bandwidth in MB/s, the size in GB, and the time in seconds, which results in a combined metric unit that we call *adjusted GB seconds* (denoted AGBs). For the rest of this paper, we use this unit to express the cost.

3.3 Performance and Cost Prediction

Due to the massive amount of resources involved, it is important to anticipate the performance and cost of running a distributed scientific application at large scale, because this enables understanding whether it is feasible to obtain the desired results within a given time or cost budget.

However, in order for such an estimation to be possible, the application needs to exhibit a well defined I/O access pattern. Luckily, a majority of high-performance computing (HPC) numerical simulations exhibit such a well defined I/O access pattern: they are composed iterative bulk-synchronous computations consisting of a large number of distributed processes that simultaneously checkpoint their state to disk at regular intervals. We choose to illustrate our estimation proposal on this class of applications.

More specifically, we assume n VMs need to checkpoint the same amount of information at regular intervals. We denote the size of the checkpoint dumped by each VM as S_c. Furthermore, users typically know how many iterations I they need to run (e.g., number of timesteps in a simulation), how much compute time I_t is needed per iteration and how many checkpoints per VM (K) will be dumped during the application runtime (i.e., number of intervals). Even if S_c or I_t is not known in advance, such information can be obtained by running the application in benchmarking mode for a short period of time until at least one set of checkpoints can be captured and analyzed (i.e., K=1). Assuming that the required information about the application was collected one way or another, the completion time T can be estimated as follows:

$$T = I \cdot I_t + \frac{K \cdot S_c}{B\left(S_c\right)}$$

In the above equation, B(x) denotes the sustained throughput for writing a dataset of size x and is assumed to be known.

In addition to the completion time, we are interested in an estimation of the overall adjusted storage accumulation C_a, which is the sum of the individual accumulation C of each VM. Since the checkpoint size S_c remains fixed throughout the application runtime, there is a size $M(S_c)$ of the caching device that corresponds to an optimal performance-cost trade-off. For the purpose of this section, we assume that $M(S_c)$ is given, while zooming later on how to choose $M(S_c)$. Furthermore, in a typical scenario, the application performs an I/O initialization step where each VM dumps S_i GB worth of data corresponding to an initial state. Accounting for this additional initialization phase, C_a can be estimated as follows:

$$C = B_b \cdot N \cdot \left(T + \frac{S_i}{D(S_i)} \right) + B_c \cdot M(S_i) \cdot D(S_i) + K \cdot B_c \cdot M(S_c) \cdot D(S_c)$$

$$C_a = n \cdot C$$

In the above equation, $D(x)$ denotes the duration for which the caching device is attached while writing a dataset of size x and is assumed to be known.

Note that due to the complex interactions between the backing device and the caching device, it is not easy to determine $B(x)$ and $D(x)$ analytically. However, $B(x)$ and $D(x)$ depend on three parameters: throughput of the backing device B_b, throughput of the caching device B_c and size of the caching device M. Thus, we propose to establish $B(x)$ and $D(x)$ experimentally by selecting a series of representative values for x and M and running I/O intensive microbenchmarks (e.g. using *dd*) to directly measure $B(x)$ and $D(x)$. We refer to this process as *calibration*.

In a minimal configuration, two possible values for x (S_i and S_c) and M ($M(S_i)$ and $M(S_c)$) are enough to calibrate for a single scenario. However, the calibration can be extended to additional values for x and M in order to obtain multiple points that can be interpolated to estimate additional "what-if" scenarios useful for the application developer (e.g., the application developer may want to study what happens if the checkpoint size doubles as a consequence of increasing the floating point precision from single to double).

3.4 Optimal Cache Size Selection Based on Performance and Cost Prediction

In the previous section we introduced a cost estimation technique based on a calibration phase that is able to anticipate the completion time and total adjusted storage accumulation for bulk-synchronous HPC applications that checkpoint at regular intervals. This was possible because of the assumption that the checkpoint size remains constant, which leads to a situation where there optimal checkpointing cache size $M(S_c)$ also remains constant. In this section we introduce a technique that is able to recommend $M(S_c)$ for this particular scenario in advance, which can be used to enhance the generic adaptive cache sizing strategy.

At first sight, a good choice seems $M(S_c)=S_c$, because it enables the cache to be large enough to hold all checkpointing data, which in turn enables the checkpointing to proceed at maximum speed. At the same time, it minimizes the adjusted storage accumulation required to do so, because the cache is not larger than absolutely necessary. However, this line of reasoning does not necessarily lead to an optimal configuration: if performance is not the top priority, then it could be beneficial to reduce $M(S_c)$ in order to obtain a lower adjusted storage accumulation. The opposite is also true: due to various overheads encountered in practice, it may be beneficial to increase $M(S_c)$ beyond S_c in order to achieve the best throughput. Ultimately, both aspects introduce a level of complexity that makes it non-trivial to analytically determine an optimal $M(S_c)$.

To address this challenge, we propose a solution that is based on the cost estimation technique introduced in the previous section. The key idea behind our proposal is to perform an extended calibration phase that determines $B_M(x)$ and $D_M(x)$ for M in a range of values that facilitates an extended search around S_c according to the remarks mentioned above. Although this extended calibration may seem expensive, it is important to note that the microbenchmarks are independent of the users and applications, therefore cloud providers can cache the results to expose and reuse them later.

Once the results are available one way or another, T and C_a can be easily computed for all M. If there is a constraint on the maximum acceptable completion time (denoted T_{max}), then we keep only those $M(S_c)$ for which $T \leq T_{max}$. Subsequently, for the remaining $M(S_c)$, we compute the corresponding C_a and keep a single value that minimizes C_a, which is the recommended value.

3.5 Architecture

The simplified architecture of our approach is depicted in Figure 1. We assume that the VMs are deployed on an IaaS cloud that enables users to provision raw storage as virtual disks. Furthermore, we assume that the cloud hypervisor can dynamically attach and detach virtual disks to the VM instances (a standard feature in most production-ready hypervisors).

Once booted, the VM instance initializes an *adaptive block device* that uses a non-expensive virtual disk of limited throughput as the *backing device*. The adaptive block device is exposed inside the guest OS as a standard block device and can be leveraged as such (e.g., it can be formatted by using a file system).

Once the adaptive block device is running, a *controller* daemon collects I/O statistics about it at fine granularity (e.g., sustained throughput); and, based on these statistics, it implements the design principles described in Section 3.1. Specifically, during an I/O-intensive phase, it interacts with a standardized *IaaS API* in order to

Figure 1. Integration of our approach into an IaaS cloud architecture; components that are part of our design are highlighted with a darker background.

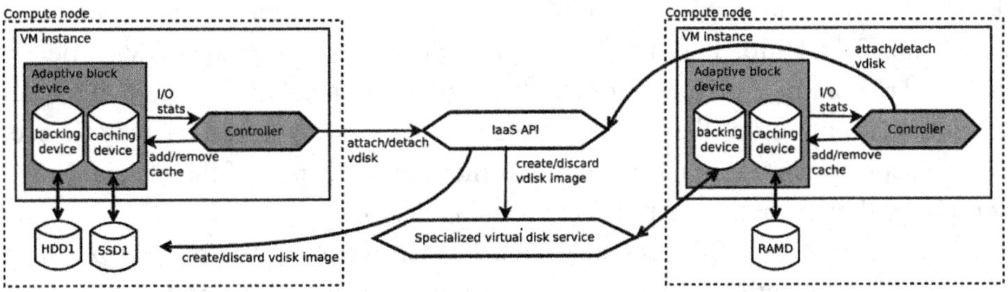

attach a virtual disk of optimized size (based on the experience from the previous I/O intensive phases) that will act as the *caching device*. Once the VM instance has recognized the caching device, it incorporates the corresponding guest-level block device into the adaptive block device. All interactions between the caching device and the backing device are handled transparently by our adaptive block device based on the principles mentioned in Section 3.1. Once the I/O-intensive phase completes, the controller signals the adaptive block device to start flushing. After the flushing has completed, it detaches the corresponding virtual disk from the VM instance using the IaaS API and destroys the disk, thus stopping the accumulation of storage costs due to caching.

How to provision a virtual disk is open to a wide range of choices: various types of devices (e.g., HDDs, SSDs, RAM-disks) can be directly leveraged by the hypervisor and exposed as virtual disks inside the VM instance. If devices need to be shared, another option is to use virtual disk images of various formats (e.g., raw, QCOW2 (QCOW2, n.d.)), hosted either locally or remotely on different types of devices. Virtual disks also may be provided by specialized services, such as Amazon EBS (AmazonEBS, n.d.) or our own previous work (Nicolae et al., 2011). Our approach is agnostic to any of these choices as long as they are handled through a standardized IaaS API.

3.6 Implementation Details

In this section, we briefly introduce a prototype that implements the components presented in Section 3.5.

We rely on *Bcache* (BCache, n.d.) to implement the *adaptive block device*. Our choice was motivated by several factors. First, it offers out-of-the-box support to cache hot blocks of designated devices on other devices, while offering support to activate/deactivate caching in an online fashion. Second, it is highly configurable and offers detailed statistics about I/O utilization. In particular, the ability to control the caching strategy and the interaction between the backing device and caching device was crucial in enabling the implementation of the design principles presented in Section 3.1. Third, it is implemented at the kernel level and is specifically designed to minimize performance overhead. Since we need to handle another level of indirection on top of the virtualized nature of the backing and caching device, this aspect is important in our context. Furthermore, it is part of the official Linux kernel and thus enjoys widespread exposure and adoption.

The *controller* was implemented as a Python daemon. We rely on *psutil* to get per-disk I/O statistics. The interaction with Bcache is implemented directly through the *sysfs* interface. We note also certain nontrivial aspects related to the management of virtual disks, in particular how to detect inside the guest when the disk is recognized by the kernel. To this end, we rely on *pyudev*, which implements an accessible interface to *libudev*, including asynchronous monitoring of devices in a dedicated background thread.

4. EXPERIMENTAL EVALUATION

This section presents the experimental evaluation of our approach. We introduce the experimental setup and methodology (Section 4.1), and discuss results for microbenchmarks (Section 4.2) and two real-life HPC applications (Section 4.3 and Section 4.4).

4.1 Experimental Setup

Our experiments were performed on the *Shamrock* testbed of the Exascale Systems group of IBM Research in Dublin. For this work, we used a reservation of 32 nodes interconnected with Gigabit Ethernet, each of which features an Intel Xeon X5670 CPU (12 cores), HDD local storage of 1 TB, and 128 GB of RAM.

We simulate a cloud environment using *QEMU/KVM* 1.6 as the hypervisor. The VM instances run a recent Debian Sid (3.12 Linux kernel) as the guest operating system. The network interface of each VM uses the *virtio* driver and is bridged on the host with the physical interface in order to enable point-to-point communication between any pair of VMs.

We compare three approaches throughout our evaluation:

Static Preallocation Using a Slow Virtual Disk

In this setting, a large, fixed-size virtual disk is created on the local HDD of each host as a RAW file and attached to each VM instance after booting. The maximum I/O bandwidth of the virtio driver is fixed by using the hypervisor monitor, and the host-side caching is disabled to avoid interference. After booting the VM instances, all virtual disks are formatted by using the *ext4* file system, and the corresponding mount points are used for all I/O generated during the experiments. We refer to this setting as *static-slow*.

Static Preallocation Using a Fast Virtual Disk

This setting is similar to the one described above, except that the fixed-sized virtual disk is hosted as a RAW file in a RAM-disk. Again, the maximum bandwidth available to the guest operating system is fixed. However, it is several times higher than in the previous case and is intended to simulate a faster device, such as an SSD. We refer to this setting as *static-fast*.

Transparent Throughput Elasticity Using Our Approach

In this setting, we use a virtual disk with properties identical to those in the *static-slow* case as a backing device. Whenever more bandwidth is needed, a new virtual disk with properties identical to those in the *static-fast* case is used as a caching device to temporarily boost I/O throughput. The size of the caching device, as well as the moment when to attach and detach it, is automatically determined by our approach during runtime (as explained in Section 3.1). Furthermore, the utilization threshold *UT* is set to 30%, and the inactivity delay *ID* is set to 30s. We refer to this setting as *adaptive*.

These approaches are compared based on the following metrics:

- **Performance Overhead:** The difference in performance observed between *static-fast*, which is used as a baseline for the best possible performance, and the other two approaches that leverage slower virtual disks. In the case of microbenchmarks, performance refers to the sustained I/O throughput as perceived by the application. In the case of real-life applications, performance refers to the completion time, which measures the overall end-impact of each approach on the application runtime.

- **Total Adjusted Storage Accumulation:** The sum of the adjusted storage accumulation for all VM instances involved in the experiment. It is used to quantify storage-related costs for the entire application deployment according to the cost model introduced in Section 3.2.
- **Evolution of I/O Activity:** Represents the total I/O bandwidth utilization (due to reads and writes to virtual disks) for all VM instances. In the *static-fast* and *static-slow* cases, it overlaps with the sustained I/O throughput as perceived by the application. In the *adaptive* case, it measures all background I/O activity to the backing device and caching device (which can be higher than *static-fast* when both devices are active simultaneously). This metric is important for studying how the compute phases interleave with the I/O phases and how the backing device interacts with the caching device during this interleaving.

4.2 Microbenchmarks

Our first series of experiments focuses on the I/O performance of all three approaches in synthetic settings. For this purpose, we use *Bonnie++*, a standard I/O benchmarking tool that measures read, write, and rewrite throughput when using 32 KB blocks (default value used in the experiments). We focus on these values because they are the most representative of real-life large-scale scientific applications (as opposed to byte-by-byte read/write throughput or other file-system related statistics that are reported).

We run the following experiment: a single VM instance is booted and Bonnie++ is launched three times in a row, with a 120 second pause between each run. We repeat the experiment for each approach three times and record the average of the relevant Bonnie++ statistics. The memory allocated to the VM is fixed at 2 GB. The virtual disk settings are as follows: the size of the backing device is fixed at 10 GB, with a reserved bandwidth of 60 MB/s for both *static-slow* and *adaptive* and a reserved bandwidth of 128 MB/s for *static-fast*. For *adaptive*, the reserved bandwidth of the caching device is fixed at 128 MB/s.

The Bonnie++ statistics are depicted in Figure 2. Since our approach automatically adjusts the size of the caching device after the first iteration, we depict the results for the first run and the remaining two runs separately. The initial cache size is set to 10 GB, which is lowered by our approach to 6 GB for the consecutive iterations. We denote the first iteration *adaptive-first*, and the average of the second and third iteration *adaptive-rest*.

Figure 2. Bonnie++: I/O performance under different access patterns and its corresponding I/O activity. a. Throughput for block-write (BlockW), block-overwrite (BlockO), and block-read (BlockR); b. I/O activity (reads and writes from the backing device and, if applicable, caching device)

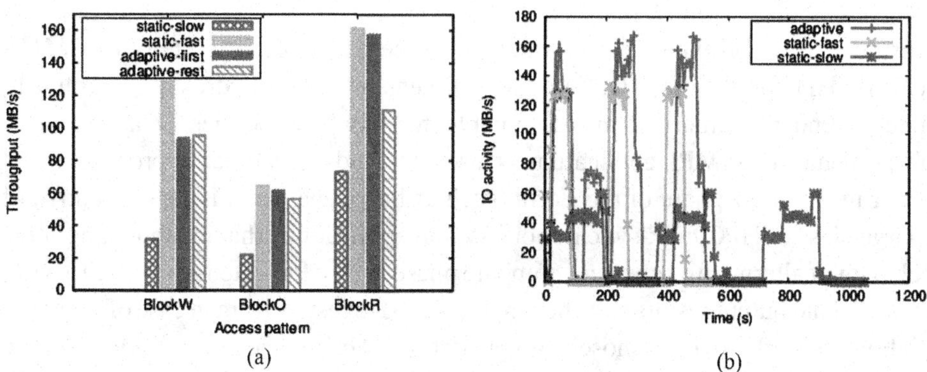

As can be observed, in the case of *static-slow*, the backing HDD limits the write throughput to 33 MB/s (out of 60 MB/s), which is not the case for *static-fast*, where the maximum write throughput of 128 MB/s can be achieved). At approximately 100 MB/s, both adaptive approaches have an overhead of 30% of write throughput compared with *static-fast*. With respect to overwrite throughput, all approaches suffer performance degradation compared with a simple write, which is due to the read, seek back, and write cycle employed by Bonnie++ for each block. The large gap between *static-slow* and the rest is still present; however, this time the overhead between the two adaptive approaches and *static-fast* is almost negligible. With respect to read throughput, a considerable increase is present for all approaches as a result of caching. Also, for the first time, a visible difference is noticeable between the two adaptive approaches: *adaptive-first* is comparable to *static-fast* whereas *adaptive-rest* has an overhead 25%. This overhead is due to the smaller size of the caching device, which forces writeback to the backing device earlier (and thus causes reads from the caching device).

To understand the interaction between the backing device and the caching device better, we depict the evolution of I/O activity (as measured at five-second granularity) in Figure 2(b). As expected, both static approaches have a highly deterministic behavior, with a flatter and elongated pattern observable for *static-slow*. In the case of *adaptive*, an initial burst is observable for the first run, which is followed by a smaller secondary burst. This secondary burst corresponds to cache flushing after *ID* elapsed that triggers the detach request. Thanks to the automatic adjustment of the size of the caching device to a smaller value, we observe earlier writeback. This causes a shorter flush burst that is fused into the primary burst, effectively enabling the caching device to be detached sooner (which reduces utilization cost).

4.3 Case Study: CM1

Our next series of experiments evaluates the behavior of our system for *CM1*, a real-life HPC application that is a three-dimensional, non-hydrostatic, nonlinear, time-dependent numerical model suitable for idealized studies of atmospheric phenomena. This MPI application is used to study small-scale processes that occur in the atmosphere of the Earth (such as hurricanes) and is representative of a large class of HPC bulk-synchronous stencil applications that exhibit an iterative behavior of alternating between a compute phase and an I/O-intensive phase to write intermediate output results and checkpoints (used to restart from in case of failures).

For this work, we have chosen as input data a 3D hurricane that is a version of the Bryan and Rotunno simulations (Bryan & Rotunno, 2009). We run the simulation of this 3D hurricane on 32 VMs, with each VM hosted on a separate physical node and equipped with 11 virtual cores (out of which 10 are reserved for CM1 and 1 reserved for guest OS overhead). Furthermore, 1 core is reserved for the hypervisor. Each VM is allocated 18 GB of RAM, enough to fill the need of the MPI processes. Thus, the overall setup totals 320 MPI processes that generate a heavy load on the underlying nodes. The output/checkpointing frequency is set at 50 simulation time steps, out of a total of 160 time steps. This setup leads to the following access pattern: right after initialization, the application dumps the initial state, which causes a first I/O-intensive phase. After that there follow three more I/O-intensive phases of higher magnitude that are interleaved with computational phases.

The settings are as follows: the size of the backing device is fixed at 50 GB, while the reserved bandwidth is fixed at 33 MB/s for *static-slow* and *adaptive* (according the maximum write throughput observed in microbenchmarks in order to avoid over-provisioning). The bandwidth in the case of *static-fast* is fixed at 128 MB/s. The caching device has a bandwidth of 128 MB/s and an initial size of 10 GB. Each experiment is repeated five times for all three approaches, and the results are averaged.

Performance results are summarized in Table 1. As can be observed, speeding the I/O phase can lead to a significant boost in overall completion time: compared with *static-fast*, which is used as a baseline, *adaptive* has a small overhead of 3.3%, which contrasts with the large overhead of 23% observed for *static-slow*. These results are significant both directly (the users want a minimal time to solution) and indirectly (longer runtimes mean the VMs need to stay up longer and thus generate more costs).

Table 1. CM1 (numerical model designed for idealized studies of atmospheric phenomena): Performance results

Approach	Completion Time	Overhead
static-slow	1471s	23%
static-fast	1190s	–
adaptive	1231s	3.3%

Even if the overhead of *adaptive* is small, it is justifiable only if the storage space and bandwidth utilization can be significantly lowered according to the cost model introduced in Section 3.2. To quantify these costs, we compute the adjusted storage accumulation for all three approaches. More specifically, for each VM instance *i*, in the case of *static-slow* we have $C_i(t)$, while for *static-fast* we have $C_i(t)$. For *adaptive*, we have:

$$C_i(t) = 33 \cdot 50 \cdot t + 128 \cdot \int_0^t M_i(x)\,dx$$

$M_i(x)$ is the size of the caching device for VM instance *i* at moment *x* and is automatically determined by our approach (0 if the caching device is not in use). To facilitate the calculation of $C_i(t)$ in practice, we assume a discretization of time at five-second granularity (i.e., we probe for the value $M_i(x)$ every five seconds and assume it stays constant during this interval). Since we have a total of 32 VM instances, the total cost in each of the three cases is:

$$C_a(t) = \sum_{i=1}^{32} C_i(t)$$

C_a is expressed in AGBs (introduced in Section 3.2) and is depicted in Figure 3. One can see a large gap between *static-slow* and *static-fast*, which steadily grows as the application progresses in time. However, not only is *adaptive* very close to *static-slow*, but overall it even manages to reduce the total adjusted storage accumulation by almost 7% because the application finishes faster. Compared with *static-fast*, this amounts to a reduction of 65% in cost, which is a large gain for the price of 3.3% performance overhead.

Figure 3. CM1 (numerical model designed for idealized studies of atmospheric phenomena): a real-life HPC application that runs on 32 VMs (each on a different node) using 10 MPI processes/node. a. Evolution of total adjusted storage accumulation for all 32 VM instances (lower is better); b. Total I/O activity (reads and writes from all backing devices and, if applicable, caching devices of all 32 VM instances)

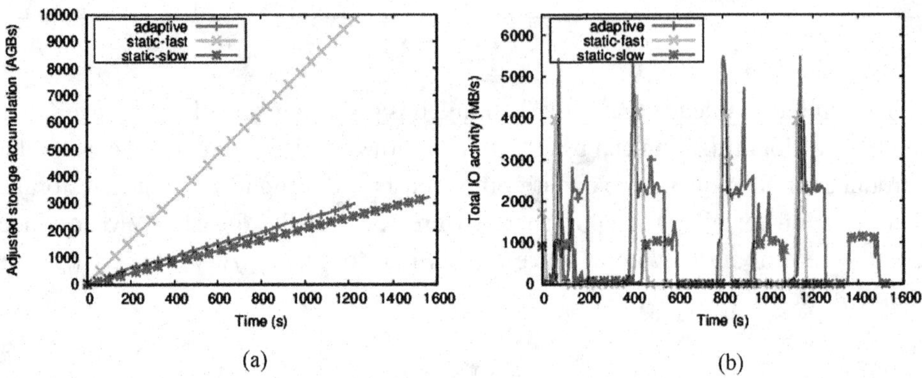

The evolution of total I/O activity in depicted in Figure 3(b). To calculate it, we divide the time (x axis) in five-second intervals and sum the I/O throughput (expressed in MB/s) observed during each interval for all VM instances (y axis). Since the application is bulk-synchronous, the I/O-intensive phases and the compute intensive phases overlap for all VM instances at the same time, leading to a clear delimitation in terms of I/O activity for all three approaches.

In the case of *static-fast* and *static-slow*, the I/O phases are short but of high amplitude and, respectively, longer but of lower amplitude. These results directly correspond to the ability of the underlying backing device to handle a fixed amount of I/O activity using a high and, respectively, low reserved bandwidth. With our approach, the behavior is more complex: the first I/O phase of the application generates a high I/O burst, followed by a clearly visible flush period. Since the first I/O phase is less intensive than the rest (for all three approaches), our approach picks a 4 GB cache device for the second phase, which then is increased to 6 GB for the last two phases. All I/O phases except the first exhibit an I/O burst that is fused to the flush period, with only a small difference noticeable between the second phase and the third, which itself is almost identical to the fourth. Intuitively, this hints at the ability of our approach to optimally adjust the cache size based on the previous I/O-intensive phases.

4.4 Case Study: LAMMPS

A second real-life HPC application we use to demonstrate the benefits of our approach is *LAMMPS* (Plimpton, 1995), a large-scale atomic/molecular massively parallel simulator. LAMMPS can be used to model atoms or, more generically, particles at the atomic, meso, or continuum scale. Such modeling is useful in understanding and designing solid-state materials (metals, semiconductors), soft matter (biomolecules, polymers), and coarse-grained or mesoscopic systems. Similar to CM1, it exhibits an iterative behavior of alternating between a compute phase and an I/O-intensive phase to write intermediate output results and checkpoints, which are used for restart in case of failures.

For this work, we have chosen as input data a 3D Lennard-Jones melting scenario. Melting, the phenomenon of phase transition from a crystalline solid state to a liquid state, is one of the most important phase transformations in the processing and applications of materials, playing an important role in materials science and engineering (Das & Singh, 2013). As in the case of CM1, we run the simulation on 32 VMs, with each VM hosted on a separate physical node and equipped with 11 virtual cores, each of which corresponds to a physical core, with the remaining physical core reserved for the hypervisor. Inside each VM, 10 of the virtual cores are reserved for MPI processes, while the remaining core is reserved for operating system overhead. Each MPI process is responsible for a 20x160x160 subdomain. Thus, the total deployment amounts to 320 MPI processes that are evenly spread over 32 VMs and process a 6400x160x160 grid. The output/checkpointing frequency is set at 30 simulation time steps, out of a total of 100 time steps. This results in an initial I/O- intensive phase to dump the initial state, followed by three I/O- intensive phases interleaved with computational phases.

The settings are identical to the setup used in Section 4.3 for CM1: the size of the backing device is fixed at 50 GB, with a reserved bandwidth of 33 MB/s for *static-slow* and *adaptive*. The bandwidth of the backing device is fixed at 128 MB/s for *static-fast*. The caching device has a bandwidth of 128 MB/s and an initial size of 10 GB. Each experiment is repeated five times for all three approaches, and the results are averaged.

Performance results are depicted in Table 2, where *static-fast* is used as a baseline for the fastest possible completion time. As can be observed, using a slow backing device in the case of *static-slow* leads to a significant increase (15.5%) in overall completion time when compared with *static-fast* because of the longer I/O phases. On the other hand, *adaptive* successfully reduces the overhead of the I/O phases to such extent that the overall increase in completion time becomes negligible (i.e., around 1%).

Figure 4. LAMMPS (Large-scale Atomic/Molecular Massively Parallel Simulator): a real-life HPC application that runs on 32 VMs (each on a different node) using 10 MPI processes/node. a. Evolution of total adjusted storage accumulation for all 32 VM instances (lower is better); b. Total I/O activity (reads and writes from all backing devices and, if applicable, caching devices of all 32 VM instances)

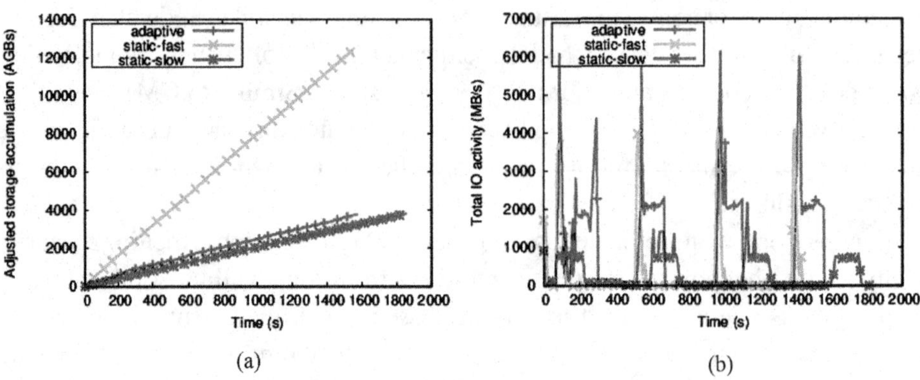

Table 2. LAMMPS (Large-scale Atomic/Molecular Massively Parallel Simulator): Performance results

Approach	Completion Time	Overhead
static-slow	1680s	15.5%
static-fast	1454s	–
adaptive	1476s	1.01%

For this negligible increase in completion time, our approach achieves massive reductions in cost when compared with *static-fast* and even a moderate reduction in cost when compared to *static-slow*. These results are depicted in Figure 4 as the total adjusted storage accumulation for all instances ($C_a(t)$). For all three approaches, $C_a(t)$ is calculated in the same way as is described in Section 4.3 (since we use the same configuration as in the case of CM1).

More specifically, *adaptive* reduces the storage accumulation by more than 70% when compared with *static-fast* and marginally by 1% compared with *static-slow* (thanks to the fact that it finishes faster), effectively making it a double winner over *static-slow* in terms of both performance and cost.

To understand how the interaction between backing devices and caching devices contributes to the results, we again analyze the total I/O activity. In Figure 4(b) a pattern similar to the case of CM1 is observable: *static-fast* and *static-slow* exhibit a short but intense I/O burst vs. a longer but milder I/O burst, with our approach successfully attaching the caching device at the right time and adapting its size based on the past experience (demonstrated by the shorter and more regular flush periods after the initial burst for the last three I/O-intensive phases when compared with the initial I/O-intensive phase where the optimal cache size is unknown).

4.5 Prediction and Optimization of Performance and Cost

In this section, we apply the techniques presented in Section 3.3 and Section 3.4 to the two HPC applications introduced above: CM1 and LAMMPS. We aim to understand: (1) how accurately our estimation is compared to the results observed in real life; (2) what cache size is recommended by our optimization technique and what impact this would have.

As a first step, we perform an extended calibration using *dd* to write a variable dataset size (3 GB, 4 GB, 6 GB and 9 GB) in chunks of 1 MB. These dataset sizes match the write patterns observed for the applications: in the case of CM1, there is an initial dump of state amounting to S_i=5 GB, while the checkpoint size S_c=4 GB. In the case of LAMMPS, S_i=4 GB, while S_c=3 GB. The cache size ranges from 2 GB to 12 GB, using an increment of 2 GB. Figure 5 depicts the results of the calibration in terms of sustained throughput (Figure 5(a)) and for how long the cache remained attached (Figure 5(b)).

With respect to the sustained throughput, there are several important observations. First, the maximum sustained throughput (i.e., 100 MB/s) is below the maximum

Figure 5. Calibration phase: Sustained throughput and cache attach duration using a variable cache size. a. Sustained throughput using dd to write a fixed-sized dataset (higher is better); b. Amount of time for which the caching device stays attached (lower is better)

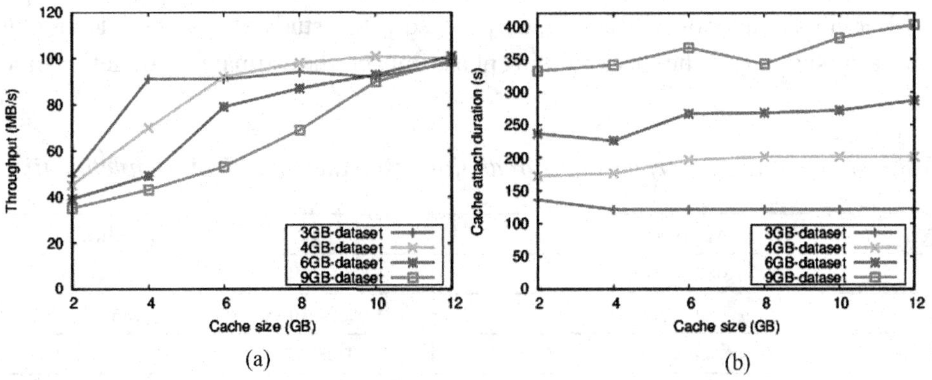

bandwidth of the caching device (i.e., 128 MB/s), which is expected because there is a delay between the moment when the I/O intensive phase starts and the moment when caching device gets attached and can accelerate the *dd* writes. Second, as anticipated in Section 3.4, it can be observed that the peak throughput is achieved when the cache size is larger than the dataset size, due to the extra overhead in managing two block devices simultaneously. Interesting to note is that the increase continues well beyond the dataset size. Conversely, when the cache size is smaller than the dataset size, the sustained throughput drops considerably. Analyzing the duration for which the caching device remains attached, it can be observed that the cache size has much less impact than the dataset size. This result is expected, as the caching device needs to stay attached only for as long as it is necessary to accumulate the written data and then flush it, which is not dependent on cache size.

Using these measurements, our first goal is to assess how accurate the estimation of the completion time and adjusted storage accumulation is when compared with the real-life results presented in Section 4.3 and Section 4.4. To this end, we first measure the baseline (i.e. completion time when running without any checkpointing), which corresponds to $I \cdot I_t$: for CM1 we obtained 1100s, while for LAMMPS we obtained 1380s. Then, using the equations for T and C_a (introduced in Section 3.3), we compute the corresponding estimations for all three approaches: for *static-fast* and *static-slow*, we use B_c=0 and fix $B(x)$=128 and, respectively, $B(x)$=33. For *adaptive*, the initial cache size is $M(S_i)$=10 GB (matching the setting used for the real-life experiments), while $M(S_c)=S_c$+2 GB, which is the dynamic cache size selected by the access pattern aware cache sizing during the checkpointing phase. Since there are three checkpoints, K=3. The estimations for T and C_a are then normalized to their real-life counterparts to obtain the accuracy. The results are summarized in Table 3 and, respectively, Table 4. As can be observed, the completion time can be predicted with high accuracy: the error is at most 1.3% underestimation, with virtually no overestimation (i.e. less than 0.5%). On the other hand, the total adjusted storage accumulation is harder to predict with the same level of accuracy: the maximum error ranges from a 4% underestimation to a 10% overestimation.

For the reminder of this section, we proceed with a study of how the selection of the cache size during the checkpointing phase impacts the estimated completion time

Table 3. Accuracy of performance prediction: estimated over real completion time

Approach	CM1	LAMMPS
static-slow	1.0009270132	0.9876623377
static-fast	1.0050420168	0.9986244842
adaptive	1.0020838484	1.003573662

Table 4. Accuracy of cost prediction: estimated over real total adjusted storage accumulation

Approach	CM1	LAMMPS
static-slow	1.0399457837	0.9613944238
static-fast	0.9888	0.9605177994
adaptive	1.1063781856	0.9898244917

and total adjusted storage accumulation. This illustrates how our proposal introduced in Section 3.4 can be used to optimize the access pattern aware cache sizing strategy in order to achieve a minimal cost for a given maximum acceptable completion time. To this end, we use the same parameters as before, but vary $M(S_c) \in [2..12]$ in the calculation of T and C_a for *adaptive*, which are then normalized against their estimated (fixed) counterparts from *static-fast*. The results are depicted in Figure 6(a)and Figure 6(b).

As expected, a higher cache size leads to a smaller estimated degradation of performance compared with *static-fast*. However, the benefits for using a $M(S_c)$ larger than 6 GB for CM1 and 4 GB for LAMMPS are becoming marginal. On the other hand, the estimated storage accumulation is minimized by fixing $M(S_c)$=4 GB in both cases. Thus, for LAMMPS the minimum cost and performance degradation coincide, whereas for CM1 it is not possible to aim for the minimum cost unless a performance degradation of 7% is acceptable. In both cases, using $M(S_c)$ less than 4 GB leads to severe degradation of performance, which also raises the cost (because of longer runtime).

Figure 6. Predicted impact of cache size on performance and cost. a. Estimated completion time, normalized to static-fast (lower is better); b. Estimated storage accumulation, normalized to static-fast (lower is better)

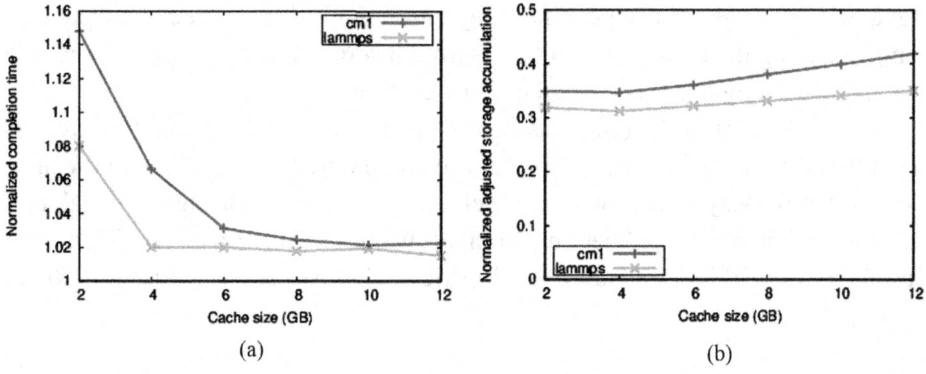

5. DISCUSSION

Cloud storage is becoming increasingly heterogeneous, as a response to user demand for differentiated quality of service. This trend is visible both with commercial and open-source providers. Amazon EBS (AmazonEBS, n.d.) has long offered both SSD and HDD based virtual disks, each with differentiated performance characteristics. Specifically, SSD based virtual disks are optimized either for general purpose I/O or to sustain high IOPS (provisioned IOPS). Similarly, HDD based virtual disks are optimized either for cold storage or to sustain high throughput. Container orchestration systems (such as Borg, Omega, Kubernetes) (Burns, Grant, Oppenheimer, Brewer, & Wilkes, 2016) typically support several volume types from various cloud services. OpenStack Cinder (OpenStack Cinder, n.d.) allows users to define their own volume type with an associated QoS. The heterogeneity aspect is further complicated by the fact that the notion of quality of service is hardly standardized between cloud providers. In many cases, it does not provide minimum I/O throughput guarantees, but rather averages and/or maximums. Such QoS metrics make it more difficult to design a performance model, but they do not impact the adaptive caching strategy, as it naturally converges to an optimal cache size even if the initial guess was incorrect. Therefore, we believe a transparent solution for I/O throughput elasticity is highly desirable and possible despite increasing complexity.

As a response to increasing complexity and heterogeneity of cloud storage, tiered solutions have become increasingly popular with users to help balance cost, access latency, reliability and capacity (Branch, Tjeerdsma, Wilson, Hurley, & McConnell, 2014). For example, OctopusFS (Kakoulli & Herodotou, 2017) utilizes multiple storage media, including memory, SSDs, HDDs and remote storage to improve the controllability and automatability of the storage system, as well as I/O performance. Scalability and high availability are also important features emphasizes by efforts such as (H. Wang & Varman, 2014; Ghoshal & Ramakrishnan, 2017). One challenge of using tiered storage is costly (in terms of performance) data movement among the tiers, which can be addressed by using caching (Zhang et al., 2010). Therefore, we argue that our proposal can become a key building block for tiered cloud storage, complementing the management of long-lived heterogeneous storage devices with ephemeral caching to lower the operational costs even further.

Hybrid cloud bursting (i.e., leasing temporary off-premise cloud resources to boost the overall capacity of an on-premise cloud during peak utilization) can be a cost-effective way to deal with the increasing complexity of big data analytics, especially for iterative applications. In this context, our previous work (Clemente-Castelló et al., 2015; Clemente-Castelló, Nicolae, Mayo, & Fernández, 2018) has introduced several efficient data management techniques and a performance model for MapReduce to enable dynamic migration of data off-premise and efficient exploitation of data locality, which key principle of big data analytics. Data migration is an effective way to improve locality and access performance, but it needs to be complemented with an elasticity dimension to keep the cost low. Therefore, we believe that our adaptive caching proposal can address this gap.

In addition to data locality, our previous work has also emphasized data shuffling as a key building block of big data analytics that has a major impact on the overall performance. Data shuffling can can be a limiting factor not only for MapReduce, but an entire family of related big data analytics frameworks, such as such as Spark (Nicolae, Costa, Misale, Katrinis, & Park, 2017). With increasing complexity of big data analytics applications, a shift from embarrassingly parallel patterns (map-intensive) to more tightly coupled patterns (reduce-intensive) that rely on data-shuffling can be noticed. When running such applications on the cloud, optimized cloud storage that can address data shuffling efficiently is needed. To this end, we envision an approach similar to our proposal for managing the I/O throughput elasticity, but specifically tailored for the I/O patterns exhibited by data shuffling.

Disaggregation allows datacenters to be architected as a collection of standalone resources instead of aggregated servers, which enables greater modularity and flexibility of growing/upgrading each type of resource independently. In this context, disaggregated memory that is shared by multiple nodes in a data-center is a promising direction, especially when considering that memory is the main scalability limitation for modern Exascale infrastructures. However, memory disaggregation is much more challenging due to the fact that processors need extremely fast access to memory, but the bandwidth required between memory and the CPU is too large and network latency is too high. Rao et al. (Rao & Porter, 2016) performed a series of experiments on Spark SQL and concluded that it is possible to disaggregate the memory using currently available network hardware and improvements in software architecture can help in performing better in a disaggregated memory environment. Recent research on memory disaggregation introduces a new architecture building block, known as the memory blade (K. Lim et al., 2009), which shares similar ideas with our approach by using fast-slow layered design but without the elasticity dimension. Overall, very little research was done in the context of disaggregated memory for cloud where elasticity plays an important role. In this context, we see our approach as a facilitator for the notion of elastic disaggregated memory: the local memory is temporarily provisioned as needed to act as a cache, while the actual permanent memory is allocated on cheap resources that live outside of the node.

6. CONCLUSION

In this paper we have described a solution that relies on a specialized block device exposed inside the guest operating system in order to intercept all I/O to a potentially slow virtual disk and enhance its throughput during I/O peaks by leveraging an additional faster, short-lived virtual disk that acts as a caching layer. Our approach offers low-level transparency that enables any higher-level storage abstraction to benefit from throughput elasticity, including those not originally designed to run on IaaS clouds. Furthermore, it relies solely on standard virtual disks to operate, which offers a high degree of compatibility with a wide range of cloud providers.

We demonstrated the benefits of this approach through experiments that involve dozens of nodes, using both microbenchmarks and two representative real-life HPC applications: CM1 and LAMMPS. Compared with static approaches that over-provision fast virtual disks to accommodate the I/O peaks, our approach demonstrates a reduction of storage cost in real life (using a cost model that charges users proportionally to disk size and reserved bandwidth) of 66%–70%, all of which is possible with a negligible performance overhead (1%–3.3%) when compared with the fastest and more expensive solution. Furthermore, our findings show that using slow virtual disks to minimize storage costs is not the optimal solution: because of higher performance degradation (15%–23%), applications end up using the cheap virtual disks for longer, thereby resulting in an overall increase in cost compared with our approach (1%–7%).

Furthermore, we have introduced a performance and cost prediction model specifically for HPC applications that interleave computationally intensive phases with write intensive phases corresponding to checkpointing. In this case, our approach aims to estimate the completion time and total adjusted storage accumulation. We have validated our proposal for the two real-life HPC application case studies: compared with the real-life results, our estimations have a maximal error of 1.3% for completion time and 10% for adjusted storage accumulation, with a best case scenario of less than 0.5% error otherwise. We also introduced a methodology to optimize the cache size used during checkpointing in order to achieve minimal cost depending on maximum acceptable completion time, which complements our the generic access pattern aware cache sizing strategy. This approach was illustrated for both real-life HPC applications.

We believe our contribution is highly relevant as a general transparent caching solution for cloud storage, as it can deliver high I/O performance without the need to over-provision devices with high QoS guarantees, for which cloud providers typically ask for premium prices. Specifically, we have identified several challenges associated with modern cloud storage (increasing heterogeneity of storage options and increasing complexity of pricing models) and have discussed how to adapt our proposal accordingly. Furthermore, we have identified several use cases beyond the original scope, both at application-level (big data analytics) and system-level (tiered storage, disaggregated memory) that can leverage our proposal and are interesting to explore as future work.

ACKNOWLEDGMENT

This material is based in part on work supported in part by the U.S. Department of Energy, Office of Science, under contract DE-AC02-06CH11357.

REFERENCES

Amazon Elastic Block Storage (S3). (n.d.). Retrieved from http://aws.amazon.com/s3/

Amazon Elastic Block Storage (EBS). (n.d.). Retrieved from http://aws.amazon.com/ebs/

BCache. (n.d.). Retrieved from http://bcache.evilpiepirate.org

Branch, R., Tjeerdsma, H., Wilson, C., Hurley, R., & McConnell, S. (2014). Cloud computing and big data: A review of current service models and hardware perspectives. *Journal of Software Engineering and Applications*, *7*(08), 686–693. doi:10.4236/jsea.2014.78063

Bryan, G. H., & Rotunno, R. (2009). The maximum intensity of tropical cyclones in axisymmetric numerical model simulations. *Journals of the American Meteorological Society*, *137*, 1770–1789.

Burns, B., Grant, B., Oppenheimer, D., Brewer, E., & Wilkes, J. (2016). Borg, omega, and kubernetes. *Queue*, *14*(1), 10:70–10:93.

Carra, D., Neglia, G., & Michiardi, P. (2018). Elastic provisioning of cloud caches: A cost-aware ttl approach. In Socc '18: The 2018 ACM symposium on cloud computing (pp. 526–526). Academic Press. doi:10.1145/3267809.3275468

Chang, Y.-H., Hsu, P.-Y., Lu, Y.-F., & Kuo, T.-W. (2011, June). A driver-layer caching policy for removable storage devices. *Trans. Storage*, *7*(1), 1:1–1:23.

Chen, J., Douglas, C., Mutsuzaki, M., Quaid, P., Ramakrishnan, R., Rao, S., & Sears, R. (2012). Walnut: A unified cloud object store. In *Sigmod '12: Proceedings of the 2012 acm sigmod international conference on management of data* (pp. 743–754). Scottsdale, AZ: ACM. 10.1145/2213836.2213947

Chiu, D., Shetty, A., & Agrawal, G. (2010). Elastic cloud caches for accelerating service-oriented computations. In *Proceedings of the 2010 acm/ieee international conference for high performance computing, networking, storage and analysis* (pp. 1–11). New Orleans, LA: IEEE Computer Society. 10.1109/SC.2010.21

Clemente-Castelló, F. J., Nicolae, B., Katrinis, K., Rafique, M. M., Mayo, R., Fernández, J. C., & Loreti, D. (2015). Enabling Big Data Analytics in the Hybrid Cloud Using Iterative MapReduce. In *Ucc'15: 8th IEEE/ACM international conference on utility and cloud computing* (pp. 290–299). Limassol, Cyprus: IEEE/ACM.

Clemente-Castelló, F. J., Nicolae, B., Mayo, R., & Fernández, J. C. (2018). Performance model of mapreduce iterative applications for hybrid cloud bursting. *IEEE Transactions on Parallel and Distributed Systems*, *29*(8), 1794–1807. doi:10.1109/TPDS.2018.2802932

Cooper, B. F., Ramakrishnan, R., Srivastava, U., Silberstein, A., Bohannon, P., Jacobsen, H.-A., … Yerneni, R. (2008, August). Pnuts: Yahoo!'s hosted data serving platform. *Proc. VLDB Endow.*, *1*(2), 1277–1288. 10.14778/1454159.1454167

Das, C., & Singh, J. (2013). Melting transition of confined lennard-jones solids in slit pores. *Theoretical Chemistry Accounts*, *132*(4), 1351. doi:10.100700214-013-1351-y

Forney, B. C., Arpaci-Dusseau, A. C., & Arpaci-Dusseau, R. H. (2002). Storage-aware caching: Revisiting caching for heterogeneous storage systems. In *Fast'02: Proc. 1st USENIX conference on file and storage technologies* (pp. 5–5). USENIX.

Ghoshal, D., & Ramakrishnan, L. (2017). Madats: Managing data on tiered storage for scientific workflows. In *Hpdc'17: The 26th international symposium on high-performance parallel and distributed computing* (pp. 41–52). Academic Press.

Google. (2014). *Google Compute Engine Pricing*. Retrieved from https://developers.google.com/compute/pricing

Hoefler, T., Schneider, T., & Lumsdaine, A. (2010). Characterizing the influence of system noise on large-scale applications by simulation. In *Sc '10: Proceedings of the 23rd ACM/IEEE international conference for high performance computing, networking, storage and analysis* (pp. 1–11). New Orleans, LA: IEEE Computer Society. 10.1109/SC.2010.12

Hou, B., & Chen, F. (2017). Gds-lc: A latency- and cost-aware client caching scheme for cloud storage. *ACM Trans. Storage, 13*(4), 40:1–40:33.

Jo, H., Kwon, Y., Kim, H., Seo, E., Lee, J., & Maeng, S. (2010). Ssd-hdd-hybrid virtual disk in consolidated environments. In *Euro-par'09: Proc. 15th international conference on parallel processing* (pp. 375–384). Delft, The Netherlands: Academic Press.

Kakoulli, E., & Herodotou, H. (2017). Octopusfs: A distributed file system with tiered storage management. In The 2017 ACM international conference on management of data (pp. 65–78). ACM. doi:10.1145/3035918.3064023

Karampaglis, Z., Gounaris, A., & Manolopoulos, Y. (2014). A bi-objective cost model for database queries in a multi-cloud environment. In *Medes '14: The 6th international conference on management of emergent digital ecosystems* (pp. 19:109–19:116). Buraidah, Al Qassim, Saudi Arabia: Academic Press. 10.1145/2668260.2668271

Kgil, T., & Mudge, T. (2006). Flashcache: a nand flash memory file cache for low power web servers. In Cases'16: The 2006 international conference on compilers, architecture and synthesis for embedded systems (pp. 103–112). Seoul, South Korea: Academic Press. doi:10.1145/1176760.1176774

Li, C., Shilane, P., Douglis, F., Shim, H., Smaldone, S., & Wallace, G. (2014). Nitro: A capacity-optimized ssd cache for primary storage. In *Usenix annual technical conference* (pp. 501–512). USENIX.

Lim, H. C., Babu, S., & Chase, J. S. (2010). Automated control for elastic storage. In *Icac '10: Proc. 7th international conference on autonomic computing* (pp. 1–10). Washington, DC: Academic Press.

Lim, K., Chang, J., Mudge, T., Ranganathan, P., Reinhardt, S. K., & Wenisch, T. F. (2009). Disaggregated memory for expansion and sharing in blade servers. *ACM SIGARCH Computer Architecture News*, *37*(3), 267–278. doi:10.1145/1555815.1555789

Liu, M., Jin, Y., Zhai, J., Zhai, Y., Shi, Q., Ma, X., & Chen, W. (2013). Acic: Automatic cloud i/o configurator for hpc applications. In *Sc '13: The 26th international conference on high performance computing, networking, storage and analysis* (pp. 38:1–38:12). Denver, CO: Academic Press.

Luo, T., Ma, S., Lee, R., Zhang, X., Liu, D., & Zhou, L. (2013). S-cave: Effective ssd caching to improve virtual machine storage performance. In *Pact '13: Proc. 22nd international conference on parallel architectures and compilation techniques* (pp. 103–112). Edinburgh, UK: Academic Press.

Meyer, D. T., Aggarwal, G., Cully, B., Lefebvre, G., Feeley, M. J., Hutchinson, N. C., & Warfield, A. (2008, April). Parallax: Virtual disks for virtual machines. *SIGOPS Oper. Syst. Rev.*, *42*(4), 41–54. doi:10.1145/1357010.1352598

Nicolae, B., Bresnahan, J., Keahey, K., & Antoniu, G. (2011). Going back and forth: Efficient multi-deployment and multi-snapshotting on clouds. In *Hpdc '11: 20th international ACM symposium on high-performance parallel and distributed computing* (p. 147-158). San José: ACM.

Nicolae, B., & Cappello, F. (2013, May). BlobCR: Virtual disk based checkpoint-restart for HPC applications on IaaS clouds. *Journal of Parallel and Distributed Computing*, *73*(5), 698–711. doi:10.1016/j.jpdc.2013.01.013

Nicolae, B., Costa, C., Misale, C., Katrinis, K., & Park, Y. (2017). Leveraging adaptive i/o to optimize collective data shuffling patterns for big data analytics. *IEEE Transactions on Parallel and Distributed Systems*, *28*(6), 1663–1674. doi:10.1109/TPDS.2016.2627558

Nicolae, B., Karve, A., & Kochut, A. (2015). Discovering and Leveraging Content Similarity to Optimize Collective On-Demand Data Access to IaaS Cloud Storage. In *Ccgrid'15: 15th IEEE/ACM international symposium on cluster, cloud and grid computing* (p. 211-220). Shenzhen, China: IEEE/ACM. 10.1109/CCGrid.2015.156

Nicolae, B., & Rafique, M. (2013). Leveraging Collaborative Content Exchange for On-Demand VM Multi-Deployments in IaaS Clouds. In *Euro-par '13: 19th international euro-par conference on parallel processing* (pp. 305–316). Aachen, Germany: Academic Press. 10.1007/978-3-642-40047-6_32

Nicolae, B., Riteau, P., & Keahey, K. (2014a). Bursting the cloud data bubble: Towards transparent storage elasticity in iaas clouds. In *Ipdps '14: Proc. 28th IEEE international parallel and distributed processing symposium*. Phoenix, AZ: IEEE.

Nicolae, B., Riteau, P., & Keahey, K. (2014b). Transparent Throughput Elasticity for IaaS Cloud Storage Using Guest-Side Block-Level Caching. In *Ucc'14: 7th IEEE/ACM international conference on utility and cloud computing* (pp. 186–195). London, UK: IEEE/ACM. 10.1109/UCC.2014.27

Nicolae, B., Riteau, P., & Keahey, K. (2015). Towards Transparent Throughput Elasticity for IaaS Cloud Storage: Exploring the Benefits of Adaptive Block-Level Caching. *International Journal of Distributed Systems and Technologies*, *6*(4), 21–44. doi:10.4018/IJDST.2015100102

Openstack cinder. (n.d.). Retrieved from https://docs.openstack.org/cinder

Perez-Palacin, D., Calinescu, R., & Merseguer, J. (2013). Log2cloud: Log-based prediction of cost-performance trade-offs for cloud deployments. In *Sac '13: The 28th annual ACM symposium on applied computing* (pp. 397–404). Coimbra, Portugal: ACM.

Plimpton, S. (1995, March). Fast parallel algorithms for short-range molecular dynamics. *Journal of Computational Physics*, *117*(1), 1–19. doi:10.1006/jcph.1995.1039

Puttaswamy, K. P., Nandagopal, T., & Kodialam, M. (2012). Frugal storage for cloud file systems. In *Eurosys '12: The 7th ACM European conference on computer systems* (pp. 71–84). Bern, Switzerland: ACM. 10.1145/2168836.2168845

Qiu, S., & Reddy, A. L. N. (2013). Nvmfs: A hybrid file system for improving random write in nand-flash ssd. In *Msst' 13: Proc. 38th international conference on massive storage systems and technology* (p. 1-5). Academic Press. 10.1109/MSST.2013.6558434

Rao, P. S., & Porter, G. (2016). Is memory disaggregation feasible? A case study with spark sql. In Ancs'16: The 2016 symposium on architectures for networking and communications systems (pp. 75–80). Santa Clara, CA: Academic Press.

Saxena, M., Swift, M. M., & Zhang, Y. (2012). Flashtier: a lightweight, consistent and durable storage cache. In *Eurosys'12: The 7th ACM European conference on computer systems* (pp. 267–280). Bern, Switzerland: ACM. 10.1145/2168836.2168863

SoftLayer. (n.d.). Retrieved from http://www.softlayer.com/

Tesfatsion, S. K., Klein, C., & Tordsson, J. (2018). Virtualization Techniques Compared: Performance, Resource, and Power Usage Overheads in Clouds. In *ICPE '18: The 2018 ACM/SPEC International Conference on Performance Engineering* (pp. 145–156). Berlin, Germany: ACM.

The QCOW2 Image Format. (n.d.). Retrieved from https://people.gnome.org/~markmc/qcow-image-format.html

Vo, H. T., Wang, S., Agrawal, D., Chen, G., & Ooi, B. C. (2012, June). Logbase: A scalable log-structured database system in the cloud. *Proc. VLDB Endow., 5*(10), 1004–1015. 10.14778/2336664.2336673

Wang, A.-I. A., Kuenning, G., Reiher, P., & Popek, G. (2006, August). The conquest file system: Better performance through a disk/persistent-ram hybrid design. *Trans. Storage, 2*(3), 309–348. doi:10.1145/1168910.1168914

Wang, H., & Varman, P. J. (2014). Balancing fairness and efficiency in tiered storage systems with bottleneck-aware allocation. In *Fast'14: The 12th USENIX conference on file and storage technologies* (Vol. 14, pp. 229–242). USENIX.

Wang, Y., Shu, J., Zhang, G., Xue, W., & Zheng, W. (2010, July). Sopa: Selecting the optimal caching policy adaptively. *Trans. Storage, 6*(2), 7:1–7:18.

White, T. (2009). *Hadoop: The definitive guide*. O'Reilly Media, Inc.

Wu, G., He, X., & Eckart, B. (2012, February). An adaptive write buffer management scheme for flash-based ssds. *Trans. Storage, 8*(1), 1:1–1:24.

Xu, Y., Arteaga, D., Zhao, M., Liu, Y., Figueiredo, R. J. O., & Seelam, S. (2012). vPFS: Bandwidth virtualization of parallel storage systems. In *Msst' 12: Proc. 38th international conference on massive storage systems and technology* (p. 1-12). Academic Press.

Zhang, G., Chiu, L., Dickey, C., Liu, L., Muench, P., & Seshadri, S. (2010). Automated lookahead data migration in ssd-enabled multi-tiered storage systems. In *Msst'10: 26th IEEE symposium on mass storage systems and technologies* (pp. 1–6). IEEE. 10.1109/MSST.2010.5496999

Chapter 8
Accessing Data From Multiple Heterogeneous Distributed Database Systems

Shefali Trushit Naik
Ahmedabad University, India

ABSTRACT

This chapter describes the method to retrieve data from multiple heterogeneous distributed relational database management systems such as MySQL, PostgreSQL, MS SQL Server, MS Access, etc. into Oracle RDBMS using Oracle's Heterogeneous Gateway Services. The complete process starting from downloading and installation of required software, creation of data source names using open database connectivity, modification of system parameter files, checking connections, creation of synonyms for tables of remote databases into oracle, creation of database links and accessing data from non-oracle databases using database links is explained in great detail. Apart from this, data manipulation in remote databases from Oracle and execution of PL/SQL procedures to manipulate data residing on remote databases is discussed with examples. Troubleshooting common errors during this process is also discussed.

DOI: 10.4018/978-1-5225-8295-3.ch008

1. INTRODUCTION

In current era, people of all the ages use database in one or the other way directly or indirectly. Computerized Database has made our life very easy and comfortable. We can search any place, product, area, thing, etc. with the help of stored data in a fraction of seconds. People widely use e-commerce websites for sales, purchase, booking, and many other things. Massive amount of data are processed daily over networks. It is impossible to keep and process these data on a single site. Therefore, the data need to be stored at different sites, which user should be allowed to access from anywhere. To implement this functionality, the distribution of data is required. Using network topologies, operating systems, database management systems and computers, it is possible to access data stored at different sites geographically. These types of databases are called Distributed Databases.

Distributed database is a concept in which the physical database (tables) is distributed on different locations or computers known as sites. All the computers are connected through communication network with each other. The distribution of data could be full, partial or not at all. Before distribution, tables are partitioned and if needed replicas of these partitions are created and stored on different locations. There are three dimensions namely Autonomy, Distribution and Heterogeneity; which decide the strength of distributed database (Özsu & Valduriez, 2011). Presence or absence of any of these three dimensions defines the database type. There are three well-known architectures of distributed databases-client/server, peer to peer and multi-database (Breitbart, Morales, Silberschatz, & Thompson, 1990). The systems which have full distribution capacity are called peer-to-peer systems. These systems are fully distributed in nature which shares all their data with other sites to execute transaction and to manipulate the data. The sites which have partial distribution capacity are called client-server systems. This distribution is the most popular. In client-server system, the application resides on client, the data is managed on server and the communication is done by both client and server (Özsu & Valduriez, 2011). Multi-database systems are fully autonomous. These are the system in which the database is installed on each machine and they are interconnected. In DDBMS, the processing can be done at any site (Beraka, Mathkour, & Gannouni, 2011). Users sitting on these sites can access and manipulate local and remote data. On different sites, hardware and software used may be uniform or different. If they are uniform, the type of distributed database system is called Homogeneous Distributed Database System, but if different it is called Heterogeneous Distributed Database System. For ex., the database which is distributed on four different sites (computers), each having different database management systems namely Oracle,

MySQL, PostgreSQL and MS SQL Server, the distributed database system known as Heterogeneous Distributed Database. To retrieve, manipulate and store data from these type of multiple heterogeneous distributed database systems; on each site some mechanism is required which will allow to do so. Many RDBMS provide Replication to fetch and manipulate data from different databases which are created within that same RDBMS (homogeneous databases). The comparison is given in the following section. None of the RDBMS except Oracle supports data retrieval and manipulation from different RDBMS (heterogeneous databases). Oracle RDBMS provides Heterogeneous Gateway Service using which data from different non-oracle RDBMS could be retrieved, manipulated and stored back to that database. The implementation of heterogeneous distributed database system is quite challenging which is described step-wise in great detail in this chapter.

2. LITERATURE REVIEW AND RELATED WORK

There are few RDBMSs like MS SQL Server, PostgreSQL, MySQL, Oracle which provide facility to distribute data across different sites through communication network. The mechanism provided by various RDBMS is discussed here. MS SQL Server provides the architecture which needs user to configure Distributor Servers, Publisher Server and Distribution Database for Availability Group. The detailed steps are given in the documentation of Microsoft. Replicas can be added and removed in the distribution database. The limitations of this configuration are no support for local distributor, Oracle publisher, Merge replication Peer to peer replication and Transactional replication. PostgreSQL provides Replicator (Sourikova, n.d.) to build distributed database which is free. It works on top of Postgres Database. It provides peer to peer asynchronous replication. But database replication is partial because only latest updates are transferred over the network. Different companies provide forks or patches for PostgreSQL database to build distributed database. MySQL Replication (Bojovic, 2015; Microsoft, 2019) provides only Master-Slave Replication to build distributed database. In this, the replication is possible only from Master to Slave. It means only write operation is possible on Master database, while read operation is possible on multiple Slaves databases. Oracle (2019) provides Database Links to build distributed database environment. It is full proof, only thing is it is expensive. Using all these methods only homogeneous distributed database environment could be created but that is too with limitations, Oracle is the exception. It is not possible to create heterogeneous distributed database environment using these RDBMS, except Oracle.

There are many applications which use data from different databases to modify or access them. To do this, application has to create connection to each of them and open the connection which leads to complex logic (Ganesan, n.d.). This also results in data integrity issues between the databases which leads to inconsistent data. To resolve this synchronization issue, Oracle provides the concept of distributed processing, where the application connects to one local database (created in Oracle) and this local database transparently (location and database transparency) connects to the other databases (non-oracle remote databases). The data dictionary and structured query language of the Oracle database are used for the non-Oracle database through the heterogeneous gateway services using which multiple heterogeneous distributed database environment could be created. The step-wise process to create multiple heterogeneous distributed database environment and, accessing and manipulating data in this environment is discussed in the following section in detail.

3. ACCESSING DATA FROM MULTIPLE HETEROGENEOUS DISTRIBUTED DATABASES

3.1 Software Requirements

The following software are required to set up distributed database environment and to manage distributed data from Oracle in Windows operating system. Before installation of these software, check the configuration of your windows operating system. If it is 32-bit, download and install all the software for 32-bit, else install accordingly. All the software referred in this chapter are for 32-bit system. Oracle software are expensive, but it is made available for free for educational purpose on Oracle Technology Network (OTN) (Oracle, n.d.). All other software are open source which could be downloaded from internet. Install the list of software given below.

3.1.1 Oracle 11g Server and Client

Search these files- win32_11gR2_database_1of2.zip and win32_11gR2_database_2of2.zip on OTN, unzip them and run setup.exe from the first file's unzipped folder to install Oracle 11g by providing required information. This version includes functionalities of partitioning and materialized views. The SQL Plus Oracle client is also installed along with server program to access data from Oracle Server. It is installed on a stand-alone machine. The database instance and required users are created after installation to access the data.

3.1.2 Oracle 11g Client Library

Download win32_11gR2_client.zip from OTN, unzip it and install it to enable the oracle heterogeneous service.

3.1.3 Oracle 11g Heterogeneous Gateway Service

Download win32_11gR2_gateways.exe from OTN and execute. To set up the heterogeneous distributed database environment, Oracle's heterogeneous gateways (Oracle, 2012; Oracle, 2011; Oracle, 2007) are used. These gateways work as a communication channel between Oracle DBMS and non-Oracle DBMS. Using these gateways, distributed data stored on the remote databases could be accessed and manipulated from the Oracle RDBMS. It provides location and database transparency in the distributed environment, which means there is no need to provide physical address of the machine where the remote database is stored. The main advantage is, from oracle client using oracle's native commands, user can access data from the remote databases. Oracle provides gateways to many non-oracle systems such as DB2, Sybase, Informix, MS SQL Server, etc. It also provides gateways for ODBC which is general solution that uses ODBC driver to access any ODBC compliant database system such as MS Access, PostgreSQL, MySQL, MS Excel, etc.

Oracle Heterogeneous Gateway is composed of two components - Heterogeneous Service (HS) and an agent. Heterogeneous Service is common for all the non-oracle systems. It provides the technology to connect with non-oracle systems, recognize SQL, process PL/SQL and mapping to access metadata. It also maintains the transactions coordination between oracle and non-oracle databases. The agent provides datatype conversion, mappings and interface between oracle and non-oracle databases. It interacts with the Heterogeneous Service to provide transparent connectivity between oracle and remote databases. Figure 1 shows the architecture of Oracle heterogeneous gateway. To connect Oracle and non-oracle database, heterogeneous gateway and client libraries are required to be installed. The database link to connect with a non-Oracle database instance should be created in Oracle, ODBC driver of specific database to be installed and required parameter files need to be created.

The following sequence is followed to process the query from Oracle to non-Oracle database.

1. The query is sent by user application to Oracle through oracle net.
2. HS gateway converts query into the form which is understandable by non-Oracle databases.
3. Then it is sent through oracle net to the HS gateway.

Figure 1. Architecture of Oracle Heterogeneous Gateway

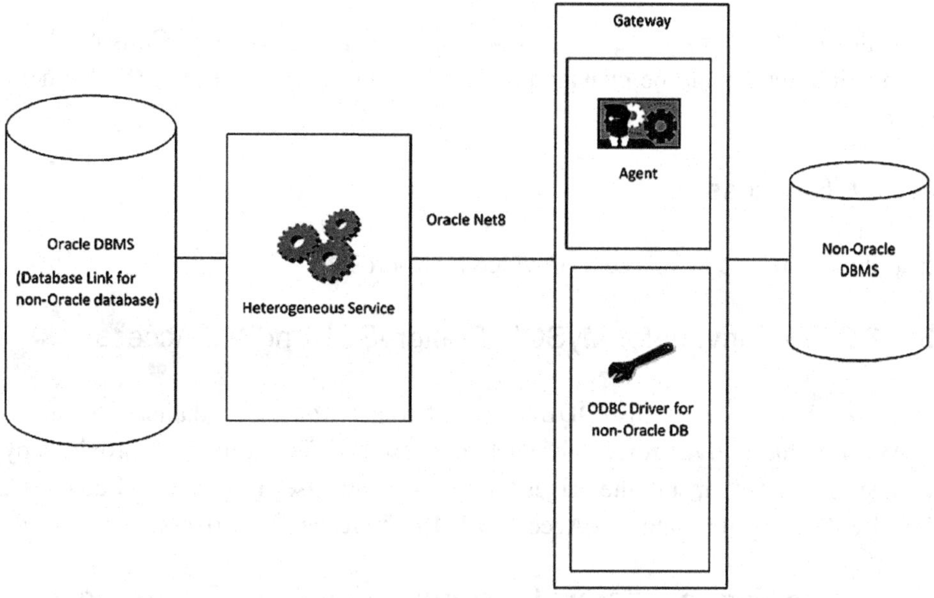

4. Using username and password specified in the database link created on oracle for the non-oracle database, the gateway logs in to non-oracle database.
5. Gateway fetches data using query statement of non-oracle database.
6. Gateway converts the fetched data into the format of oracle database.
7. Result is sent by the gateway to oracle database using oracle net.
8. Oracle sends result to the user application using oracle net.

3.1.4 MySQL (WAMP) Server

Download and run Wampserver2.4-x86.exe to access MySQL Console. WAMP (Windows, Apache, MySQL and any one of PHP, Perl or Python) Server is installed to access MySQL 5.6.12 from it. WAMP Server could be installed only on windows. Using MySQL Console, the database is accessed and data could be managed within it. MySQL ODBC 5.3 Unicode Driver is also installed to connect MySQL and Oracle databases through oracle heterogeneous gateway.

3.1.5 PostgreSQL Server

Download and run postgresql-9.2.2-1-windows.exe to access PSQL Console. After installation, data could be managed using either PGAdmin or PSQL (SQL Shell) clients.

3.1.6 MS Access

Install the database MS Access provided by Microsoft.

3.1.7 ODBC Drivers for MySQL, PostgreSQL and MS Access

Open Database Connectivity (ODBC) is used to access data from database using the ODBC interface. ODBC driver for each database is different. It is not provided by Oracle. User has to install the driver for specific database. To connect Oracle with PostgreSQL, MySQL and MS Access DBMS, the respective drivers are installed.

3.2 Set Up Heterogeneous Distributed Database Environment

There are many challenges and issues (Adiba, Chupin, Demolombe, Gardarin, & Le Bihan, 1978; Paliwal & Subash, n.d.) in distributed database implementation. One of the challenges is obtaining database transparency. Transparency means the details should be hidden from user. In other words, when users access data from multiple heterogeneous databases (Chung, 1990; Ferrier & Stangret, 1982; Fummi, Martini, Monguzzi, Perbellini, & Poncino, 2004; Khokhar, Prasanna, Shaaban, & Wang, 1993; Lee, Chapin, & Taylor, 2003; Pu, Leff, & chen, 1991; Yu, Zhang, Yang, Ding, & Wang, 2003), they do not worry about how to access data, in which format it should be stored, etc. In distributed database, there are several methods of data access from distributed databases, but it involves complicated implementation of these methods. The data access and distributed transaction execution is made very easy through this oracle heterogeneous gateway. The successful implementation of data access from multiple heterogeneous databases provides very easy and efficient access of data in Oracle using its native language/commands. Oracle user will neither have to bother about architecture nor commands of the remote databases from where data is accessed. Even user need not have to worry about the location of database. Once all the databases are connected through heterogeneous gateway, user will be able to access data and process distributed transactions efficiently from Oracle. The procedure to connect four heterogeneous databases namely PostgreSQL, MySQL, Oracle and MS Access is described in the following sections. In Distributed Database (Özsu & Valduriez, 2011) the physical database is distributed across multiple sites. One of the architecture of distributed database management system is multiple heterogeneous distributed databases (Sharaf, Chrysanthis, Labrinidis, Pruhs, 2008). In multiple heterogeneous distributed database environment, autonomous multiple databases residing on different locations (Sun, Chen, & Wu, 2005; Wang & Spooner, 1987; Yu, Zhang, Yang, Ding, Wang, 2003; Zhang & Orlowska, 1993) are connected together to access data of each other. To achieve location and database transparency, Oracle provides heterogeneous gateway service. With location transparency, user can access the data without knowledge of location of data. i.e., user doesn't have to specify the location of data in the commands. Similarly, with database transparency, user will be able to access data from many databases without knowledge of commands of all the databases. The implementation steps of accessing data from multiple heterogeneous databases are explained following. The process of establishing connection between oracle and non-oracle database require deep knowledge of databases. To access data from multiple heterogeneous databases, the respective DBMS software along with its ODBC drivers must be installed. Oracle heterogeneous service is also required which could be installed from oracle technology network. The client library of oracle is also needed. The sequence of flow given below should be followed to connect and access data from non-oracle database to oracle.

3.2.1 Multiple Heterogeneous Database Architecture

Figure 2 shows multiple heterogeneous database architecture which connects PostgreSQL, MySQL, MS Access and Oracle database using Oracle's Heterogeneous Gateway Service.

3.2.2 Steps to Connect Oracle and Non-Oracle Databases

The brief sequence given below should be followed to connect and access data from non-oracle database to oracle.

Step-1 Install Oracle Server, Oracle Client Library and Oracle Heterogeneous Gateway Service from oracle technology network.

Step-2 Install PostgreSQL, MySQL and MS Access databases with respective ODBC drivers.

Step-3 Create users in PostgreSQL and MySQL databases. Grant required privileges to the users. Create tables in specific user's account. Insert data in these tables.

Step-4 Open ODBC data source and create three system data source names for each postgreSQL, MySQL and MS Access databases. Test connections.

Step-5 After successful connections, create three initialization parameter files for each of the system DSN with name "init<DSN>.ora". Save this file in the folder

Figure 2. Multiple Heterogeneous Database Architecture

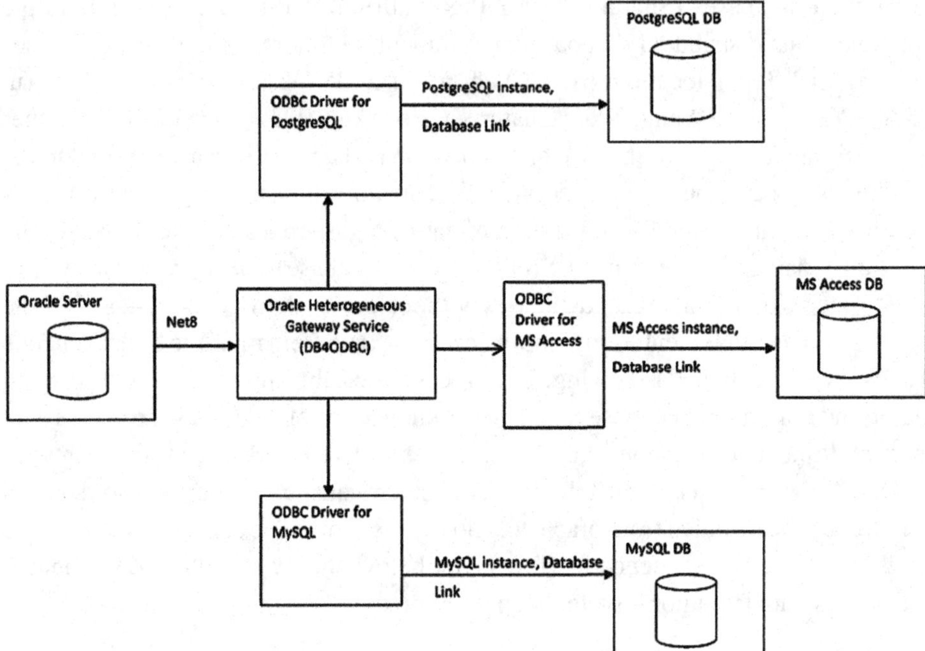

where oracle home is installed. This file will contain name of the database instance, which is system DSN name.

Step-6 Open listener.ora and tnsnames.ora files from the folder where oracle home is installed. Modify both the files with required entries and save.

Step-7 Start listener service from command prompt. Check connection of each of the database instance using “tnsping <DSN>” command.

Step-8 Create database links in oracle client to access data from non-oracle database.

Step-9 Access data from non-oracle database using query language of oracle.

3.2.3 Flowchart of Process to Connect Oracle and Non-Oracle Databases

The flowchart of whole process of oracle with non-oracle database connection and data access is given in Figure 3.

Figure 3. Flowchart of connection of oracle and non-oracle databases

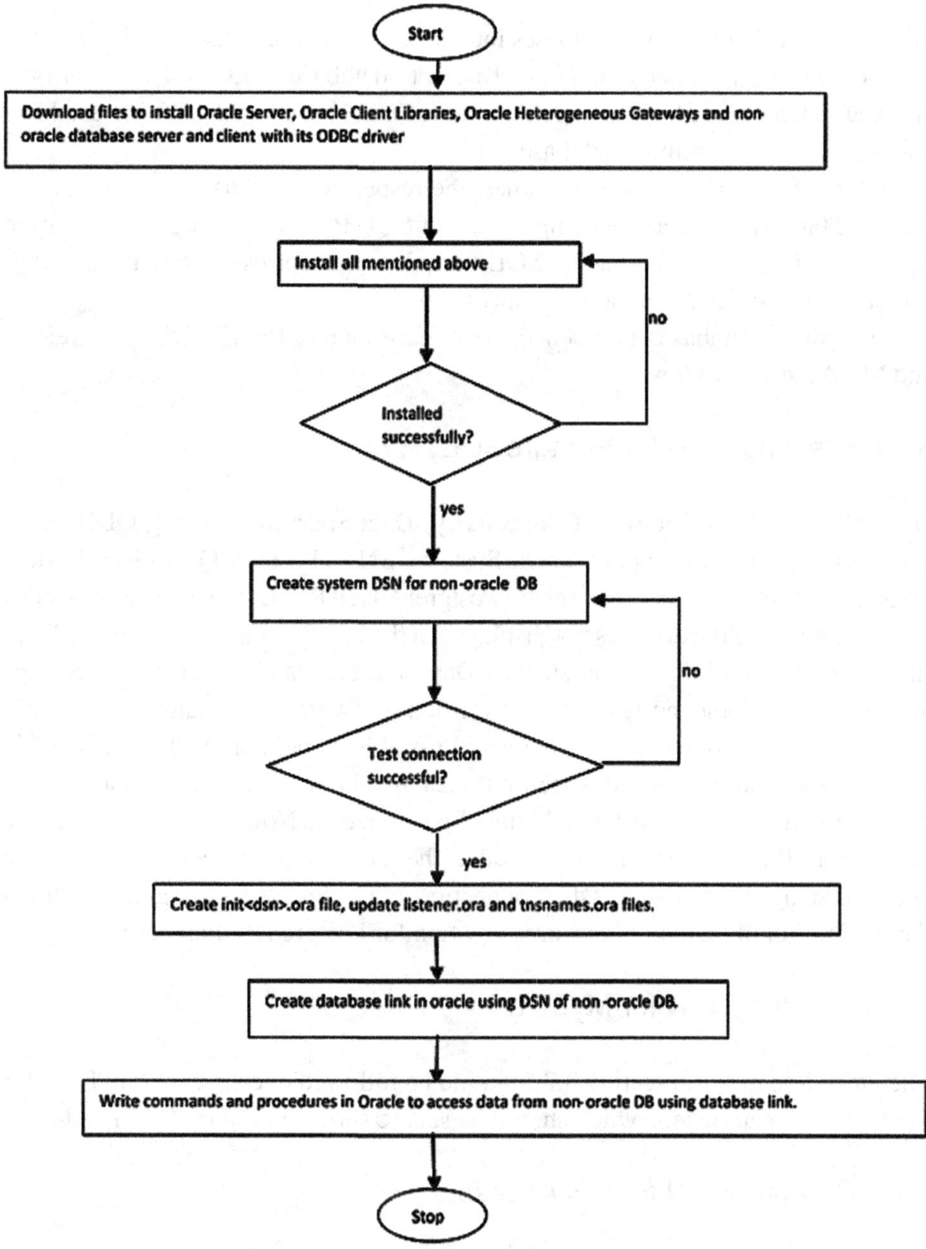

3.2.4 Creating Data Source Names (DSN)

To access data from remote databases into Oracle, database links should be created in oracle for each remote databases. To create database links, system identifiers are required. System identifiers are data source names which enable us to establish connection with the remote database.

Before we create data source names, the respective database server should be started. Start oracle database using the client SQL Plus by logging in as sys user. Start WAMP server and open MySQL console with root user. Start PostgreSQL server using psql client and login as any user.

After all the databases are opened, create data sources for MySQL, PostgreSQL and MS Access as follows.

3.2.5 Creating DSN for PostgreSQL

Open ODBC (Open DataBase Connectivity) Data Source (by typing ODBC data source in windows search box) to create System DSN for PostgreSQL. Select "System DSN" tab→click "Add" button→select "PostgreSQL ODBC Driver(Unicode)"→click "Finish" button(If the driver is not displayed in the list, first install the driver). Now, fill in the required information such as Data Source, Database: postgres, Server: localhost, User Name: postgres, Port: 5433 and Password in the dialog box which is opened. The data source name is any valid variable name. For ex., here it is "PG". The database and user within specified database should exists in the portgreSQL database before it is used here. If not, first create it. Now, click "Test" to test connection. If all the credentials are valid, the message for successful connection will be displayed. After successful connection, click "Save" button. Figure 4 shows the screen shot of ODBC data source creation for PostgreSQL database.

3.2.6 Creating DSN for MySQL

The procedure given in section 3.2.5 should be followed to create System DSN for MySQL. The parameters which should be set are shown in Figure 5 with values.

3.2.7 Creating DSN for MS Access

First create MS Access database and save it in a specific location. Now, open ODBC data sourc→Click on System DSN→ click "Add" button→Select appropriate "Microsoft Access Driver" from the list→click "Finish". Now, write any valid variable name in the "Data Source Name" text box→Write "Description"(This is

Figure 4. Creating DSN for PostgreSQL

Figure 5. Creating DSN for MySQL

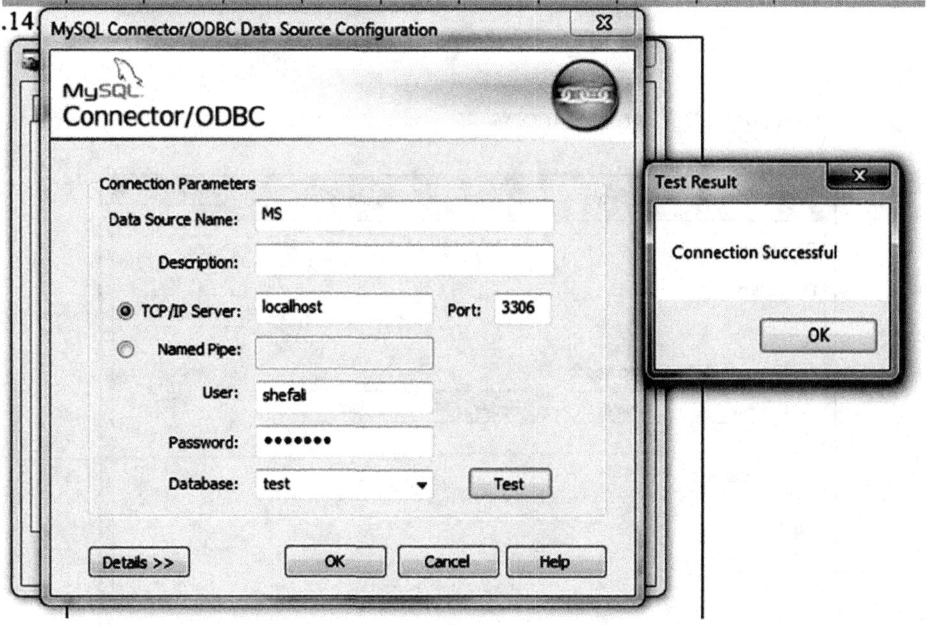

optional)→Click on "Select" button to select MS Access database which you have created before. Click "OK". Figure 6 shows the creation of DSN for MS Access.

3.2.8 Creating Initialization Parameter Files in Oracle for Non-Oracle Databases

After data source names are created for remote databases, the initialization parameter files for each remote databases should be created. These are text files which will contain name of the DSN as a System Identifier name.

The initialization parameter files should have the name init<sid>.ora where "init" is the prefix and sid is the DSN name. To create init<sid>.ora files search inithsodbc.ora file, open it and save it with the name "init + system DSN name". ora. Assume that DSN for PostgreSQL is "PG", DSN for MySQL is "MS" and DSN for MS Access is "AC". Therefore, three files with names initpg.ora, initms.ora and initac.ora need to be created for PostgreSQL, MySQL and MS Access databases respectively. These files must be saved in the folder "hs" which must be there in the folder where "oracle_home" parameter resides). To search directory of oracle_home, execute the following commands in SYS user in Oracle SQL Plus.

```
SQL> var oraclehome varchar2(500);
SQL> exec dbms_system.get_env('ORACLE_HOME',:oraclehome);
SQL> print oraclehome;
```

Figure 6. Creating DSN for MS Access

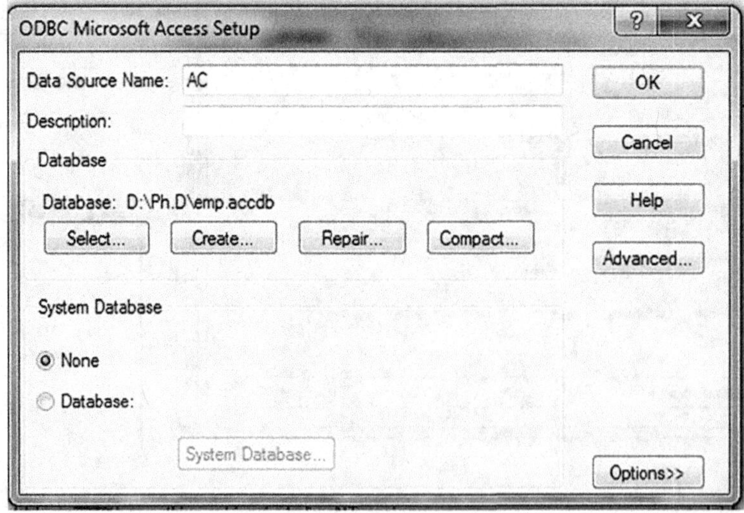

Now, open the file initpg.ora and set the parameters HS_FDS_CONNECT_INFO = PG (PG is the System DSN for PostgreSQL) and HS_FDS_TRACE_LEVEL = ON. Save the file and close it. Do the same for MySQL and MS Acess. In initms.ora set HS_FDS_CONNECT_INFO = MS (MS is the System DSN for MySQL) and HS_FDS_TRACE_LEVEL = ON. In initac.ora set HS_FDS_CONNECT_INFO = AC (AC is the System DSN for MS Access) and HS_FDS_TRACE_LEVEL = ON. Remember that additional parameters for language could also be set as per the requirement. Screen shot of initpg.ora file is given in Figure 7.

3.2.9 Modifying Listener.ora and Tnsnames.ora Files for Non-Oracle Databases

Open listener.ora file to add PostgreSQL DSN in it. Add the following code with sid_name=pg (pg is the DSN for PostgreSQL) and program=dg4odbc (note: In oracle version 11g and higher the program need to be set as dg4odbc.). Set the value of oracle_home variable as per your setting.

```
(SID_DESC = (SID_NAME = PG)
(ORACLE_HOME = D:\app\Aalap\product\11.2.0\dbhome_1) (PROGRAM =
dg4odbc))
```

Similarly, copy this code for MySQL and MS Access databases with their respective DSNs. Also, set the parameter KEY=PNPKEY. Save and close listener. ora file. Figure 8 shows the screenshot of listener.ora file.

Figure 7. Initialization parameter file named initpg.ora for PostgreSQL

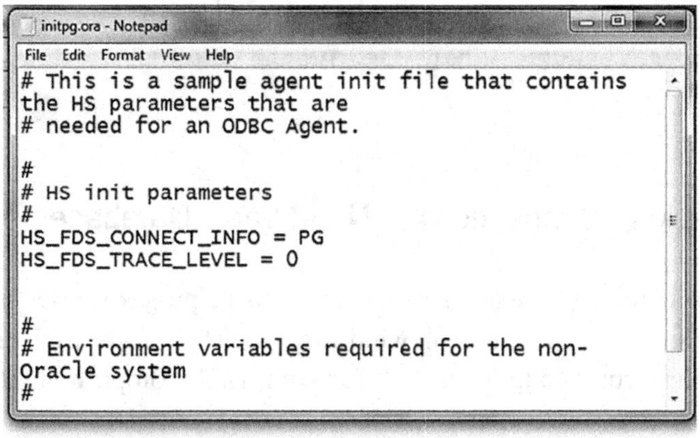

```
initpg.ora - Notepad
File Edit Format View Help
# This is a sample agent init file that contains
the HS parameters that are
# needed for an ODBC Agent.

#
# HS init parameters
#
HS_FDS_CONNECT_INFO = PG
HS_FDS_TRACE_LEVEL = 0


#
# Environment variables required for the non-
Oracle system
#
```

Figure 8. Listener.ora file

```
listener.ora - Notepad
File Edit Format View Help
SID_LIST_LISTENER =
  (SID_LIST =
    (SID_DESC =
       (SID_NAME = PG)
       (ORACLE_HOME = D:\app\Aalap\product\11.2.0\dbhome_1)
       (PROGRAM = dg4odbc)
    )

   (SID_DESC =
       (SID_NAME = AC)
       (ORACLE_HOME = D:\app\Aalap\product\11.2.0\dbhome_1)
       (PROGRAM = dg4odbc)
    )

   (SID_DESC =
     (SID_NAME = PLSExtProc)
     (ORACLE_HOME = D:\app\Aalap\product\11.2.0\dbhome_1)
     (PROGRAM = extproc)
   )

   (SID_DESC =
     (SID_NAME = CLRExtProc)
     (ORACLE_HOME = D:\app\Aalap\product\11.2.0\dbhome_1)
     (PROGRAM = extproc)
   )
  )

LISTENER =
  (DESCRIPTION_LIST =
    (DESCRIPTION =
 (ADDRESS = (PROTOCOL = IPC)(KEY = PNPKEY))
 (ADDRESS = (PROTOCOL = TCP)(HOST = Aalap-PC)(PORT = 1521))
    )
  )
```

Now, open tnsnames.ora file to add the following code for the PostgreSQL SID (DSN). Save and close the file. Figure 9 shows the screen shot of tnsnames.ora file.

```
PG = (DESCRIPTION=(ADDRESS=(PROTOCOL = TCP) (HOST = Aalap-PC)
(PORT = 1521))
(CONNECT_DATA=(SERVER = DEDICATED)(SID = PG))
(HS=OK))
```

3.2.10 Checking Connections of Non-Oracle Databases

To check the connection, execute the command tnsping <DSN> on command prompt as following. Type "cmd" in windows search box, right click on "cmd" and select the option "run as administrator". On command prompt, write the command

Figure 9. Tnsnames.ora file

```
tnsnames.ora - Notepad
File Edit Format View Help
LISTENER_ORCL =
(ADDRESS = (PROTOCOL = TCP)(HOST = localhost)(PORT = 1521))

PG =
 (DESCRIPTION=
    (ADDRESS=(PROTOCOL = TCP)(HOST = Aalap-PC)(PORT = 1521))
 (CONNECT_DATA=(SERVER = DEDICATED)(SID = PG))
 (HS=OK))
AC =
 (DESCRIPTION=
    (ADDRESS=(PROTOCOL = TCP)(HOST = Aalap-PC)(PORT = 1521))
 (CONNECT_DATA=(SERVER = DEDICATED)(SID = AC))
 (HS=OK))

XE =
  (DESCRIPTION =
    (ADDRESS = (PROTOCOL = TCP)(HOST = Aalap-PC)(PORT = 1521))
    (CONNECT_DATA =
      (SERVER = DEDICATED)
      (SERVICE_NAME = XE)
    ) )
EXTPROC_CONNECTION_DATA =
  (DESCRIPTION =
    (ADDRESS_LIST =
      (ADDRESS = (PROTOCOL = IPC)(KEY = EXTPROC_FOR_XE))
    )
    (CONNECT_DATA =
      (SID = PLSExtProc)
      (PRESENTATION = RO)
    )
  )
ORACLR_CONNECTION_DATA =
  (DESCRIPTION =
    (ADDRESS_LIST =
      (ADDRESS = (PROTOCOL = IPC)(KEY = EXTPROC_FOR_XE))
    )
    (CONNECT_DATA =
      (SID = CLRExtProc)
      (PRESENTATION = RO)
    )
  )
```

"tnsping pg" to check the connection of Oracle with PostgreSQL as follows. Here PG is DSN for PostgreSQL.

```
D:\app\Aalap\product\11.2.0\dbhome_1>tnsping pg
```

If the connection is successful, it will display "OK" with time taken to establish the connection as shown in Figure 10.

Similarly, check connections with MySQL and MS Access databases by executing the commands "tnsping MS" and "tnsping AC" respectively. If there is any problem, tnsping will display an error. If there is an error, check the path and contents of ".ora" files.

Figure 10. Issuing "tnsping" command to check connection of oracle with non-oracle databases

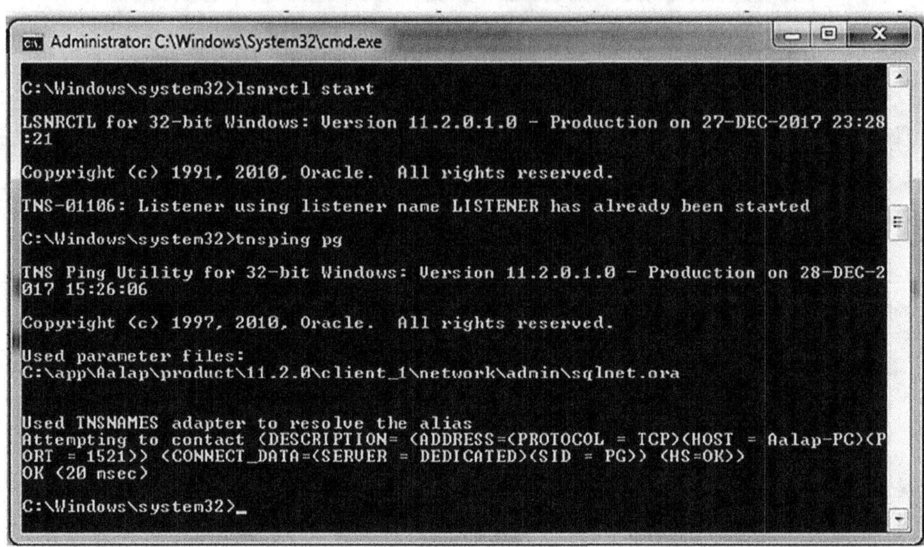

Apart from this, using listener service "lsnrctl", we can check whether the listener is listening request on the remote databases' SIDs or not. To check this, execute the command "lsnrctl start" on command prompt. If it shows the service is already running, then execute the command "lsnrctl status". This will display the details as given in Figure 11.

If there is any error, check the location from where sqlnet.ora file is referring listener.ora file.

3.2.11 Creating Database Links in Oracle to Access Data From Non-Oracle Databases

After successful connection with non-oracle databases, open oracle's client "SQL Plus" and login into SYS user as SYSDBA role. To login as SYS user type "sys as sysdba" in user name and enter password. In SYS user's account, create any user which you want to use as normal user and from which you want to access data of remote databases. For ex., create the user "shefali" with password "shefali", execute the command "create user shefali identified by password quota 4M on users". Here, "users" is the name of tablespace on which 4 MB quota to store data is assigned to

Figure 11. Starting the listener service to check status of listener

```
Administrator: C:\Windows\System32\cmd.exe
Microsoft Windows [Version 6.1.7601]
Copyright (c) 2009 Microsoft Corporation.  All rights reserved.

C:\Windows\system32>lsnrctl start

LSNRCTL for 32-bit Windows: Version 11.2.0.1.0 - Production on 27-DEC-2017 22:52
:44

Copyright (c) 1991, 2010, Oracle.  All rights reserved.

Starting tnslsnr: please wait...

TNSLSNR for 32-bit Windows: Version 11.2.0.1.0 - Production
System parameter file is C:\product\11.2.0\tg_1\network\admin\listener.ora
Log messages written to c:\product\11.2.0\tg_1\log\diag\tnslsnr\AALAP-PC\listene
r\alert\log.xml
Listening on: (DESCRIPTION=(ADDRESS=(PROTOCOL=tcp)(HOST=AALAP-PC)(PORT=1521)))

Connecting to (DESCRIPTION=(ADDRESS=(PROTOCOL=TCP)(HOST=AALAP-PC)(PORT=1521)))
STATUS of the LISTENER
------------------------
Alias                     LISTENER
Version                   TNSLSNR for 32-bit Windows: Version 11.2.0.1.0 - Produ
ction
Start Date                27-DEC-2017 22:52:50
Uptime                    0 days 0 hr. 0 min. 5 sec
Trace Level               off
Security                  ON: Local OS Authentication
SNMP                      OFF
Listener Parameter File   C:\product\11.2.0\tg_1\network\admin\listener.ora
Listener Log File         c:\product\11.2.0\tg_1\log\diag\tnslsnr\AALAP-PC\liste
ner\alert\log.xml
Listening Endpoints Summary...
  (DESCRIPTION=(ADDRESS=(PROTOCOL=tcp)(HOST=AALAP-PC)(PORT=1521)))
Services Summary...
Service "AC" has 1 instance(s).
  Instance "AC", status UNKNOWN, has 1 handler(s) for this service...
Service "CLRExtProc" has 1 instance(s).
  Instance "CLRExtProc", status UNKNOWN, has 1 handler(s) for this service...
Service "MS" has 1 instance(s).
  Instance "MS", status UNKNOWN, has 1 handler(s) for this service...
Service "ORCL" has 1 instance(s).
  Instance "ORCL", status UNKNOWN, has 1 handler(s) for this service...
Service "PG" has 1 instance(s).
  Instance "PG", status UNKNOWN, has 1 handler(s) for this service...
Service "PLSExtProc" has 1 instance(s).
  Instance "PLSExtProc", status UNKNOWN, has 1 handler(s) for this service...
The command completed successfully

C:\Windows\system32>
```

user "shefali". You may assign any tablespace and change value of quota. After user is created, grant privileges to create session, table and database link to this user by executing the command "grant create session, create table, create public database link to shefali;" in SYS user. After this, change the user to "shefali" by executing the command "connect shefali" on SQL prompt. Figure 12 shows creation of oracle user.

Now, login into PostgreSQL. To login open "psql" SQL shell. Enter server name=localhost, database=postgres, port=5433 and username=postgres. Change username if you want to login as different user. After login, create few tables and insert data in these tables. We will access and manipulate these data from oracle. Figure 13 shows the data fetched from the table "emp" of "postgres" user.

Figure 12. Logging into oracle from SQL Plus as SYS user and creating new user

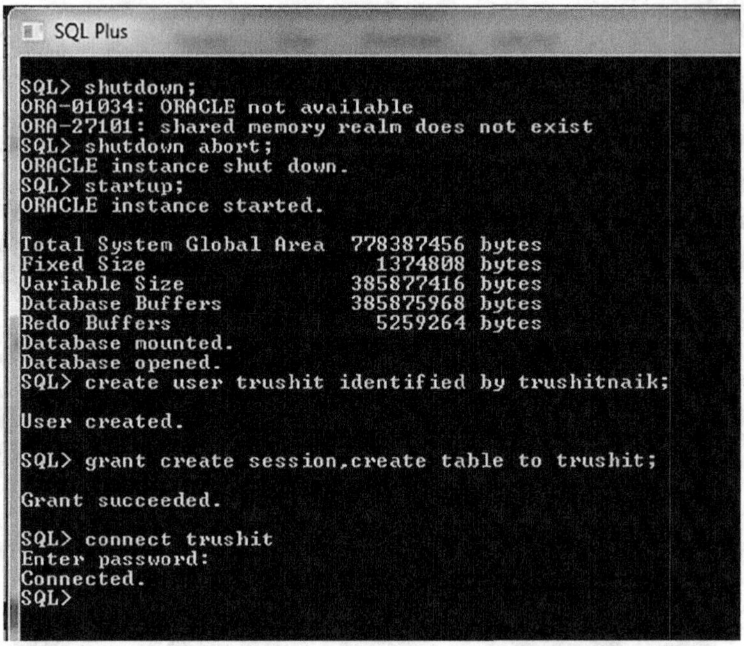

```
SQL Plus

SQL> shutdown;
ORA-01034: ORACLE not available
ORA-27101: shared memory realm does not exist
SQL> shutdown abort;
ORACLE instance shut down.
SQL> startup;
ORACLE instance started.

Total System Global Area  778387456 bytes
Fixed Size                  1374808 bytes
Variable Size             385877416 bytes
Database Buffers          385875968 bytes
Redo Buffers                5259264 bytes
Database mounted.
Database opened.
SQL> create user trushit identified by trushitnaik;

User created.

SQL> grant create session,create table to trushit;

Grant succeeded.

SQL> connect trushit
Enter password:
Connected.
SQL>
```

Figure 13. Login into PostgreSQL as "postgres" user, create table "emp" with few records

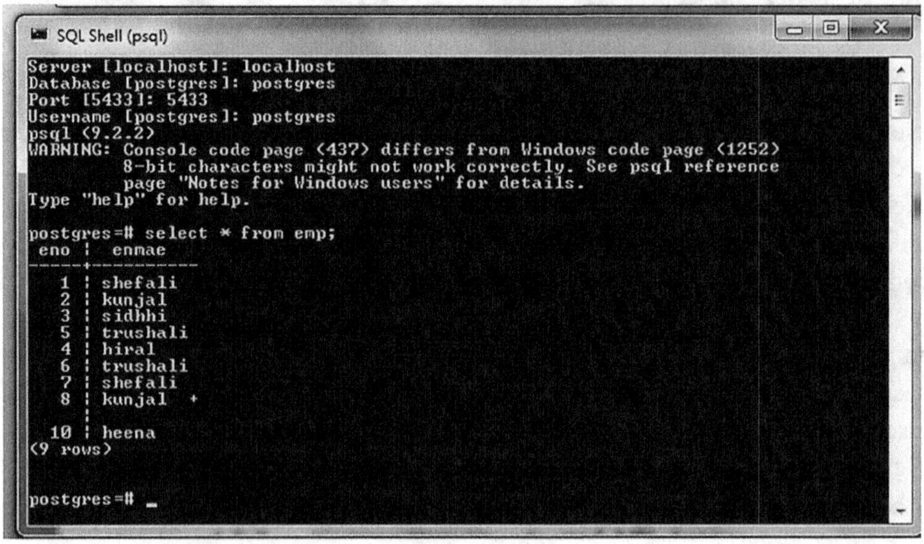

```
SQL Shell (psql)
Server [localhost]: localhost
Database [postgres]: postgres
Port [5433]: 5433
Username [postgres]: postgres
psql (9.2.2)
WARNING: Console code page (437) differs from Windows code page (1252)
         8-bit characters might not work correctly. See psql reference
         page "Notes for Windows users" for details.
Type "help" for help.

postgres=# select * from emp;
 eno |  enmae
-----+----------
   1 | shefali
   2 | kunjal
   3 | sidhhi
   5 | trushali
   4 | hiral
   6 | trushali
   7 | shefali
   8 | kunjal  +
     |
  10 | heena
(9 rows)


postgres=# _
```

Next login into MySQL. To login first start the WAMP server. After WAMP server is started, open MySQL console by right clicking on WAMP server icon. It will prompt to enter the password (The default user of MySQL is root with no password.). Press enter key without inputting anything in password. New database may be created after login or we may also use the database which is already available. After database is created, we need to change the database by issuing the command "use <database_name>". After database is in use, create table with data. For ex., the table "emp" is created in "test" database with few records. Figure 14 shows the screen shot of login as a "root" user, changing database to "test" and fetching data from "emp" table. To create "shefali" user in MySQL execute the command.

```
Create user 'shefali'@'localhost' identified by 'shefali123';
```

Also, oracle user should be assigned rights to access data from MySQL user account. Assume that "Shefali" of oracle needs right to access data from MySQL then execute the following command on MySQL prompt to grant her (oracle user) permission.

```
grant all on *.* TO 'shefali'@'%'  IDENTIFIED BY  'shefali123';
```

(Note: "Shefali" is oracle user name and "shefali123" is the password of this user)

Figure 14. Login into MySQL as "root" user, using "test" database and fetching records from "emp" table

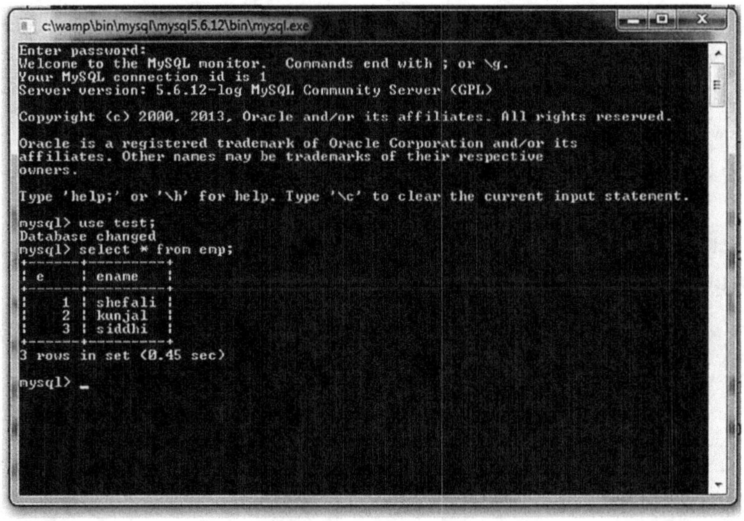

```
c:\wamp\bin\mysql\mysql5.6.12\bin\mysql.exe
Enter password:
Welcome to the MySQL monitor.  Commands end with ; or \g.
Your MySQL connection id is 1
Server version: 5.6.12-log MySQL Community Server (GPL)

Copyright (c) 2000, 2013, Oracle and/or its affiliates. All rights reserved.

Oracle is a registered trademark of Oracle Corporation and/or its
affiliates. Other names may be trademarks of their respective
owners.

Type 'help;' or '\h' for help. Type '\c' to clear the current input statement.

mysql> use test;
Database changed
mysql> select * from emp;
+------+----------+
| e    | ename    |
+------+----------+
|    1 | shefali  |
|    2 | kunjal   |
|    3 | siddhi   |
+------+----------+
3 rows in set (0.45 sec)

mysql> _
```

Similarly, create table in the MS Access database which you have created before. There is no need to login into MS Access database. User can directly create the database and tables within database. If you wish, you may set password later for this database.

We have data ready in remote databases to fetch into oracle using database links. Database link is a connection between two physical databases. Execute the following command in oracle user login to create a database link named "topg" which will fetch data from the "postgtres" user login of PostgreSQL. "PG" is DSN name, "postgres" is PostgreSQL user name and "shefali123" is password.

```
create public database link topg connect to "postgres"
identified by "shefali" using 'PG';
```

Now, create a database link named "toms" to fetch data from "shefali" user of MySQL. "MS" is DSN of MySQL.

```
create public database link toms connect to "shefali"
identified by "shefali123" using 'MS';
```

Next, execute the following command to create a database link named "toac" to fetch data from MS Access.

```
create public database link toac using 'AC';
```

After successful creation of database links for all remote databases, data stored in the tables of these databases could be retrieved and manipulated from oracle.

3.2.12 Accessing Data Into Oracle From Non-Oracle Databases Using Database Links

Login into oracle user and execute the following commands.

1. To fetch data from "emp" table of PostgreSQL using "topg" database link, execute the following query.

```
select * from "emp"@topg;
```

Figure 15 shows the result after execution of above command.

2. To fetch data from "emp" table of MySQL database using "toms" database link, execute the following query.

```
select * from "emp"@toms;
```

3. To fetch data from "salary" table of MS Access database using "toac" database link, execute the following query.

```
select * from "salary"@toac;
```

To hide the complexity of writing database link in the query, we may create synonym for remote tables. These synonyms could be used as table names in query. Execute the following command to create a synonym named "employee1" for "emp"@topg.

```
CREATE SYNONYM employee1 FOR "emp"@topg;
```

Use this synonym in select query as follows.

```
select * from employee1;
```

Figure 15. Fetchning data from "emp" table of PostgreSQL in Oracle

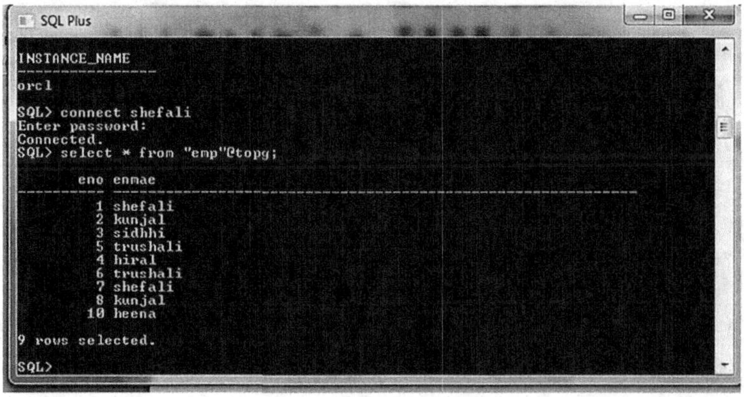

```
SQL Plus
INSTANCE_NAME
----------------
orcl
SQL> connect shefali
Enter password:
Connected.
SQL> select * from "emp"@topg;

       eno enmae
---------- ----------------------------------------------------------
         1 shefali
         2 kunjal
         3 sidhhi
         5 trushali
         4 hiral
         6 trushali
         7 shefali
         8 kunjal
        10 heena

9 rows selected.

SQL>
```

Figure 16 shows the usage of synonym.

Figure 17 shows output of the query which fetches data from four different databases.

Following query written in oracle will retrieve data from in oracle from MS Access and PostgreSQL.

```
select e."eno"||'    '||e."enmae"||'     '||s."sal_date"||'
'||s."salary" from "emp"@topg e, salary@toac s where
e."eno"=s."empno";
```

Following "insert" statement written in oracle will insert record into "emp" table of PostgreSQL database.

```
insert into "public"."emp"@topg values(10,'heena');
```

The following PL/SQL stored procedure named "disp" created in oracle will fetch and display records from two remote databases PostgreSQL and MS Access.

```
Create or replace procedure disp as
                              cursor c_emp is select * from
"public"."emp"@topg;
                  r_emp c_emp%rowtype;
                     cursor c_kg is select * from salary@toac;
                      r_kg c_kg%rowtype;
begin
                      dbms_output.put_line('Data from
```

Figure 16. Using synonym for simplicity

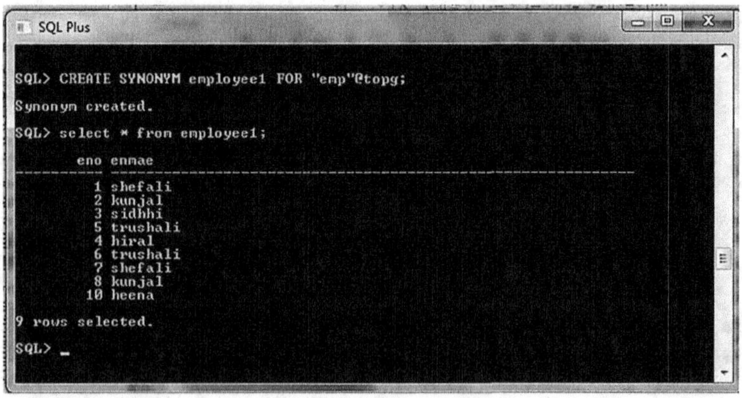

```
SQL Plus
SQL> CREATE SYNONYM employee1 FOR "emp"@topg;

Synonym created.

SQL> select * from employee1;

       eno enmae
---------- ----------------------------------------
         1 shefali
         2 kunjal
         3 sidhhi
         5 trushali
         4 hiral
         6 trushali
         7 shefali
         8 kunjal
        10 heena

9 rows selected.

SQL> _
```

Figure 17. Fetching data from multiple remote databases in a single query

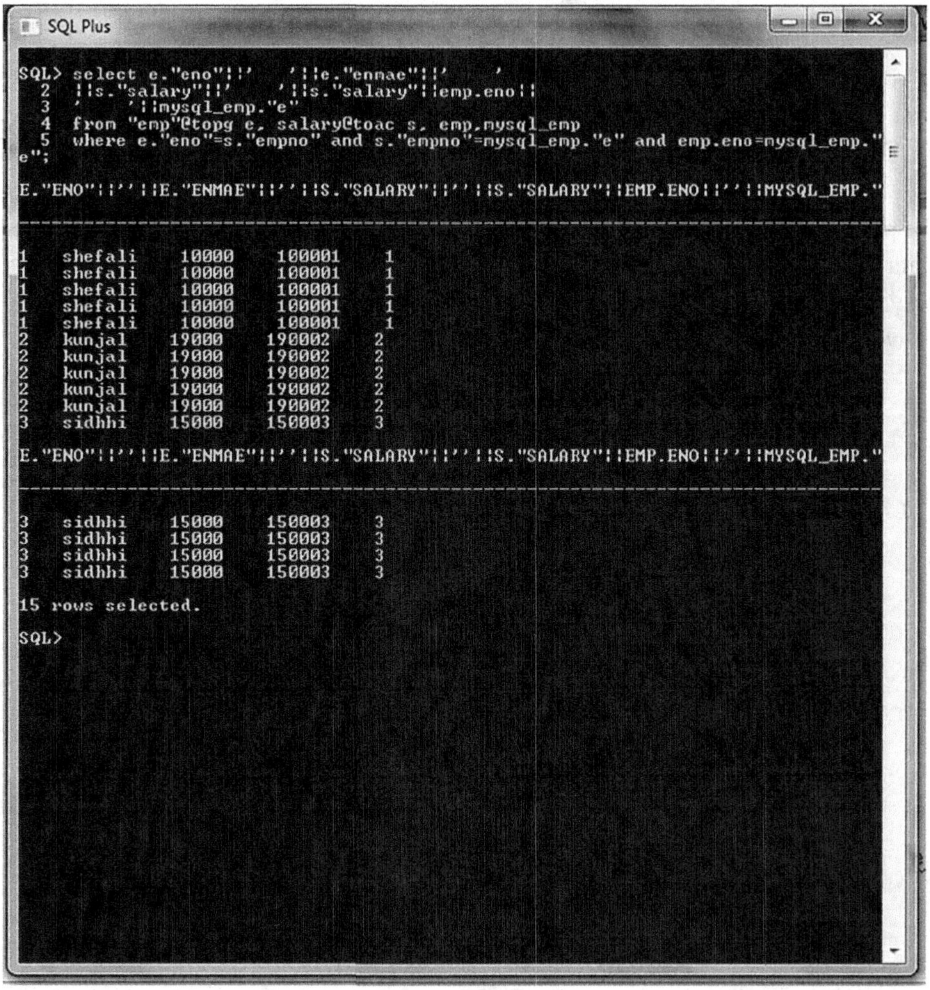

```
SQL Plus

SQL> select e."eno"||'    '||e."enmae"||'    '
  2  ||s."salary"||'    '||s."salary"||emp.eno||
  3  '    '||mysql_emp."e"
  4  from "emp"@topg e, salary@toac s, emp,mysql_emp
  5  where e."eno"=s."empno" and s."empno"=mysql_emp."e" and emp.eno=mysql_emp."
e";

E."ENO"||''||E."ENMAE"||''||S."SALARY"||''||S."SALARY"||EMP.ENO||''||MYSQL_EMP."
--------------------------------------------------------------------------------
1    shefali    10000    100001    1
1    shefali    10000    100001    1
1    shefali    10000    100001    1
1    shefali    10000    100001    1
1    shefali    10000    100001    1
2    kunjal    19000    190002    2
2    kunjal    19000    190002    2
2    kunjal    19000    190002    2
2    kunjal    19000    190002    2
2    kunjal    19000    190002    2
3    sidhhi    15000    150003    3

E."ENO"||''||E."ENMAE"||''||S."SALARY"||''||S."SALARY"||EMP.ENO||''||MYSQL_EMP."
--------------------------------------------------------------------------------
3    sidhhi    15000    150003    3
3    sidhhi    15000    150003    3
3    sidhhi    15000    150003    3
3    sidhhi    15000    150003    3

15 rows selected.

SQL>
```

```
PostgreSQL…..');
                        for r_emp in c_emp loop
dbms_output.put_line('Emp Name ==>'||r_emp. "enmae");
                        end loop;
                        dbms_output.put_line('Data from MS
Access…..');
                        for r_kg in c_kg loop
dbms_output.put_line('Emp No ==>'||r_kg. "empno");
```

```
            end loop;
end;
/
```

4. CONCLUSION

To process distributed transactions and distributed queries in oracle which access data from no-oracle databases, oracle's heterogeneous gateway service is the best way. It provides database and location transparency which make user comfortable to work with remote databases.

REFERENCES

Adiba, M. E., Chupin, J. C., Demolombe, R., Gardarin, G., & Le Bihan, J. (1978, September). Issues in distributed data base management systems: A technical overview. In *Proceedings of the fourth international conference on Very Large Data Bases-Volume 4* (pp. 89-110). VLDB Endowment.

Beraka, M., Mathkour, H., & Gannouni, S. (2011, September). Data sharing in distributed computing environment. In *Electrical and Control Engineering (ICECE), 2011 International Conference on* (pp. 4760-4763). IEEE. 10.1109/ICECENG.2011.6057414

Bojovic, I. (2015). *MySQL Master-Slave Replication on the Same Machine*. Retrieved from https://www.toptal.com/mysql/mysql-master-slave-replication-tutorial

Breitbart, Y., Morales, H., Silberschatz, A., & Thompson, G. (1990, October). Multidatabase performance evaluation. In *Information Technology, 1990.'Next Decade in Information Technology', Proceedings of the 5th Jerusalem Conference on (Cat. No. 90TH0326-9)* (pp. 507-519). IEEE. 10.1109/JCIT.1990.128323

Chung, C. W. (1990). DATAPLEX: An access to heterogeneous distributed databases. *Communications of the ACM*, *33*(1), 70–80. doi:10.1145/76372.76377

Ferrier, A., & Stangret, C. (1982, September). *Heterogeneity in the Distributed Database Management System SIRIUS-DELTA* (pp. 45–53). VLDB.

Fummi, F., Martini, S., Monguzzi, M., Perbellini, G., & Poncino, M. (2004, February). Modeling and analysis of heterogeneous industrial networks architectures. In *Proceedings of the conference on Design, automation and test in Europe-Volume 3* (p. 30342). IEEE Computer Society 10.1109/DATE.2004.1269270

Ganesan, B. (n.d.). *Oracle Heterogeneous Services*. Retrieved 29-3-2019 from http://www.dba-oracle.com/t_plsql_heterogeneous%20services.htm

Khokhar, A. A., Prasanna, V. K., Shaaban, M. E., & Wang, C. L. (1993). Heterogeneous computing: Challenges and opportunities. *Computer*, *26*(6), 18–27. doi:10.1109/2.214439

Lee, J., Chapin, S. J., & Taylor, S. (2003). Reliable heterogeneous applications. *IEEE Transactions on Reliability*, *52*(3), 330–339. doi:10.1109/TR.2003.819502

Microsoft. (2019). *Set up replication distribution database in Always On availability group*. Retrieved 28-3-2019 from https://docs.microsoft.com/en-us/sql/relational-databases/replication/configure-distribution-availability-group?view=sql-server-2017

Oracle. (2007). *Oracle Database Gateways*. Retrieved 29-3-2019 from www.oracle.com/technetwork/database/gateways/gateways-twp-131579.pdf

Oracle. (2010). *Oracle Database Gateway for ODBC*. Retrieved 29-3-2019 from https://docs.oracle.com/cd/E18283_01/gateways.112/e12070.pdf

Oracle. (2012). *Oracle Database Gateway*. Retrieved 29-3-2019 from https://docs.oracle.com/cd/E11882_01/gateways.112/e12013.pdf

Oracle. (2019). *Managing a Distributed Database*. Retrieved 28-3-2019 from https://docs.oracle.com/cd/B19306_01/server.102/b14231/ds_admin.htm#i1008852

Oracle. (n.d.). *Oracle Technology Network*. Retrieved 29-3-2019 from https://www.oracle.com/technical-resources/

Özsu, M. T., & Valduriez, P. (2011). *Principles of distributed database systems*. Springer Science & Business Media.

Paliwal, S., & Subash, V. B. (n.d.). *Performance Optimization of Oracle Distributed Databases*. Retrieved from http://citeseerx.ist.psu.edu/viewdoc/summary?doi=10.1.1.174.3872

Pu, C., Leff, A., & Chen, S. W. (1991). Heterogeneous and autonomous transaction processing. *Computer*, *24*(12), 64–72. doi:10.1109/2.116890

Sharaf, M. A., Chrysanthis, P. K., Labrinidis, A., & Pruhs, K. (2008). Algorithms and metrics for processing multiple heterogeneous continuous queries. *ACM Transactions on Database Systems*, *33*(1), 5. doi:10.1145/1331904.1331909

Sourikova, I. (n.d.). *PostgreSQL Replicator – easy way to build a distributed Postgres database*. Retrieved 28-3-2019 from https://www.racf.bnl.gov/Facility/TechnologyMeeting/Irina_Sourikova_techMeet.pdf

Sun, X. H., Chen, Y., & Wu, M. (2005, June). Scalability of heterogeneous computing. In *Parallel Processing, 2005. ICPP 2005. International Conference on* (pp. 557-564). IEEE.

Wang, C. Y., & Spooner, D. L. (1987, March). *Access Control in a Heterogeneous Distributed Database Management System*. SRDS.

Yu, H., Zhang, S. Z., Yang, N. H., Ding, H., & Wang, X. K. (2003, November). Intelligent agent-based distributed heterogeneous database system. In *Machine Learning and Cybernetics, 2003 International Conference on* (Vol. 3, pp. 1932-1935). IEEE.

Zhang, Y., & Orlowska, M. E. (1993, October). A hybrid concurrency control approach in heterogeneous distributed database systems. In *TENCON'93. Proceedings. Computer, Communication, Control and Power Engineering. 1993 IEEE Region 10 Conference on* (Vol. 1, pp. 323-326). IEEE.

Chapter 9
A P2P Architecture for Social Networking

Michele Tomaiuolo
https://orcid.org/0000-0002-6030-9435
University of Parma, Italy

Monica Mordonini
https://orcid.org/0000-0002-5916-9770
University of Parma, Italy

Agostino Poggi
https://orcid.org/0000-0003-3528-0260
University of Parma, Italy

ABSTRACT

Social networking systems are usually huge centralized systems owned by a single company. However, this solution has many drawbacks (e.g., lack of privacy, lack of anonymity, risks of censorship, and operating costs). This chapter proposes a novel P2P system that leverages existing, widespread, and stable technologies such as DHTs and BitTorrent. In particular, it introduces a key-based identity system and a model of social relations for distributing content efficiently among interested readers. The proposed system, called Blogracy, is a micro-blogging social networking system focused on (1) anonymity and resilience to censorship, (2) authenticatable content, and (3) semantic interoperability using activity streams. This chapter presents the model and the implementation of the Blogracy system, discusses the experimentations to study its behavior, and presents their results regarding (1) communication delays for some simulations of node churn, (2) delays measured in test operations over PlanetLab in direct communication, and (3) through the I2P anonymizing network.

DOI: 10.4018/978-1-5225-8295-3.ch009

INTRODUCTION

After the huge success of the early social networking systems, many other players came in the social networking market and nowadays hundreds of different social networking systems exist. Even if these social networking systems are greatly dissimilar in their user base and functionality, they are almost always centralized systems. The centralized nature allows a simple browser-based user experience and, moreover, many algorithms, e.g., friend suggestion, are far easier and more efficient to implement in this setting.

A drawback is that scaling centralized systems to tens or hundreds of millions of users is not an easy task. Certainly, existing systems demonstrate that the problem can be solved providing enough resources. However, the huge operative costs of supporting the infrastructure necessary to provide the service to millions of users can only be justified with robust business plans. While some social networking services have extremely differentiated business models (Hobart, 2011; McGrath, 2010), for most of them the primary source of income is advertisement and consequently they have a strong motive for: (i) using user provided data to increase performance for that purpose and (ii) even giving access to authorized commercial third parties to the data. This behavior poses serious threats to privacy and data protection issues and there are virtually no specific legislation or explicit guarantees.

Another problem is that many social networking systems have very demanding terms of service, essentially asking their users a non-exclusive, transferable, sub-licensable, royalty-free, worldwide license to use content that they submit. Arguably, social networking sites tend to guide their users into "walled gardens," without giving users full control over their own information because such information constitutes much of the company value (Berners-Lee, 2010; Shankland, 2010).

The last problem with centralized social networking systems is that service providers are in the position to perform a-priori or a-posteriori censorship and may be forced for legal reason: (i) to perform such actions, and (ii) to disclose all the information they have, no matter how private (Franchi, Poggi & Tomaiuolo, 2013). In fact, the recent clamor about the PRISM program and the release of classified documents by Edward Snowden (Greene, 2014) has raised many questions about the privacy issues of current social networking applications.

Thus, we believe that an approach based on peer-to-peer (P2P) or distributed technologies not only is viable but also highly desirable. First of all, P2P systems essentially achieve simpler resource scalability, in the sense that the availability of resources is roughly proportional to the number of users.

This property is especially desirable for media sharing social networking systems, considering the exceptionally high amount of resources needed. Secondly, the popularity over time of most content on such systems exhibits either a power-law or an exponential behavior (Avramova et al., 2009) and is consequently well suited for P2P distribution (Zink et al., 2009), possibly with fallback strategies for less popular content. Regarding censorship issues, a P2P system essentially solves them by design.

Without a central entity, nobody is in the position of censoring data systematically nor may be held legally responsible for the diffusion of censurable data: the sole owners and responsible of the data are the users themselves.

Attacks to distributed and P2P social platforms are yet possible, for example by introducing Sybil nodes in the network, i.e., nodes with forged identities created to subvert the reputation system in a P2P network. However, analyzing these kinds of attacks is not the focus of the article. A comprehensive list of such attacks and countermeasures is presented in (Franchi & Tomaiuolo, 2013).

The main objective of this article is to present Blogracy, a new P2P system for social networking that we implemented and tested on the PlanetLab infrastructure. Thus, some results will be presented about the feasibility and limitations encountered in the realization of a distributed social networking system layered upon a widespread file sharing network such as BitTorrent. The system is modular in the approach to the core problems of (i) data availability and resilience to censorship, (ii) content authenticability, (iii) data confidentiality, (iv) network anonymity, and (v) semantic interoperability. All these aspects are kept as much orthogonal as possible in the system. For both its architecture and its level of implementation, to our knowledge it is quite unique. Being available as open source software, it can be freely used for conducting further analysis and evaluations in the larger research area of distributed social platforms, exploring alternative architectural choices and implementations along each axis.

BACKGROUND

The landscape of distributed social platforms is quite differentiated and it is interesting to compare the various solutions that are being proposed. Apart from the centralized architecture of the most widespread social networking platforms, two main approaches can be distinguished: (i) federated systems, where a number of servers connect for distributing updates and content to interested remote users; and (ii) P2P systems, where the resources deployed by final users are fundamental for the core functioning of the whole system.

In systems developed according to the federated approach, users are allowed to register on their preferred server and then to create relationships with users of other servers. The best known federated systems include Diaspora (http://joindiaspora.com/) and StatusNet (http://status.net/ – formerly known as Laconica). Diaspora servers communicate by means of an ad-hoc federation protocol and the standard Salmon protocol for comments. Users can (i) participate in the network by setting up their own server, which is named a "pod", or (ii) exploit already existing pods. StatusNet instead adheres to the OStatus standard protocol for the interconnection of various servers. Using a number of existing protocols, StatusNet shows quite strong interoperability with other networks. In general, a drawback of federated systems is their problematic scalability. In fact, they require additional resources to be deployed by publishers of popular content, to maintain acceptable performance. This is particularly relevant in the case of users sharing large multimedia files, or publishing viral content, acquiring popularity very fast. Moreover, federated networks offer limited resilience against DoS attacks, which may simply target a certain server to impede the activities of all the users it hosts.

Other systems are designed according to a full-fledged P2P architecture, usually based on a Distributed Hash Table (DHT). These systems achieve simpler resource scalability, in the sense that the availability of resources is proportional to the number of participating users. Moreover, resources can be spread effectively, without requiring their originating node to be constantly online. The origin of these systems can be traced back to Freenet (Clarke et al., 2002), which is meant as a distributed, cooperative, uncensored and secure file system. It uses a "best-effort" unreliable routing algorithm to find content and namespaces, over both "OpenNet" and "DarkNet" connections. Freenet uses an anonymizing layer based on a variation of Chaum's mix-net scheme, which inspired also the more famous Onion routing scheme used by Tor and the one used by I2P. Another system for anonymous publishing is OsirisSPS (http://www.osiris-sps.org/ – Serverless Portal System). It is a framework for creating web portals and forums distributed over a peer-to-peer network and a Kademlia DHT, supporting (i) content replication, (ii) anonymity, (iii) signature and (iv) encryption of messages. The distributed management of reputation and the possibility to realize so-called Anarchist portals are the most distinguishing aspects of the program.

Specifically, in the field of social networking, various systems are being proposed, mostly at the design level, on the basis of P2P communications and DHT indexing, including PeerSoN (Buchegger et al., 2009), Safebook (Cutillo, Molva & Strufe, 2009), Persona (Baden et al., 2009), LotusNet (Aiello and Ruffo, 2010) and LifeSocial (Graffi et al., 2010).

PeerSoN (Buchegger et al., 2009) is a system designed to provide encryption, decentralization and direct data exchange in the field of social networks, dealing with privacy and connectivity issues. The system is designed to use a DHT. Unfortunately, the originally chosen DHT implementation, OpenDHT, later became overloaded and unusable and had to be replaced by a centralized service, for testing and evaluation. The DHT should be used to trace the user's network presence. An index file, containing a list of new content generated by the user, should also be registered in the DHT. With regards to identity management, the first prototype of PeerSoN is designed around a Public Key Infrastructure (PKI). Given the centralized or hierarchical nature of PKI, this solution hardly matches the needs of a decentralized network. In fact, authors hint at some studies being conducted for removing a centralized PKI and for developing a more efficient approach, but the result is not yet clear.

Safebook (Cutillo, Molva & Strufe, 2009) is based on a DHT and a network of socially close peers, defined Matryoshka. Peers in a user's Matryoshka are trusted and support the user by anonymizing communications and replicating content and profile information. However, the idea of this new overlay architecture has yet to be evaluated, both for performance and security. Other systems, including Blogracy, have a design which is orthogonal to the problem of network-level anonymity and can thus rely on available anonymizing protocols, based on mix-net schemes. About user identity, Safebook exploits a more traditional certification authority. In fact, a user's public key cannot be calculated from his identity, and all public/private key pairs are generated locally by the peers.

Persona is designed as a set of social networking services. The first prototype implementation consists of two main services (for storage and management of collaborative data). The most developed and interesting aspect of Persona is its model for confidentiality of users' profiles and data. It uses an interesting Attribute-Based Encryption protocol for protecting access to users' content, sharing the approach of Blogracy. This approach allows each user to create various groups of "friends", by assigning proper attribute credentials. Content can then be associated with a publication policy and made available only to a restricted audience.

LotusNet (Aiello & Ruffo, 2010) is a model of a social network to be built over Likir. Likir itself is an implementation of a secured Kademlia DHT, which requires a user to be authenticated before participating in the network. During the registration phase, the user's private key is calculated by a globally trusted Certification Authority, on the sole basis of the user's identity (e.g., OpenId or email address) and a unique private master key. The corresponding public key can be generated by everyone, from the user's identity and the public master key of the system. This architecture, however, presents a clear single point of failure in the central authority, which may leak users' keys, sign or decrypt cyphertexts without being noticed, according to the key escrow problem, which is well known for identity based schemes.

LifeSocial (Graffi et al., 2010) is a prototype developed over FreePastry for DHT indexing and PAST for data replication. It is among the ones in a more mature implementation stage. Lifesocial is composed of various mandatory modules, for managing profile, friends, groups and photos. Additional modules are available for chat and whiteboard functionalities. Blogracy differentiates from Lifesocial in using BitTorrent instead of Pastry and PAST. This way, it better integrates into existing networks, augmenting the social aspects of already existing file-sharing communities. Moreover, Blogracy uses standard formats, thus integrating with other social networks. In fact, it has been already tested in conjunction with other networks based on Activity Streams, RSS feeds, and Twitter. Finally, Lifesocial uses a traditional encryption scheme, where a secret session key is encrypted with the public keys of intended receivers. Instead, Blogracy uses a more scalable approach based on Attribute-Based Encryption.

DiDuSoNet (Guidi et al., 2015) is a P2P distributed online social network that provide a full access control on their user data. In particular, it offers data persistence and consistence and guarantees data availability even when users are offline by distributing storage on trusted friend nodes.

Finally, it is worth mentioning some systems focused on the P2P distribution of feeds and updates. Though not providing social networking features, these systems provide support for some typical operations of generic content sharing applications. Some of these systems share the dependency on the Pastry DHT and possibly Scribe (Castro et al., 2002), an application level multicast infrastructure built on top of it. These include Cuckoo (Xu, Chen, & Fu, 2009), FeedTree (Sandler et al., 2005) and Megaphone (Perfitt & Englert, 2010).

BLOGRACY

Blogracy shares some architectural choices with other distributed social networking systems, as we have discussed above. In fact, it uses DHT mechanisms (which are also used by many of the alternative systems, in different ways) for indexing users and files; it uses Attribute-Based Encryption for confidentiality (similarly to Persona); and it uses mix-net schemes for network anonymity (similarly to Freenet and many following systems, including Safebook). Its distinguishing features lay mainly in the adoption of an open and simple key-based identity system, and the use of interoperable protocols and widespread technologies. There's virtually no current P2P social networking system that can leverage the BitTorrent network, or other already existing and widespread DHTs. In this sense, to our knowledge Blogracy is the first concrete attempt to cross the border between one of the most popular file-sharing platforms and the growing sphere of distributed and interoperable social networking applications. Currently, it is one of the few systems which is available as a working prototype. The core functionalities of Blogracy have been already tested on PlanetLab. The whole system is freely available as open source software. In our opinion, it represents an important resource for further analysis and testing in the whole research area of distributed social networks.

DESIGN

While many authors argue for the distribution and openness of social networking and micro-blogging services, few usable implementations exist, either in the field of federated networks or as fully distributed solutions. Considering the existing or proposed solutions, we therefore present a new system, which we named Blogracy (http://www.blogracy.net/). Our new system is built incrementally over popular services; in fact, from the very beginning, we chose to leverage existing and widespread networks for file sharing, and providing those large communities with specific features for microblogging applications and for publishing personal activity streams.

The architecture of the application (Figure 1) is modular and is built around two basic components: (i) an underlying BitTorrent module for basic file sharing and DHT operations, exploiting an existing implementation, and (ii) an OpenSocial container, i.e., a module providing the services of the social platform to the local user, to be accessed through a web interface. Additionally, the system supports the future extension of its core functionalities by means of autonomous agents providing (i) recommendations of both users and content, (ii) personalization of results, (iii) trust negotiation mechanisms (Poggi & Tomaiuolo, 2011; Agazzi & Tomaiuolo, 2013; Tomaiuolo, 2014).

For its basic operation, Blogracy exploits a P2P file-sharing mechanism and two logically separated DHTs. Users in Blogracy have a profile and a semantically

Figure 1. Blogracy architecture

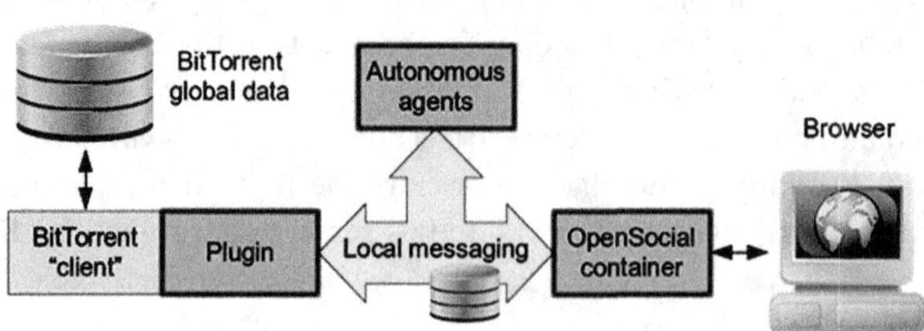

meaningful activity stream, which contains their actions in the system (e.g., add a post, tag a picture, comment a video). One DHT maps the user's identifier with a reference to his activity stream. The user's activity stream is represented in a standard format, which we will briefly describe in the following pages. It is encoded as a JSON file which also contains a reference to the user's profile and references to user generated content (e.g., posts, comments). All these references, in the form of magnet URIs (Sauermann, Cyganiak & Völkel, 2007), are keys of the second DHT, which are then resolved to the actual files. The files are delivered using the underlying P2P file-sharing mechanism.

In the following sections we will describe the most distinguishing features realized in Blogracy over this extensible architecture and how they relate to other existing systems and abstract architectures.

User Identity and Privacy

For all practical purposes, individual users of large networks have to be associated with numerical identifiers or unique strings, since names used in real life are hardly unique. Moreover, anonymity or pseudonymity are often a requirement of users of micro-blogging and other Internet applications (Chawki, 2010).

Even under anonymity or pseudonymity, user content needs to be verified for authenticity and integrity, properties which can be easily enforced by means of public-key cryptography and digital signatures. Usually, a public key is associated to a person or a legal entity (Fornacciari et al., 2018) through a certificate issued by a globally acknowledged authority. Instead, in a key-based identity scheme (Li, 2000), a user can be represented directly though his own, locally generated, public key. This way, all content produced by the user can be easily verified against his public key, which is also his own main identifier. Alternatively, a cryptographic hash of the public key can be used without loss of security (Li, 2000), and this is exactly the scheme adopted in Blogracy. This simple approach to identity management has its roots in Trust Management systems (Rivest and Lampson, 1996; Yan, Zhang, & Vasilakos, 2014; Tomaiuolo, 2014). In those systems, the decision to delegate a task and the required privileges to some other entity is based on a local notion of trust, in principle based on socio-cognitive considerations (Falcone & Castelfranchi, 2001).

Since a user's identity corresponds to his public key, and he is required to sign his own social data files, then verifying the information authenticity and integrity is immediate and can be performed quite cheaply either by the receiving users, or directly by the network infrastructure, i.e., by the DHT nodes that host the references to the updated pieces of information. This way, a user can join the Blogracy network simply by creating a public/private key pair, alongside additional optional profile information. Then, he can reach other users only after obtaining their ID, i.e., the hash of their public key. This ID can either be published on generic websites and web-based index pages, or obtained from contacts in the personal social network, possibly from an initial introducer. Personal contacts are then stored locally, on the peer node. After obtaining an ID, a user can download the corresponding social data, which also contains the associated public key. The public key can then be verified against the ID, i.e., its hash, and used to verify the integrity and authenticity of the social data.

A signature scheme is used for attesting the authenticity of DHT entries, in particular the magnet-URIs used as values in the DHT1. The scheme is based on the JWS (JSON Web signature), which is currently an Internet Draft (Jones, Bradley, & Sakimura, 2015). In fact, JWS is a quite practical specification, based on simple JSON objects and Base64 encoded strings. In particular, the header is a JSON object which specifies the cryptographic algorithms to use; the payload contains the signed message, which may be a JSON object or any byte sequence. Both the header and payload are encoded as Base64 strings, which are concatenated (separated though a dot). A signature is then calculated, encoded as a Base64 string, and concatenated to the previously obtained text. At the end of the process, the JWS is represented as a concatenation of the three Base64 strings (header, payload, signature), separated by two dots (an example is shown in Figure 2, taken from the draft specification).

As shown in Figure 3, the header object in use by Blogracy currently refers to the quite usual SHA256withRSA algorithm, named HS256 in the specifications. The "kid" field is an identifier for the signing key: in Blogracy the user's main public key is numbered as 0. The hash of this public key is also the user's unique identifier. Additional signing keys, corresponding to different kid values, may be added in the

Figure 2. An example JWS serialization


```
EyJ0eXAiOiJKV1QiLA0KICJhbGciOiJIUzI1NiJ9
.
eyJpc3MiOiJqb2UiLA0KICJleHAiOjEzMDA4MTkzODAsDQogImh0dHA6Ly9leGFt
cGxlLmNvbS9pc19yb290Ijp0cnVlfQ
.
dBjftJeZ4CVP-mB92K27uhbUJU1p1r_wW1gFWFOEjXk
```


Figure 3. A typical Blogracy JWS header


```
{
  "alg": "HS256",
  "kid": "0"
}
```

user's profile (which is included in the file containing all the user's social data, as an OpenSocial Person object).

The payload, instead, is simply the magnet-URI for the updated user's social data file. Verifying a DHT entry is handy, since the signing key corresponding to a certain kid can be found easily into the user's profile and then it can be stored locally by the user's followers for faster access (each signing key must itself be signed by the user's main public key). This way, the authenticity of an entry can be verified and the typical pollution of keyword-based DHT indexes can be easily detected (Montassier et al., 2011).

As a simpler alternative (which was used in early experiments), in a JWS it is possible to specify the signing key directly, through the definition of a "jwk" (JSON Web Key) Header Parameter. This way, a verifier could match directly the hash of the signing key with the DHT key under which the value is published. However, this would force the use of (i) a single signing key, which must always correspond to the DHT key, and (ii) a short signing key, according to the limitations of the used DHT protocol, which may reserve only a constrained space for each DHT value. Therefore, this simpler scheme has been abandoned.

Attribute Authorities

Being mainly a platform for resilient micro-blogging, Blogracy is designed to assure new posts are published and distributed as widely as possible, exploiting the most popular and effective file-sharing infrastructure available today. However, since the core sharing system is completely agnostic with respect to published content, data can be easily encrypted with any cryptographic algorithm, either symmetric or asymmetric. In fact, Blogracy supports an Attribute-Based Encryption scheme. Blogracy privacy model uses attribute credentials for protecting access to sensible content, creating a sort of very flexible personal circles of contacts, i.e., parametrized roles to be assigned to users for granting a certain set of access rights. The encryption scheme is based on the CP-ABE protocol (Bethencourt, Sahai and Waters, 2007), though introducing some extensions for operation in a multi-authority scenario.

In the current security model of Blogracy, each user is considered an authority for his own groups of contacts, in a typical Targeted Broadcast scheme. Each user can thus grant attributes and authorizations to his own contacts, and attributes are intended as defined in a namespace local to that user, without possible overlapping. However, this way a message cannot be easily encoded according to a complex policy, which could possibly include attributes defined by different authorities. Conversely, in this setting key escrow is resolved by design, in the sense that each authority (i.e. each user) can only generate the keys for decoding messages originated locally, and thus already known.

However, this scheme does not allow to define access policies with attributes assigned by multiple authorities. A naive approach would simply use multiple encryption shells for cyphering the secret key of a message. The shells could be either nested or placed in a threshold gate, thus composing a number of rules, each one with attributes defined by a certain authority. Secret splitting algorithms could help to distribute the secret key under all the shells. However, all those schemes do not offer resistance to collusion, which is an important feature of typical ABE schemes.

According to the design of Blogracy, it is not possible to identify a globally trusted central authority, even if distributed over a limited number of entities. It is not even possible to restrict the number of attributes and attribute authorities, which would coordinate their operation at set-up time. Finally, Blogracy users are free to join the network, and they do not need or want to receive any identifier or secret from any authority. These requirements exclude both hierarchical schemes, managed centrally by a master authority, and coordinated schemes, with a predefined set of attribute authorities. Moreover, apart from trust considerations, a central entity is an unacceptable bottleneck and a single point of failure in a large P2P system.

In Blogracy, the CP-ABE scheme is adapted to the particular P2P environment. Attributes are attested by means of signed certificates (or delegation chains), originated by locally trusted attribute authorities. Such signed certificates may be used also to attest membership in a public group and may be inserted into a user's profile, either for public or restricted access. This solution is similar to the simple engineered scheme discussed in (Lewko and Waters, 2011)., but adapted for targeted broadcast in a P2P network. Thus, each user is allowed to issue attribute keys in its own space. Other authorities can be taken into account, by allowing a user to show some attribute certificates. If the user proves to be eligible and the remote authority is trusted for those attributes, the user is issued a local attribute key. In addition, it has to be considered that delegation is a feature already incorporated in the original design of CP-ABE, and in fact, in the development of the Blogracy prototype, we integrated an implementation of this delegation mechanism into an open source library for CP-ABE (https://github.com/junwei-wang/cpabe). Some eventual development of this scheme may be considered in future, since at the moment a concrete substitute for the random oracle is still missing.

Since each user is also an attribute authority for accessing his own social activities, then all relevant information is stored directly into his own JSON file, containing all the user's social data. In particular, in the "people" section, a list of acknowledged users can be created, as OpenSocial Person objects, where each user can be associated with a particular private attribute key. Each private attribute key is generated by the local user, using his own local master key MK and a set of attributes S to associate with the acknowledged user. To keep the generated attribute key confidential, it is encrypted used the public key of the remote user. Additionally, the social data file of a user also contains his own public parameters (the PK data, according to the ABE scheme). Currently, encrypted SK data and plaintext PK data for the ABE scheme are stored in the appData section of OpenSocial Person objects.

Assigned attributes serve to mark group membership, and thus some social activities may be disclosed only to a certain set of groups. This is obtained by encrypting sensible social data, according to the desired policy. In Blogracy, an access policy for a resource is essentially a list of groups which are authorized for access. In fact, each object in the social data file can be encrypted according to a different policy; otherwise, it is kept as a plaintext JSON object.

Network Anonymity

Blogracy does not require users to expose their real identity and offers instead a pseudonimity mechanism based on public keys. However, anonymity is an issue also at the lower network level. In fact, if communications among users are based on direct connections, or file locations are expressed as plain network addresses, these can be easily associated with a particular person or entity. Various network technologies are being developed, which promise to guarantee a certain level of anonymity for their users, disguising their real network location. One of the best known is Tor (The Onion Router), but other similar networks are also available, which in fact may be more adequate for an application based on file sharing techniques. In particular, I2P is an anonymizing P2P overlay network, implementing a protocol similar to Tor. It routes data through multiple peers, with multiple layers of cryptography, to render tracing much harder (Schimmer, 2009).

I2P is a software framework built as middleware layer. Its core component is the router and each node of the network is required to run a local instance of it. It guarantees connectivity for various applications, which can either provide services for other peers, or access darknet services provided by others, in a typical P2P fashion. The whole network is fully decentralized and runs as an overlay on top of IP. At its core, the network is based on a packet switching, connectionless protocol called SSU, which can be roughly described as an UDP-like protocol. But, on top of it, I2P provides also a TCP-like protocol, called NTCP. Using a classical layered encryption scheme, the sender encrypts its messages multiple times. For each different layer, it uses the public key of the next node on the chosen route. The so-called garlic protocol of I2P allows multiple messages to be stored inside the innermost layer. Each node then uses its own private key to decrypt one layer of encryption and reveal the next node in the route, to which it will forward the packet. Though being still experimental and not entirely reliable, the I2P network is growing in popularity. It is estimated that in February 2013, there were about 20,000 users online at the same time, up from around 14,000 one year before (Egger, 2013). Some weaknesses and possible attacks related to the current architecture and implementation of I2P are still discussed in (Egger, 2013).

Tor and I2P share many functionalities and mechanisms, as they both use layered cryptography and ordered paths. However, while Tor is at its core a circuit switched network, I2P is instead fundamentally a packet switched network. This makes it easier for I2P to route around congestion and failures, to create redundant paths and to balance load over available resources. Moreover, since Tor relies on well-known directory servers, it can be described as an essentially trusted, centralized system. Instead, I2P relies on a completely distributed and self-organizing database, based on Kademlia. Consequently, each peer has to profile other routers, to collaborate in determining how to select the best nodes for operating the database. Another difference is that I2P does not provide outproxy functionality out of the box, while Tor facilitates it through integrated outproxy discovery and selection. Also in I2P such outproxy mechanisms are perfectly possible, but they have to be realized directly by interested applications, running on top of the I2P middleware. In fact, this is an important difference in the focus of the two projects, more than a technical one. While Tor privileges anonymous web browsing, I2P is focused on darknet services, isolated inside the Internet. A range of applications are provided with I2P, to exploit the network for anonymous browsing of so-called eepsites, chatting, file-sharing and e-mailing.

In this sense, the focus of Tor and I2P projects are quite complementary. Technically, however, both can be used to either browse the web through outproxies or access internal hidden services, they have different strengths and weaknesses at this regard. In particular, since the I2P architecture is more distributed and focused on darknet-type services, it welcomes file sharing applications running inside the network (and thus separated from the larger communities operating on the plain Internet). Instead, Tor discourages the use of file sharing applications for not overloading its own outproxies.

Since Blogracy currently relies on Vuze for its file sharing operations (http://dev.vuze.com/), it is important to notice that Vuze can be configured to rely on I2P, for communication with both tracker servers and other peers. A plugin is available, though it has many rough edges and requires the manual setup of a number of services. Moreover, the I2P plugin does not support any Distributed Database, so it requires a tracker, preferably operating over I2P. In fact, it is possible to configure the internal tracker provided with Vuze, to operate over I2P.

The operation of Vuze over I2P requires the creation of a number of tunnels at each participant (router). Since an I2P route can only be used in one direction, two types of tunnels are needed for communicating. In practice, the exit point of an outbound tunnel must be joined to the entry point of an inbound tunnel. When creating each tunnel, users can determine its length, i.e., how many hops it should use. Thus security and latency can be balanced according to the needs of a particular application. The Kademplia-based network database (NetDB) then stores the public contact information of online services, i.e., the entry point of their inbound tunnel. For Vuze, an inbound tunnel has to be created and associated with the port of normal BitTorrent TCP and UDP connections. The plugin integrates a SOCKS proxy, which has to be used for Vuze outbound connections. For running an anonymous tracker, an additional inbound I2P tunnel has to be created. Vuze allows to setup the tracker to use the I2P tunnel as its externally communicated address.

Social Activities and Interoperability

Once users can be distinguished by their IDs, i.e., the hash of their public key, it is also possible to associate additional information with them, including personal profile and personal activity stream. The activities of a user are represented as a flow, which friends and followers are interested in and want to subscribe to. Blogracy adopts Activity Streams, an ongoing and well supported effort to standardize typical users' activities in social networks. This is an open JSON format specification for the syndication of activities performed in social web applications and services. It is currently developed by the Social Web Working Group of the W3C (http://www.w3.org/wiki/Activity_Streams/) for facilitating the integration of social activities performed on diverse sites (Dingli & Seychell, 2012).

In Blogracy, personal activities are included into a standard JSON feed, which is eventually signed according to the JSON Web Signature format to avoid tampering. This feed is shared using the underlying file-sharing platform. Essentially, a hash of its content and a magnet URI are used for identification and retrieval.

Since we expect feeds to be updated rather often and without a specific pattern, the magnet URI of a feed file is not sufficient to follow a user's activities. Adding new activities to the feed would change its contents and consequently its hash, resulting in an entirely different entity on the DHT.

This is the reason we have two logical DHTs: (i) the first DHT (DHT1) associates the user's key with the last version of his activity stream, in the form of a magnet URI; (ii) the second DHT (DHT2) is just a regular DHT and it is used to resolve the references to the resources actually mentioned in the activity stream. Although the two DHTs are two distinct logical entities, they can be implemented on a single DHT. When a user generates and shares new content, he also updates his own activity feed and shares the updated feed as well. Eventually, he updates the association in the first DHT linking his ID with the new magnet URI of his feed. The strategy is inevitably more complex than the one centralized systems adopt, considering that they can simply push notifications. On the other hand, in a decentralized context, these events have to be advertised in a public and open way, i.e., by means of an updated feed file listing a user's activity.

When a user comes online and desires to check the feed of one of his followees, the follower has to search for the followee's key on the second DHT; then, if the magnet URI is different from the last observed, the file containing the updated feed is retrieved. Since feeds are signed, it is possible to trust their authenticity and integrity, and since they are marked with a publication date, it is possible to discard older copies.

In Blogracy, searching for a user's feed happens at startup and it does not imply the repeated transfer of the whole feed, possibly unchanged. Instead, when requested, only a magnet URI is retrieved, and the whole feed is downloaded only if the URI changed. The download process itself is fully distributed among available seeds and thus it becomes more and more efficient as the number of followers grows.

Afterwards, new activities are notified directly among interested nodes. In fact, information pushing is handy in the case of fast interactions between users (Lombardo et al., 2018). In those cases, for example commenting or tagging over recent resources, direct message passing among users interested in the same shared resource is used to improve system responsiveness. Consequently, Blogracy benefits from P2P messaging facility, as provided by the file-sharing protocol. In fact, for their basic operation, file sharing systems usually need to keep track of the peers that are currently seeding or downloading a certain file (sometimes collectively defined as a "swarm"). So, advertising about a new feed is simply a matter of contacting the peers that are sharing the superseded version of the user's feed.

Concretely, since Blogracy handles users' feeds in the form of activity streams, it can also manage similar feeds obtained in other ways, seamlessly integrating content from web blogs and from the P2P network. Interoperability with more traditional news-feeds, web-based micro-blogging posts, and content distributed over the P2P network has been proven in some basic scenarios. Practical tests have verified the bidirectional integration of (i) Blogracy and Twitter, and (ii) Blogracy and RSS-based web feeds.

Delays Due to Node Churn

One of the more fundamental issues we have to face is the data availability, i.e., the problem to ensure that content placed on the network is accessible after the publisher disconnected. In fact, popular content (Seddiki and Benchaïba, 2015) will quickly gain lots of seeds, while posts published by peripheral users, with few contacts and sparse online presence, will instead suffer poor availability to the extent that it is possible that the publisher remains the only seed for his own new posts.

While this problem, due to the discontinuous online presence of nodes (the typical "churn" phenomenon of P2P file sharing system), is intuitive, we tried to analyze its effects in a quantitative way in various conditions.

In particular, the availability of a new content depends solely on the connection pattern of the source node and its followers (Angiani et al., 2016; Franchi, Poggi, & Tomaiuolo, 2016). Having a larger number of followers who share the new data, possibly with a longer online time, will certainly increase the availability of the data itself. It's worth underlining that just a single follower with very high availability can guarantee an almost perfect diffusion of data, since every follower in the social graph is also a seed in the file sharing application. For this reason, (i.e., for obtaining meaningful results, with nonzero delays) we excluded the case of constantly connected nodes from our simulations. Nevertheless, we actually foster the introduction of such nodes in real networks, for example in the form of shared nodes, which can host more users' profiles and allow them to start publishing their data more easily.

For measuring the effects of churn, we considered different scenarios and result data in various simulations (simulation scripts are available from the Blogracy website). Excluding for simplicity the possible viral diffusion of content to distant nodes (Wu et al., 2014), we conservatively limited the simulations to the network of nodes directly following a certain source. In Figure 4 shows the mean notification delay, which we measured as the instant of reception of a new message, with respect to the optimal reception time. If a follower node is online at the instant when a new message is published, then the optimal reception time is the instant of publication. Otherwise, the optimal reception time is the first time the node goes online again, after the publication.

We considered two kinds of nodes: (i) nodes connecting quite occasionally (three times a day, according to a Bernoulli process, for fifteen minutes in total); and (ii) more stable nodes, which both reproduce the median length of BitTorrent sessions (Bellissimo, Levine and Shenoy, 2004) and simulate usage in a collaborative work scenario (Franchi, Poggi, & Tomaiuolo, 2013) or a file-sharing session (both averaging to 8 hours a day). The simulated delays (shown in Figure 4) are quite severe in the

Figure 4. Simulation results showing the notification delay due to churn. The first graph is a function of the number of followers. The second graph is a function of the percentage (0%-25%) of stable nodes. A stable node is a node connected for ~8h a day. The solid lines are guides for the eye.

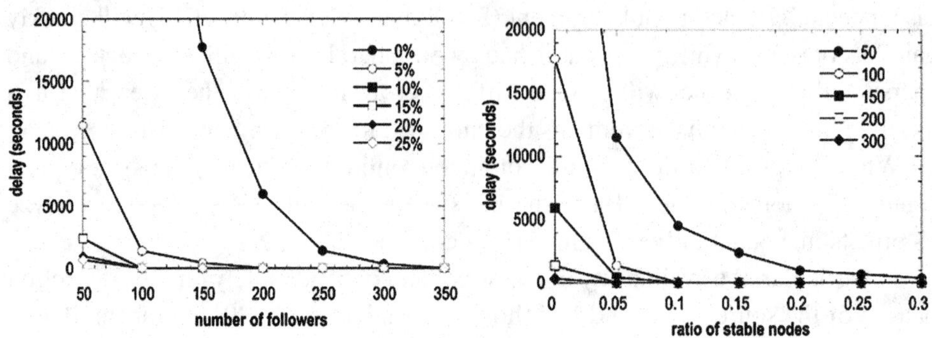

case of few followers, without stable nodes. However, when a user has more than 100-150 followers, the delays are negligible with just 5-10% of stable nodes. Thus, some aid has to be provided to newly joined users, in the form of resource hosting by other users, in addition to the small group of followers.

IMPLEMENTATION

In the previous section, we mainly described our system without referring to a specific platform, as long as it provides DHT and file-sharing mechanism. Specifically, we choose BitTorrent as the file-sharing protocol. BitTorrent is extremely popular and nowadays many applications written in various languages and for various environments interoperate using BitTorrent.

In Figure 1, we have highlighted the two main architectural components of Blogracy: (i) the BitTorrent module for basic file sharing and DHT operations, and (ii) the OpenSocial module for realizing the social platform, which can be accessed by the local user through a web interface.

The BitTorrent module is designed for providing four main services to the OpenSocial container: (i) the StoreService handles requests for storing new key-value pairs in the DHT, (ii) the LookupService finds values associated with a requested key in the DHT, (iii) the SeedService prepares a new torrent and seeds it, for a new file to share, and (iv) the DownloadService adds a new file to the download queue and signals the requester when the file is eventually available, locally.

Specifically, the popular BitTorrent client Azureus (now called Vuze) was the first program to introduce a working DHT based implementation. The processes we described in Subsection 4.2 require the possibility to use arbitrary keys (the user identifiers) on the DHT. The Vuze original DHT offers a set of primitive queries that we found suitable for our purposes. Regarding the Vuze platform, it has a modular architecture, where functionality can be added with plug-ins. The main application exposes to the plug-ins only a restricted interface, which is nonetheless sufficient for implementing our services. Consequently, we decided to implement Blogracy as a Vuze plug-in. We are gathering the ongoing implementation efforts in Blogracy own development website (http://dev.blogracy.net/).

The OpenSocial module realizes the social aspects of Blogracy, in the form of a Web application. In particular, it uses the services provided by the BitTorrent module. It is designed according to a Model-View-Controller architecture. The controller distributes responsibilities for various operations among few main classes, namely: (i) Distributed Hash Table, providing a representation of the global DHT in the context of Web application, (ii) File Sharing, managing the seeding and downloading of files, (iii) MediaController, specifically handling multimedia galleries, (iv) ActivitiesController, handling and updating the activity streams of local users and their remote friends, and (v) Chat Controller, for the management of chat channels, which are used both for direct communications among users and for the transparent push of status updates among interested peers.

While the BitTorrent module is quite agnostic about the type of application using its services, the OpenSocial Module maintains all information about a user's social identity, i.e., his cryptographic keys, profile, friends list. The local user's private key is stored enciphered in a standard Java key store, along with the public keys of his friends. All other information is stored in JSON files (possibly partially encrypted according to the ABE scheme). Except for the Java key store, all other files are shared on the BitTorrent network. Each user signs his own updated Activity Stream according to the JSON Web Signature format.

ANONYMIZATION

Blogracy doesn't require users to expose their real identity and offers instead a pseudonimity mechanism based on public keys. However, anonymity is an issue also at the lower network level. In fact, if communications among users are based on direct connections, or file locations are expressed as plain network addresses, these can be easily associated with a particular person or entity. Various network technologies are being developed, which promise to guarantee a certain level of anonymity for their users, disguising their real network location. One of the best known is Tor (The Onion Router), but other similar networks are also available, which in fact may be more adequate for an application based on file sharing techniques. In particular, I2P is a anonymizing P2P overlay network, implementing a protocol similar to Tor. However, the focus of Tor and I2P projects are quite complementary. Technically, both can be used to either browse the web through outproxies or access internal hidden services, they have different strengths and weaknesses at this regard. In particular, since I2P architecture is more distributed and focused on darknet-type services, it welcomes file sharing applications running inside the network (and thus separated from the larger communities operating on the plain Internet). Instead, Tor discourages the use of file sharing applications for not overloading its own outproxies.

Since Blogracy relies on Vuze for its current implementation, it is important to notice that Vuze can be configured to rely on I2P, for communication with both tracker servers and other peers. A plugin is available, though it has many rough edges and requires the manual setup of a number of services. Moreover, the I2P plugin does not support any Distributed Database, so it requires a tracker, preferably operating over I2P. In fact, it is possible to configure the internal tracker provided with Vuze, to operate over I2P.

The operation of Vuze over I2P requires the creation of a number of tunnels at each participant (router). Since an I2P route can only be used in one direction, two types of tunnels are needed for communicating. In practice, the exit point of an outbound tunnel must be joined to the entry point of an inbound tunnel. When creating each tunnel, users can determine its length, i.e., how many hops it should use. Thus security and latency can be balanced according to the needs of a particular application.

The Kademlia-based network database (NetDB) then stores the public contact information of online services, i.e., the entry point of their inbound tunnel. For Vuze, an inbound tunnel has to be created and associated with the port of normal BitTorrent TCP and UDP connections. The plugin integrates a SOCKS proxy, which has to be used for Vuze outbound connections. For running an anonymous tracker, an additional inbound I2P tunnel has to be created. Vuze allows to setup the tracker to use the I2P tunnel as its externally communicated address.

EXPERIMENTATION

Even if several large data analyses have been conducted over the BitTorrent network and the Vuze DHT (Falkner, 2007), we decided to test the actual functioning of Blogracy, which is quite particular, both for the usage of the DHT at different levels, and for the distribution of small social data files (essentially, some activity streams) instead of large archives and multimedia files (which nevertheless may be advertised through Blogracy messages). In particular, twelve instances of Blogracy were executed over different remote nodes of PlanetLab Europe. For simplicity and consistency, the nodes were arranged in a small fully connected social network (i.e., each node follows all the others).

Over this testbed, the functionality of the pushing mechanism was verified. It allows a source node to notify its followers in a timely and effective way about the availability of update in the local social data file. This kind of notification exploits the chat module of Vuze. Since it occurs directly between interested nodes (those participating in a swarm) it is virtually instantaneous.

Here, instead, an evaluation of the basic polling mechanism is presented, which involves sending various queries overs the DHT, downloading a torrent file and finally passing through download queues, before receiving the latest messages. It is worth noting that in a real system, this mechanism would be used only at the node startup, for receiving interesting activities produced when it was offline. Afterwards, push notifications would be more effective. In the tests, the polling cycle was set at two minutes, i.e., the availability of new messages from a certain source node was checked every two minutes.

Probably, the more interesting result is the delay in the reception of new messages at follower nodes. The delays shown in the first graph of Figure 5 are those concretely measured. In this setting, 90% of messages are received in 4.5 minutes. However, the measured times include a delay due to the polling cycle, which on average accounts for 1 minute. Thus, in the mean delay of 4.5 minutes, 3.5 minutes are effectively

Figure 5. Cumulative distribution of the notification delay in the reception of messages over the PlanetLab testbed; the polling cycle, repeated every two minutes, accounts on average for one minute. The first graph shows the case of normal Internet communications. The second graph shows the case of communications over I2P.

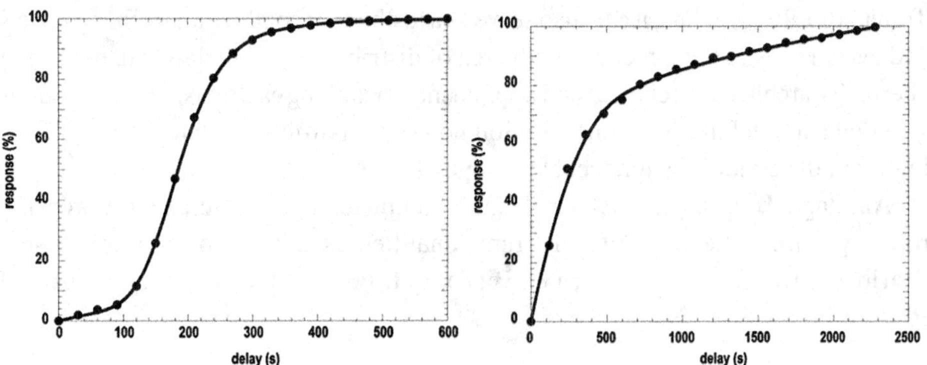

due to DHT and BitTorrent download mechanisms. To evaluate the effectiveness of actually running a distributed social network on top of I2P, some empirical tests were conducted. These were performed on PlanetLab, with a dozen of Blogracy nodes running on I2P. An additional node was configured to host a tracker service on I2P, using the internal tracker of Vuze. The cumulative distribution of measured delays is shown in the second graph of Figure 5. The reception of 90% of messages requires around 20 minutes. With respect to direct connections, delays increase roughly by a factor of 4. It is possible that results could be improved slightly through finer setup, reducing the length of tunnels (and thus the level of anonymity). In any case, these results are not surprising, being in accordance with more extensive performance tests conducted over I2P. In (Ehlert, 2011), for example, authors measure that simple web browsing through IP2 increases the latency by a factor of 3, with respect to direct access. This is not a cheap price, but it is what is necessary to pay, in terms of performances, for I2P network anonymity.

CONCLUSION AND FUTURE RESEARCH DIRECTIONS

This chapter discussed a P2P system that leverages existing, widespread and stable technologies such as DHTs and BitTorrent for supporting the development of a social networking system called Blogracy. Although the primitives offered by those technologies were created with other goals in mind, however, they could be effectively adapted for our system. In particular, we introduced a key-based identity system and a model of social relations for distributing resources efficiently among interested readers.

We designed Blogracy as a micro-blogging social networking system, and we gave priority to the features more important for micro-blogging, such as: (i) data availability and resilience to censorship, (ii) content authenticability, (iii) data confidentiality, (iv) network anonymity, and (v) semantic interoperability. All these aspects are kept as much orthogonal as possible in the system (Franchi, Poggi and Tomaiuolo, 2016). Thus, it can also serve as a testbed for conducting further analysis and evaluations in the larger research area of distributed social platform, exploring alternative architectural choices and implementations along each axis. The simulations we conducted, taking into consideration nodes with different connection patterns, highlight the conditions for acceptable operation.

Although Blogracy is not yet feature-complete, we have created a working prototype, implementing all core functionalities as a layer over a well-tested distributed file sharing system, i.e., BitTorrent. Performance analysis shows that the basic mechanism of polling for new content is functional. However, practically it is required mainly at system startup, since afterwards it is replaced by a more efficient push strategy. The system has also been tested over the I2P anonymizing network, which is designed to support anonymous services and also file sharing applications. Moreover, since it uses activity streams and weak semantic data formats for contacts and profiles, the system has been easily integrated with other existing social platforms (e.g. Twitter) and RSS-based content streams, as either a data source or a data sink.

We plan to extend the system further. Areas for study and improvements include: (i) privacy, where algorithms based on multiple independent authorities for attribute certification could improve extendibility and flexibility of disclosure policies; (ii) cooperation and incentive mechanisms, for allowing smooth introduction of new users into the network; (iii) distributed reputation mechanisms, based on social relations, for strengthening also the basic functionalities of the underlying P2P network. Finally, we plan to improve the implementation of the Blogracy system by taking advantage of an actor-based software framework that should improve the integration of its software components (Bergenti, Poggi and Tomaiuolo, 2014; Bergenti et al., 2016).

REFERENCES

Agazzi, F., & Tomaiuolo, M. (2013). Trust Negotiation for Automated Service Integration. *Proceedings of the 14th Workshop on Objects and Agents (WOA 2013).*

Aiello, L. M., & Ruffo, G. (2010). LotusNet: Tunable privacy for distributed online social network services. *Computer Communications*, *35*(1), 75–88. doi:10.1016/j.comcom.2010.12.006

Angiani, G., Fornacciari, P., Mordonini, M., Tomaiuolo, M., & Iotti, E. (2016). Models of participation in social networks. In Social Media Performance Evaluation and Success Measurements (pp. 196-224). Academic Press.

Avramova, Z., Wittevrongel, S., Bruneel, H., & De Vleeschauwer, D. (Aug.2009). Analysis and modeling of video popularity evolution in various on-line video content systems. *Proceedings of the 1st International Conference on Evolving Internet (INTERNET '09)*, 95-100.

Baden, R., Bender, A., Spring, N., Bhattacharjee, B., & Starin, D. (2009). Persona: an online social network with user-defined privacy. In *Proceedings of the ACM conference on Data communication (SIGCOMM '09)* (pp. 135–146). ACM. 10.1145/1592568.1592585

Bellissimo, A., Levine, B. N., & Shenoy, P. (2004). *Exploring the use of BitTorrent as the basis for a large trace repository (Technical Report)*. University of Massachusetts.

Bergenti, B., Poggi, A., & Tomaiuolo, M. (2014). An Actor Based Software Framework for Scalable Applications. In *Proceedings of the International Conference on Internet and Distributed Computing Systems* (pp. 26-35). Springer. 10.1007/978-3-319-11692-1_3

Bergenti, F., Iotti, E., Poggi, A., & Tomaiuolo, M. (2016). Concurrent and Distributed Applications with ActoDeS. *MATEC Web of Conferences, 6*(04043). 10.1051/matecconf/20167604043

Berners-Lee, T. (2010). Long Live the Web: A Call for Continued Open Standards and Neutrality. *Scientific American Magazine*. Retrieved from http://www.scientificamerican.com/article.cfm?id=long-live-the-web

Bethencourt, J., Sahai, A., & Waters, B. (2007). Ciphertext-Policy Attribute-Based Encryption. In *IEEE Symposium on Security and Privacy* (pp. 321-334). IEEE.

Buchegger, S., Schiöberg, D., Vu, L., & Datta, A. (2009). PeerSoN: P2P social networking: early experiences and insights. In *Proceedings of the Second ACM EuroSys Workshop on Social Network Systems* (pp. 46-52). ACM.

Castro, M., Druschel, P., Kermarrec, A. M., & Rowstron, A. (2002). Scribe: A large-scale and decentralized application-level multicast infrastructure. *IEEE Journal on Selected Areas in Communications*, *20*(8), 1489–1499. doi:10.1109/JSAC.2002.803069

Chawki, M. (2010). Anonymity in cyberspace: Finding the balance between privacy and security. *International Journal of Technology Transfer and Commercialisation*, *9*(3), 183–199. doi:10.1504/IJTTC.2010.030209

Clarke, I., Miller, S., Hong, T., Sandberg, O., & Wiley, B. (2002). Protecting free expression online with Freenet. *Internet Computing*, *6*(1), 40–49. doi:10.1109/4236.978368

Cutillo, L. A., Molva, R., & Strufe, T. (2009). Safebook: A Privacy Preserving Online Social Network Leveraging on Real-Life Trust. *IEEE Communications Magazine*, *47*(12), 94–101. doi:10.1109/MCOM.2009.5350374

Dimmock, N., Bacon, J., Ingram, D., & Moody, K. (2005). Risk models for trust-based access control (TBAC). In Trust Management (pp. 364-371). Academic Press.

Dingli, A., & Seychell, D. (2012). Taking Social Networks to the Next Level. *International Journal of Distributed Systems and Technologies*, *3*(4), 24–33. doi:10.4018/jdst.2012100103

Fornacciari, P., Mordonini, M., Poggi, A., Sani, L., & Tomaiuolo, M. (2018). A holistic system for troll detection on Twitter. *Computers in Human Behavior*, *89*, 258–268. doi:10.1016/j.chb.2018.08.008

Franchi, E., Poggi, A., & Tomaiuolo, M. (2013). Open social networking for online collaboration. *International Journal of e-Collaboration*, *9*(3), 50–68. doi:10.4018/jec.2013070104

Franchi, E., Poggi, A., & Tomaiuolo, M. (2014). Multi-Agent Active Services for Online Social Networks. In Handbook of Research on Demand-Driven Web Services: Theory, Technologies, and Applications. Academic Press. doi:10.4018/978-1-4666-5884-4.ch004

Franchi, E., Poggi, A., & Tomaiuolo, M. (2015). Information and Password Attacks on Social Networks: An Argument for Cryptography. *Journal of Information Technology Research*, *8*(1), 25–42. doi:10.4018/JITR.2015010103

Franchi, E., Poggi, A., & Tomaiuolo, M. (2016). Blogracy: A peer-to-peer social network. *International Journal of Distributed Systems and Technologies*, *7*(2), 37–56. doi:10.4018/IJDST.2016040103

Franchi, E., Poggi, A., & Tomaiuolo, M. (2016). Social media for online collaboration in firms and organizations. *International Journal of Information System Modeling and Design*, *7*(1), 18–31. doi:10.4018/IJISMD.2016010102

Franchi, E., & Tomaiuolo, M. (2013). Distributed Social Platforms for Confidentiality and Resilience. In *Social Network Engineering for Secure Web Data and Services* (pp. 114–136). Hershey, PA: IGI Global. doi:10.4018/978-1-4666-3926-3.ch006

Franchi, E., & Tomaiuolo, M. (2014). A Unified Framework for Traditional and Agent-Based Social Network Modeling. In Interdisciplinary Applications of Agent-Based Social Simulation and Modeling (p. 184). Academic Press. doi:10.4018/978-1-4666-5954-4.ch011

Graffi, K., Groß, C., Mukherjee, P., Kovacevic, A., & Steinmetz, R. (2010). LifeSocial. KOM: A P2Pbased Platform for Secure Online Social Networks. In *Proceedings of the 10th IEEE International Conference onP2PComputing IEEE P2P'10* (pp. 554-558). IEEE.

Greene, M. (2014). Where has privacy gone? How surveillance programs threaten expectations of privacy. *The John Marshall Journal of Information Technology & Privacy Law*, *30*(4), 795–827.

Guidi, B. (2015). *DiDuSoNet: A P2P architecture for distributed Dunbar-based social networks*. Retrieved from https://etd.adm.unipi.it/theses/available/etd-11202015-225158/

Hobart, B. (2011). *What a deep dive into LinkedIn's S-1 reveals about the company's growth potential*. Retrieved from http://read.bi/hzHD1b

Li, N. (July2000). Local Names in SPKI/SDSI. In *Proceedings of the 13th IEEE workshop on Computer Security Foundations (CSFW '00)* (pp. 2-15). IEEE Computer Society Press. 10.1109/CSFW.2000.856921

Lombardo, G., Fornacciari, P., Mordonini, M., Sani, L., & Tomaiuolo, M. (2018). A combined approach for the analysis of support groups on Facebook - The case of patients of hidradenitis suppurativa. *Multimedia Tools and Applications*, 1–19.

McGrath, R. G. (2010). Business Models: A Discovery Driven Approach. *Long Range Planning*, *43*(2-3), 247–261. doi:10.1016/j.lrp.2009.07.005

Perfitt, T., & Englert, B. (2010). *Megaphone: Fault Tolerant, Scalable, and Trustworthy*. Microblogging.

Poggi, A., & Tomaiuolo, M. (2011). Integrating Peer-to-Peer and Multi-agent Technologies for the Realization of Content Sharing Applications. In Information Retrieval and Mining in Distributed Environments, SCI (Vol. 324, pp. 93-107). Springer.

Sandler, D., Mislove, A., Post, A., & Druschel, P. (2005). Feedtree: Sharing web micronews with P2P event notification. In P2P Systems IV, LNCS (Vol. 3640, pp. 141-151). Springer.

Sauermann, L., Cyganiak, R., & Völkel, M. (2007). *Cool URIs for the semantic web*. Academic Press.

Schimmer, L. (2009). Peer Profiling and Selection in the I2P Anonymous Network 1 I2P Overview. *Proceedings of PET-CON '09*, 1-12.

Seddiki, M., & Benchaïba, M. (2015). Gpop: A Global File Popularity Measurement for Unstructured P2P Networks. *International Journal of Distributed Systems and Technologies*, *6*(3), 51–64. doi:10.4018/IJDST.2015070104

Shankland, S. (2010). *Facebook blocks contact exporting tool.* Retrieved from http://news.cnet.com/8301-30685_3-20076774-264/facebook-blocks-contact-exporting-tool/

Tomaiuolo, M. (2013). dDelega: Trust management for web services. *International Journal of Information Security and Privacy*, *7*(3), 53–67. doi:10.4018/jisp.2013070104

Tomaiuolo, M. (2014). Trust Management and Delegation for the Administration of Web Services. In I. Portela & F. Almeida (Eds.), *Organizational, Legal, and Technological Dimensions of Information System Administration* (pp. 18–37). Hershey, PA: IGI Global. doi:10.4018/978-1-4666-4526-4.ch002

Wu, T. Y., Lee, W. T., Guizani, N., & Wang, T. M. (2014). Incentive mechanism for p2p file sharing based on social network and game theory. *Journal of Network and Computer Applications*, *41*, 47–55. doi:10.1016/j.jnca.2013.10.006

Xu, T., Chen, Y., & Fu, X. (2010). Twittering by Cuckoo: decentralized and socio-aware online microblogging services. In *Proceedings of the ACM SIGCOMM 2010 Conference* (pp. 473—475). ACM. 10.1145/1851182.1851270

Zink, M., Suh, K., Gu, Y., & Kurose, J. (2009). *Watch global, cache local: Youtube network traffic at a campus network - measurements and implications. In Proceedings of SPIE 6818.* San Jose, CA: International Society for Optical Engineering.

KEY TERMS AND DEFINITIONS

Anonymity: State of being unknown or unacknowledged to the others.

Peer-to-Peer System: A network-based system in which each node can act as both client and server for the other ones of the system.

Privacy: The right to be secluded from the presence or view of others.

Social Network: Social structure made by individuals and organizations that are connected by relationships; relationships that may represent various kinds of ties between member and that can be either symmetrical or asymmetrical.

Social Networking System: A software system that allows users to manipulate a representation of their online social networks and to interact with the other users in the system, especially collaboratively discussing user-produced resources.

Chapter 10
Failure Detectors of Strong S and Perfect P Classes for Time Synchronous Hierarchical Distributed Systems

Anshul Verma
Banaras Hindu University, India

Mahatim Singh
Banaras Hindu University, India

Kiran Kumar Pattanaik
Atal Bihari Vajpayee Indian Institute of Information Technology and Management Gwalior, India

ABSTRACT

Present failure detection algorithms for distributed systems are designed to work in asynchronous or partially synchronous environments on mesh (all-to-all) connected systems and maintain status of every other process. Several real-time systems are hierarchically connected and require working in strict synchronous environments. Use of existing failure detectors for such systems would generate excess computation and communication overhead. The chapter describes two suspicion-based failure detectors of Strong S and Perfect P classes for hierarchical distributed systems working in time synchronous environments. The algorithm of Strong S class is capable of detecting permanent crash failures, omission failures, link failures, and timing failures. Strong completeness and weak accuracy properties of the algorithm are evaluated. The failure detector of Perfect P class is capable of detecting crash failures, crash-recovery failures, omission failures, link failures, and timing failures. Strong completeness and strong accuracy properties of the failure detector are evaluated.

DOI: 10.4018/978-1-5225-8295-3.ch010

INTRODUCTION

In distributed systems failure detectors are used to maintain information about the operational states of other processes. Information provided by a failure detector is assumed unreliable because it can suspect a correct process or not suspect a faulty process. The operational status information of a process provided by two failure detectors at different processes may differ (Cortinas, 2011). In such scenarios *completeness* and *accuracy* are the two properties to assess the reliability of failure detectors. Completeness has been further defined into two variations: strong and weak; while, accuracy has been defined into four variations: strong, weak, eventual strong, and eventual weak (Chandra & Toueg, 1996). The *strong completeness* represents that eventually every process that crashes is permanently suspected by every correct process. Whereas, *strong accuracy* represents that no correct process is suspected by any process. *Weak accuracy* represents that some correct process is never suspected, means some correct processes can be suspected. The failure detectors that satisfy *strong completeness* and *weak accuracy* properties belong to *Strong S* class. However, those satisfy *strong completeness* and *strong accuracy* properties belong to the *Perfect P* class. Similarly, there are eight pairs, each pair forming a new failure detector class (see Table 1) formed by selecting one of the two completeness properties and one of the four accuracy properties.

Failure detectors adopt mainly two methods for status monitoring of other processes: *polling* and *heartbeat. Polling* is basically a *query/reply* (or pull) based status monitoring technique (Larrea, Arévalo, & Fernández, 1999; Larrea, Fernández, & Arévalo, 2004). Whereas, in *heartbeat*, every process *q* periodically sends a heartbeat message to all its neighbours processes *p* to inform them that *q* is alive, thus termed as push based. Absence of the heartbeat message implies a fault (Aguilera, Chen, & Toueg, 1997; Soraluze, Cortiñas, Lafuente, Larrea, & Freiling, 2011). Some failure detectors return a list of suspected processes as output fall under *suspicion based* (Chandra & Toueg, 1996), and those return a list of trusted (correct) processes as output fall under *trust based* failure detectors (Chandra, Hadzilacos, & Toueg, 1996).

Taxonomy of distributed systems is presented in Figure 1 which is based on the physical arrangement of nodes (*topology aspect*), and events' completion time bound (*time aspect*). In *time aspects* based classification, systems are classified into three categories: synchronous, asynchronous, and partially synchronous, on the basis of two time attributes. First, the time taken for message transmission between two processes, and second the time taken by a processor to execute a task (Cortinas, 2011). Synchronous systems have lower and upper time bound defined

Table 1. Classification of failure detectors

Completeness	Accuracy			
	Strong	Weak	Eventual Strong	Eventual Weak
Strong	*Perfect* P	*Strong* S	*Eventually Perfect* $\Diamond P$	*Eventually Strong* $\Diamond S$
Weak	Q	*Weak* W	$\Diamond Q$	*Eventually Weak* $\Diamond W$

(Chandra & Toueg, 1996)

Figure 1. Taxonomy of distributed systems
(Verma & Pattanaik, 2016)

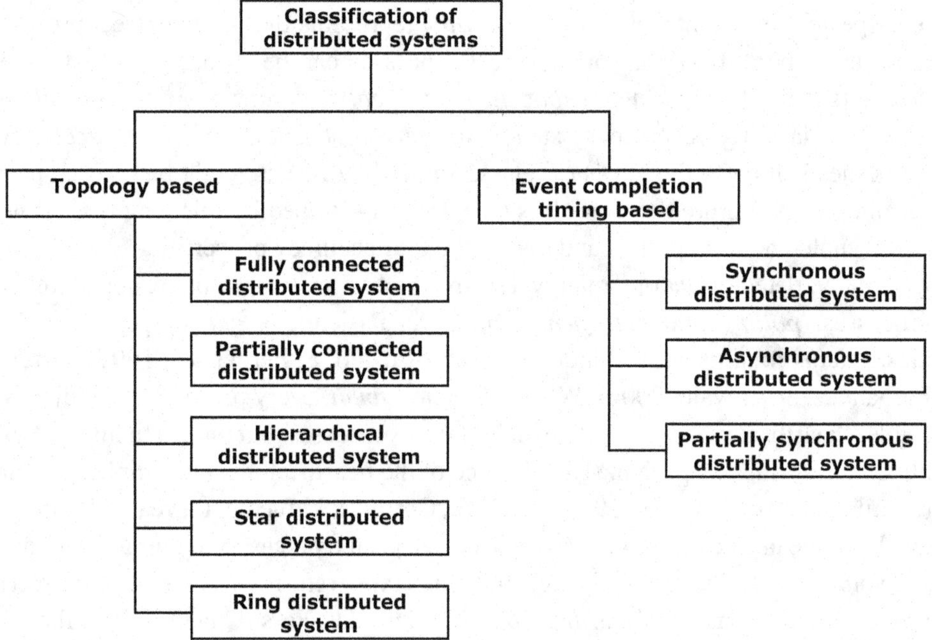

for message transmission and task execution (Hadzilacos & Toueg, 1994). Whereas, asynchronous systems do not have time bound for message transmission and task execution events (Chandra & Toueg, 1996). Partially synchronous systems follow the characteristics of synchronous and asynchronous systems (Dolev, Dwork, & Stockmeyer, 1987; Dwork, Lynch, & Stockmeyer, 1988; Widder & Schmid, 2009).

Failure detectors for all-to-all process connected (mesh) networks discussed in the literature are designed for asynchronous or partially synchronous environments in which each process maintains the status of every other process in the system. Such failure detectors result in undesired computation and communication overhead when applied on hierarchical topology based real time applications, e.g. cable TV networks, domain name server systems, network time protocol systems, wireless networks for military, multi-agent based train control systems (Verma, Pattanaik, & Goel, 2014; Verma & Pattanaik, 2014; Verma & Pattanaik, 2015a; Verma & Pattanaik, 2015b), etc. that do not require maintaining status of every other processes at each process. In hierarchical networks, a process should only bother about the status of its children (descendant) processes in the hierarchy. Hence, the root process will have aggregate information about the status of all processes in the network. Most of the existing failure detectors provide system wide information about the individual suspected or trusted processes. Such information although reflects the status of the individual processes, the relational (parent-child) information requirement of hierarchical networks can't be determined from that. Thus a new failure detector algorithm of *Perfect P* class has been proposed by the authors of this chapter (Verma & Pattanaik, 2016) for the hierarchical topology based systems.

In this chapter, that failure detector is thoroughly described along with generic discussion on several terminologies whose understanding is necessary to understand and develop a new failure detector. The chapter deeply discussed *suspicion based* failure detector algorithms of *Strong S* and *Perfect P* classes for the hierarchical distributed systems working in time synchronous environments. The *Strong S* class algorithm shows early stage of failure detector algorithm development for the time synchronous hierarchical distributed system. It is able to detect permanent *crash failure*, *omission failure*, *link failure*, and *timing failure*. The correctness proof is evaluated in terms of *strong completeness* and *weak accuracy* properties of the algorithm. The algorithm has several limitations those are addressed by *Perfect P* class algorithm. The *Perfect P* class algorithm is capable to detect *crash failures*, *crash-recovery failures*, *omission failures*, *link failures*, and *timing failures*. The mechanism satisfies the *strong completeness* and *strong accuracy* properties of *Perfect P* class.

The rest of the chapter is organized as follow. Section 2 presents the related work, and Section 3 describes the generic definition of failure detector and its related terminologies. Section 4 describes the system model of the hierarchical time synchronous systems. Section 5 describes a new failure detector algorithm of *Strong S* class followed by its correctness proof in Section 6. Detailed failure detector algorithm of *Perfect P class* is discussed in Section 7 followed by its correctness proof in Section 8. A case study is discussed in Section 9 that describes the use of proposed failure detector algorithm in a real life hierarchical time synchronous system. Finally Section 10 concludes the chapter.

RELATED WORK

Failure detector algorithms of different classes are discussed in the literature for asynchronous and partially synchronous systems. Those follow either *polling* or *heartbeat* approach for failure monitoring and provide either a list of suspected processes or trusted processes as output. Such algorithms are developed for all-to-all process communication model, and are capable to deal with a majority of failures. In the following, some of the failure detector algorithms are discussed on the basis of their class, failure monitoring approach, output, and addressed failures.

The concept of unreliable failure detectors was introduced in (Chandra & Toueg, 1996) to solve the consensus problem in asynchronous systems while detecting only *crash failures*. The paper discusses *suspicion based* failure detector for asynchronous systems with *crash failures*. The unreliable failure detectors were categorised into eight classes in terms of *completeness* and *accuracy* properties. Authors prove that the consensus can be solved by unreliable failure detectors and the same can be used for atomic broadcast. However, the message *omission failures* and *link failures* in synchronous or partially synchronous environments are not discussed.

A non-suspicion algorithm based Heartbeat failure detector proposed in (Aguilera, Chen, & Toueg, 1997) achieves reliable communication with quiescent algorithms and deals with *crash failures* and *link failures*. It is used for consensus, k-set agreement, atomic broadcast, atomic commitment, etc. It provides only a list of suspected process in matrix form that shows correct and faulty processes. Since, it is designed for asynchronous systems and does not use timeout concept it is not suitable for synchronous systems.

An all-to-all process communication pattern based failure detector algorithm, given in (Chandra & Toueg, 1996), exchanges a number of messages periodically that is quadratic on the number of processes. An enhancement of this failure detector algorithm is presented in (Larrea, Fernández, & Arévalo, 2004) that uses a logical ring arrangement of the processes and periodically exchanges at most linear number of messages. The algorithm uses the *polling* concept for detecting *crash failures* in partially synchronous system and assumes there is always a majority of correct processes, links are reliable, and *crash failures* are permanent and such assumptions are not true in real networks.

A transformation of failure detector Ω (Chandra, Hadzilacos, & Toueg, 1992) is presented in (Gallet, Fauconnier, Freiling, Penso, & Tielmann, 2007) is the weakest failure detector for consensus in an asynchronous environment. The impact of *omission failure* is studied on the algorithms of asynchronous systems with *crash-stop failures*. The proposed algorithm deals with the *crash-stop* and permanent *omission failures* with the assumption of majority of correct processes. The algorithm does not consider timing and is intended for asynchronous systems hence not suitable for synchronous and partially synchronous systems.

A *suspicion based* partially perfect failure detector, working on *polling* concept, is discussed in (Macêdo & Gorender, 2009) for partitioned (partially) synchronous systems. Some properties (i.e., strong partition synchrony and timeliness oracle) were introduced that must be valid to develop a failure detector of *Perfect P* class for such systems. The algorithm is developed for all-to-all process connected partially synchronous systems, hence is not suitable for time synchronous hierarchical networks.

A communication efficient failure detector of *eventual Perfect* $\Diamond P$ class is proposed in (Soraluze, Cortiñas, Lafuente, Larrea, & Freiling, 2011) for the *general omission failure* model that deals with the process *crash failures* and *omission failures* while sending or receiving messages. The algorithm uses the *heartbeat* approach for failure monitoring in partially synchronous all-to-all process connected network. The algorithm represents both correct and faulty processes in the form of a matrix. It is communication efficient as it uses only a linear number of links for message transmission. Since, the algorithm is designed according to the requirements of partially synchronous all-to-all process connected networks, it is not directly applicable for time critical hierarchical networks working in synchronous environment.

New failure detector classes $H\Omega$ and $H\Sigma$ for homonymous distributed systems are introduced in (Arevalo, Anta, Imbs, Jimenez, & Raynal, 2012) that are the counterpart of weakest failure detector classes Ω and Σ. Two failure detector algorithms of these classes are designed to solve the consensus problem in homonymous systems with the assumption of majority of correct processes. These algorithms are *trust based*, use *polling* approach for failure monitoring, and deal with process *crash failures*. The algorithms are developed for asynchronous systems and do not address message *omission failures*.

A *suspicion based* failure detector $M*$, is presented in (Park, Lee, & Yu, 2013) to solve non-blocking atomic commitment problem in a crash-prone asynchronous system. The developed failure detector is weaker than the *Perfect P* class, but stronger than the *eventually Perfect* $\Diamond P$ class. It uses *heartbeat* approach for failure monitoring and assumes majority of correct processes. It is intended for asynchronous systems and does not address message *omission failures*.

To the best of our understanding none of the above works focused on the development of failure detector algorithms for the real time hierarchical networks working in the synchronous environments. Therefore, it is important to develop a new failure detector for real time hierarchical networks focussing on *crash failures*, *crash-recovery failures*, *omission failures*, *link failures*, and *timing failures*.

FAILURE DETECTOR

Failure detectors were introduced by (Chandra & Toueg, 1996) to solve the problem of consensus. Here, the introduction of failure detector and its basic terminologies are presented. For detailed introduction and further information, readers can refer the following works: (Mostefaoui, Mourgaya, & Raynal, 2002; Raynal, 2005; Guerraoui & Rodrigues, 2006; Guerraoui, 2008; Raynal, 2010; Freiling, Guerraoui, & Kouznetsov, 2011).

General Definition

Failure detector is an algorithm/module located at each process in the distributed system. It collects operational state information of other processes in the system and provides to its owner to make aware of faulty processes in the system. The collected operational state information of other processes may be unreliable because failure detectors can suspect a non-faulty process or not suspect a faulty process. This information can vary from one process to another at the same time and in the same distributed system.Failure detectors reliability is measured through two properties: *completeness* and *accuracy*.

The failure detectors that provide a list of suspected processes as output, known as *suspicion based* (Chandra & Toueg, 1996), for example the eventually perfect failure detector ($\Diamond P$). Other types of failure detectors output a list of non-suspected processes and known as *trust based* (Hutle, 2005), for example eventual leader failure detector (Ω).

Classification of Failure Detectors

Failure detectors are classified according to two properties: *completeness* and *accuracy* (Chandra & Toueg, 1996). Completeness represents the capability of suspecting faulty processes, whereas accuracy represents the degree of mistakes the failure detector can make during suspecting faulty processes. Both properties are complementary to each other. For example, only completeness can be achieved by suspecting every process in the system, in the same way, only accuracy can be achieved by suspecting none of the processes. Therefore, a good balance between both properties is essential according to the requirement of failure detectors because neither of both is useful separately. Variations of both properties are described in the following.

Completeness: There are two variations of the completeness property that a failure detector can satisfy.

- **Strong Completeness:** Eventually every process that crashes is permanently suspected by *every* correct process. Means, every correct process will eventually and permanently suspect every faulty process.
- **Weak Completeness:** Eventually every process that crashes is permanently suspected by *some* correct process. Means, every faulty process will be eventually and permanently suspected by at least one correct process.

Accuracy: Four variations of the accuracy property are available in literature.

- **Strong Accuracy:** No process is suspected before it crashes. Means, no correct process can ever be suspected.
- **Weak Accuracy:** Some correct process is never suspected. Means, some correct processes can be suspected.
- **Eventual Strong Accuracy:** There is a time after which correct processes are not suspected by any correct process. Means, eventually no false suspicion will be made.
- **Eventual Weak Accuracy:** There is a time after which some correct process is never suspected by any correct process. Means, eventually some false suspicion will not be made.

According to the above discussed properties, failure detectors are classified into eight different classes by combining a completeness and an accuracy properties(Chandra & Toueg, 1996), which are shown in Table 1.

Apart from these classes, a new failure detector class was introduced, denoted by *Omega* (Ω), to elect a correct leader among all correct processes in a system (Chandra, Hadzilacos & Toueg, 1996). Notice that the previous ones are *suspicion based* failure detectors, whereas Ω is a *trust based* failure detector class (Cortinas, 2011).

Monitoring Approaches

Failure detectors are abstract concepts or mechanisms, i.e., they do not depend on a specific implementation. They can be implemented by following any approach as long as the approach meets the properties of the desired class. As discussed earlier, failure detectors monitor operational state of other processes. They mainly use one of the two approaches for monitoring operational state of other processes: *polling* and *heartbeat*.

- **Polling (or Query/Reply):** Each process sends "are-you-alive?" message to each other process in the system and waits for the reply from each process within a predefined time. If it does not receive "I-am-alive" message from a corresponding process within predefined time, it suspects the process as faulty. In this way, each process maintains a list of suspected (faulty) processes in the system. Failure detectors based on *polling* approach can be seen in (Larrea, Arévalo, & Fernández, 1999; Larrea, Fernández, & Arévalo, 2004).
- **Heartbeat:** Each process periodically sends "I-am-alive" message to each other process in the system as well as receives the same message from each other process. If a process does not receive "I-am-alive" message from any process within a predefined time, it suspects the process as faulty. In this way, each process maintains a list of suspected (faulty) processes in the system. Failure detectors based on *heartbeat* approach have been proposed in (Park, Lee, & Yu, 2013; Soraluze, Cortiñas, Lafuente, Larrea, & Freiling, 2011).

Communication Patterns

In addition to the monitoring approaches, communication pattern between processes is also an important aspect of failure detectors specifically when considering communication efficiency. For example, all-to-all processes communication pattern has some advantages such as more possibility of communication, but lacks efficiency in terms of number of message transmission. On the other hand, a linear communication pattern highly reduces the number of message transmission, but lacks the possibility of communication.

The efficiency of a communication pattern highly depends on the physical arrangement (topology) of the processes in the distributed system. For example, if all-to-all processes communication pattern is followed in ring or bus or tree topology based networks, it will generate extra overhead in terms of number of message transmission and message processing. Whereas, the communication efficiency can be improved by developing a communication pattern according to the network topology.

Another factor that affects the communication patter is timing model of the system. If the system is synchronous, the message transmission and processing times are already known and should be set beforehand. Whereas, if the system is partially synchronous, a mechanism to eventually find out the message transmission and processing times, and adjust the communication pattern accordingly is necessary. However, the time bound is absent in asynchronous systems, therefore should not be considered in communication pattern. In the following section, an efficient failure detector is discussed that is developed for time synchronous and hierarchical topology based distributed systems (Verma & Pattanaik, 2016).

SYSTEM MODEL FOR TIME SYNCHRONOUS HIERARCHICAL DISTRIBUTED SYSTEMS

The system model defines the characteristics, assumptions, and constraints of the system around which the failure detector algorithm is developed. When developing a failure detector algorithm, one of the most important tasks is defining a system model in which the algorithm will work. An algorithm is best suited for those real life systems whose characteristics meet with system model properties. System model also plays a great role in modification of an existing algorithm to make it compatible with different systems. This section describes the system model of the failure detector for real time hierarchical distributed systems working in synchronous environments.

Processes

In a setup of one process per processor or site (or node) every process executes its own copy of the failure detector algorithm and maintains a local state of that execution. The system has a finite set Π of n processes, denoted by $\Pi = \{P_1, P_2, P_3, \ldots, P_n\}$, which are connected through pairwise bidirectional communication channels in a hierarchical topology. A parent process is represented by P_i and its child process is represented by P_iC_j. A process may be *correct* or *faulty* depending on the characteristics related to the hierarchical system model.

- *Correct process*: Process that behaves according to its specification, i.e., a process that does not experience any failure and able to communicate with the root process timely.

- *Faulty process*: Process that suffers a failure and might affect its specification or a correct process that is not connected with the root process due to any type of failure between the path such as intermediate process or link failure.

Event Generation

The system follows both *time-driven* and *event-driven* approaches. In the former approach a process periodically sends "Are-you-alive?" messages to its child processes. Whereas, in the latter approach child processes reply with "I-am-alive" message only on the reception of "Are-you-alive?" message.

Communication Links

Processes are connected through bidirectional communication links. The links are unreliable and can drop messages or delay the transmission of messages.

Time and Timing Models

Each process has a local clock to synchronize the execution of events within the process. As the system environment is synchronous every event execution and message transmission are time bounded. The main concern of synchronous systems is that the time bounds must be defined correctly in the worst case (Cortinas, 2011). Although it is difficult to find systems that meet these properties, but there are several real time safety critical systems that require a strict time bound for the execution of events. Violation of these timing restrictions in such systems causes serious errors.

Failure Models

A distributed system may suffer by *crash failures*, *crash-recovery failures*, *omission failures*, *link failures*, *timing failures*, and *byzantine failures* (Cortinas, 2011). The solutions pertaining to the above failures are categorized into two classes. First deals with *byzantine failures* and second deals with the rest of the failures. In case of *byzantine failure*, components of a system fail in arbitrary ways, i.e., the process produces incorrect or inconsistent outputs. Whereas, in case of other failures, process crashes and does not produce any output or a message is omitted. The solution strategy to solve *byzantine failures* is different from other type of failures. The proposed final failure detector algorithm addresses all failures except the *byzantine failures*. A *Byzantine failure* detection mechanism is discussed in (Benenson, Fort,

Freiling, Kesdogan, & Penso, 2006) that uses tamper proof security modules (e.g., smart card) and a generalization of this concept is given in (Veríssimo, 2006). The other failures are described in the following.

- **Crash Failure:** In a process crash, the process stops all its event executions e.g. process execution, sending and receiving messages. Crashes that are permanent and do not recover are termed as *crash-stop* or *crash-prone*.
- **Crash-Recovery Failure**: Process subjected to crash may recover eventually.
- **Omission Failure:** In this type of failures, messages are omitted in the process during transmission, not in the communication link. This happens due to buffer overflow or malicious dropping of messages. Such failures are classified into *send-omission* and *receive-omission* type. In the former, a process executes *send-message* instruction but the message never reaches the outgoing link, whereas in the latter type of omission fault a message reaches its destination process, but *receive-message* instruction is never executed at the destination. *Crash failure*, *send-omission* and *receive-omission* collectively termed as *general-omission failure*. The final proposed failure detector algorithm is capable of dealing with both permanent and transient *omission failures*.
- **Link Failure:** It occurs when a link is unable to transmit a message between two processes specifically due to link break-down or congestion.
- **Timing Failure:** This occurs when a process takes more time than the specified time bound to execute an event, or a link takes more time than an acceptable time bound to transmit a message.

Failure Detector Properties

Each process executes its copy of the failure detector algorithm and eventually constructs its local health monitoring tree (HMT). HMT of a process represents a sub-tree containing all its child processes, that it is monitoring, and their operational status. The root process generates a global HMT from the information about faulty processes supplied by other processes. The global HMT represents the operational status of the complete system. The *strong completeness* and *strong accuracy* properties pertaining to the proposed failure detector of *Perfect P* class are defined as:

- **Strong Completeness:** Every faulty process (according to hierarchical system model) will eventually be detected by its all parent processes in upward hierarchy.
- **Strong Accuracy:** No correct process is suspected by any correct process.

FAILURE DETECTOR ALGORITHM OF *STRONG S* CLASS

The proposed failure detector algorithm belongs to *Strong S* class hence achieves the *strong completeness* and the *weak accuracy* properties. The algorithm is able to detect permanent *crash failure*, *omission failure*, *link failure*, and *timing failure*. The algorithm works on *polling* approach whereby it sends "Are-you-alive?" messages, and waits for "I-am-alive" messages indicating the polled processes are up and running. The response message consists of faulty process information FP_iC_j. Faulty process information received from children processes by parent processes is used to construct parents' HMTs. If response is not received or received beyond the timeout the monitored process is perceived as faulty and its identity is inserted in the list of faulty processes F_i. The variables used in the algorithm and their description are given in Table 2.

The algorithm of failure detector mechanism comprises four tasks as shown in Algorithm 1. At the beginning of Task 1, failure detector of process P_i periodically

Table 2. Variables used in algorithm and their description

Variable	Description
HMT_{Root}	Pointer of root process node in HMT
P_i	A parent process
P_iC_j	A child process of P_i
P_kC_l	A recovered process
F_i	Faulty process list of P_i
FP_iC_j	Faulty process list of P_iC_j
f_i	A process in the list FP_iC_j
$To_i\left[P_iC_j\right]$	Timeout of respond message from P_iC_j
$CTree$	Pointer of a recovered process node in HMT
$FTree$	Pointer of a faulty process node in HMT

sends "Are-you-alive?" messages to all its child processes P_iC_j at the next level in the hierarchy (line 4). It estimates a timeout (line 3) for the reception of corresponding "I-am-alive" messages. Where $Time(\ )$ denotes the current time of process P_i, $OutT$ and InT are the upper time-bound of incoming and outgoing links for message transmission. Whereas, α is a safety margin that represents the total of time taken to execute Task 4 and allowable clock skew between two processes.

Upon receipt of "I-am-alive" message from P_iC_j Task 2 is executed. P_i checks if the expected messages are received within timeout (line 7) and all timely receipts are considered to be healthy. Thereafter P_i checks if the P_iC_j was earlier a faulty process (line 8). If yes, P_iC_j is removed from F_i (line 9) and HMT is updated accordingly (lines 10, 11) as it is not a faulty process. P_iC_j also sends a list of faulty processes FP_iC_j detected by its failure detector along with "I-am-alive" message. P_i merges FP_iC_j with F_i (line 13) to learn about faulty processes detected by P_iC_j. The timeout defined for the reception of the message from P_iC_j is ignored (line 14). P_i updates its HMT according to the contents of updated F_i (lines 15 to 18). If "I-am-alive" message is received after the timeout period, P_i just ignores this message.

Task 3 is executed when "I-am-alive" message is not received from P_iC_j within its timeout. If P_iC_j was not a faulty process and its timeout expires without the reception of "I-am-alive" message (lines 22, 23), P_i declares it as faulty and updates F_i (line 24), based on which the HMT is constructed (lines 25, 26). If P_iC_j was already a faulty process, nothing happens.

When a child process P_iC_j receives "Are-you-alive?" message from its parent P_i (line 30), Task 5 is executed. P_iC_j sends "I-am-alive" message along with FP_iC_j to P_i (line 31).

During the execution of tasks 2 and 3 each time F_i updates (lines 9, 13, 24) the corresponding HMT is updated. When a process fails or a failed process recovers subsequently its status is updated at F_i and HMT. Figure 2 depicts HMT of a process Z, in which the process *P2* is faulty and therefore all its child processes become faulty for Z. HMT is updated in two steps: first, the location of the child process is searched on HMT for which changes are to be made, second, the status of the all child processes including that process is updated according to the operation (correct or fault). The pseudo-code of procedures to manage HMT is presented in algorithm

Algorithm 1. Failure detector algorithm of Strong S class

$HMT_{Root} = Root\, process\, address\, of\, HMT$

Task 1: Send message to children processes at every monitoring interval

$for\, \forall\, P_iC_j,\, P_i\, do$

$\quad To_i\left[P_iC_j\right] = Time(\ ) + OutT + InT + \alpha$

$\quad send$ "Are-you-alive?" $to P_iC_j$

end

Task 2: Received acknowledgement from child process

$when$ "I-am-alive" $+\, FP_iC_j\, is\, received\, from\, P_iC_j,\, P_i\, do$

$\quad if\left(To_i\left[P_iC_j\right] \geq Time(\ )\right)$

$\quad\quad if\left(P_iC_j \in F_i\right)$

$\quad\quad\quad F_i = F_i \cap P_iC_j$

$\quad\quad\quad CTree = Search\left(P_iC_j, HMT_{Root}, \text{"correct"}\right)$

$\quad\quad\quad UpdateHMT\left(CTree, \text{"correct"}\right)$

$\quad\quad endif$

$\quad\quad F_i = F_i \cup FP_iC_j$

$\quad\quad To_i\left[P_iC_j\right] = \infty$

$\quad\quad for\, \forall f_i \in FP_iC_j\, do$

$\quad\quad\quad FTree = Search\left(f_i, HMT_{Root}, \text{"fault"}\right)$

$\quad\quad\quad UpdateHMT\left(FTree, \text{"fault"}\right)$

$\quad\quad end$

$\quad endif$

end

Task 3: Not received acknowledgement from child process

$when$ "I-am-alive" $+\, FP_iC_j\, is\, not\, received\, from\, P_iC_j\, within\, To_i\left[P_iC_j\right],\, P_i\, do$

$\quad if\left(To_i\left[P_iC_j\right] < Time(\ )\right)$

$\quad\quad if\left(P_iC_j \notin F_i\right)$

$\quad\quad\quad F_i = F_i \cup P_iC_j$

$\quad\quad\quad FTree = Search\left(P_iC_j, HMT_{Root}, \text{"fault"}\right)$

continued on following page

Algorithm 1. Continued

```
                UpdateHMT(FTree, "fault")
        endif
    endif
end
Task 4: Received message from parent process
when "Are-you-alive?" is received from P_i, P_iC_j do
    send "I-am-alive" + FP_iC_j to P_i
end
```

Figure 2. Example HMT of process Z
(Verma & Pattanaik, 2016)

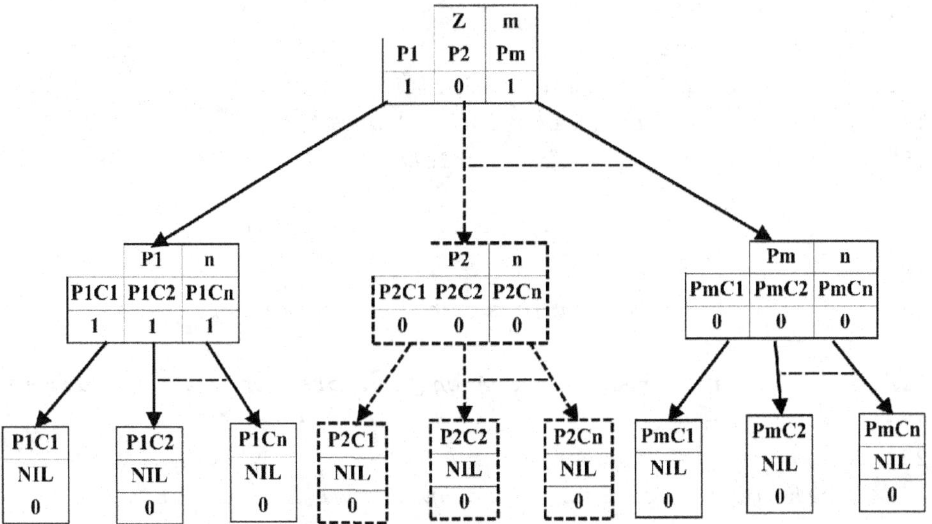

2. It contains two recursive procedures: *Search* and *UpdateHMT*. *Search* procedure takes process name, HMT root address, and operation as input and searches that particular process and returns its parent's address as output. *UpdateHMT* procedure takes a process address and operation as input and updates the status of all its child processes according to the operation.

The algorithm is not able to update the information of a recovered process at all processes above its parent process upward in the hierarchy. Hence, it does not work well for recovered failed processes. The algorithm does not address if the

Algorithm 2. Pseudo-code of procedures to manage HMT (Verma & Pattanaik, 2016)

```
//structure of a node in HMT
structure process
{
string pname                    // process name
integer n                 // number of children processes
structure process *chl[n]    // address of children processes
integer chlstatus[n]          // status of children processes
} *HMT_Root                    // root process pointer
// Searching a process node in HMT
structure process* Search(string pnm, structure process
*prs, string operation)
integer i;
if (prs is not empty)
    i=0
    when (i < prs->n)
            if (pnm = *prs->chl[i])
                    if (operation = "fault")
                            prs->chlstatus[i] = 0
                    else
                            prs->chlstatus[i] = 1
                    endif
                    return (prs->chl[i]) to main procedure
            endif
            call procedure Search(pnm, prs->chl[i], operation)
            i++
    end
    call procedure Search(pnm, prs->chl[i], operation)
endif
end procedure
// Updating sub-tree of a process in HMT
void UpdateHMT(structure process *pprs, string operation)
integer i;
if (pprs is not empty)
    i = 0
    while (i < pprs->n)
            if (operation = "fault")
                    pprs->chlstatus[i] = 0
```

continued on following page

Algorithm 2. Continued

```
        else
                pprs->chlstatus[i] = 1
        endif
        call procedure UpdateHMT(pprs->chl[i], operation)
        i++
    end
    call procedure UpdateHMT(pprs->chl[i], operation)
endif
end procedure
```

reply messages are delayed due to the congestion and are not in sequence. These limitations are addressed by the algorithm given in next section.

CORRECTNESS PROOF

The *strong completeness* and the *weak accuracy* properties of the proposed failure detector algorithm of *Strong S* class are evaluated. Furthermore, the efficacy of the algorithm is evaluated in terms of its ability to detect permanent *crash failure*, *omission failure*, *link failure*, and *timing failure*.

Theorem 1

The failure detector algorithm satisfies the *strong completeness* property in which every faulty process (according to hierarchical system model) will eventually be detected by all its parent processes up in the hierarchy.

Proof

When a parent process P_i sends "Are-you-alive?" message at time t (task 1) to its child process P_iC_j and P_iC_j fails, there may be two situations. First, if P_iC_j fails before the reception of "Are-you-alive?" message, it does not respond. Consequently, just after time $\left(t + OutT + InT + \alpha\right)$ P_i detects P_iC_j (task 3). Second, if P_iC_j fails after sending "I-am-alive" message and received by P_i within $\left(t + OutT + InT + \alpha\right)$, P_i does not have any information about this failure and still considers healthy. However, this failure is detected in the next time window $\left(t' + OutT + InT + \alpha\right)$.

A faulty process is detected by its parent within maximum two time windows. In next time window, P_i sends detected faulty process list F_i to its parent process (task 2). In this way, in each time window, a faulty process information is transmitted to its parent processes at the next level up in the hierarchy and the respective HMTs are updated. Thus the information of all affected child processes of a faulty process is maintained in HMT and justifies the *strong completeness* property. Observe also that the crash of internal processes can lead to the hierarchal structure partition, separating distinct and un-communicable correct processes. These correct processes are unable to communicate with root process and called faulty processes according to the definition of faulty process of hierarchical system model.

Theorem 2

The failure detector algorithm satisfies *weak accuracy* property in which some correct process is never suspected. Means, some correct processes can be suspected.

Proof

A parent process P_i sends "Are-you-alive?" message at time t (task 1) to its child process P_iC_j, if P_iC_j is correct it sends an acknowledgement within time $\left(t + OutT + InT + \alpha\right)$ to P_i. Consequently, condition

$$\left(t + OutT + InT + \alpha\right) < Time\left(\ \right)$$

is never satisfied (line 22) and P_i does not execute task 3 to detect P_iC_j. If P_iC_j was previously faulty then condition $P_iC_j \in F_i$ of task 2 is true (line 8), further it is removed from the faulty process list F_i by executing line 9 of task 2, and status of P_iC_j and all its child processes are updated at HMT of P_i (line 10, 11). But the recovered child process will remain as faulty for all the processes above its parent process in the hierarchy. Because all parent processes union their faulty processes list F_i with the faulty processes list FP_iC_j received from their child processes. But the processes do not intersect their faulty processes list with the faulty processes list received from their child processes. Therefore, a recovered process is only updated as correct in its parent's faulty processes list, whereas it is remain as faulty for all processes above its parent process upward in the hierarchy. A correct recovered process is suspected by some other correct processes hence achieves *weak accuracy*.

Theorem 3

The failure detector algorithm detects only permanent *crash failure*, *omission failure*, *link failure*, and *timing failure*.

Proof

When P_i does not receive "I-am-alive" message from P_iC_j within the timeout $\left(t + OutT + InT + \alpha\right)$, it detects that the said process has been crashed (task 3).

Omission failure may occur at both parent P_i and child P_iC_j processes during message exchange between them. Due to any *omission failure*, whether it occurs on P_i or P_iC_j, P_i detects P_iC_j as a faulty process (task 3) because P_i is unable to communicate with P_iC_j. For example, in the case of *send-omission* at P_i, P_i sends "Are-you-alive?" message to P_iC_j, but the message does not reach at the link, which means it does not reach at P_iC_j, therefore P_iC_j does not reply for that, and after the timeout of corresponding "Are-you-alive?" message P_i declares P_iC_j as faulty. In case of *receive-omission* at P_iC_j, "Are-you-alive?" message reaches at P_iC_j but it is not delivered to P_iC_j, therefore P_iC_j does not reply for that, and after the timeout of corresponding "Are-you-alive?" message P_i declares P_iC_j as faulty. In case of *send-omission* at P_iC_j, "Are-you-alive?" message is delivered to P_iC_j, P_iC_j sends "I-am-alive" message to P_i but it does not reach at the link, which means it does not reach at P_i and P_i detects P_iC_j as faulty. In case of *receive-omission* at P_i, "I-am-alive" message of the corresponding "Are-you-alive?" message reaches at P_i from P_iC_j, but it is not delivered to P_i, and P_i declares P_iC_j as faulty after corresponding timeout. The algorithm only detects *permanent omission failures*, means if an omission failure process recovers its information is not updated at all processes above its parent process upward in the hierarchy.

Processes are connected with their parents through bidirectional links which are basically two single directional links, one from parent to child and other from child to parent. When a link from parent P_i to child P_iC_j fails, "Are-you-alive?" message does not reach at P_iC_j. Consequently, P_iC_j does not reply and P_i detects P_iC_j after corresponding timeout (task 3). When a link from P_iC_j to P_i fails, "I-am-alive" message of P_iC_j does not reach at P_i. As a result, P_i waits for the timeout of corresponding "Are-you-alive?" message and thereafter detects P_iC_j as faulty (task 3).

Timing failure occurs when either a process execution or message transmission takes time beyond their corresponding allowable timeout. The timeout includes incoming and outgoing links' time bound, and the event execution time bound. Due to non-receipt of the reply from child process on account of *timing failure* P_i declares P_iC_j as faulty (task 3). Whereas, the algorithm is unable to differentiate whether the received "I-am-alive" message belongs to the reply of current "Are-you-alive?" message or some older. Hence, the algorithm is not able to detect *Timing failure* completely.

FAILURE DETECTOR ALGORITHM OF PERFECT P CLASS

Similar to Algorithm 1, the failure detector mechanism (Algorithm 3) works on *polling* approach whereby it sends "Are-you-alive?" messages, and waits for "I-am-alive" messages indicating the polled processes are up and running. The response message consists of faulty process information FP_iC_j and message identity $M_{id}P_iC_j$. Faulty process information received from children processes by parent processes is used to construct parents' HMTs. Message identity ensures the reply received is for the intended request and within a timeout period. If response is not received or received beyond the timeout the monitored process is perceived as faulty and its identity is inserted in the list of faulty processes F_i. The variables used in the Algorithm 3 (except those are defined in Table 2) and their description are given in Table 3.

The algorithm of failure detector mechanism comprises five tasks as shown in Algorithm 3 (Verma & Pattanaik, 2016). At the beginning of Task 1, failure detector of process P_i periodically sends "Are-you-alive?" messages to all its child processes P_iC_j at the next level in the hierarchy (line 8). It estimates a timeout (line 7) for the reception of corresponding "I-am-alive" messages. Where $Time()$ denotes the

Table 3. Variables used in algorithm and their description

Variable	Description
$S_{id}P_iC_j$	Sequence number of next message to be sent to P_iC_j
$R_{id}P_iC_j$	Sequence number of next expected message from P_iC_j
$M_{id}P_iC_j$	Sequence number of respond message from P_iC_j

current time of process P_i, $OutT$ and InT are the upper time-bound of incoming and outgoing links for message transmission. Whereas, α is a safety margin that represents the total of time taken to execute Task 5 and allowable clock skew between two processes. Sequence number $S_{id}P_iC_j$ of the next message to be sent to P_iC_j is incremented (line 9).

Upon receipt of "I-am-alive" message from P_iC_j Task 2 executes. P_i checks if the expected messages are received within timeout (line 12) and all timely receipts are considered to be healthy. Thereafter P_i checks if the P_iC_j was earlier a faulty process (line 13). If yes, P_iC_j is removed from F_i (line 14) and HMT is updated accordingly (line 16) as it is not a faulty process, and a message to that effect is sent to the parent process of P_i for the removal of P_iC_j from the faulty process list (line 17). P_iC_j also sends a list of faulty processes FP_iC_j detected by its failure detector along with "I-am-alive" message. P_i merges FP_iC_j with F_i (line 19) to learn about faulty processes detected by P_iC_j. The timeout defined for the reception of the message from P_iC_j is ignored (line 20). The sequence number $R_{id}P_iC_j$ of the next expected message from P_iC_j is incremented (line 21) to reflect in sequence reception. P_i updates its HMT according to the contents of updated F_i (lines 22 to 25). If "I-am-alive" message is received in the incorrect sequence or after the timeout period, P_i just ignores this message.

Task 3 is executed when "I-am-alive" message is not received from P_iC_j within its timeout. If P_iC_j was not a faulty process and its timeout expires without the reception of "I-am-alive" message (lines 29, 30), P_i declares it as faulty and updates F_i (line 31) based on which the HMT is constructed (lines 33, 34). The sequence number $R_{id}P_iC_j$ of next expected message from P_iC_j is also incremented (line 32) to reflect in sequence reception. If P_iC_j was already a faulty process, only sequence number of next expected message is incremented (line 36).

Subsequent process recovery requires update of F_i at all parent processes up in the hierarchy (Task 4). When the message is received from child process P_iC_j to remove a faulty process P_kC_l from F_i, P_i removes P_kC_l (line 42) and its corresponding HMT is updated (lines 43, 44). P_i also forwards the message to its parent process (line 45).

When a child process P_iC_j receives "Are-you-alive?" message from its parent P_i (line 48), Task 5 is executed. P_iC_j sends "I-am-alive" message along with FP_iC_j

Algorithm 3. Failure detector algorithm of Perfect P class (Verma & Pattanaik, 2016)

```
Initialization
$HMT_{Root} = Root\ process\ address\ of\ HMT$
$for \forall P_iC_j,\ P_i\ do$
    $S_{id}P_iC_j = 1$
    $R_{id}P_iC_j = 1$
$end$
Task 1: Send message to children processes at every monitoring interval
$for \forall P_iC_j,\ P_i\ do$
    $To_i[P_iC_j] = Time() + OutT + InT + \alpha$
    $send\ S_{id}P_iC_j + \text{"Are-you-alive?"}\ to P_iC_j$
    $S_{id}P_iC_j{+}{+}$
$end$
Task 2: Received acknowledgement from child process
    $when\ M_{id}P_iC_j + \text{"I-am-alive"} + FP_iC_j\ is\ received\ from\ P_iC_j,\ P_i\ do$
    $if\left(\left(To_i[P_iC_j] \geq Time()\right) \wedge \left(M_{id}P_iC_j = R_{id}P_iC_j\right)\right)$
        $if\left(P_iC_j \in F_i\right)$
            $F_i = F_i \cap P_iC_j$
            $CTree = Search\left(P_iC_j, HMT_{Root}, \text{"correct"}\right)$
            $UpdateHMT\left(CTree, \text{"correct"}\right)$
            $send\ RemoveCorrect\left(P_iC_j\right) to\ parent\ process\ of\ P_i$
        $endif$
        $F_i = F_i \cup FP_iC_j$
        $To_i[P_iC_j] = \infty$
        $R_{id}P_iC_j{+}{+}$
        $for \forall f_i \in FP_iC_j\ do$
            $FTree = Search\left(f_i, HMT_{Root}, \text{"fault"}\right)$
            $UpdateHMT\left(FTree, \text{"fault"}\right)$
        $end$
    $endif$
$end$
```

continued on following page

Algorithm 3. Continued

Task 3: Not received acknowledgement from child process

$when\ M_{id}P_iC_j + \text{"I-am-alive"} + FP_iC_j\ is\ not\ received\ from\ P_iC_j\ within\ To_i\left[P_iC_j\right],\ P_i\ do$

    $if\left(To_i\left[P_iC_j\right] < Time(\ )\right)$

        $if\left(P_iC_j \notin F_i\right)$

            $F_i = F_i \cup P_iC_j$

            $R_{id}P_iC_j ++$

            $FTree = Search\left(P_iC_j\ , HMT_{Root}, \text{"}fault\text{"}\right)$

            $UpdateHMT\left(FTree, \text{"}fault\text{"}\right)$

        $else$

            $R_{id}P_iC_j ++$

        $endif$

    $endif$

end

Task 4: Received message from child process for removing correct process from faulty list

$when\ RemoveCorrect\left(P_kC_l\right) is\ received\ from\ P_iC_j,\ P_i\ do$

    $if\left(P_kC_l \in F_i\right)$

        $F_i = F_i \cap P_kC_l$

        $CTree = Search\left(P_kC_l, HMT_{Root}, \text{"}correct\text{"}\right)$

        $UpdateHMT\left(CTree, \text{"}correct\text{"}\right)$

        $send\ RemoveCorrect\left(P_kC_l\right) to\ parent\ process\ of\ P_i$

    $endif$

end

Task 5: Received message from parent process

$when\ M_{id}P_iC_j + \text{"Are-you-alive?"} is\ received\ from\ P_i,\ P_iC_j\ do$

    $send\ M_{id}P_iC_j + \text{"I-am-alive"} + FP_iC_j\ to\ P_i$

end

and $M_{id}P_iC_j$ to P_i (line 49). $M_{id}P_iC_j$ represents acknowledgement identity for the corresponding $S_{id}P_iC_j$.

During the execution of tasks 2, 3 and 4 each time F_i updates (lines 14, 19, 31, 42) the corresponding HMT is updatedby the Algorithm 2. When a process fails or a failed process recovers subsequently its status is updated at F_i and HMT.

CORRECTNESS PROOF

The *strong completeness* and the *strong accuracy* properties of the proposed failure detector algorithm of *Perfect P* class are evaluated(Verma & Pattanaik, 2016). Furthermore, the efficacy of the algorithm is evaluated in terms of its ability to detect *crash failure*, *crash-recovery failure*, *omission failure*, *link failure*, and *timing failure*..

Theorem 1

The failure detector algorithm satisfies the *strong completeness* property in which every faulty process (according to hierarchical system model) will eventually be detected by all its parent processes up in the hierarchy.

Proof

Same as described in the proof of theorem 1 of Algorithm 1.

Theorem 2

The failure detector algorithm satisfies *strong accuracy* property in which correct process is not suspected by any correct process.

Proof

A parent process P_i sends "Are-you-alive?" message at time t (task 1) to its child process P_iC_j, if P_iC_j is correct it sends an acknowledgement within time $\left(t + OutT + InT + \alpha\right)$ to P_i. Consequently, condition

$$\left(t + OutT + InT + \alpha\right) < Time\left(\ \right)$$

is never satisfied (line 29) and P_i does not execute task 3 to detect P_iC_j. If P_iC_j was previously faulty then condition $P_iC_j \in F_i$ of task 2 is true (line 13), further it is removed from the faulty process list F_i by executing line 14 of task 2, and status of P_iC_j and all its child processes are updated at HMT of P_i (line 15, 16). A message $RemoveCorrect\left(P_iC_j\right)$ is also sent to the parent process of P_i to remove P_iC_j from the list of faulty processes (line 17). A parent process removes a faulty process P_kC_l from the list upon receiving the message. Accordingly, changes are made on HMT, and this message is further sent to the parent process (task 4). As a result, eventually a correct process is never suspected by any correct process.

Theorem 3

The failure detector algorithm detects *crash failure*, *crash-recovery failure*, *omission failure*, *link failure*, and *timing failure*.

Proof

When P_i does not receive "I-am-alive" message from P_iC_j within the timeout $\left(t + OutT + InT + \alpha\right)$, it detects that the said process has been crashed (task 3).

Crash-recovery failure is similar to *crash failure* except that crashed process may recover. When a crashed process recovers it starts replying for "Are-you-alive?" message. When a parent process P_i receives "I-am-alive" message from a recovered child process P_iC_j, P_i detects it by condition $P_iC_j \in F_i$ of task 2 (line 13). P_i removes P_iC_j form F_i and updates HMT accordingly, thereafter sends this message to its parent to update F_i and HMT as described in the proof of *theorem 2*.

Omission failure may occur at both parent P_i and child P_iC_j processes during message exchange between them. Due to any *omission failure*, whether it occurs on P_i or P_iC_j, P_i detects P_iC_j as a faulty process (task 3) because P_i is unable to communicate with P_iC_j. For example, in the case of *send-omission* at P_i, P_i sends "Are-you-alive?" message to P_iC_j, but the message does not reach at the link, which means it does not reach at P_iC_j, therefore P_iC_j does not reply for that, and after the timeout of corresponding "Are-you-alive?" message P_i declares P_iC_j as faulty.

In case of *receive-omission* at P_iC_j, "Are-you-alive?" message reaches at P_iC_j but it is not delivered to P_iC_j, therefore P_iC_j does not reply for that, and after the timeout of corresponding "Are-you-alive?" message P_i declares P_iC_j as faulty. In case of *send-omission* at P_iC_j, "Are-you-alive?" message is delivered to P_iC_j, P_iC_j sends "I-am-alive" message to P_i but it does not reach at the link, which means it does not reach at P_i and P_i detects P_iC_j as faulty. In case of *receive-omission* at P_i, "I-am-alive" message of the corresponding "Are-you-alive?" message reaches at P_i from P_iC_j, but it is not delivered to P_i, and P_i declares P_iC_j as faulty after corresponding timeout. The proposed failure detector algorithm is capable of dealing with both permanent and transient *omission failures*.

Processes are connected with their parents through bidirectional links which are basically two single directional links, one from parent to child and other from child to parent. When a link from parent P_i to child P_iC_j fails, "Are-you-alive?" message does not reach at P_iC_j. Consequently, P_iC_j does not reply and P_i detects P_iC_j after corresponding timeout (task 3). When a link from P_iC_j to P_i fails, "I-am-alive" message of P_iC_j does not reach at P_i. As a result, P_i waits for the timeout of corresponding "Are-you-alive?" message and thereafter detects P_iC_j as faulty (task 3).The algorithm is capable to handle break-down as well as congestion link failures.

The algorithm is able to differentiate whether the received "I-am-alive" message belongs to the reply of current "Are-you-alive?" message or belongs to some older one by comparing with sequence number $R_{id}P_iC_j$ of the next expected message and sequence number $M_{id}P_iC_j$ of the received message (line 12, task 2).Hence, the algorithm is able to detect *Timing failure* even reply messages are out of order. The timeout includes incoming and outgoing links' time bound, and the event execution time bound. Due to non receipt of the reply from child process with in predefine time-bound, P_i declares P_iC_j as faulty (task 3).

Case Study: Application to Railways Systems

As discussed earlier, previously failure detectors were developed according to the requirements of traditional distributed computer networks those were mostly mesh connected and worked in asynchronous or partially synchronous environments.

Whereas, there are several real life networks those are hierarchically connected and work in strict time synchronous environments. Therefore, the developments of new failure detectors are necessary to cope with the requirements of such systems. This section presents a case of time synchronous hierarchical multi-agent *communication based train control* (CBTC) system developed for Indian Railways, named *Indian railways management system* (IRMS) (Verma & Pattanaik, 2015a; Verma & Pattanaik, 2015b) to illustrate the use of proposed failure detector in a real world application (Verma & Pattanaik, 2016).

A train control system is a time critical (i.e. real-time response) and mission critical (i.e. reliability) system. Any operational or equipment fault can cause disaster, therefore safety is the prime concern. In IRMS, health of the system depends on proper working of the agents and communication among them. An agent crash or communication link failure may cause serious hazards. Therefore, it is necessary to develop a health monitoring or failure detector mechanism that detects failures timely and helps to take necessary actions to prevent accidents. An agent is representing a process in this section.

IRMS works on moving block signaling system in which moving authority is calculated at run time (dynamically) by computers on the basis of train characteristics and ahead track status. Moving authority is a command given to a train indicating the train to move in a given direction at a given speed. Continuous communication between train's cab signaling system and the central signaling system is required to exchange control information.

The software agent based CBTC rail track infrastructure (Verma & Pattanaik, 2015a) is divided into areas or regions, each area under the control of a Zone controller (ZC) and each with its own radio transreceiving system with reliable and continuous radio link. Figure 3 shows the high level architecture of IRMS describing the important functional components and their corresponding agents. It consists of four principal components: ZC, Station controller (SC), Trackside device control system (TSDCS), and Onboard device control system (OBDCS). Each train's OBDCS consist of the several train borne equipments those collect the relevant information and periodically sends to their respective ZC. Upon receiving of this information, respective ZC computes safe moving authority and communicates to the respective trains. Further, ZC gives the instructions to SC to create the route by interlocking for the arrival or departure of trains in Station section. Each Station section has a single SC responsible for establishing or releasing a route for the arrival or departure of trains. SC gives instruction one by one to TSDCS to fix each switch in a required position. Switches falling under a particular Station section are controlled by the respective TSDCS. It is responsible to fix each individual switch in a required position. TSDCS also continuously monitors the health and status of all its switches, and reports to respective SC.

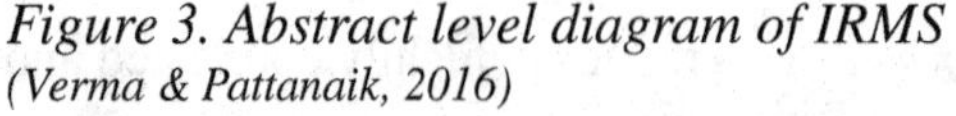

Figure 3. Abstract level diagram of IRMS
(Verma & Pattanaik, 2016)

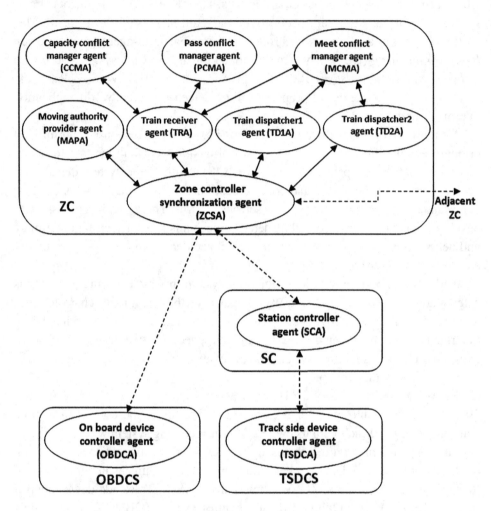

Each sub-system contains one or more identified software agents to carry specific task(s) as shown in Figure 3. The functionality of agents is further divided into several sub-agents. The agents follow a predefined workflow and operate in a collaborative manner to perform the goal of each sub-system and finally achieve the overall system goal. The agents' interactions form a hierarchical network as shown in Figure 4 in which ZCSA is on top most position (root). Only sub-agents of agent MAPA is shown in Figure 4, the sub-agents of other agents are not expended to retain the simplicity. For the expansion of certain abbreviations used in Figure 4 the reader may refer to Table 4. ZSCA creates a bridge between agents working

Table 4. Abbreviation used in Figure 4

Abbreviation	Description
RFMA	RFID fault manager agent
TTFMA	Train technical fault manager agent
TPFMA	Train partition fault manager agent
STMA	Successor trains manager agent
TFMA	Track fault manager agent
TRSCA	Turnout restricted speed calculator agent
TRMA	Train restart manager agent
SBDCA	Safe braking distance calculator agent
ORSCA	Object restricted speed calculator agent
ERSCA	Emergency brake restricted speed calculator agent
ITPIA	Initial trains position initializer agent
IDA	Information distributor agent
CMA	Curve manager agent
GMA	Grade manager agent

Figure 4. Agents' hierarchy in IRMS
(Verma & Pattanaik, 2016)

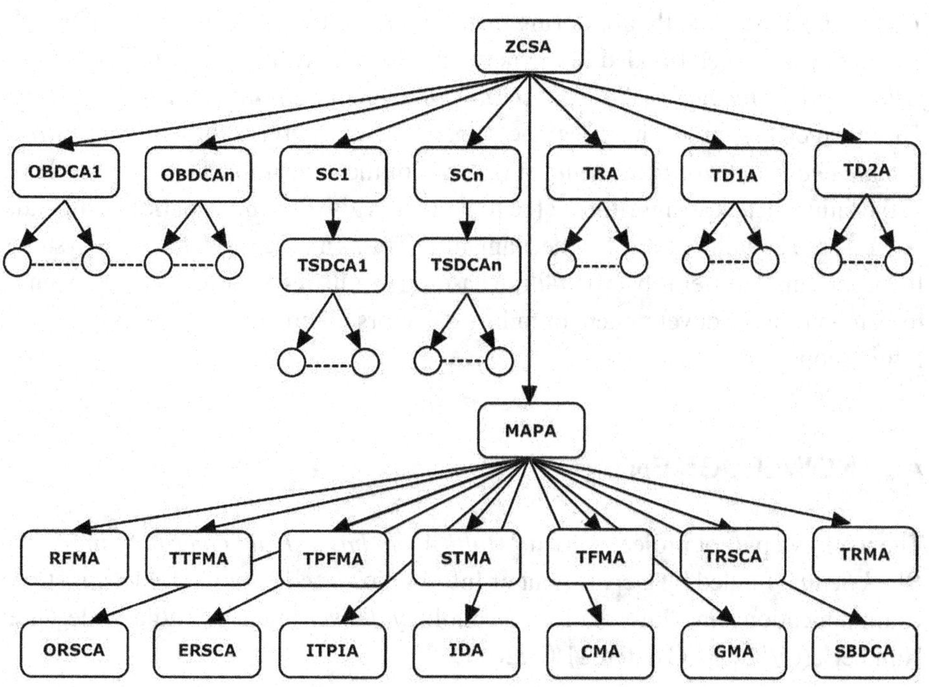

on trains, stations, and ZC. Each agent should be connected with ZCSA through direct or indirect path for its proper functioning. If a failure occurs (agent crash, link failure, timing failure, or omission failure) at an agent, the agent and all its children loose interaction with ZCSA as a consequence the system is unable to provide respective functionalities. The proposed failure detector is developed to full fill the requirement of such systems.

CONCLUSION

The chapter presented a generic definition of failure detectors along with discussion on several terminologies whose understanding is necessary to understand and develop a new failure detector algorithm. The chapter deeply discussed *suspicion based* failure detector algorithms of *Strong S* and *Perfect P* classes for the hierarchical distributed systems working in synchronous environments. The *Strong S* class algorithm shows early stage of failure detector algorithm development for the time synchronous hierarchical distributed system. The correctness proof is evaluated in terms of *strong completeness* and *weak accuracy* properties of the algorithm. The algorithm has several limitations those are addressed in *Perfect P* class algorithm. The *Perfect P* class algorithm generates $2\left(n-1\right)$ number of messages in a time window and each process maintains operational status of all its children processes. The *polling* based health monitoring methodology is the key to the reduction in the number of messages flooded in the network. The algorithm is able to detect *crash failures*, *crash-recovery failures*, *omission failures*, *link failures*, and *timing failures*. The correctness proof justifies the functional correctness in terms of *strong completeness* and *strong accuracy* properties of the algorithm. The resulting HMT of the failure detector algorithm at the root process gives the information of all faulty processes. The failure detector mechanism serves as a base for many such systems. Incorporating a system specific failure cases to test its responsiveness may open up research vistas for development of failure detectors for emerging systems can be the future scope.

ACKNOWLEDGMENT

The work is a part of project named "*Multi-Agent based Train Operation in Moving Block Setup*" funded by Department of Information Technology (DIT), Ministry of Communications and Information Technology, Government of India, vide Grant Number 2(6)/2010-EC dated 21/03/2011.

REFERENCES

Aguilera, M. K., Chen, W., & Toueg, S. (1997). Heartbeat: A timeout-free failure detector for quiescent reliable communication. *Distributed Algorithms. Lecture Notes in Computer Science*, *1320*, 126–140. doi:10.1007/BFb0030680

Arevalo, S., Anta, A. F., Imbs, D., Jimenez, E., & Raynal, M. (2012). Failure detectors in homonymous distributed systems (with an application to consensus). In *32nd International Conference on Distributed Computing Systems* (pp. 275-284). IEEE Computer Society. 10.1109/ICDCS.2012.13

Benenson, Z., Fort, M., Freiling, M. C., Kesdogan, D., & Penso, L. D. (2006). Trusted Pals: Secure multiparty computation implemented with smart cards. Lecture Notes in Computer Science, 4189, 34–48.

Chandra, T. D., Hadzilacos, V., & Toueg, S. (1992). The weakest failure detector for solving consensus. In *11th Annual ACM Symposium on Principles of Distributed Computing* (pp. 147-158). Vancouver, BC, Canada: ACM. 10.21236/ADA253611

Chandra, T. D., Hadzilacos, V., & Toueg, S. (1996). The weakest failure detector for solving consensus. *Journal of the Association for Computing Machinery*, *43*(4), 685–722. doi:10.1145/234533.234549

Chandra, T. D., & Toueg, S. (1996). Unreliable failure detectors for reliable distributed systems. *Journal of the Association for Computing Machinery*, *43*(2), 225–267. doi:10.1145/226643.226647

Cortinas, R. (2011). *Failure detectors and communication efficiency in the crash and general omission failure models* (Unpublished doctoral dissertation). University of the Basque Country.

Dolev, D., Dwork, C., & Stockmeyer, L. J. (1987). On the minimal synchronism needed for distributed consensus. *Journal of the Association for Computing Machinery*, *34*(1), 77–97. doi:10.1145/7531.7533

Dwork, C., Lynch, N. A., & Stockmeyer, L. J. (1988). Consensus in the presence of partial synchrony. *Journal of the Association for Computing Machinery*, *35*(2), 288–323. doi:10.1145/42282.42283

Freiling, F. C., Guerraoui, R., & Kuznetsov, P. (2011). The failure detector abstraction. *ACM Computing Surveys*, *43*(2), 9. doi:10.1145/1883612.1883616

Gallet, C. D., Fauconnier, H., Freiling, F. C., Penso, L. D., & Tielmann, A. (2007). From crash-stop to permanent omission: Automatic transformation and weakest failure detectors. Lecture Notes in Computer Science, 4731, 165–178.

Guerraoui, R. (2008). Failure Detectors. In Encyclopedia of Algorithms (pp. 1-99). Springer US. doi:10.1007/978-0-387-30162-4_140

Guerraoui, R., & Rodrigues, L. (2006). *Introduction to reliable distributed programming*. Springer Science & Business Media.

Hadzilacos, V., & Toueg, S. (1994). *A modular approach to fault-tolerant broadcasts and related problems (Technical Report)*. Ithaca, NY: Cornell University.

Hutle, M. (2005). *Failure detection in sparse networks* (PhD THESIS). Technischen Universitat Wien Fakultat fur Informatik.

Larrea, M., Arévalo, S., & Fernández, A. (1999). Efficient algorithms to implement unreliable failure detectors in partially synchronous systems. Lecture Notes in Computer Science, 1693, 34-49.

Larrea, M., Fernández, A., & Arévalo, S. (2004). On the implementation of unreliable failure detectors in partially synchronous systems. *IEEE Transactions on Computers*, *53*(7), 815–828. doi:10.1109/TC.2004.33

Macêdo, R. J., & Gorender, S. (2009). Perfect failure detection in the partitioned synchronous distributed system model. In *International Conference on Availability, Reliability and Security* (pp. 273-280). Fukuoka Institute of Technology. 10.1109/ARES.2009.165

Mostefaoui, A., Mourgaya, E., & Raynal, M. (2002). An introduction to oracles for asynchronous distributed systems. *Future Generation Computer Systems*, *18*(6), 757–767. doi:10.1016/S0167-739X(02)00048-1

Park, S. H., Lee, J. Y., & Yu, S. C. (2013). Non-blocking atomic commitment algorithm in asynchronous distributed systems with unreliable failure detectors. *10th International Conference on Information Technology: New Generations*, 33-38. 10.1109/ITNG.2013.13

Raynal, M. (2010). Communication and agreement abstractions for fault-tolerant asynchronous distributed systems. *Synthesis Lectures on Distributed Computing Theory*, *1*(1), 1–273.

Reynal, M. (2005). A short introduction to failure detectors for asynchronous distributed systems. *ACM SIGACT News, 36*(1), 53–70. doi:10.1145/1052796.1052806

Soraluze, I., Cortiñas, R., Lafuente, L., Larrea, M., & Freiling, F. (2011). Communication-efficient failure detection and consensus in omission environments. *Information Processing Letters, Elsevier, 111*(6), 262–268. doi:10.1016/j.ipl.2010.12.008

Veríssimo, P. (2006). Travelling through wormholes: A new look at distributed systems models. *SIGACT News, 37*(1), 66–81. doi:10.1145/1122480.1122497

Verma, A., & Pattanaik, K. K. (2014). Mobile agent based train control system for mitigating meet conflict at turnout. *Procedia Computer Science, Elsevier, 32*, 317–324. doi:10.1016/j.procs.2014.05.430

Verma, A., & Pattanaik, K. K. (2015a). Multi-agent CBTC system for Indian railways: The structural design. *Journal of Software (JSW), 10*(3), 250–259.

Verma, A., & Pattanaik, K. K. (2015b). Multi-agent CBTC system for Indian railways: The behavior analysis. *Journal of Modern Transportation, 23*(4), 272–286. doi:10.100740534-015-0083-1

Verma, A., & Pattanaik, K. K. (2016). Failure Detector of *Perfect P* Classfor Synchronous HierarchicalDistributed Systems. *International Journal of Distributed Systems and Technologies*, *7*(2), 57–74. doi:10.4018/IJDST.2016040104

Verma, A., Pattanaik, K. K., & Goel, P. P. (2014). Mobile agent based CBTC system with moving block signalling for Indian railways. In *2nd International Conference on Railway Technology: Research, Development and Maintenance (Railways 2014)*. Civil-Comp Press.

Widder, J., & Schmid, U. (2009). The Theta-Model: Achieving synchrony without clocks. *Distributed Computing*, *22*(1), 29–47. doi:10.100700446-009-0080-x

KEY TERMS AND DEFINITIONS

Distributed Systems: A distributed system is a collection of independent computers and software that appears to its users as a single coherent system. The software components located on networked computers communicate and coordinate with each other by passing messages in order to achieve a common goal.

Failure Detector Classes: Failure detectors are classified according to two properties: *completeness* and *accuracy*. There are two variations of the *completeness* property and four variations of the *accuracy* property. Failure detectors are classified into eight different classes by combining two variations, one from *completeness* and another from *accuracy* properties.

Failure Detectors: Failure detector is an algorithm/module located at each process in the distributed system. It collects operational state information of other processes in the system and provides to its owner process to make him aware of faulty processes in the system. Failure detectors reliability is measured through two properties: *completeness* and *accuracy*.

Hierarchical Systems: In hierarchical systems, processes/nodes are arranged in hierarchy or reverse tree like structure. The system is structured using different levels of authority and chain of commands in which higher levels control lower levels of the hierarchy. If a link breaks, the higher authorities do not have control on the levels below the failure.

Synchronous Systems: A synchronous system has a clear time bound for each event occurs in the system. There are clear lower and upper time bound for each event execution and message transmission. Every clock has a known, bounded deviation from the real time. Time bound violation by any event is considered as a failure.

Compilation of References

Aamodt, A., & Nygard, M. (1995). Different roles and mutual dependencies of data, information, and knowledge — An AI perspective on their integration. *Data & Knowledge Engineering*, *16*(3), 191–222. doi:10.1016/0169-023X(95)00017-M

Aazam, M., & Huh, E. N. (2016). Fog computing: The cloud-IoT/IoE middle- ware paradigm. *IEEE Potentials*, *35*(3), 40–44. doi:10.1109/MPOT.2015.2456213

Adiba, M. E., Chupin, J. C., Demolombe, R., Gardarin, G., & Le Bihan, J. (1978, September). Issues in distributed data base management systems: A technical overview. In *Proceedings of the fourth international conference on Very Large Data Bases-Volume 4* (pp. 89-110). VLDB Endowment.

Afzal, B., Umair, M., Shah, G. A., & Ahmed, E. (2017). Enabling IoT platforms for social IoT applications: Vision, feature mapping, and challenges. *Future Generation Computer Systems*.

Agazzi, F., & Tomaiuolo, M. (2013). Trust Negotiation for Automated Service Integration. *Proceedings of the 14th Workshop on Objects and Agents (WOA 2013).*

Aguilera, M. K., Chen, W., & Toueg, S. (1997). Heartbeat: A timeout-free failure detector for quiescent reliable communication. *Distributed Algorithms. Lecture Notes in Computer Science*, *1320*, 126–140. doi:10.1007/BFb0030680

Aiello, L. M., & Ruffo, G. (2010). LotusNet: Tunable privacy for distributed online social network services. *Computer Communications*, *35*(1), 75–88. doi:10.1016/j.comcom.2010.12.006

Akatyev, N., & James, J. I. (2017). Evidence identification in IoT networks based on threat assessment. *Future Generation Computer Systems*.

Alaba, F. A., Othman, M., Ibrahim, A. T. H., & Alotaibi, F. (2017). Internet of Things security: A survey. *Journal of Network and Computer Applications, 88*, 10-28.

Al-Ali, A. R., Zualkernan, I. A., Rashid, M., Gupta, R., & Alikarar, M. (2017). A smart home energy management system using IoT and big data analytics approach. *IEEE Transactions on Consumer Electronics*, *63*(4), 426–434. doi:10.1109/TCE.2017.015014

Amazon Elastic Block Storage (EBS). (n.d.). Retrieved from http://aws.amazon.com/ebs/

Amazon Elastic Block Storage (S3). (n.d.). Retrieved from http://aws.amazon.com/s3/

Angiani, G., Fornacciari, P., Mordonini, M., Tomaiuolo, M., & Iotti, E. (2016). Models of participation in social networks. In Social Media Performance Evaluation and Success Measurements (pp. 196-224). Academic Press.

Arevalo, S., Anta, A. F., Imbs, D., Jimenez, E., & Raynal, M. (2012). Failure detectors in homonymous distributed systems (with an application to consensus). In *32nd International Conference on Distributed Computing Systems* (pp. 275-284). IEEE Computer Society. 10.1109/ICDCS.2012.13

Avramova, Z., Wittevrongel, S., Bruneel, H., & De Vleeschauwer, D. (Aug.2009). Analysis and modeling of video popularity evolution in various on-line video content systems. *Proceedings of the 1st International Conference on Evolving Internet (INTERNET '09)*, 95-100.

AWS. (2019). Retrieved from https://aws.amazon.com/serverless/?nc2=h_m2

Bacon, J., Evans, D., Eyers, D. M., Migliavacca, M., Pietzuch, P., & Shand, B. (2010). Enforcing End-to-End Application Security in the Cloud. In Middleware 2010 (pp. 293-312). Springer Berlin Heidelberg. doi:10.1007/978-3-642-16955-7_15

Baden, R., Bender, A., Spring, N., Bhattacharjee, B., & Starin, D. (2009). Persona: an online social network with user-defined privacy. In *Proceedings of the ACM conference on Data communication (SIGCOMM '09)* (pp. 135–146). ACM. 10.1145/1592568.1592585

Banerjee, S., Bhattacharjee, B., & Kommareddy, C. (2002). Scalable application layer multicast. In *Proceedings of ACM/IEEE Sigcomm 2002* (pp. 205-217). ACM/IEEE.

Bao, Y., Ren, L., Zhang, L., Zhang, X., & Luo, Y. (2012). Massive Sensor Data Management Framework in Cloud Manufacturing Based on Hadoop. *IEEE10th International Conference on Industrial Informatics*, 397-401. doi: 10.1109/INDIN.2012.6301192

BCache. (n.d.). Retrieved from http://bcache.evilpiepirate.org

Belli, L., Cirani, S., Davoli, L., Ferrari, G., Melegari, L., & Picone, M. (2016). Applying Security to a Big Stream Cloud Architecture for the Internet of Things. *International Journal of Distributed Systems and Technologies*, *7*(1), 37–58. doi:10.4018/IJDST.2016010103

Belli, L., Cirani, S., Davoli, L., Melegari, L., Mònton, M., & Picone, M. (2015). An Open-Source Cloud Architecture for Big Stream IoT Applications. In I. Podnar Žarko, K. Pripužić, & M. Serrano (Eds.), *Interoperability and Open-Source Solutions for the Internet of Things* (Vol. 9001, pp. 73–88). Springer International Publishing; doi:10.1007/978-3-319-16546-2_7

Belli, L., Cirani, S., Ferrari, G., Melegari, L., & Picone, M. (2014). A Graph-Based Cloud Architecture for Big Stream Real-Time Applications in the Internet of Things. In *Advances in Service-Oriented and Cloud Computing* (Vol. 508, pp. 91–105). Springer International Publishing. doi:10.1007/978-3-319-14886-1_10

Bellissimo, A., Levine, B. N., & Shenoy, P. (2004). *Exploring the use of BitTorrent as the basis for a large trace repository (Technical Report)*. University of Massachusetts.

Benenson, Z., Fort, M., Freiling, M. C., Kesdogan, D., & Penso, L. D. (2006). Trusted Pals: Secure multiparty computation implemented with smart cards. Lecture Notes in Computer Science, 4189, 34–48.

Beraka, M., Mathkour, H., & Gannouni, S. (2011, September). Data sharing in distributed computing environment. In *Electrical and Control Engineering (ICECE), 2011 International Conference on* (pp. 4760-4763). IEEE. 10.1109/ICECENG.2011.6057414

Bergenti, F., Iotti, E., Poggi, A., & Tomaiuolo, M. (2016). Concurrent and Distributed Applications with ActoDeS. *MATEC Web of Conferences, 6*(04043). 10.1051/matecconf/20167604043

Bergenti, B., Poggi, A., & Tomaiuolo, M. (2014). An Actor Based Software Framework for Scalable Applications. In *Proceedings of the International Conference on Internet and Distributed Computing Systems* (pp. 26-35). Springer. 10.1007/978-3-319-11692-1_3

Berners-Lee, T. (2010). Long Live the Web: A Call for Continued Open Standards and Neutrality. *Scientific American Magazine*. Retrieved from http://www.scientificamerican.com/article.cfm?id=long-live-the-web

Bethencourt, J., Sahai, A., & Waters, B. (2007). Ciphertext-Policy Attribute-Based Encryption. In *IEEE Symposium on Security and Privacy* (pp. 321-334). IEEE.

Bharambe, A., Rao, S., Padmanabhan, V., Seshan, S., & Zhang, H. (2005). The impact of heterogeneous bandwidth constraints on DHT-based multicast protocols. In *Proceedings of the 4th International Conference on Peer-to-Peer Systems* (pp. 115-126). Academic Press. 10.1007/11558989_11

Bianchi, G., Melazzi, N. B., Bracciale, L., Piccolo, F. L., & Salsano, S. (2010). Streamline: An optimal distribution algorithm for peer-to-peer real-time streaming. *IEEE Transactions on Parallel and Distributed Systems*, *21*(6), 857–871. doi:10.1109/TPDS.2009.114

Biswas, K., & Muthukkumarasamy, V. (2016, December). Securing Smart Cities Using Blockchain Technology. In *High Performance Computing and Communications; IEEE 14th International Conference on Smart City; IEEE 2nd International Conference on Data Science and Systems (HPCC/SmartCity/DSS), 2016 IEEE 18th International Conference on* (pp. 1392-1393). IEEE. 10.1109/HPCC-SmartCity-DSS.2016.0198

Bojovic, I. (2015). *MySQL Master-Slave Replication on the Same Machine*. Retrieved from https://www.toptal.com/mysql/mysql-master-slave-replication-tutorial

Bonomi, F., Milito, R., Natarajan, P., & Zhu, J. (2014). Fog Computing: A Platform for Internet of Things and Analytics. In Big Data and Internet of Things: A Roadmap for Smart Environments (pp. 169-186). Springer International Publishing. doi:10.1007/978-3-319-05029-4_7

Bonomi, F., Milito, R., Zhu, J., & Addepalli, S. (2012). *Fog computing and its role in the internet of things. In Mobile cloud computing* (pp. 13–16). ACM.

Botta, A., de Donato, W., Persico, V., & Pescapé, A. (2016). Integration of Cloud computing and Internet of Things: A survey. *Future Generation Computer Systems, 56*, 684-700. doi:10.1016/j.future.2015.09.021

Branch, R., Tjeerdsma, H., Wilson, C., Hurley, R., & McConnell, S. (2014). Cloud computing and big data: A review of current service models and hardware perspectives. *Journal of Software Engineering and Applications*, *7*(08), 686–693. doi:10.4236/jsea.2014.78063

Breitbart, Y., Morales, H., Silberschatz, A., & Thompson, G. (1990, October). Multidatabase performance evaluation. In *Information Technology, 1990.'Next Decade in Information Technology', Proceedings of the 5th Jerusalem Conference on (Cat. No. 90TH0326-9)* (pp. 507-519). IEEE. 10.1109/JCIT.1990.128323

Bryan, G. H., & Rotunno, R. (2009). The maximum intensity of tropical cyclones in axisymmetric numerical model simulations. *Journals of the American Meteorological Society*, *137*, 1770–1789.

Buchegger, S., Schiöberg, D., Vu, L., & Datta, A. (2009). PeerSoN: P2P social networking: early experiences and insights. In *Proceedings of the Second ACM EuroSys Workshop on Social Network Systems* (pp. 46-52). ACM.

Burakowski, W., Beben, A., van den Berg, H., Bosman, J. W., Hasslinger, G., Kertesz, A., ... Stiller, B. (2018). Traffic Management for Cloud Federation. *Springer, LNCS, 10768*, 269–312.

Burns, B., Grant, B., Oppenheimer, D., Brewer, E., & Wilkes, J. (2016). Borg, omega, and kubernetes. *Queue, 14*(1), 10:70–10:93.

Bushmaker, J. (2018). *Cryptocurrencies*. Retrieved from https://www.investinblockchain.com/top-cryptocurrencies/

Callegati, F., Giallorenzo, S., Melis, A., & Prandini, M. (2018). Cloud-of-Things meets Mobility-as-a-Service: An insider threat perspective. *Computers & Security, 74*, 277-295. doi:10.1016/j.cose.2017.10.006

Carra, D., Neglia, G., & Michiardi, P. (2018). Elastic provisioning of cloud caches: A cost-aware ttl approach. In Socc '18: The 2018 ACM symposium on cloud computing (pp. 526–526). Academic Press. doi:10.1145/3267809.3275468

Castro, M., Druschel, P., Kermarrec, A. M., Nandi, A., Rowstron, A., & Singh, A. (2003). SplitStream: High-bandwidth multicast in cooperative environments. In *Proceedings of 19th ACM Symposium on Operating Systems Principles* (pp. 298-313). ACM.

Castro, M., Druschel, P., Kermarrec, A. M., & Rowstron, A. (2002). Scribe: A large-scale and decentralized application-level multicast infrastructure. *IEEE Journal on Selected Areas in Communications, 20*(8), 1489–1499. doi:10.1109/JSAC.2002.803069

Cerullo, G., Mazzeo, G., Papale, G., Ragucci, B., & Sgaglione, L. (2018). IoT and Sensor Networks Security. In Intelligent Data-Centric Systems (pp. 77-101). Academic Press. doi:10.1016/B978-0-12-811373-8.00004-5

Chandra, T. D., Hadzilacos, V., & Toueg, S. (1992). The weakest failure detector for solving consensus. In *11th Annual ACM Symposium on Principles of Distributed Computing* (pp. 147-158). Vancouver, BC, Canada: ACM. 10.21236/ADA253611

Chandra, T. D., Hadzilacos, V., & Toueg, S. (1996). The weakest failure detector for solving consensus. *Journal of the Association for Computing Machinery, 43*(4), 685–722. doi:10.1145/234533.234549

Chandra, T. D., & Toueg, S. (1996). Unreliable failure detectors for reliable distributed systems. *Journal of the Association for Computing Machinery*, *43*(2), 225–267. doi:10.1145/226643.226647

Chang, Y.-H., Hsu, P.-Y., Lu, Y.-F., & Kuo, T.-W. (2011, June). A driver-layer caching policy for removable storage devices. *Trans. Storage, 7*(1), 1:1–1:23.

Chawki, M. (2010). Anonymity in cyberspace: Finding the balance between privacy and security. *International Journal of Technology Transfer and Commercialisation*, *9*(3), 183–199. doi:10.1504/IJTTC.2010.030209

Chen, J., Douglas, C., Mutsuzaki, M., Quaid, P., Ramakrishnan, R., Rao, S., & Sears, R. (2012). Walnut: A unified cloud object store. In *Sigmod '12: Proceedings of the 2012 acm sigmod international conference on management of data* (pp. 743–754). Scottsdale, AZ: ACM. 10.1145/2213836.2213947

Chen, F., Guo, K., Lin, J., & Porta, T. L. (2012). Intra-Cloud Lightning: Building CDNs in the Cloud. *Proceedings - IEEE INFOCOM*, 433–444.

Chibelushi, Eardley, & Arabo. (2013). Identity Management in the Internet of Things: the Role of MANETs for Healthcare Applications. *Computer Science and Information Technology, 1*(2), 73-81.

Chifor, B.-C., Bica, I., Patriciu, V.-V., & Pop, F. (2017). A security authorization scheme for smart home Internet of Things devices. *Future Generation Computer Systems*.

Chiu, D., Shetty, A., & Agrawal, G. (2010). Elastic cloud caches for accelerating service-oriented computations. In *Proceedings of the 2010 acm/ieee international conference for high performance computing, networking, storage and analysis* (pp. 1–11). New Orleans, LA: IEEE Computer Society. 10.1109/SC.2010.21

Choo, K.-K. R., Bishop, M., Glisson, W., & Nance, K. (2018). Internet- and cloud-of-things cybersecurity research challenges and advances. *Computers & Security, 74*, 275-276. doi:10.1016/j.cose.2018.02.008

ChrisC. (2018). Retrieved from https://www.youtube.com/watch?v=LikdmXfWO2A&t=2312s

Chung, C. W. (1990). DATAPLEX: An access to heterogeneous distributed databases. *Communications of the ACM*, *33*(1), 70–80. doi:10.1145/76372.76377

Cicco, L. D., Mascolo, S., & Calamita, D. (2013). A Resource Allocation Controller for Cloud-based Adaptive Video Streaming. *IEEE International Conference on Communications: IEEE ICC'13 - 1st International Workshop on Mobile Cloud Computing and Services*, 723-727.

Cirani, S., Picone, M., & Veltri, L. (2015). mjCoAP: An Open-Source Lightweight Java CoAP Library for Internet of Things Applications. In Interoperability and Open-Source Solutions for the Internet of Things. Springer. Doi:10.1007/978-3-319-16546-2_10

Cirani, S., Davoli, L., Picone, M., & Veltri, L. (2014, Jul). Performance Evaluation of a SIP-based Constrained Peer-to-Peer Overlay. In *2014 IEEE International Conference on High Performance Computing Simulation* (pp. 432-435). IEEE. 10.1109/HPCSim.2014.6903717

Cirani, S., Picone, M., & Veltri, L. (2013). CoSIP: A Constrained Session Initiation Protocol for the Internet of Things. In *Advances in Service-Oriented and Cloud Computing* (Vol. 393, pp. 13–24). Springer Berlin Heidelberg. doi:10.1007/978-3-642-45364-9_2

Cisco. (2017). *Cisco Delivers Vision of Fog Computing to Accelerate Value from Billions of Connected Devices.* Press Release. Available: https://newsroom.cisco.com/press-release-content?type=webcontent&articleId=1334100

Clarke, I., Miller, S., Hong, T., Sandberg, O., & Wiley, B. (2002). Protecting free expression online with Freenet. *Internet Computing*, *6*(1), 40–49. doi:10.1109/4236.978368

Clemente-Castelló, F. J., Nicolae, B., Katrinis, K., Rafique, M. M., Mayo, R., Fernández, J. C., & Loreti, D. (2015). Enabling Big Data Analytics in the Hybrid Cloud Using Iterative MapReduce. In *Ucc'15: 8th IEEE/ACM international conference on utility and cloud computing* (pp. 290–299). Limassol, Cyprus: IEEE/ACM.

Clemente-Castelló, F. J., Nicolae, B., Mayo, R., & Fernández, J. C. (2018). Performance model of mapreduce iterative applications for hybrid cloud bursting. *IEEE Transactions on Parallel and Distributed Systems*, *29*(8), 1794–1807. doi:10.1109/TPDS.2018.2802932

Cloud Manufacturing. (2017). In *Wikipedia.* Retrieved from https://en.wikipedia.org/wiki/Cloud_manufacturing

Collina, M., Corazza, G. E., & Vanelli-Coralli, A. (2012). Introducing the QEST broker: Scaling the IoT by bridging MQTT and REST. In *2012 IEEE 23rd International Symposium on Personal Indoor and Mobile Radio Communications* (pp. 36-41). IEEE. DOI: 10.1109/PIMRC.2012.6362813

Cooper, B. F., Ramakrishnan, R., Srivastava, U., Silberstein, A., Bohannon, P., Jacobsen, H.-A., … Yerneni, R. (2008, August). Pnuts: Yahoo!'s hosted data serving platform. *Proc. VLDB Endow., 1*(2), 1277–1288. 10.14778/1454159.1454167

Cortinas, R. (2011). *Failure detectors and communication efficiency in the crash and general omission failure models* (Unpublished doctoral dissertation). University of the Basque Country.

Cutillo, L. A., Molva, R., & Strufe, T. (2009). Safebook: A Privacy Preserving Online Social Network Leveraging on Real-Life Trust. *IEEE Communications Magazine*, *47*(12), 94–101. doi:10.1109/MCOM.2009.5350374

D¨unhaupt, S. (2012). *Vulnerabilities of Industrial Automation Systems*. RUHR-University Bochum, Seminar Thesis report.

Dang, T. D., & Hoang, D. (2018). A Data Protection Model for Fog Computing. *Second International Conference on Fog and Mobile Edge computing (FMEC)*, 32-38.

Das, C., & Singh, J. (2013). Melting transition of confined lennard-jones solids in slit pores. *Theoretical Chemistry Accounts*, *132*(4), 1351. doi:10.100700214-013-1351-y

Dastjerdi, A. V., Gupta, H., Calheiros, R. N., Ghosh, S. K., & Buyya, R. (2016). Fog computing: Principles, architectures, and applications. In Internet of Things (pp. 61-75). Academic Press.

Davoli, L., Belli, L., Veltri, L., & Ferrari, G. (2018). THORIN: An Efficient Module for Federated Access and Threat Mitigation in Big Stream Cloud Architectures. *IEEE Cloud Computing*, *5*(1), 38–48. doi:10.1109/MCC.2018.011791713

Deering, S. E., & Cheriton, D. R. (1990). Multicast routing in datagram internetworks and ex- tended LANs. *International Journal ACM Transactions on Computer Systems*, *8*(2), 85–110. doi:10.1145/78952.78953

Devare, M. (2018). Low Power Communication Protocols for IoT Enabled Applications. In *Protocols and Applications for the Industrial Internet of Things*. IGI Global.

Devare, M. H. (2019). Challenges and Opportunities in High Performance Cloud Computing. In S. Singh & R. Mohan Sharma (Eds.), *Handbook of Research on the IoT, Cloud Computing, and Wireless Network Optimization* (pp. 85–114). Hershey, PA: IGI Global. doi:10.4018/978-1-5225-7335-7.ch005

Dimmock, N., Bacon, J., Ingram, D., & Moody, K. (2005). Risk models for trust-based access control (TBAC). In Trust Management (pp. 364-371). Academic Press.

Ding, T., Yan, G., Lei, Y., & Xu, X. (2016). Research on Critical Technologies of Manufacturing Execution Based on Cloud-Service. *3rd International Conference on Information Science and Control Engineering*, 538-542.

Dingli, A., & Seychell, D. (2012). Taking Social Networks to the Next Level. *International Journal of Distributed Systems and Technologies*, *3*(4), 24–33. doi:10.4018/jdst.2012100103

Disterhöft, A., Sandkühler, P., Ippisch, A., & Graffi, K. (2018). Mr. Tree: Multiple Realities in Tree-based Monitoring Overlays for Peer-to-Peer Networks. In *Proceedings of 2018 International Conference on Computing, Networking and Communications (ICNC)* (pp. 354-360). Academic Press. 10.1109/ICCNC.2018.8390361

Dolev, D., Dwork, C., & Stockmeyer, L. J. (1987). On the minimal synchronism needed for distributed consensus. *Journal of the Association for Computing Machinery*, *34*(1), 77–97. doi:10.1145/7531.7533

Dorri, A., Kanhere, S. S., Jurdak, R., & Gauravaram, P. (2017, March). Blockchain for IoT Security and Privacy: The Case Study of a Smart Home. In *Pervasive Computing and Communications Workshops (PerCom Workshops), 2017 IEEE International Conference on* (pp. 618-623). IEEE.

Dwork, C., Lynch, N. A., & Stockmeyer, L. J. (1988). Consensus in the presence of partial synchrony. *Journal of the Association for Computing Machinery*, *35*(2), 288–323. doi:10.1145/42282.42283

El-Ansary, S., Alima, L. O., Brand, P., & Haridi, S. (2003). Efficient broadcast in structured P2P networks. *Proceedings of 2nd International Workshop on Peer-To-Peer Systems (IPTPS'03).*

Elmisery, A. M., Rho, S., & Botvich, D. (2014). A Fog Based Middleware for Automated Compliance with OECD Privacy Principles in Internet of Healthcare Things. *IEEE Access: Practical Innovations, Open Solutions*, *4*, 8418–8841. doi:10.1109/ACCESS.2016.2631546

Eltoweissy, M., Olariu, S., & Younis, M. (2010). Towards autonomous vehic-ular clouds. Ad hoc Networks, 49, 1-16.

Esposito, C., Castiglione, A., Martini, B., & Choo, K. K. R. (2016). Cloud Manufacturing: Security, Privacy, and Forensic Concerns. *Computers & Society*, 16–22.

European Union. (2016). *Interoperability of Heterogeneous IoT Platforms (INTER-IoT)*. Retrieved from https://cordis.europa.eu/project/rcn/199587_en.html

European Union. (2017). *Aggregate Farming in the Cloud (AFarCloud)*. Retrieved from https://cordis.europa.eu/project/rcn/216117_en.html

Farahani, B., Firouzi, F., Chang, V., Badaroglu, M., Constant, N., & Mankodiya, K. (2018). Towards fog-driven IoT eHealth: Promises and challenges of IoT in medicine and healthcare. *Future Generation Computer Systems, 78*(2), 659-676.

Farahzadi, A., Shams, P., Rezazadeh, J., & Farahbakhsh, R. (2017). Middleware technologies for cloud of things-a survey. *Digital Communications and Networks*. doi:10.1016/j.dcan.2017.04.005

Farris, I., Orsino, A., Militano, L., Iera, A., & Araniti, G. (2018). Federated IoT services leveraging 5G technologies at the edge. *Ad Hoc Networks, 68*, 58-69.

Ferrier, A., & Stangret, C. (1982, September). *Heterogeneity in the Distributed Database Management System SIRIUS-DELTA* (pp. 45–53). VLDB.

Fornacciari, P., Mordonini, M., Poggi, A., Sani, L., & Tomaiuolo, M. (2018). A holistic system for troll detection on Twitter. *Computers in Human Behavior, 89*, 258–268. doi:10.1016/j.chb.2018.08.008

Forney, B. C., Arpaci-Dusseau, A. C., & Arpaci-Dusseau, R. H. (2002). Storage-aware caching: Revisiting caching for heterogeneous storage systems. In *Fast'02: Proc. 1st USENIX conference on file and storage technologies* (pp. 5–5). USENIX.

FowlerM. (2017). Retrieved from https://martinfowler.com/articles/serverless.html

Franchi, E., & Tomaiuolo, M. (2014). A Unified Framework for Traditional and Agent-Based Social Network Modeling. In *Interdisciplinary Applications of Agent-Based Social Simulation and Modeling* (p. 184). Academic Press. doi:10.4018/978-1-4666-5954-4.ch011

Franchi, E., Poggi, A., & Tomaiuolo, M. (2014). Multi-Agent Active Services for Online Social Networks. In Handbook of Research on Demand-Driven Web Services: Theory, Technologies, and Applications. Academic Press. doi:10.4018/978-1-4666-5884-4.ch004

Franchi, E., Poggi, A., & Tomaiuolo, M. (2013). Open social networking for online collaboration. *International Journal of e-Collaboration*, *9*(3), 50–68. doi:10.4018/jec.2013070104

Franchi, E., Poggi, A., & Tomaiuolo, M. (2015). Information and Password Attacks on Social Networks: An Argument for Cryptography. *Journal of Information Technology Research*, *8*(1), 25–42. doi:10.4018/JITR.2015010103

Franchi, E., Poggi, A., & Tomaiuolo, M. (2016). Blogracy: A peer-to-peer social network. *International Journal of Distributed Systems and Technologies*, *7*(2), 37–56. doi:10.4018/IJDST.2016040103

Franchi, E., Poggi, A., & Tomaiuolo, M. (2016). Social media for online collaboration in firms and organizations. *International Journal of Information System Modeling and Design*, *7*(1), 18–31. doi:10.4018/IJISMD.2016010102

Franchi, E., & Tomaiuolo, M. (2013). Distributed Social Platforms for Confidentiality and Resilience. In *Social Network Engineering for Secure Web Data and Services* (pp. 114–136). Hershey, PA: IGI Global. doi:10.4018/978-1-4666-3926-3.ch006

Freiling, F. C., Guerraoui, R., & Kuznetsov, P. (2011). The failure detector abstraction. *ACM Computing Surveys*, *43*(2), 9. doi:10.1145/1883612.1883616

Fremantle, P., Aziz, B., Scott, P., & Kopecky, J. (2014, Sep). Federated Identity and Access Management for the Internet of Things. *3rd International Workshop on the Secure IoT*. 10.1109/SIoT.2014.8

Fummi, F., Martini, S., Monguzzi, M., Perbellini, G., & Poncino, M. (2004, February). Modeling and analysis of heterogeneous industrial networks architectures. In *Proceedings of the conference on Design, automation and test in Europe-Volume 3* (p. 30342). IEEE Computer Society 10.1109/DATE.2004.1269270

Gaetani, E., Aniello, L., Baldoni, R., Lombardi, F., Margheri, A., & Sassone, V. (2017). *Blockchain-based database to ensure data integrity in cloud computing environments*. Academic Press.

Gallet, C. D., Fauconnier, H., Freiling, F. C., Penso, L. D., & Tielmann, A. (2007). From crash-stop to permanent omission: Automatic transformation and weakest failure detectors. Lecture Notes in Computer Science, 4731, 165–178.

Ganesan, B. (n.d.). *Oracle Heterogeneous Services*. Retrieved 29-3-2019 from http://www.dba-oracle.com/t_plsql_heterogeneous%20services.htm

Gao, J. (2014). *Machine Learning Applications for Data Center Optimization*. Google.

Georgakopoulos, D., Jayaraman, P. P., Fazia, M., Villari, M., & Ranjan, R. (2016). Internet of Things and Edge Cloud Computing Roadmap for Manufacturing. *Computers & Society*, 66–73.

Ghahramani, Zhou, & Hon. (2017). Toward Cloud Computing QoS Architecture: Analysis of Cloud Systems and Cloud Services. *IEEE/CAA Journal of Automatica Sinica, 4*, 5-17.

Ghoshal, D., & Ramakrishnan, L. (2017). Madats: Managing data on tiered storage for scientific workflows. In *Hpdc'17: The 26th international symposium on high-performance parallel and distributed computing* (pp. 41–52). Academic Press.

Gong, Y., Zhang, C., Fang, Y., & Sun, J. (2012). Protecting Location Privacy for Task Allocation in Ad Hoc Mobile Cloud Computing. *IEEE Transactions on Emerging Topics in Computing*, 1–12.

Google. (2014). *Google Compute Engine Pricing*. Retrieved from https://developers.google.com/compute/pricing

Google. (2018). *Google Cloud IoT Core*. Retrieved from: https://cloud.google.com/iot/docs/

Graffi, K., Groß, C., Mukherjee, P., Kovacevic, A., & Steinmetz, R. (2010). LifeSocial.KOM: A P2Pbased Platform for Secure Online Social Networks. In *Proceedings of the 10th IEEE International Conference onP2PComputing IEEE P2P'10* (pp. 554-558). IEEE.

Greene, M. (2014). Where has privacy gone? How surveillance programs threaten expectations of privacy. *The John Marshall Journal of Information Technology & Privacy Law, 30*(4), 795–827.

Guerraoui, R. (2008). Failure Detectors. In Encyclopedia of Algorithms (pp. 1-99). Springer US. doi:10.1007/978-0-387-30162-4_140

Guerraoui, R., & Rodrigues, L. (2006). *Introduction to reliable distributed programming*. Springer Science & Business Media.

Guidi, B. (2015). *DiDuSoNet: A P2P architecture for distributed Dunbar-based social networks*. Retrieved from https://etd.adm.unipi.it/theses/available/etd-11202015-225158/

Hadzilacos, V., & Toueg, S. (1994). *A modular approach to fault-tolerant broadcasts and related problems (Technical Report)*. Ithaca, NY: Cornell University.

Hardt, D. (2012). *RFC 6749: The OAuth 2.0 Authorization Framework*. Retrieved from http://tools.ietf.org/html/rfc6749

Hobart, B. (2011). *What a deep dive into LinkedIn's S-1 reveals about the company's growth potential*. Retrieved from http://read.bi/hzHD1b

Hoefler, T., Schneider, T., & Lumsdaine, A. (2010). Characterizing the influence of system noise on large-scale applications by simulation. In *Sc '10: Proceedings of the 23rd ACM/IEEE international conference for high performance computing, networking, storage and analysis* (pp. 1–11). New Orleans, LA: IEEE Computer Society. 10.1109/SC.2010.12

Hong, Y., Liu, W. M., & Wang, L. (2017). Privacy preserving smart meter streaming against information leakage of appliance status. *IEEE Transactions on Information Forensics and Security*, *12*(9), 2227–2241. doi:10.1109/TIFS.2017.2704904

Hosseini, M., Ahmed, D. T., Shirmohammadi, S., & Georganas, N. D. (2007). A survey of application-layer multicast protocols. *Journal IEEE Communications Surveys and Tutorials*, *9*(3), 58–74. doi:10.1109/COMST.2007.4317616

Hou, B., & Chen, F. (2017). Gds-lc: A latency- and cost-aware client caching scheme for cloud storage. *ACM Trans. Storage, 13*(4), 40:1–40:33.

Huanga, K., & Zhang, D. (2010). DHT-based lightweight broadcast algorithms in large-scale computing infrastructures. *Future Generation Computer Systems*, *26*(3), 29–310.

Huang, C., Li, J., & Ross, K. W. (2007). Can internet video-on-demand be profitable? In *Proceedings of ACM SIGCOMM'*07 (pp.133-144). ACM.

Hua, P., Dhelima, S., Ning, H., & Qiu, T. (2017). Survey on fog computing: Architecture, key technologies, applications and open issues. *Journal of Network and Computer Applications*, *98*, 27–42. doi:10.1016/j.jnca.2017.09.002

Huebsch, R. (2003). *Content-based multicast: Comparison of implementation options (Tech. Rep. UCB/ CSD-03-1229)*. Berkeley, CA: University of California.

Hu, H., Wen, Y., Chua, T. S., Huang, J., Zhu, W., & Li, X. (2016). Joint Content Replication and Request Routing for Social Video Distribution Over Cloud CDN: A Community Clustering Method. *IEEE Transactions on Circuits and Systems for Video Technology*, *26*(7), 1320–1333. doi:10.1109/TCSVT.2015.2455712

Hu, H., Wen, Y., Chua, T. S., Huang, J., Zhu, W., & Wu, D. (2014). Community-Based Effective Social Video Contents Placement in Cloud Centric CDN Network. *Proceedings of IEEE ICME*. 10.1109/ICME.2014.6890134

Hu, M., Luo, J., Wang, Y., & Veeravalli, B. (2014). Practical Resource Provisioning and Caching with Dynamic Resilience for Cloud-Based Content Distribution Networks. *IEEE Transactions on Parallel and Distributed Systems*, *25*(8), 2169–2179. doi:10.1109/TPDS.2013.287

Hutle, M. (2005). *Failure detection in sparse networks* (PhD THESIS). Technischen Universitat Wien Fakultat fur Informatik.

Ian Wright. (2017). *What Can Augmented Reality Do for Manufacturing?* Retrieved from https://www.engineering.com/AdvancedManufacturing/ArticleID/14904/What-Can-Augmented-Reality-Do-for-Manufacturing.aspx

IBM. (2018). *IBM Watson IoT*. Retrieved from https://www.ibm.com/internet-of-things

Jeong, H. Y., Park, J. H., & Lee, J. D. (2014). The Cloud Storage Model for Manufacturing System in Global Factory Automation. *28th International Conference on Advanced Information Networking and Applications Workshops*, 895- 899. 10.1109/WAINA.2014.138

Jia, Z., & Tian, X. (2013). A Novel Security Private Cloud Solution Based on ECryptfs. *6th International Conference on Information Management, Innovation Management and Industrial Engineering*, 38- 41. 10.1109/ICIII.2013.6703598

Jiming, Y., Zhiping, G., & Rongbo, S. (2012). Perception of Manufacturing Resources In Cloud-Manufacturing System. *International Conference on Computer Science and Service System, IEEE Computer Society*, 1993-1996. 10.1109/CSSS.2012.497

Jo, H., Kwon, Y., Kim, H., Seo, E., Lee, J., & Maeng, S. (2010). Ssd-hdd-hybrid virtual disk in consolidated environments. In *Euro-par'09: Proc. 15th international conference on parallel processing* (pp. 375–384). Delft, The Netherlands: Academic Press.

Kaa. (2018). Retrieved from https://www.kaaproject.org/

Kakoulli, E., & Herodotou, H. (2017). Octopusfs: A distributed file system with tiered storage management. In The 2017 ACM international conference on management of data (pp. 65–78). ACM. doi:10.1145/3035918.3064023

Karagiannis, V., Chatzimisios, P., Vazquez-Gallego, F., & Alonso-Zarate, J. (2015). A survey on application layer protocols for the internet of things. *Transaction on IoT and Cloud Computing*, *3*(1), 11–17.

Karampaglis, Z., Gounaris, A., & Manolopoulos, Y. (2014). A bi-objective cost model for database queries in a multi-cloud environment. In *Medes '14: The 6th international conference on management of emergent digital ecosystems* (pp. 19:109–19:116). Buraidah, Al Qassim, Saudi Arabia: Academic Press. 10.1145/2668260.2668271

Kgil, T., & Mudge, T. (2006). Flashcache: a nand flash memory file cache for low power web servers. In Cases'16: The 2006 international conference on compilers, architecture and synthesis for embedded systems (pp. 103–112). Seoul, South Korea: Academic Press. doi:10.1145/1176760.1176774

Khan & Salah. (2017). IoT security: Review, blockchain solutions, and open challenges. *Future Generation Computer Systems*. doi:10.1016/j.future.2017.11.022

Khanna, A., & Anand, R. (n.d.). IoT based smart parking system. *International Conference on Internet of Things and Applications (IOTA)*, 266-270.

Khokhar, A. A., Prasanna, V. K., Shaaban, M. E., & Wang, C. L. (1993). Heterogeneous computing: Challenges and opportunities. *Computer*, *26*(6), 18–27. doi:10.1109/2.214439

Kim, E., Kaspar, D., & Vasseur, J. (2012, Apr). *Design and application spaces for ipv6 over low-power wireless personal area networks (6LoWPANs)* (No. 6568). RFC 6568 (Informational). IETF. Retrieved from http://www.ietf.org/rfc/rfc6568

Kitcharoen, N., Kamolsantisuk, S., Angsomboon, R., & Achalakul, T. (2013). RapidMiner Framework for Manufacturing Data Analysis on the Cloud. *10th International Joint Conference on Computer Science and Software Engineering*. 10.1109/JCSSE.2013.6567336

Koo, D., & Hur, J. (2018). Privacy-preserving deduplication of encrypted data with dynamic ownership management in fog computing. *Future Generation Computer Systems*, *78*, 739–752. doi:10.1016/j.future.2017.01.024

Kshetri, N. (2017). Can blockchain strengthen the internet of things? *IT Professional*, *19*(4), 68–72. doi:10.1109/MITP.2017.3051335

Kundan, K., & Malik, L. G. (2015). TTS: A Study of Trusted Tenant System in Cloud Computing Environment. *IEEE Sponsored 2nd International Conference on Innovations in Information Embedded and Communication Systems*, 1-5.

Lagutin, D., Visala, K., Zahemszky, A., Burbridge, T., & Marias, G. F. Roles and security in a publish/subscribe network architecture. In *2010 IEEE Symposium on Computers and Communications* (pp. 68-74). IEEE. 10.1109/ISCC.2010.5546746

Larrea, M., Arévalo, S., & Fernández, A. (1999). Efficient algorithms to implement unreliable failure detectors in partially synchronous systems. Lecture Notes in Computer Science, 1693, 34-49.

Larrea, M., Fernández, A., & Arévalo, S. (2004). On the implementation of unreliable failure detectors in partially synchronous systems. *IEEE Transactions on Computers*, *53*(7), 815–828. doi:10.1109/TC.2004.33

Lartigau, J., Nie, L., Xu, X., Zhan, D., & Mou, T. (2012). Scheduling Methodology for Production Services in Cloud Manufacturing. *International Joint Conference on Service Sciences, IEEE Computer Society*, 34-39. 10.1109/IJCSS.2012.19

Lavinia, A., Dobre, C., Pop, F., & Cristea, V. (2010). A failure detection system for large scale distributed systems. *International Journal of Distributed Systems and Technologies*, *2*(3), 64–87. doi:10.4018/jdst.2011070105

Law, Palaniswami, Kounga, & Lo. (2013). WAKE: Key management scheme for wide area measurement systems in smart grid. *IEEE Communication Managements, l51*, 34-41.

Leavitt, N. (2013). Storage challenge: Where will all that Big Data go? *Computer*, *46*(9), 22–25. doi:10.1109/MC.2013.326

Lee, J., Chapin, S. J., & Taylor, S. (2003). Reliable heterogeneous applications. *IEEE Transactions on Reliability*, *52*(3), 330–339. doi:10.1109/TR.2003.819502

Lee, K., Kim, D., Ha, D., Rajput, U., & Oh, H. (2015). On Security and Privacy Issues of Fog Computing Supported Internet of Things environment. *6th International Conference on the Network of the Future (NOF)*, 1-3. 10.1109/NOF.2015.7333287

Li, C., Shilane, P., Douglis, F., Shim, H., Smaldone, S., & Wallace, G. (2014). Nitro: A capacity-optimized ssd cache for primary storage. In *Usenix annual technical conference* (pp. 501–512). USENIX.

Liang, C., Liu, Y., & Ross, K. W. (2009). Topology optimization in multi-tree based P2P streaming system. In *Proceedings of 21st International Conference on Tools with Artificial Intelligence (ICTAI '09)* (pp. 806–813). Academic Press.

Liang, X., Shetty, S., Tosh, D., Kamhoua, C., Kwiat, K., & Njilla, L. (2017, May). Provchain: A blockchain-based data provenance architecture in cloud environment with enhanced privacy and availability. In *Proceedings of the 17th IEEE/ACM International Symposium on Cluster, Cloud and Grid Computing* (pp. 468-477). IEEE Press. 10.1109/CCGRID.2017.8

Li, C., Qin, Z., Novak, E., & Li, Q. (2017). *Securing SDN Infrastructure of IoT-Fog Network from MitM Attacks. IEEE Internet of Things Journal.*

Li, J., Sollins, K., & Lim, D. Y. (2005). Implementing aggregation and broadcast over distributed hash tables. *Newsletter ACM SIGCOMM Computer Communication Review*, *35*(1), 81–92. doi:10.1145/1052812.1052813

Lim, H. C., Babu, S., & Chase, J. S. (2010). Automated control for elastic storage. In *Icac '10: Proc. 7th international conference on autonomic computing* (pp. 1–10). Washington, DC: Academic Press.

Lim, K., Chang, J., Mudge, T., Ranganathan, P., Reinhardt, S. K., & Wenisch, T. F. (2009). Disaggregated memory for expansion and sharing in blade servers. *ACM SIGARCH Computer Architecture News*, *37*(3), 267–278. doi:10.1145/1555815.1555789

Li, N. (July2000). Local Names in SPKI/SDSI. In *Proceedings of the 13th IEEE workshop on Computer Security Foundations (CSFW '00)* (pp. 2-15). IEEE Computer Society Press. 10.1109/CSFW.2000.856921

Lin, C. F., Leu, M. C., Chang, C. W., & Yuan, S. M. (2011). The Study and Methods for Cloud-based CDN. *International Conference on Cyber-Enabled Distributed Computing and Knowledge Discovery*, 470-475. 10.1109/CyberC.2011.82

Linthicum, D. S. (2016). The Technical Case for Mixing Cloud Computing and Manufacturing. *IEEE Cloud Computing*, 12-15.

Li, S. (2017). Security Requirements in IoT Architecture. In *Securing the Internet of Things* (pp. 97–108). Boston: Syngress. doi:10.1016/B978-0-12-804458-2.00005-6

Liu, M., Jin, Y., Zhai, J., Zhai, Y., Shi, Q., Ma, X., & Chen, W. (2013). Acic: Automatic cloud i/o configurator for hpc applications. In *Sc '13: The 26th international conference on high performance computing, networking, storage and analysis* (pp. 38:1–38:12). Denver, CO: Academic Press.

Liu, N., Li, X., & Wang, Q. (2011). A resource & capability virtualization method for Cloud Manufacturing Systems. IEEE.

Li, W., Zhu, C., Yang, L. T., Shu, L., Ngai, E. C. H., & Ma, Y. (2017). Subtask Scheduling for Distributed Robots in Cloud Manufacturing. *IEEE Systems Journal, 11*(2), 941–950. doi:10.1109/JSYST.2015.2438054

Li, Y., Shen, Y., & Liu, Y. (2012). Utilizing Content Delivery Network in Cloud Computing. *Proceedings of, ICCP2012*, 137–143.

Lombardo, G., Fornacciari, P., Mordonini, M., Sani, L., & Tomaiuolo, M. (2018). A combined approach for the analysis of support groups on Facebook - The case of patients of hidradenitis suppurativa. *Multimedia Tools and Applications*, 1–19.

Lowe, S. D. (2017). *All-Flash Data Centers for Dummies, Pure Storage Edition, Published by*. John Wiley & Sons, Inc.

Luan, H., Cai, L. X., Chen, J., Shen, X., & Bai, F. (2011). Vtube: Towardsthe media rich city life with autonomous vehicular content distribution. *IEEE Communications Society Conference on Sensor, Mesh and AdHoc Communications and Networks (SECON)*. 10.1109/SAHCN.2011.5984918

Luan, H., Kwong, K. W., Hei, X., & Danny, H. K. T. (2010). Adaptive topology formation for peer-to-peer video streaming. *Journal Peer-to-Peer Networking and Applications, 3*(3), 186–207. doi:10.100712083-009-0048-4

Luo, T., Ma, S., Lee, R., Zhang, X., Liu, D., & Zhou, L. (2013). S-cave: Effective ssd caching to improve virtual machine storage performance. In *Pact '13: Proc. 22nd international conference on parallel architectures and compilation techniques* (pp. 103–112). Edinburgh, UK: Academic Press.

Lv, Z., Song, H., Basanta-Val, P., Steed, A., & Jo, M. (2017). Next-Generation Big Data Analytics: State of the Art, Challenges, and Future Research Topics. *IEEE Transactions on Industrial Informatics, 13*(4), 1891–1899. doi:10.1109/TII.2017.2650204

Macêdo, R. J., & Gorender, S. (2009). Perfect failure detection in the partitioned synchronous distributed system model. In *International Conference on Availability, Reliability and Security* (pp. 273-280). Fukuoka Institute of Technology. 10.1109/ARES.2009.165

Magharei, N., & Rejaie, R. (2010). PRIME: Peer- to-peer receiver- driven mesh-based streaming. *Journal IEEE/ACM Transactions on Networking, 17*(4), 1052-1065.

Mahmoud, Rodrigues, Saleem, Al-Muhtadi, Kumar, & Korotaev. (2018). Towards energy-aware fog-enabled cloud of things for healthcare. *Computers & Electrical Engineering, 67*, 58-69. .2018.02.047 doi:10.1016/ j.compeleceng

Malek, Y. N., Kharbouch, A., El Khoukhi, H., Bakhouya, M., De Florio, V., El Ouadghiri, D., Latre, S., & Blondia, C. (2017). *On the use of IoT and Big Data Technologies for Real-time Monitoring and Data Processing*. Academic Press. DOI: . doi:10.1016/j.procs.2017.08.281

Mamata, R. B. P. (2018). Communication Improvement and Traffic Control Based on V2I in Smart City Framework. *International Journal of Vehicular Telematics and Infotainment Systems*, *2*(1).

McGrath, R. G. (2010). Business Models: A Discovery Driven Approach. *Long Range Planning*, *43*(2-3), 247–261. doi:10.1016/j.lrp.2009.07.005

Meng, Q., & Gong, C. (2013). Research of Cloud Computing Security in Digital Library. *6th IEEE International Conference on Information Management, Innovation Management and Industrial Engineering*, 41-44. 10.1109/ICIII.2013.6703173

Mera Pérez, D., Batko, M., & Zezula, P. (2014). Towards Fast Multimedia Feature Extraction: Hadoop or Storm. *2014 IEEE International Symposium on Multimedia*, 106-109. 10.1109/ISM.2014.60

Mercan, S., & Yuksel, M. (2016). Virtual direction multicast: An efficient overlay tree construction algorithm. *Journal of Communications and Networks (Seoul)*, *18*(3), 446–459. doi:10.1109/JCN.2016.000060

Meyer, D. T., Aggarwal, G., Cully, B., Lefebvre, G., Feeley, M. J., Hutchinson, N. C., & Warfield, A. (2008, April). Parallax: Virtual disks for virtual machines. *SIGOPS Oper. Syst. Rev.*, *42*(4), 41–54. doi:10.1145/1357010.1352598

Microsoft. (2018). *Azure IoT: the Internet of Things (IoT) for every business*. Retrieved from https://azure.microsoft.com/en-us/overview/iot/

Microsoft. (2019). *Set up replication distribution database in Always On availability group*. Retrieved 28-3-2019 from https://docs.microsoft.com/en-us/sql/relational-databases/replication/configure-distribution-availability-group?view=sql-server-2017

Mineraud, J., Mazhelis, O., Su, X., & Tarkoma, S. (2016). A gap analysis of Internet-of-Things platforms. *Computer Communications*, *89*, 5–16. doi:10.1016/j.comcom.2016.03.015

Mostefaoui, A., Mourgaya, E., & Raynal, M. (2002). An introduction to oracles for asynchronous distributed systems. *Future Generation Computer Systems*, *18*(6), 757–767. doi:10.1016/S0167-739X(02)00048-1

Mukherjee & Biswas. (2017). Networking for IoT and applications using existing communication technology. *Egyptian Informatics Journal*. doi:10.1016/j.eij.2017.11.002

Murphy, J., & Roser, M. (2017). *Internet*. Retrieved from https://ourworldindata.org/internet/

Nadareishvili, I., Mitra, R., McLarty, M., & Amundsen, M. (2016). *Micro-Service Architecture Aligning Principles, Practices, and Culture*. O'Reilly Media.

Nan, Li, Bao, Delicato, Pires, & Zomaya. (2018). A dynamic tradeoff data processing framework for delay-sensitive applications in Cloud of Things systems. *Journal of Parallel and Distributed Computing, 112*(1), 53-66. doi:10.1016/j.jpdc.2017.09.009

Nicolae, B., & Rafique, M. (2013). Leveraging Collaborative Content Exchange for On-Demand VM Multi-Deployments in IaaS Clouds. In *Euro-par '13: 19th international euro-par conference on parallel processing* (pp. 305–316). Aachen, Germany: Academic Press. 10.1007/978-3-642-40047-6_32

Nicolae, B., Bresnahan, J., Keahey, K., & Antoniu, G. (2011). Going back and forth: Efficient multi-deployment and multi-snapshotting on clouds. In *Hpdc '11: 20th international ACM symposium on high-performance parallel and distributed computing* (p. 147-158). San José: ACM.

Nicolae, B., Karve, A., & Kochut, A. (2015). Discovering and Leveraging Content Similarity to Optimize Collective On-Demand Data Access to IaaS Cloud Storage. In *Ccgrid'15: 15th IEEE/ACM international symposium on cluster, cloud and grid computing* (p. 211-220). Shenzhen, China: IEEE/ACM. 10.1109/CCGrid.2015.156

Nicolae, B., Riteau, P., & Keahey, K. (2014a). Bursting the cloud data bubble: Towards transparent storage elasticity in iaas clouds. In *Ipdps '14: Proc. 28th IEEE international parallel and distributed processing symposium*. Phoenix, AZ: IEEE.

Nicolae, B., Riteau, P., & Keahey, K. (2014b). Transparent Throughput Elasticity for IaaS Cloud Storage Using Guest-Side Block-Level Caching. In *Ucc'14: 7th IEEE/ACM international conference on utility and cloud computing* (pp. 186–195). London, UK: IEEE/ACM. 10.1109/UCC.2014.27

Nicolae, B., & Cappello, F. (2013, May). BlobCR: Virtual disk based checkpoint-restart for HPC applications on IaaS clouds. *Journal of Parallel and Distributed Computing, 73*(5), 698–711. doi:10.1016/j.jpdc.2013.01.013

Nicolae, B., Costa, C., Misale, C., Katrinis, K., & Park, Y. (2017). Leveraging adaptive i/o to optimize collective data shuffling patterns for big data analytics. *IEEE Transactions on Parallel and Distributed Systems*, *28*(6), 1663–1674. doi:10.1109/TPDS.2016.2627558

Nicolae, B., Riteau, P., & Keahey, K. (2015). Towards Transparent Throughput Elasticity for IaaS Cloud Storage: Exploring the Benefits of Adaptive Block-Level Caching. *International Journal of Distributed Systems and Technologies*, *6*(4), 21–44. doi:10.4018/IJDST.2015100102

Nijim, S., & Pagano, B. (2017). APIs for Dummies. John Wiley & Sons, Inc.

Numms, J. (n.d.). *Salesforce turns to Amazon Web Services for Internet of Things Cloud*. Retrieved from https://www.cbronline.com/emerging-technology/

Onica, E., Felber, P., Mercier, H., & Riviére, E. (2016). Confidentiality-preserving publish/subscribe: A survey. *ACM Computing Surveys*, *49*(2), 1–41. doi:10.1145/2940296

Openstack cinder. (n.d.). Retrieved from https://docs.openstack.org/cinder

Oracle Executive. (2017). *Why End-to-End Visibility Is Key to a Modern Manufacturing Process*. Oracle Executive Paper.

Oracle. (2007). *Oracle Database Gateways*. Retrieved 29-3-2019 from www.oracle.com/technetwork/database/gateways/gateways-twp-131579.pdf

Oracle. (2010). *Oracle Database Gateway for ODBC*. Retrieved 29-3-2019 from https://docs.oracle.com/cd/E18283_01/gateways.112/e12070.pdf

Oracle. (2012). *Oracle Database Gateway*. Retrieved 29-3-2019 from https://docs.oracle.com/cd/E11882_01/gateways.112/e12013.pdf

Oracle. (2019). *Managing a Distributed Database*. Retrieved 28-3-2019 from https://docs.oracle.com/cd/B19306_01/server.102/b14231/ds_admin.htm#i1008852

Oracle. (n.d.). *Oracle Technology Network*. Retrieved 29-3-2019 from https://www.oracle.com/technical-resources/

Overton, J., & Brigham, J. C. (2017). *The Digital Twin, Data-Driven Simulations Innovate the Manufacturing Process*. DXC Technology White Paper.

Özsu, M. T., & Valduriez, P. (2011). *Principles of distributed database systems*. Springer Science & Business Media.

Paliwal, S., & Subash, V. B. (n.d.). *Performance Optimization of Oracle Distributed Databases*. Retrieved from http://citeseerx.ist.psu.edu/viewdoc/summary?doi=10.1.1.174.3872

Paris, C. J., Laflen, J. B., Grabb, M. L., & Kalitan, D. M. (2017). *The Future for The Industrial Services: The Digital Twin, Infosys Insight.* General Electric, White Paper.

Park, J. H., & Park, J. H. (2017). Blockchain Security in Cloud Computing: Use Cases, Challenges, and Solutions. *Symmetry*, *9*(8), 164. doi:10.3390ym9080164

Park, S. H., Lee, J. Y., & Yu, S. C. (2013). Non-blocking atomic commitment algorithm in asynchronous distributed systems with unreliable failure detectors. *10th International Conference on Information Technology: New Generations*, 33-38. 10.1109/ITNG.2013.13

Pattanayak, B., & Rath, M. (2014). A Mobile Agent Based Intrusion Detection System Architecture For Mobile Ad Hoc Networks. *Journal of Computational Science*, *10*(6), 970–975. doi:10.3844/jcssp.2014.970.975

Perez, B. D., Szefer, J., & Lee, R. B. (2013). Characterizing Hypervisor Vulnerabilities in Cloud Computing Servers. *Proceedings of the Workshop on Security in Cloud Computing (SCC).*

Perez-Palacin, D., Calinescu, R., & Merseguer, J. (2013). Log2cloud: Log-based prediction of cost-performance trade-offs for cloud deployments. In *Sac '13: The 28th annual ACM symposium on applied computing* (pp. 397–404). Coimbra, Portugal: ACM.

Perfitt, T., & Englert, B. (2010). *Megaphone: Fault Tolerant, Scalable, and Trustworthy*. Microblogging.

Peris, A. D., Hern, J. M., & Huedo, E. (2012). Evaluation of the broadcast operation in Kademlia. In *2012 IEEE 14th International Conference on High Performance Computing and Communication & 2012 IEEE 9th International Conference on Embedded Software and Systems* (pp. 756-763). IEEE. 10.1109/HPCC.2012.107

Peris, A. D., Hernández, J. M., & Huedo, E. (2016). Evaluation of alternatives for the broadcast operation in Kademlia under churn. *Peer-to-Peer Networking and Applications*, *9*(2), 313–327. doi:10.100712083-015-0338-y

Petersen, J. L. (1994). *Estimating the parameters of a pareto distribution* (Master thesis). Retrieved October 16th, 2018, from http://www.math.umt.edu/gideon/pareto.pdf

Plimpton, S. (1995, March). Fast parallel algorithms for short-range molecular dynamics. *Journal of Computational Physics*, *117*(1), 1–19. doi:10.1006/jcph.1995.1039

Poggi, A., & Tomaiuolo, M. (2011). Integrating Peer-to-Peer and Multi-agent Technologies for the Realization of Content Sharing Applications. In Information Retrieval and Mining in Distributed Environments, SCI (Vol. 324, pp. 93-107). Springer.

Poonguzhali, E., Priyadarsini, A., Magnifique, P., & Asvini, S. (2015). A Security Model For Timing Attack in Cloud Environment. *IEEE Sponsored 2nd International Conference on Innovations in Information Embedded and Communication Systems ICIIECS'15*, 1-5.

Pu, C., Leff, A., & Chen, S. W. (1991). Heterogeneous and autonomous transaction processing. *Computer*, *24*(12), 64–72. doi:10.1109/2.116890

Puthal, D., Mohanty, S. P., Nanda, P., & Choppali, U. (2017). Building Security Perimeters to Protect Network Systems Against Cyber Threats. *IEEE Consumer Electronics Magazine*, *6*(4), 24–27. doi:10.1109/MCE.2017.2714744

Puthal, D., Nepal, S., Ranjan, R., & Chen, J. (2016). Threats to networking cloud and edge datacenters in the internet of things. *IEEE Cloud Computing*, *3*(3), 64–71. doi:10.1109/MCC.2016.63

Puttaswamy, K. P., Nandagopal, T., & Kodialam, M. (2012). Frugal storage for cloud file systems. In *Eurosys '12: The 7th ACM European conference on computer systems* (pp. 71–84). Bern, Switzerland: ACM. 10.1145/2168836.2168845

Qiu, S., & Reddy, A. L. N. (2013). Nvmfs: A hybrid file system for improving random write in nand-flash ssd. In *Msst' 13: Proc. 38th international conference on massive storage systems and technology* (p. 1-5). Academic Press. 10.1109/MSST.2013.6558434

Quang, H. V., Maurizio, C., Rasool, A., Ali, S., Fadi, A. E., & Theo, D. (2015). Secure Cloud Storage: A framework for Data Protection as a Service in the multi-Cloud environment. *1st Workshop on Security and Privacy in the Cloud*, 638-642.

Quantumrealmgames. (2018). Retrieved from http://quantumrealmgames.com/#qcrules

Raiciu, C., & Rosenblum, D. S. (2006). *Enabling Confidentiality in Content-Based Publish/Subscribe Infrastructures*. Securecomm and Workshops. doi:10.1109/SECCOMW.2006.359552

Rao, P. S., & Porter, G. (2016). Is memory disaggregation feasible? A case study with spark sql. In Ancs'16: The 2016 symposium on architectures for networking and communications systems (pp. 75–80). Santa Clara, CA: Academic Press.

Rashmi, V. (2015). Understanding DDoS attack & its effects in cloud environment. *Procedia of Computer Science, Elsevier, 49*, 202–210. doi:10.1016/j.procs.2015.04.245

Rath & Oreku. (2018). Security Issues in Mobile Devices and Mobile Adhoc Networks. In Mobile Technologies and Socio-Economic Development in Emerging Nations. IGI Global. doi:10.4018/978-1-5225-4029-8.ch009

Rath & Pattanayak. (2019). Security Protocol with IDS Framework Using Mobile Agent in Robotic MANET. *International Journal of Information Security and Privacy, 3*(1), 46-58.

Rath, M. (2018). Smart Traffic Management System for Traffic Control using Automated Mechanical and Electronic Devices. *I Mater. Sci. Eng., 377*. doi:/377/1/01220110.1088/1757-899X

Rath, M. (2018a). An Exhaustive Study and Analysis of Assorted Application and Challenges in Fog Computing and Emerging Ubiquitous Computing Technology. *International Journal of Applied Evolutionary Computation, 9*(2), 17-32. Retrieved from www.igi-global.com/ijaec

Rath, M. (2018c). Effective Routing in Mobile Ad-hoc Networks With Power and End-to-End Delay Optimization: Well Matched With Modern Digital IoT Technology Attacks and Control in MANET. In *Advances in Data Communications and Networking for Digital Business Transformation*. IGI Global. Doi:10.4018/978-1-5225-5323-6.ch007

Rath, M. (2018d). An Analytical Study of Security and Challenging Issues in Social Networking as an Emerging Connected Technology. In *Proceedings of 3rd International Conference on Internet of Things and Connected Technologies*. Malaviya National Institute of Technology. Retrieved from https://ssrn.com/abstract=3166509

Rath, M., & Panda, M. R. (2017). MAQ system development in mobile ad-hoc networks using mobile agents. *IEEE 2nd International Conference on Contemporary Computing and Informatics (IC3I)*, 794-798.

Rath, M., & Panigrahi, C. (2016). Prioritization of Security Measures at the Junction of MANET and IoT. In *Second International Conference on Information and Communication Technology for Competitive Strategies*. ACM Publication. 10.1145/2905055.2905187

Rath, M., & Pattanayak, B. K. (2014). A methodical survey on real time applications in MANETS: Focussing On Key Issues. *International Conference on, High Performance Computing and Applications (IEEE ICHPCA)*. 10.1109/ICHPCA.2014.7045301

Rath, M., & Pattanayak, B. K. (2018). Monitoring of QoS in MANET Based Real Time Applications. In Information and Communication Technology for Intelligent Systems (ICTIS 2017) (vol. 84, pp. 579-586). Springer. doi:10.1007/978-3-319-63645-0_64

Rath, M., & Pattanayak, B. K. (2019). Performance Evaluation of Optimized Protocol in MANET. International Journal of Information and Computer Security.

Rath, M., Pati, B., & Pattanayak, B. (2015). Delay and power based network assessment of network layer protocols in MANET. *2015 International Conference on Control, Instrumentation, Communication and Computational Technologies (IEEE ICCICCT)*, 682-686. 10.1109/ICCICCT.2015.7475365

Rath, M., Pati, B., & Pattanayak, B. (2016). Comparative analysis of AODV routing protocols based on network performance parameters in Mobile Adhoc Networks. In Foundations and Frontiers in Computer, Communication and Electrical Engineering (pp. 461-466). CRC Press, Taylor & Francis.

Rath, M., Pati, B., & Pattanayak, B. (2016). QoS Satisfaction in MANET Based Real Time Applications. *International Journal of Control Theory and Applications, 9*(7), 3069-3083.

Rath, M., Pati, B., & Pattanayak, B. K. (2016). Inter-Layer Communication Based QoS Platform for Real Time Multimedia Applications in MANET. Wireless Communications, Signal Processing and Networking (IEEE WiSPNET), 613-617. doi:10.1109/WiSPNET.2016.7566203

Rath, M., Pati, B., & Pattanayak, B. K. (2018). Relevance of Soft Computing Techniques in the Significant Management of Wireless Sensor Networks. In Soft Computing in Wireless Sensor Networks (pp. 86-106). Chapman and Hall/CRC, Taylor & Francis Group. doi:10.1201/9780429438639-4

Rath, M., Pati, B., & Pattanayak, B. K. (2019). Design and Development of Secured Framework for Efficient Routing in Vehicular Ad-hoc Network. Int'l Journal of Business and Data Communication Network, 15(2).

Rath. (2019). Information Security Problem and Solution Approaches in Social Applications. In Cyber-Physical Systems for Social Applications (pp. 207-220). IGI Global.

Rath, M. (2017). Resource provision and QoS support with added security for client side applications in cloud computing. *International Journal of Information Technology*, *9*(3), 1–8.

Rath, M. (2017). Resource Provision and Qos Support with Added Security for Client Side Applications in Cloud Computing. *International Journal of Information Technology*, *9*(3), 1–8.

Rath, M., & Pati, B. (2017). *Load balanced routing scheme for MANETs with power and delay optimisation. International Journal of Communication Network and Distributed Systems,* 19.

Rath, M., Pati, B., & Pattanayak, B. (2015). Energy Competent Routing Protocol Design in MANET with Real time Application Provision. *International Journal of Business Data Communications and Networking*, *11*(1), 50–60. doi:10.4018/IJBDCN.2015010105

Rath, M., Pati, B., & Pattanayak, B. (2016). Energy Efficient MANET Protocol Using Cross Layer Design for Military Applications. *Defence Science Journal*, *66*(2), 146. doi:10.14429/dsj.66.9705

Rath, M., Pati, B., & Pattanayak, B. (2016). Resource Reservation and Improved QoS for Real Time Applications in MANET. *Indian Journal of Science and Technology*, *9*(36). doi:10.17485/ijst/2016/v9i36/100910

Rath, M., Pati, B., & Pattanayak, B. K. (2017). Cross layer based QoS platform for multimedia transmission in MANET. *11th International Conference on Intelligent Systems and Control (ISCO)*, 402-407. 10.1109/ISCO.2017.7856026

Rath, M., Pati, B., & Pattanayak, B. K. (2019). Mobile Agent-Based Improved Traffic Control System in VANET. In A. Krishna, K. Srikantaiah, & C. Naveena (Eds.), *Integrated Intelligent Computing, Communication and Security. Studies in Computational Intelligence* (Vol. 771). Singapore: Springer. doi:10.1007/978-981-10-8797-4_28

Rath, M., & Pattanayak, B. (2016). A Contemporary Survey and Analysis of Delay and Power Based Routing Protocols in MANET. *Journal of Engineering and Applied Sciences (Asian Research Publishing Network)*, *11*(1), 536–540.

Rath, M., & Pattanayak, B. (2017). MAQ:A Mobile Agent Based QoS Platform for MANETs. *International Journal of Business Data Communications and Networking, IGI Global*, *13*(1), 1–8. doi:10.4018/IJBDCN.2017010101

Rath, M., & Pattanayak, B. K. (2018). SCICS: A Soft Computing Based Intelligent Communication System in VANET. Smart Secure Systems – IoT and Analytics Perspective. *Communications in Computer and Information Science*, *808*, 255–261. doi:10.1007/978-981-10-7635-0_19

Rath, M., Pattanayak, B. K., & Pati, B. (2017). *Energetic Routing Protocol Design for Real-time Transmission in Mobile Ad hoc Network. In Computing and Network Sustainability, Lecture Notes in Networks and Systems* (Vol. 12). Singapore: Springer.

Rath, M., Rout, U. P., & Pujari, N. (2017). *Congestion Control Mechanism for Real Time Traffic in Mobile Adhoc Networks, Computer Communication, Networking and Internet Security. In Lecture Notes in Networks and Systems* (Vol. 5, pp. 149–156). Singapore: Springer.

Rath, M., Swain, J., Pati, B., & Pattanayak, B. K. (2018). *Attacks and Control in MANET. In Handbook of Research on Network Forensics and Analysis Techniques* (pp. 19–37). IGI Global.

Ratnasamy, S., Handley, M., Karp, R., & Shenker, S. (2001). Application-level multicast using content-addressable networks. In Proceedings of Networked Group Communication (pp. 14-29). Academic Press. doi:10.1007/3-540-45546-9_2

Ratnasamy, S., Francis, P., Handley, M., & Karp, R. (2001). Scalable content-addressable network. In *Proceedings of ACM SIGCOMM'*01 (pp. 161-172). ACM.

Rauscheckerl, U., & Stohrl, M. (2012). Using Manufacturing Service Descriptions for flexible Integration of Production Facilities to Manufacturing Clouds. *Proceedings of the 18th International Conference on Engineering, Technology, and Innovation.*

Raynal, M. (2010). Communication and agreement abstractions for fault-tolerant asynchronous distributed systems. *Synthesis Lectures on Distributed Computing Theory*, *1*(1), 1–273.

Rego, P. A. L., Bonfim, M. S., Ortiz, M. D., & Bezerra, J. M. (2015). *An OpenFlow-based Elastic Solution for Cloud-CDN Video Streaming Service*. IEEE. doi:10.1109/GLOCOM.2015.7417789

Reynal, M. (2005). A short introduction to failure detectors for asynchronous distributed systems. *ACM SIGACT News*, *36*(1), 53–70. doi:10.1145/1052796.1052806

Rhea, S., Geels, D., Roscoe, T., & Kubiatowicz, J. (2004). Handling churn in a DHT. *Proceedings of the USENIX Annual Technical Conference.*

Rodd, S., & Carlton, B. (2013). *Exclusive Story- Cloud Technology Boosts Oil and Gas Operations*. Available at https://www.aogr.com/web-exclusives/exclusive-story/cloud-technology-boosts-oil-and-gas-operations

Romdhani, I. (2017). Confidentiality and Security for IoT Based Healthcare. In *Securing the Internet of Things* (pp. 133–139). Boston: Syngress. doi:10.1016/B978-0-12-804458-2.00009-3

Romdhani, I. (2017). Existing Security Scheme for IoT. In *Securing the Internet of Things* (pp. 119–130). Boston: Syngress. doi:10.1016/B978-0-12-804458-2.00007-X

Rowstron, A., & Druschel, P. (2001).Pastry: Scalable, distributed object location and routing for large-scale peer-to-peer systems. In *Proceedings of IFIP/ACM International Conference on Distributed Systems Platforms* (pp. 329–350). IFIP/ACM. 10.1007/3-540-45518-3_18

Ruth, M. (2018). A Methodical Analysis of Application of Emerging Ubiquitous Computing Technology with Fog Computing and IoT in Diversified Fields and Challenges of Cloud Computing. *International Journal of Information Communication Technologies and Human Development, 10*(2). Doi:10.4018/978-1-5225-4100-4.ch002

Ruth, M. (2017). Resource provision and QoS support with added security for client-side applications in cloud computing. *Springer International Journal of Information Technology*, *9*(3), 1–8.

Saad, M. I. M., Jalil, K. A., & Manaf, M. (2013). Data Provenance Trusted Model in Cloud Computing. *3rd International Conference on Research and Innovation in Information Systems (ICRIIS'13)*, 257-262. 10.1109/ICRIIS.2013.6716719

Sahmim & Gharsellaoui. (2017). Privacy and Security in Internet-based Computing: Cloud Computing, Internet of Things, Cloud of Things: A Review. *Procedia Computer Science, 112*, 1516-1522. doi:10.1016/j.procs.2017.08.050

Sahoo, J., & Rath, M. (2017). Study and Analysis of Smart Applications in Smart City Context. *2017 International Conference on Information Technology (ICIT)*, 225-228. 10.1109/ICIT.2017.38

Sandler, D., Mislove, A., Post, A., & Druschel, P. (2005). Feedtree: Sharing web micronews with P2P event notification. In P2P Systems IV, LNCS (Vol. 3640, pp. 141-151). Springer.

Saravanan, K. (2017). Cloud Robotics: Robot Rides on the Cloud – Architecture, Applications, and Challenges. In R. Kumar, P. Pattnaik, & P. Pandey (Eds.), *Detecting and Mitigating Robotic Cyber Security Risks* (pp. 261–274). Hershey, PA: IGI Global. doi:10.4018/978-1-5225-2154-9.ch017

Saravanan, K., & Radhakrishnan, A. (2018). *Energy Aware Resource Allocation Model for IaaS Optimization. In Cloud Computing for Optimization: Foundations, Applications, Challenges, Studies in Big data*. Springer. doi:10.1007/978-3-319-73676-1_3

Saravanan, K., & Saraniya, S. (2018). Cloud IOT based novel livestock monitoring and identification system using UID. *Sensor Review*, *38*(1), 21–33. doi:10.1108/SR-08-2017-0152

Saravanan, K., & Srinivasan, P. (2017). Examining IoT's Applications Using Cloud Services. In P. Tomar & G. Kaur (Eds.), *Examining Cloud Computing Technologies Through the Internet of Things* (pp. 147–163). Hershey, PA: IGI Global. doi:10.4018/978-1-5225-3445-7.ch008

Sarkar, S., Chatterjee, S., & Misra, S. (2018). Assessment of the suitability of fog computing in the context of Internet of things. *IEEE Transaction on Cloud Computing*, *6*(1), 46–59. doi:10.1109/TCC.2015.2485206

Satyanarayanan, M., Chen, Z., Ha, K., Hu, W., Richter, W., & Pil-lai, P. (2014). Cloudlets: at the leading edge of mobile-cloud convergence. *IEEE International Conference on Mobile Computing, Applications and Services (MobiCASE)*, 1-9. 10.4108/icst.mobicase.2014.257757

Sauermann, L., Cyganiak, R., & Völkel, M. (2007). *Cool URIs for the semantic web*. Academic Press.

Saxena, M., Swift, M. M., & Zhang, Y. (2012). Flashtier: a lightweight, consistent and durable storage cache. In *Eurosys'12: The 7th ACM European conference on computer systems* (pp. 267–280). Bern, Switzerland: ACM. 10.1145/2168836.2168863

Scarfò, A. (2018). The Cyber Security Challenges in the IoT Era. In Intelligent Data-Centric Systems. Academic Press.

Schimmer, L. (2009). Peer Profiling and Selection in the I2P Anonymous Network 1 I2P Overview. *Proceedings of PET-CON '09*, 1-12.

Seddiki, M., & Benchaïba, M. (2015). Gpop: A Global File Popularity Measurement for Unstructured P2P Networks. *International Journal of Distributed Systems and Technologies*, *6*(3), 51–64. doi:10.4018/IJDST.2015070104

Shankland, S. (2010). *Facebook blocks contact exporting tool*. Retrieved from http://news.cnet.com/8301-30685_3-20076774-264/facebook-blocks-contact-exporting-tool/

Sharaf, M. A., Chrysanthis, P. K., Labrinidis, A., & Pruhs, K. (2008). Algorithms and metrics for processing multiple heterogeneous continuous queries. *ACM Transactions on Database Systems*, *33*(1), 5. doi:10.1145/1331904.1331909

Sharma, P. K., Moon, S. Y., & Park, J. H. (2017). Block-VN: A distributed blockchain based vehicular network architecture in smart City. *Journal of Information Processing Systems*, *13*(1), 84.

Shelby, Z., Hartke, K., Bormann, C., & Frank, B. (2014). *RFC 7252: The Constrained Application Protocol (CoAP)*. Internet Engineering Task Force.

Shitole, A., & Devare, M. (2018). Machine Learning Supported Statistical Analysis of IoT Enabled Physical Location Monitoring Data. *International Conference On Computational Vision and Bio-Inspired Computing, Springer Lecture Notes in Computational Science and Engineering*.

Singh, H., & Sachdev, A. (2014). The Quantum Way of Cloud Computing. *International Conference on Reliability, Optimization and Information Technology – ICROIT*, 397-400.

Smith, R., Curtis, M. J., & Zeng, W. J. (2016). *A Practical Quantum Instruction Set Architecture*. Retrieved from https://arxiv.org/abs/1608.03355

SoftLayer. (n.d.). Retrieved from http://www.softlayer.com/

Sohal, A. S., Sandhu, R., Sood, S. K., & Chang, V. (2018). A cybersecurity framework to identify malicious edge device in fog computing and cloud-of-things environments. *Computers & Security, 74*, 340-354. .2017.08.016 doi:10.1016/j.cose

Sohal, A. S., Sandhu, R., Sood, S. K., & Chang, V. (2017). *A cybersecurity framework to identify malicious edge device in fog computing and cloud-of-things environments. In Computers & Security* (pp. 1–15). Elsevier.

Soleymani, S. A., Abdullah, A. H., Zareei, M., Anisi, M. H., Vargas-Rosales, C., Khan, M. K., & Goudarzi, S. (2017). A Secure Trust Model based on Fuzzy Logic in Vehicular Ad Hoc Networks with Fog computing. *IEEE Access: Practical Innovations, Open Solutions*, *99*, 1–10.

Soraluze, I., Cortiñas, R., Lafuente, L., Larrea, M., & Freiling, F. (2011). Communication-efficient failure detection and consensus in omission environments. *Information Processing Letters, Elsevier*, *111*(6), 262–268. doi:10.1016/j.ipl.2010.12.008

Sourikova, I. (n.d.). *PostgreSQL Replicator – easy way to build a distributed Postgres database*. Retrieved 28-3-2019 from https://www.racf.bnl.gov/Facility/TechnologyMeeting/Irina_Sourikova_techMeet.pdf

Stansberry, M. (2016). *Data Center Industry Survey. Making Your Asset Smarter with the Digital Twin*. DNVGL.

Stergiou, C., Psannis, K. E., Kim, B.-G., & Gupta, B. (2018). Secure integration of IoT and Cloud Computing. *Future Generation Computer Systems*, *78*(3), 964–975. doi:10.1016/j.future.2016.11.031

Stoica, I., Morris, R., Karger, D., Kaashoek, M. F., & Balakrisnan, H. (2001). Chord: A scalable peer- to-peer lookup service for Internet applications. In *Proceedings of ACM SIGCOMM'*01 (pp. 149-160). ACM. 10.1145/383059.383071

Sun, J., Sun, S., Li, K., Dan, L., Sangaiah, A. K., & Chang, V. (2018). Efficient algorithm for traffic engineering in Cloud-of-Things and edge computing. *Computers & Electrical Engineering*. doi:10.1016/j.compeleceng.2018.02.016

Sun, X. H., Chen, Y., & Wu, M. (2005, June). Scalability of heterogeneous computing. In *Parallel Processing, 2005. ICPP 2005. International Conference on* (pp. 557-564). IEEE.

Sun, E., Zhang, X., & Li, Z. (2012). The internet of things (IOT) and cloud computing (CC) based tailings dam monitoring and pre-alarm system in mines. *Safety Science*, *50*(4), 811–815. doi:10.1016/j.ssci.2011.08.028

Tao, F., Zhang, L., Liu, Y., Cheng, Y., Wang, L., & Xu, X. (2015). Manufacturing Service Management in Cloud Manufacturing: Overview and Future Research Directions. *Journal of Manufacturing Science and Engineering*, *137*(4), 040912. doi:10.1115/1.4030510

Tao, Y. S., & Lee, H. Y. (2015). Certifying SaaS in the MTCS Framework. *2015 International Conference on Cloud Computing Research and Innovation*, 15-18.

Tesfatsion, S. K., Klein, C., & Tordsson, J. (2018). Virtualization Techniques Compared: Performance, Resource, and Power Usage Overheads in Clouds. In *ICPE '18: The 2018 ACM/SPEC International Conference on Performance Engineering* (pp. 145–156). Berlin, Germany: ACM.

Thamizhselvan, M., Raghuraman, R., Manoj, S. G., & Paul, P. V. (2015). A Novel Security Model For Cloud Using Trusted Third-Party Encryption. *IEEE Sponsored 2nd International Conference on Innovations in Information Embedded and Communication Systems ICIIECS'15*, 1-5.

The QCOW2 Image Format. (n.d.). Retrieved from https://people.gnome.org/~markmc/qcow-image-format.html

Tomaiuolo, M. (2013). dDelega: Trust management for web services. *International Journal of Information Security and Privacy*, *7*(3), 53–67. doi:10.4018/jisp.2013070104

Tomaiuolo, M. (2014). Trust Management and Delegation for the Administration of Web Services. In I. Portela & F. Almeida (Eds.), *Organizational, Legal, and Technological Dimensions of Information System Administration* (pp. 18–37). Hershey, PA: IGI Global. doi:10.4018/978-1-4666-4526-4.ch002

Tran, D. A., Hua, K. A., & Do, T. T. (2004). A peer- to-peer architecture for media streaming. *Journal IEEE JSAC Special Issue on Advances in Service Overlay Networks*, *22*(1), 121–133.

Trezor. (2018). *Trezor: The safe place for your coins*. Retrieved from https://trezor.io/

Triwinarko, A. (2002). *Elliptic Curve Digital Signature Algorithm (ECDSA)*. Makalah TA, Departemen Teknik Informatika ITB.

Tsuneizumi, I., Aikebaier, A., Ikeda, M., Enokido, T., & Takizawa, M. (2011). Design and implementation of hybrid time (HT) group communication protocol for homogeneous broadcast groups. *International Journal of Distributed Systems and Technologies*, *2*(3), 37–48. doi:10.4018/jdst.2011070103

Uzunov, A. V. (2016). A survey of security solutions for distributed publish/subscribe systems. *Computers & Security*, *61*, 94–129. doi:10.1016/j.cose.2016.04.008

Venkataraman, V., Francis, P., & Calandrino, J. (2006). Chunkyspread: Heterogeneous unstructured tree-based peer-to-peer multicast. In *Proceedings of the 2006 IEEE International Conference on Network Protocols* (pp. 2–11). IEEE. 10.1109/ICNP.2006.320193

Veríssimo, P. (2006). Travelling through wormholes: A new look at distributed systems models. *SIGACT News*, *37*(1), 66–81. doi:10.1145/1122480.1122497

Verma, A., Pattanaik, K. K., & Goel, P. P. (2014). Mobile agent based CBTC system with moving block signalling for Indian railways. In *2nd International Conference on Railway Technology: Research, Development and Maintenance (Railways 2014)*. Civil-Comp Press.

Verma, A., & Pattanaik, K. K. (2014). Mobile agent based train control system for mitigating meet conflict at turnout. *Procedia Computer Science, Elsevier*, *32*, 317–324. doi:10.1016/j.procs.2014.05.430

Verma, A., & Pattanaik, K. K. (2015a). Multi-agent CBTC system for Indian railways: The structural design. *Journal of Software (JSW)*, *10*(3), 250–259.

Verma, A., & Pattanaik, K. K. (2015b). Multi-agent CBTC system for Indian railways: The behavior analysis. *Journal of Modern Transportation*, *23*(4), 272–286. doi:10.100740534-015-0083-1

Verma, A., & Pattanaik, K. K. (2016). Failure Detector of *Perfect P* Classfor Synchronous HierarchicalDistributed Systems. *International Journal of Distributed Systems and Technologies*, *7*(2), 57–74. doi:10.4018/IJDST.2016040104

Vinodhini, A. N., & Ayyasamy, S. (2017). Prevention of Personal Data in Cloud Computing Using Bio-Metric. *IEEE International Conference on Innovations in Green Energy and Healthcare Technologies*, 1-6. 10.1109/IGEHT.2017.8094085

Vo, H. T., Wang, S., Agrawal, D., Chen, G., & Ooi, B. C. (2012, June). Logbase: A scalable log-structured database system in the cloud. *Proc. VLDB Endow.*, *5*(10), 1004–1015. 10.14778/2336664.2336673

Volkmann, D. (2016). *The Rise of Digital Twins*. Retrieved from https://www.ge.com/digital/blog/rise-digital-twins

Wang, H., & Varman, P. J. (2014). Balancing fairness and efficiency in tiered storage systems with bottleneck-aware allocation. In *Fast'14: The 12th USENIX conference on file and storage technologies* (Vol. 14, pp. 229–242). USENIX.

Wang, W., & Liu, F. (2012). *The Research of Cloud Manufacturing Resource Discovery Mechanism.* The 7th International Conference on Computer Science & Education, Melbourne, Australia.

Wang, Y., Shu, J., Zhang, G., Xue, W., & Zheng, W. (2010, July). Sopa: Selecting the optimal caching policy adaptively. *Trans. Storage, 6*(2), 7:1–7:18.

Wang, A.-I. A., Kuenning, G., Reiher, P., & Popek, G. (2006, August). The conquest file system: Better performance through a disk/persistent-ram hybrid design. *Trans. Storage*, *2*(3), 309–348. doi:10.1145/1168910.1168914

Wang, C. Y., & Spooner, D. L. (1987, March). *Access Control in a Heterogeneous Distributed Database Management System.* SRDS.

Wang, Q., Chen, D., Zhang, N., Ding, Z., & Qin, Z. (2017). PCP: A Privacy-Preserving Content-Based Publish-Subscribe Scheme with Differential Privacy in Fog computing. *IEEE Access: Practical Innovations, Open Solutions*, *5*, 17962–17986. doi:10.1109/ACCESS.2017.2748956

Wang, T., Li, Y., Chen, Y., Tian, H., Cai, Y., Jia, W., & Wang, B. (2017). Fog-Based Evaluation Approach for Trustworthy Communication in Sensor-Cloud System. *IEEE Communications Letters*, *14*, 1–4.

Warehouse. (2016). *Wearable Technology in the Warehouse*. Retrieved from https://www.supplychain247.com/ article/wearable_technology_in_the_warehouse

White, E. (n.d.). Retrieved from http://hp.sys-con.com/node/3250225/CloudandInternetofThings

White, T. (2009). *Hadoop: The definitive guide*. O'Reilly Media, Inc.

Widder, J., & Schmid, U. (2009). The Theta-Model: Achieving synchrony without clocks. *Distributed Computing*, *22*(1), 29–47. doi:10.100700446-009-0080-x

WIP. (2019). *World Intellectual Property Indicators, Economics and Statistics Series by WIPO, Info-graphics, Comparison 2015-16*. WIP.

Wu, Chen, Choo, & He. (2018). Efficient and secure searchable encryption protocol for cloud-based Internet of Things. *Journal of Parallel and Distributed Computing, 111*, 152-161. .2017.08.007 doi:10.1016/j.jpdc

Wu, G., He, X., & Eckart, B. (2012, February). An adaptive write buffer management scheme for flash-based ssds. *Trans. Storage, 8*(1), 1:1–1:24.

Wu, Y., Peng, G., Chen, L., & Zhang, H. (2016). Service Architecture and evaluation model of distributed 3D printing based on Cloud manufacturing. *IEEE International Conference on Systems, Man, and Cybernetics*, 2762-2767.

Wu, T. Y., Lee, W. T., Guizani, N., & Wang, T. M. (2014). Incentive mechanism for p2p file sharing based on social network and game theory. *Journal of Network and Computer Applications*, *41*, 47–55. doi:10.1016/j.jnca.2013.10.006

Xiang, F., Xu, L., & Jiang, G. Z. (2016). Green Manufacturing Service Composition in Cloud Manufacturing System: An Introduction. *Proceedings of IEEE 11th Conference on Industrial Electronics and Applications*, 1988-1993. 10.1109/ICIEA.2016.7603915

Xia, Y., Hong, H., Lin, G., & Sun, Z. (2017). A Secure and Efficient Cloud Resource Allocation Scheme with Trust Evaluation Mechanism Based on Combinatorial Double Auction. KSII. *Transactions on Internet and Information Systems (Seoul)*, *9*, 4197–4219.

Xinjuan, J., & Quan, L. (2016). Research on the On-Demand Service Mode in Cloud Manufacturing. IEEE.

Xu, Y., Arteaga, D., Zhao, M., Liu, Y., Figueiredo, R. J. O., & Seelam, S. (2012). vPFS: Bandwidth virtualization of parallel storage systems. In *Msst' 12: Proc. 38th international conference on massive storage systems and technology* (p. 1-12). Academic Press.

Xu, T., Chen, Y., & Fu, X. (2010). Twittering by Cuckoo: decentralized and socio-aware online microblogging services. In *Proceedings of the ACM SIGCOMM 2010 Conference* (pp. 473—475). ACM. 10.1145/1851182.1851270

Xu, W., Yu, J., Zhou, Z., Xie, Y., Pham, D. T., & Ji, C. (2015). Dynamic Modeling of Manufacturing Equipment Capability Using Condition Information in Cloud Manufacturing. *Journal of Manufacturing Science and Engineering*, *137*(4), 1–14. doi:10.1115/1.4030079

Yang, J., Wang, C., Zhao, Q., Jiang, B., Zhihan, L., & Sangaiah, A. K. (2018). Marine surveying and mapping system based on Cloud Computing and Internet of Things. *Future Generation Computer Systems, 85*, 39-50. .future.2018.02.032 doi:10.1016/j

Yang, K., Zhang, K., Jia, X., Hasan, M. A., & Shen, X. S. (2017). Privacy-preserving attribute-keyword based data publish-subscribe service on cloud platforms. *Information Sciences*, *387*, 116–131. doi:10.1016/j.ins.2016.09.020

Yu, H., Zhang, S. Z., Yang, N. H., Ding, H., & Wang, X. K. (2003, November). Intelligent agent-based distributed heterogeneous database system. In *Machine Learning and Cybernetics, 2003 International Conference on* (Vol. 3, pp. 1932-1935). IEEE.

Zaslavsky, A., Perera, C., & Georgakopoulos, D. (2013). *Sensing as a Service and Big Data.* Retrieved from http://arxiv.org/abs/1301.0159

Zhang, G., Chiu, L., Dickey, C., Liu, L., Muench, P., & Seshadri, S. (2010). Automated lookahead data migration in ssd-enabled multi-tiered storage systems. In *Msst'10: 26th IEEE symposium on mass storage systems and technologies* (pp. 1–6). IEEE. 10.1109/MSST.2010.5496999

Zhang, Y., & Orlowska, M. E. (1993, October). A hybrid concurrency control approach in heterogeneous distributed database systems. In *TENCON'93. Proceedings. Computer, Communication, Control and Power Engineering. 1993 IEEE Region 10 Conference on* (Vol. 1, pp. 323-326). IEEE.

Zhang, X., Wang, L., Li, Y., & Sun, M. (2017). A centralized optimization solution for application layer multicast tree. *IEEE eTransactions on Network and Service Management*, *14*(3), 771–785. doi:10.1109/TNSM.2017.2731521

Zhang, Z., Chen, S., Ling, Y., & Chow, R. (2005). Resilient capacity-aware multicasting based on overlay networks. In *Proceedings of the 25th IEEE International Conference on Distributed Computing Systems* (pp. 565–574). IEEE.

Zheng, H., Feng, Y., & Tan, J. (2017). A Hybrid Energy-aware Resource Allocation Approach in Cloud Manufacturing Environment. IEEE.

Zheng, W. B., Zhou, M. C., Xia, Y. N., Wu, L., Luo, X., Pang, S. C., & Zhu, Q. S. (2017). Percentile performance estimation of unreliable IaaS clouds and their cost-optimal capacity decision. *IEEE Access: Practical Innovations, Open Solutions*, *5*, 2808–2818. doi:10.1109/ACCESS.2017.2666793

Zink, M., Suh, K., Gu, Y., & Kurose, J. (2009). *Watch global, cache local: Youtube network traffic at a campus network - measurements and implications. In Proceedings of SPIE 6818*. San Jose, CA: International Society for Optical Engineering.

Related References

To continue our tradition of advancing academic research, we have compiled a list of recommended IGI Global readings. These references will provide additional information and guidance to further enrich your knowledge and assist you with your own research and future publications.

Abed, S., Khir, T., & Ben Brahim, A. (2016). Thermodynamic and Energy Study of a Regenerator in Gas Turbine Cycle and Optimization of Performances. *International Journal of Energy Optimization and Engineering*, *5*(2), 25–44. doi:10.4018/IJEOE.2016040102

Abu Bakar, W. A., Abdullah, W. N., Ali, R., & Mokhtar, W. N. (2016). Polymolybdate Supported Nano Catalyst for Desulfurization of Diesel. In T. Saleh (Ed.), *Applying Nanotechnology to the Desulfurization Process in Petroleum Engineering* (pp. 263–280). Hershey, PA: IGI Global. doi:10.4018/978-1-4666-9545-0.ch009

Addo-Tenkorang, R., Helo, P., & Kantola, J. (2016). Engineer-To-Order Product Development: A Communication Network Analysis for Supply-Chain's Sustainable Competitive Advantage. In R. Addo-Tenkorang, J. Kantola, P. Helo, & A. Shamsuzzoha (Eds.), *Supply Chain Strategies and the Engineer-to-Order Approach* (pp. 43–59). Hershey, PA: IGI Global. doi:10.4018/978-1-5225-0021-6.ch003

Adebiyi, I. D., Popoola, P. A., & Pityana, S. (2016). Mitigation of Wear Damage by Laser Surface Alloying Technique. In E. Akinlabi, R. Mahamood, & S. Akinlabi (Eds.), *Advanced Manufacturing Techniques Using Laser Material Processing* (pp. 172–196). Hershey, PA: IGI Global. doi:10.4018/978-1-5225-0329-3.ch007

Ahmad, W. (2016). Sulfur in Petroleum: Petroleum Desulfurization Techniques. In T. Saleh (Ed.), *Applying Nanotechnology to the Desulfurization Process in Petroleum Engineering* (pp. 1–52). Hershey, PA: IGI Global. doi:10.4018/978-1-4666-9545-0.ch001

Ahmed, I., Ahmad, N., Mehmood, I., Haq, I. U., Hassan, M., & Khan, M. U. (2016). Applications of Nanotechnology in Transportation Engineering. In A. Khitab & W. Anwar (Eds.), *Advanced Research on Nanotechnology for Civil Engineering Applications* (pp. 180–207). Hershey, PA: IGI Global. doi:10.4018/978-1-5225-0344-6.ch006

Aikhuele, D. (2018). A Study of Product Development Engineering and Design Reliability Concerns. *International Journal of Applied Industrial Engineering*, *5*(1), 79–89. doi:10.4018/IJAIE.2018010105

Al-Najar, B. T., & Bououdina, M. (2016). Bioinspired Nanoparticles for Efficient Drug Delivery System. In M. Bououdina (Ed.), *Emerging Research on Bioinspired Materials Engineering* (pp. 69–103). Hershey, PA: IGI Global. doi:10.4018/978-1-4666-9811-6.ch003

Al-Shebeeb, O. A., Rangaswamy, S., Gopalakrishan, B., & Devaru, D. G. (2017). Evaluation and Indexing of Process Plans Based on Electrical Demand and Energy Consumption. *International Journal of Manufacturing, Materials, and Mechanical Engineering*, *7*(3), 1–19. doi:10.4018/IJMMME.2017070101

Alexakis, H., & Makris, N. (2016). Validation of the Discrete Element Method for the Limit Stability Analysis of Masonry Arches. In V. Sarhosis, K. Bagi, J. Lemos, & G. Milani (Eds.), *Computational Modeling of Masonry Structures Using the Discrete Element Method* (pp. 292–325). Hershey, PA: IGI Global. doi:10.4018/978-1-5225-0231-9.ch012

AlMegren, H. A., Gonzalez-Cortes, S., Huang, Y., Chen, H., Qian, Y., Alkinany, M., ... Xiao, T. (2016). Preparation of Deep Hydrodesulfurzation Catalysts for Diesel Fuel using Organic Matrix Decomposition Method. In H. Al-Megren & T. Xiao (Eds.), *Petrochemical Catalyst Materials, Processes, and Emerging Technologies* (pp. 216–253). Hershey, PA: IGI Global. doi:10.4018/978-1-4666-9975-5.ch009

Alshammari, A., Kalevaru, V. N., Bagabas, A., & Martin, A. (2016). Production of Ethylene and its Commercial Importance in the Global Market. In H. Al-Megren & T. Xiao (Eds.), *Petrochemical Catalyst Materials, Processes, and Emerging Technologies* (pp. 82–115). Hershey, PA: IGI Global. doi:10.4018/978-1-4666-9975-5.ch004

Amel, M. (2016). Synthesis, Characterizations, and Biological Effects Study of Some Quinoline Family. In M. Bououdina (Ed.), *Emerging Research on Bioinspired Materials Engineering* (pp. 160–196). Hershey, PA: IGI Global. doi:10.4018/978-1-4666-9811-6.ch006

Amna, T., Haasan, M. S., Khil, M., & Hwang, I. (2016). Impact of Electrospun Biomimetic Extracellular Environment on Proliferation and Intercellular Communication of Muscle Precursor Cells: An Overview – Intercellular Communication of Muscle Precursor Cells with Extracellular Environment. In M. Bououdina (Ed.), *Emerging Research on Bioinspired Materials Engineering* (pp. 247–265). Hershey, PA: IGI Global. doi:10.4018/978-1-4666-9811-6.ch009

Amuda, M. O., Lawal, T. F., & Akinlabi, E. T. (2017). Research Progress on Rheological Behavior of AA7075 Aluminum Alloy During Hot Deformation. *International Journal of Materials Forming and Machining Processes*, *4*(1), 53–96. doi:10.4018/IJMFMP.2017010104

An, M., & Qin, Y. (2016). Challenges of Railway Safety Risk Assessment and Maintenance Decision Making. In B. Rai (Ed.), *Handbook of Research on Emerging Innovations in Rail Transportation Engineering* (pp. 173–211). Hershey, PA: IGI Global. doi:10.4018/978-1-5225-0084-1.ch009

Anil, M., Ayyildiz-Tamis, D., Tasdemir, S., Sendemir-Urkmez, A., & Gulce-Iz, S. (2016). Bioinspired Materials and Biocompatibility. In M. Bououdina (Ed.), *Emerging Research on Bioinspired Materials Engineering* (pp. 294–322). Hershey, PA: IGI Global. doi:10.4018/978-1-4666-9811-6.ch011

Armutlu, H. (2018). Intelligent Biomedical Engineering Operations by Cloud Computing Technologies. In U. Kose, G. Guraksin, & O. Deperlioglu (Eds.), *Nature-Inspired Intelligent Techniques for Solving Biomedical Engineering Problems* (pp. 297–317). Hershey, PA: IGI Global. doi:10.4018/978-1-5225-4769-3.ch015

Arokiyaraj, S., Saravanan, M., Bharanidharan, R., Islam, V. I., Bououdina, M., & Vincent, S. (2016). Green Synthesis of Metallic Nanoparticles Using Plant Compounds and Their Applications: Metallic Nanoparticles Synthesis Using Plants. In M. Bououdina (Ed.), *Emerging Research on Bioinspired Materials Engineering* (pp. 1–34). Hershey, PA: IGI Global. doi:10.4018/978-1-4666-9811-6.ch001

Atik, M., Sadek, M., & Shahrour, I. (2017). Single-Run Adaptive Pushover Procedure for Shear Wall Structures. In V. Plevris, G. Kremmyda, & Y. Fahjan (Eds.), *Performance-Based Seismic Design of Concrete Structures and Infrastructures* (pp. 59–83). Hershey, PA: IGI Global. doi:10.4018/978-1-5225-2089-4.ch003

Aydin, A., Akyol, E., Gungor, M., Kaya, A., & Tasdelen, S. (2018). Geophysical Surveys in Engineering Geology Investigations With Field Examples. In N. Ceryan (Ed.), *Handbook of Research on Trends and Digital Advances in Engineering Geology* (pp. 257–280). Hershey, PA: IGI Global. doi:10.4018/978-1-5225-2709-1.ch007

Azevedo, N. M., Lemos, J. V., & Rocha de Almeida, J. (2016). Discrete Element Particle Modelling of Stone Masonry. In V. Sarhosis, K. Bagi, J. Lemos, & G. Milani (Eds.), *Computational Modeling of Masonry Structures Using the Discrete Element Method* (pp. 146–170). Hershey, PA: IGI Global. doi:10.4018/978-1-5225-0231-9.ch007

Bamufleh, H. S., Noureldin, M. M., & El-Halwagi, M. M. (2016). Sustainable Process Integration in the Petrochemical Industries. In H. Al-Megren & T. Xiao (Eds.), *Petrochemical Catalyst Materials, Processes, and Emerging Technologies* (pp. 150–163). Hershey, PA: IGI Global. doi:10.4018/978-1-4666-9975-5.ch006

Banerjee, S., Gautam, R. K., Gautam, P. K., Jaiswal, A., & Chattopadhyaya, M. C. (2016). Recent Trends and Advancement in Nanotechnology for Water and Wastewater Treatment: Nanotechnological Approach for Water Purification. In A. Khitab & W. Anwar (Eds.), *Advanced Research on Nanotechnology for Civil Engineering Applications* (pp. 208–252). Hershey, PA: IGI Global. doi:10.4018/978-1-5225-0344-6.ch007

Bas, T. G. (2017). Nutraceutical Industry with the Collaboration of Biotechnology and Nutrigenomics Engineering: The Significance of Intellectual Property in the Entrepreneurship and Scientific Research Ecosystems. In T. Bas & J. Zhao (Eds.), *Comparative Approaches to Biotechnology Development and Use in Developed and Emerging Nations* (pp. 1–17). Hershey, PA: IGI Global. doi:10.4018/978-1-5225-1040-6.ch001

Beale, R., & André, J. (2017). *Design Solutions and Innovations in Temporary Structures*. Hershey, PA: IGI Global. doi:10.4018/978-1-5225-2199-0

Behnam, B. (2017). Simulating Post-Earthquake Fire Loading in Conventional RC Structures. In P. Samui, S. Chakraborty, & D. Kim (Eds.), *Modeling and Simulation Techniques in Structural Engineering* (pp. 425–444). Hershey, PA: IGI Global. doi:10.4018/978-1-5225-0588-4.ch015

Ben Hamida, I., Salah, S. B., Msahli, F., & Mimouni, M. F. (2018). Distribution Network Reconfiguration Using SPEA2 for Power Loss Minimization and Reliability Improvement. *International Journal of Energy Optimization and Engineering*, *7*(1), 50–65. doi:10.4018/IJEOE.2018010103

Benjamin, S. R., de Lima, F., & Rathoure, A. K. (2016). Genetically Engineered Microorganisms for Bioremediation Processes: GEMs for Bioremediaton. In A. Rathoure & V. Dhatwalia (Eds.), *Toxicity and Waste Management Using Bioremediation* (pp. 113–140). Hershey, PA: IGI Global. doi:10.4018/978-1-4666-9734-8.ch006

Bhaskar, S. V., & Kudal, H. N. (2017). Effect of TiCN and AlCrN Coating on Tribological Behaviour of Plasma-nitrided AISI 4140 Steel. *International Journal of Surface Engineering and Interdisciplinary Materials Science, 5*(2), 1–17. doi:10.4018/IJSEIMS.2017070101

Bhowmik, S., Sahoo, P., Acharyya, S. K., Dhar, S., & Chattopadhyay, J. (2016). Effect of Microstructure Degradation on Fracture Toughness of 20MnMoNi55 Steel in DBT Region. *International Journal of Manufacturing, Materials, and Mechanical Engineering, 6*(3), 11–27. doi:10.4018/IJMMME.2016070102

Bhutto, A. W., Abro, R., Abbas, T., Yu, G., & Chen, X. (2016). Desulphurization of Fuel Oils Using Ionic Liquids. In H. Al-Megren & T. Xiao (Eds.), *Petrochemical Catalyst Materials, Processes, and Emerging Technologies* (pp. 254–284). Hershey, PA: IGI Global. doi:10.4018/978-1-4666-9975-5.ch010

Bhuyan, D. (2018). Designing of a Twin Tube Shock Absorber: A Study in Reverse Engineering. In K. Kumar & J. Davim (Eds.), *Design and Optimization of Mechanical Engineering Products* (pp. 83–104). Hershey, PA: IGI Global. doi:10.4018/978-1-5225-3401-3.ch005

Bouloudenine, M., & Bououdina, M. (2016). Toxic Effects of Engineered Nanoparticles on Living Cells. In M. Bououdina (Ed.), *Emerging Research on Bioinspired Materials Engineering* (pp. 35–68). Hershey, PA: IGI Global. doi:10.4018/978-1-4666-9811-6.ch002

Brunetti, A., Sellaro, M., Drioli, E., & Barbieri, G. (2016). Membrane Engineering and its Role in Oil Refining and Petrochemical Industry. In H. Al-Megren & T. Xiao (Eds.), *Petrochemical Catalyst Materials, Processes, and Emerging Technologies* (pp. 116–149). Hershey, PA: IGI Global. doi:10.4018/978-1-4666-9975-5.ch005

Bügler, M., & Borrmann, A. (2016). Simulation Based Construction Project Schedule Optimization: An Overview on the State-of-the-Art. In F. Miranda & C. Abreu (Eds.), *Handbook of Research on Computational Simulation and Modeling in Engineering* (pp. 482–507). Hershey, PA: IGI Global. doi:10.4018/978-1-4666-8823-0.ch016

Calderon, F. A., Giolo, E. G., Frau, C. D., Rengel, M. G., Rodriguez, H., Tornello, M., ... Gallucci, R. (2018). Seismic Microzonation and Site Effects Detection Through Microtremors Measures: A Review. In N. Ceryan (Ed.), *Handbook of Research on Trends and Digital Advances in Engineering Geology* (pp. 326–349). Hershey, PA: IGI Global. doi:10.4018/978-1-5225-2709-1.ch009

Carmona-Murillo, J., & Valenzuela-Valdés, J. F. (2016). Motivation on Problem Based Learning. In D. Fonseca & E. Redondo (Eds.), *Handbook of Research on Applied E-Learning in Engineering and Architecture Education* (pp. 179–203). Hershey, PA: IGI Global. doi:10.4018/978-1-4666-8803-2.ch009

Ceryan, N. (2016). A Review of Soft Computing Methods Application in Rock Mechanic Engineering. In P. Samui (Ed.), *Handbook of Research on Advanced Computational Techniques for Simulation-Based Engineering* (pp. 1–70). Hershey, PA: IGI Global. doi:10.4018/978-1-4666-9479-8.ch001

Ceryan, N., & Can, N. K. (2018). Prediction of The Uniaxial Compressive Strength of Rocks Materials. In N. Ceryan (Ed.), *Handbook of Research on Trends and Digital Advances in Engineering Geology* (pp. 31–96). Hershey, PA: IGI Global. doi:10.4018/978-1-5225-2709-1.ch002

Ceryan, S. (2018). Weathering Indices Used in Evaluation of the Weathering State of Rock Material. In N. Ceryan (Ed.), *Handbook of Research on Trends and Digital Advances in Engineering Geology* (pp. 132–186). Hershey, PA: IGI Global. doi:10.4018/978-1-5225-2709-1.ch004

Chandrasekaran, S., Silva, B., Patil, A., Oo, A. M., & Campbell, M. (2016). Evaluating Engineering Students' Perceptions: The Impact of Team-Based Learning Practices in Engineering Education. *International Journal of Quality Assurance in Engineering and Technology Education*, *5*(4), 42–59. doi:10.4018/IJQAETE.2016100103

Chen, H., Padilla, R. V., & Besarati, S. (2017). Supercritical Fluids and Their Applications in Power Generation. In L. Chen & Y. Iwamoto (Eds.), *Advanced Applications of Supercritical Fluids in Energy Systems* (pp. 369–402). Hershey, PA: IGI Global. doi:10.4018/978-1-5225-2047-4.ch012

Chen, L. (2017). Principles, Experiments, and Numerical Studies of Supercritical Fluid Natural Circulation System. In L. Chen & Y. Iwamoto (Eds.), *Advanced Applications of Supercritical Fluids in Energy Systems* (pp. 136–187). Hershey, PA: IGI Global. doi:10.4018/978-1-5225-2047-4.ch005

Clementi, F., Di Sciascio, G., Di Sciascio, S., & Lenci, S. (2017). Influence of the Shear-Bending Interaction on the Global Capacity of Reinforced Concrete Frames: A Brief Overview of the New Perspectives. In V. Plevris, G. Kremmyda, & Y. Fahjan (Eds.), *Performance-Based Seismic Design of Concrete Structures and Infrastructures* (pp. 84–111). Hershey, PA: IGI Global. doi:10.4018/978-1-5225-2089-4.ch004

Cortés-Polo, D., Calle-Cancho, J., Carmona-Murillo, J., & González-Sánchez, J. (2017). Future Trends in Mobile-Fixed Integration for Next Generation Networks: Classification and Analysis. *International Journal of Vehicular Telematics and Infotainment Systems*, *1*(1), 33–53. doi:10.4018/IJVTIS.2017010103

Cui, X., Zeng, S., Li, Z., Zheng, Q., Yu, X., & Han, B. (2018). Advanced Composites for Civil Engineering Infrastructures. In K. Kumar & J. Davim (Eds.), *Composites and Advanced Materials for Industrial Applications* (pp. 212–248). Hershey, PA: IGI Global. doi:10.4018/978-1-5225-5216-1.ch010

Dalgıç, S., & Kuşku, İ. (2018). Geological and Geotechnical Investigations in Tunneling. In N. Ceryan (Ed.), *Handbook of Research on Trends and Digital Advances in Engineering Geology* (pp. 482–529). Hershey, PA: IGI Global. doi:10.4018/978-1-5225-2709-1.ch014

de la Varga, D., Soto, M., Arias, C. A., van Oirschot, D., Kilian, R., Pascual, A., & Álvarez, J. A. (2017). Constructed Wetlands for Industrial Wastewater Treatment and Removal of Nutrients. In Á. Val del Río, J. Campos Gómez, & A. Mosquera Corral (Eds.), *Technologies for the Treatment and Recovery of Nutrients from Industrial Wastewater* (pp. 202–230). Hershey, PA: IGI Global. doi:10.4018/978-1-5225-1037-6.ch008

del Valle-Zermeño, R., Chimenos, J. M., & Formosa, J. (2016). Flue Gas Desulfurization: Processes and Technologies. In T. Saleh (Ed.), *Applying Nanotechnology to the Desulfurization Process in Petroleum Engineering* (pp. 337–377). Hershey, PA: IGI Global. doi:10.4018/978-1-4666-9545-0.ch011

Delgado, J. M., Henriques, A. A., & Delgado, R. M. (2016). Structural Non-Linear Models and Simulation Techniques: An Efficient Combination for Safety Evaluation of RC Structures. In F. Miranda & C. Abreu (Eds.), *Handbook of Research on Computational Simulation and Modeling in Engineering* (pp. 540–584). Hershey, PA: IGI Global. doi:10.4018/978-1-4666-8823-0.ch018

Delgado, P. S., Arêde, A., Pouca, N. V., & Costa, A. (2016). Numerical Modeling of RC Bridges for Seismic Risk Analysis. In F. Miranda & C. Abreu (Eds.), *Handbook of Research on Computational Simulation and Modeling in Engineering* (pp. 457–481). Hershey, PA: IGI Global. doi:10.4018/978-1-4666-8823-0.ch015

Deng, Y., & Liu, S. (2016). Catalysis with Room Temperature Ionic Liquids Mediated Metal Nanoparticles. In H. Al-Megren & T. Xiao (Eds.), *Petrochemical Catalyst Materials, Processes, and Emerging Technologies* (pp. 285–329). Hershey, PA: IGI Global. doi:10.4018/978-1-4666-9975-5.ch011

Deperlioglu, O. (2018). Intelligent Techniques Inspired by Nature and Used in Biomedical Engineering. In U. Kose, G. Guraksin, & O. Deperlioglu (Eds.), *Nature-Inspired Intelligent Techniques for Solving Biomedical Engineering Problems* (pp. 51–77). Hershey, PA: IGI Global. doi:10.4018/978-1-5225-4769-3.ch003

Dias, G. L., Magalhães, R. R., Ferreira, D. D., & Vitoriano, F. A. (2016). The Use of a Robotic Arm for Displacement Measurements in a Cantilever beam. *International Journal of Manufacturing, Materials, and Mechanical Engineering*, *6*(3), 45–57. doi:10.4018/IJMMME.2016070104

Dimitratos, N., Villa, A., Chan-Thaw, C. E., Hammond, C., & Prati, L. (2016). Valorisation of Glycerol to Fine Chemicals and Fuels. In H. Al-Megren & T. Xiao (Eds.), *Petrochemical Catalyst Materials, Processes, and Emerging Technologies* (pp. 352–384). Hershey, PA: IGI Global. doi:10.4018/978-1-4666-9975-5.ch013

Dixit, A. (2018). Application of Silica-Gel-Reinforced Aluminium Composite on the Piston of Internal Combustion Engine: Comparative Study of Silica-Gel-Reinforced Aluminium Composite Piston With Aluminium Alloy Piston. In K. Kumar & J. Davim (Eds.), *Composites and Advanced Materials for Industrial Applications* (pp. 63–98). Hershey, PA: IGI Global. doi:10.4018/978-1-5225-5216-1.ch004

Drei, A., Milani, G., & Sincraian, G. (2016). Application of DEM to Historic Masonries, Two Case-Studies in Portugal and Italy: Aguas Livres Aqueduct and Arch-Tympana of a Church. In V. Sarhosis, K. Bagi, J. Lemos, & G. Milani (Eds.), *Computational Modeling of Masonry Structures Using the Discrete Element Method* (pp. 326–366). Hershey, PA: IGI Global. doi:10.4018/978-1-5225-0231-9.ch013

Dutta, S., Roy, P. K., & Nandi, D. (2016). Optimal Allocation of Static Synchronous Series Compensator Controllers using Chemical Reaction Optimization for Reactive Power Dispatch. *International Journal of Energy Optimization and Engineering*, *5*(3), 43–62. doi:10.4018/IJEOE.2016070103

Dutta, S., Roy, P. K., & Nandi, D. (2016). Quasi Oppositional Teaching-Learning based Optimization for Optimal Power Flow Incorporating FACTS. *International Journal of Energy Optimization and Engineering*, *5*(2), 64–84. doi:10.4018/IJEOE.2016040104

Eloy, S., Dias, M. S., Lopes, P. F., & Vilar, E. (2016). Digital Technologies in Architecture and Engineering: Exploring an Engaged Interaction within Curricula. In D. Fonseca & E. Redondo (Eds.), *Handbook of Research on Applied E-Learning in Engineering and Architecture Education* (pp. 368–402). Hershey, PA: IGI Global. doi:10.4018/978-1-4666-8803-2.ch017

Elsayed, A. M., Dakkama, H. J., Mahmoud, S., Al-Dadah, R., & Kaialy, W. (2017). Sustainable Cooling Research Using Activated Carbon Adsorbents and Their Environmental Impact. In T. Kobayashi (Ed.), *Applied Environmental Materials Science for Sustainability* (pp. 186–221). Hershey, PA: IGI Global. doi:10.4018/978-1-5225-1971-3.ch009

Ercanoglu, M., & Sonmez, H. (2018). General Trends and New Perspectives on Landslide Mapping and Assessment Methods. In N. Ceryan (Ed.), *Handbook of Research on Trends and Digital Advances in Engineering Geology* (pp. 350–379). Hershey, PA: IGI Global. doi:10.4018/978-1-5225-2709-1.ch010

Erinosho, M. F., Akinlabi, E. T., & Pityana, S. (2016). Enhancement of Surface Integrity of Titanium Alloy with Copper by Means of Laser Metal Deposition Process. In E. Akinlabi, R. Mahamood, & S. Akinlabi (Eds.), *Advanced Manufacturing Techniques Using Laser Material Processing* (pp. 60–91). Hershey, PA: IGI Global. doi:10.4018/978-1-5225-0329-3.ch004

Farag, H., & Kishida, M. (2016). Kinetic Models for Complex Parallel–Consecutive Reactions Assessment of Reaction Network and Product Selectivity. In H. Al-Megren & T. Xiao (Eds.), *Petrochemical Catalyst Materials, Processes, and Emerging Technologies* (pp. 330–351). Hershey, PA: IGI Global. doi:10.4018/978-1-4666-9975-5.ch012

Faroz, S. A., Pujari, N. N., Rastogi, R., & Ghosh, S. (2017). Risk Analysis of Structural Engineering Systems Using Bayesian Inference. In P. Samui, S. Chakraborty, & D. Kim (Eds.), *Modeling and Simulation Techniques in Structural Engineering* (pp. 390–424). Hershey, PA: IGI Global. doi:10.4018/978-1-5225-0588-4.ch014

Fernando, P. R., Hamigah, T., Disne, S., Wickramasingha, G. G., & Sutharshan, A. (2018). The Evaluation of Engineering Properties of Low Cost Concrete Blocks by Partial Doping of Sand with Sawdust: Low Cost Sawdust Concrete Block. *International Journal of Strategic Engineering*, *1*(2), 26–42. doi:10.4018/IJoSE.2018070103

Fragiadakis, M., Stefanou, I., & Psycharis, I. N. (2016). Vulnerability Assessment of Damaged Classical Multidrum Columns. In V. Sarhosis, K. Bagi, J. Lemos, & G. Milani (Eds.), *Computational Modeling of Masonry Structures Using the Discrete Element Method* (pp. 235–253). Hershey, PA: IGI Global. doi:10.4018/978-1-5225-0231-9.ch010

Gaines, T. W., Williams, K. R., & Wagener, K. B. (2016). ADMET: Functionalized Polyolefins. In H. Al-Megren & T. Xiao (Eds.), *Petrochemical Catalyst Materials, Processes, and Emerging Technologies* (pp. 1–21). Hershey, PA: IGI Global. doi:10.4018/978-1-4666-9975-5.ch001

Garg, H. (2016). Bi-Criteria Optimization for Finding the Optimal Replacement Interval for Maintaining the Performance of the Process Industries. In P. Vasant, G. Weber, & V. Dieu (Eds.), *Handbook of Research on Modern Optimization Algorithms and Applications in Engineering and Economics* (pp. 643–675). Hershey, PA: IGI Global. doi:10.4018/978-1-4666-9644-0.ch025

Gaspar, P. D., Dinho da Silva, P., Gonçalves, J. P., & Carneiro, R. (2016). Computational Modelling and Simulation to Assist the Improvement of Thermal Performance and Energy Efficiency in Industrial Engineering Systems: Application to Cold Stores. In F. Miranda & C. Abreu (Eds.), *Handbook of Research on Computational Simulation and Modeling in Engineering* (pp. 1–68). Hershey, PA: IGI Global. doi:10.4018/978-1-4666-8823-0.ch001

Ge, H., Tang, M., & Wen, X. (2016). Ni/ZnO Nano Sorbent for Reactive Adsorption Desulfurization of Refinery Oil Streams. In T. Saleh (Ed.), *Applying Nanotechnology to the Desulfurization Process in Petroleum Engineering* (pp. 216–239). Hershey, PA: IGI Global. doi:10.4018/978-1-4666-9545-0.ch007

Ghosh, S., Mitra, S., Ghosh, S., & Chakraborty, S. (2017). Seismic Reliability Analysis in the Framework of Metamodelling Based Monte Carlo Simulation. In P. Samui, S. Chakraborty, & D. Kim (Eds.), *Modeling and Simulation Techniques in Structural Engineering* (pp. 192–208). Hershey, PA: IGI Global. doi:10.4018/978-1-5225-0588-4.ch006

Gil, M., & Otero, B. (2017). Learning Engineering Skills through Creativity and Collaboration: A Game-Based Proposal. In R. Alexandre Peixoto de Queirós & M. Pinto (Eds.), *Gamification-Based E-Learning Strategies for Computer Programming Education* (pp. 14–29). Hershey, PA: IGI Global. doi:10.4018/978-1-5225-1034-5.ch002

Gill, J., Ayre, M., & Mills, J. (2017). Revisioning the Engineering Profession: How to Make It Happen! In M. Gray & K. Thomas (Eds.), *Strategies for Increasing Diversity in Engineering Majors and Careers* (pp. 156–175). Hershey, PA: IGI Global. doi:10.4018/978-1-5225-2212-6.ch008

Gopal, S., & Al-Hazmi, M. H. (2016). Advances in Catalytic Technologies for Selective Oxidation of Lower Alkanes. In H. Al-Megren & T. Xiao (Eds.), *Petrochemical Catalyst Materials, Processes, and Emerging Technologies* (pp. 22–52). Hershey, PA: IGI Global. doi:10.4018/978-1-4666-9975-5.ch002

Goyal, N., Ram, M., Bhardwaj, A., & Kumar, A. (2016). Thermal Power Plant Modelling with Fault Coverage Stochastically. *International Journal of Manufacturing, Materials, and Mechanical Engineering*, *6*(3), 28–44. doi:10.4018/IJMMME.2016070103

Goyal, N., Ram, M., & Kumar, P. (2017). Welding Process under Fault Coverage Approach for Reliability and MTTF. In M. Ram & J. Davim (Eds.), *Mathematical Concepts and Applications in Mechanical Engineering and Mechatronics* (pp. 222–245). Hershey, PA: IGI Global. doi:10.4018/978-1-5225-1639-2.ch011

Gray, M., & Lundy, C. (2017). Engineering Study Abroad: High Impact Strategy for Increasing Access. In M. Gray & K. Thomas (Eds.), *Strategies for Increasing Diversity in Engineering Majors and Careers* (pp. 42–59). Hershey, PA: IGI Global. doi:10.4018/978-1-5225-2212-6.ch003

Guha, D., Roy, P. K., & Banerjee, S. (2016). Application of Modified Biogeography Based Optimization in AGC of an Interconnected Multi-Unit Multi-Source AC-DC Linked Power System. *International Journal of Energy Optimization and Engineering*, *5*(3), 1–18. doi:10.4018/IJEOE.2016070101

Guha, D., Roy, P. K., & Banerjee, S. (2016). Grey Wolf Optimization to Solve Load Frequency Control of an Interconnected Power System: GWO Used to Solve LFC Problem. *International Journal of Energy Optimization and Engineering*, *5*(4), 62–83. doi:10.4018/IJEOE.2016100104

Gupta, A. K., Dey, A., & Mukhopadhyay, A. K. (2016). Micromechanical and Finite Element Modeling for Composites. In S. Datta & J. Davim (Eds.), *Computational Approaches to Materials Design: Theoretical and Practical Aspects* (pp. 101–162). Hershey, PA: IGI Global. doi:10.4018/978-1-5225-0290-6.ch005

Guraksin, G. E. (2018). Internet of Things and Nature-Inspired Intelligent Techniques for the Future of Biomedical Engineering. In U. Kose, G. Guraksin, & O. Deperlioglu (Eds.), *Nature-Inspired Intelligent Techniques for Solving Biomedical Engineering Problems* (pp. 263–282). Hershey, PA: IGI Global. doi:10.4018/978-1-5225-4769-3.ch013

Hansman, C. A. (2016). Developing Mentoring Programs in Engineering and Technology Education. *International Journal of Quality Assurance in Engineering and Technology Education*, *5*(2), 1–15. doi:10.4018/IJQAETE.2016040101

Hasan, U., Chegenizadeh, A., & Nikraz, H. (2016). Nanotechnology Future and Present in Construction Industry: Applications in Geotechnical Engineering. In A. Khitab & W. Anwar (Eds.), *Advanced Research on Nanotechnology for Civil Engineering Applications* (pp. 141–179). Hershey, PA: IGI Global. doi:10.4018/978-1-5225-0344-6.ch005

Hejazi, T., & Akbari, L. (2017). A Multiresponse Optimization Model for Statistical Design of Processes with Discrete Variables. In M. Ram & J. Davim (Eds.), *Mathematical Concepts and Applications in Mechanical Engineering and Mechatronics* (pp. 17–37). Hershey, PA: IGI Global. doi:10.4018/978-1-5225-1639-2.ch002

Hejazi, T., & Hejazi, A. (2017). Monte Carlo Simulation for Reliability-Based Design of Automotive Complex Subsystems. In M. Ram & J. Davim (Eds.), *Mathematical Concepts and Applications in Mechanical Engineering and Mechatronics* (pp. 177–200). Hershey, PA: IGI Global. doi:10.4018/978-1-5225-1639-2.ch009

Hejazi, T., & Poursabbagh, H. (2017). Reliability Analysis of Engineering Systems: An Accelerated Life Testing for Boiler Tubes. In M. Ram & J. Davim (Eds.), *Mathematical Concepts and Applications in Mechanical Engineering and Mechatronics* (pp. 154–176). Hershey, PA: IGI Global. doi:10.4018/978-1-5225-1639-2.ch008

Henao, J., & Sotelo, O. (2018). Surface Engineering at High Temperature: Thermal Cycling and Corrosion Resistance. In A. Pakseresht (Ed.), *Production, Properties, and Applications of High Temperature Coatings* (pp. 131–159). Hershey, PA: IGI Global. doi:10.4018/978-1-5225-4194-3.ch006

Huirache-Acuña, R., Alonso-Nuñez, G., Rivera-Muñoz, E. M., Gutierrez, O., & Pawelec, B. (2016). Trimetallic Sulfide Catalysts for Hydrodesulfurization. In T. Saleh (Ed.), *Applying Nanotechnology to the Desulfurization Process in Petroleum Engineering* (pp. 240–262). Hershey, PA: IGI Global. doi:10.4018/978-1-4666-9545-0.ch008

Ilori, O. O., Adetan, D. A., & Umoru, L. E. (2017). Effect of Cutting Parameters on the Surface Residual Stress of Face-Milled Pearlitic Ductile Iron. *International Journal of Materials Forming and Machining Processes*, *4*(1), 38–52. doi:10.4018/IJMFMP.2017010103

Imam, M. H., Tasadduq, I. A., Ahmad, A., Aldosari, F., & Khan, H. (2017). Automated Generation of Course Improvement Plans Using Expert System. *International Journal of Quality Assurance in Engineering and Technology Education*, *6*(1), 1–12. doi:10.4018/IJQAETE.2017010101

Injeti, S. K., & Kumar, T. V. (2018). A WDO Framework for Optimal Deployment of DGs and DSCs in a Radial Distribution System Under Daily Load Pattern to Improve Techno-Economic Benefits. *International Journal of Energy Optimization and Engineering*, *7*(2), 1–38. doi:10.4018/IJEOE.2018040101

Ishii, N., Anami, K., & Knisely, C. W. (2018). *Dynamic Stability of Hydraulic Gates and Engineering for Flood Prevention*. Hershey, PA: IGI Global. doi:10.4018/978-1-5225-3079-4

J., J., Chowdhury, S., Goyal, P., Samui, P., & Dalkiliç, Y. (2016). Determination of Bearing Capacity of Shallow Foundation Using Soft Computing. In P. Saxena, D. Singh, & M. Pant (Eds.), *Problem Solving and Uncertainty Modeling through Optimization and Soft Computing Applications* (pp. 292-328). Hershey, PA: IGI Global. doi:10.4018/978-1-4666-9885-7.ch014

Jagan, J., Gundlapalli, P., & Samui, P. (2016). Utilization of Classification Techniques for the Determination of Liquefaction Susceptibility of Soils. In S. Bhattacharyya, P. Banerjee, D. Majumdar, & P. Dutta (Eds.), *Handbook of Research on Advanced Hybrid Intelligent Techniques and Applications* (pp. 124–160). Hershey, PA: IGI Global. doi:10.4018/978-1-4666-9474-3.ch005

Jayapalan, S. (2018). A Review of Chemical Treatments on Natural Fibers-Based Hybrid Composites for Engineering Applications. In K. Kumar & J. Davim (Eds.), *Composites and Advanced Materials for Industrial Applications* (pp. 16–37). Hershey, PA: IGI Global. doi:10.4018/978-1-5225-5216-1.ch002

Jeet, K., & Dhir, R. (2016). Software Module Clustering Using Bio-Inspired Algorithms. In P. Vasant, G. Weber, & V. Dieu (Eds.), *Handbook of Research on Modern Optimization Algorithms and Applications in Engineering and Economics* (pp. 445–470). Hershey, PA: IGI Global. doi:10.4018/978-1-4666-9644-0.ch017

Joshi, S. D., & Talange, D. B. (2016). Fault Tolerant Control for a Fractional Order AUV System. *International Journal of Energy Optimization and Engineering*, *5*(2), 1–24. doi:10.4018/IJEOE.2016040101

Julião, D., Ribeiro, S., de Castro, B., Cunha-Silva, L., & Balula, S. S. (2016). Polyoxometalates-Based Nanocatalysts for Production of Sulfur-Free Diesel. In T. Saleh (Ed.), *Applying Nanotechnology to the Desulfurization Process in Petroleum Engineering* (pp. 426–458). Hershey, PA: IGI Global. doi:10.4018/978-1-4666-9545-0.ch014

Kamthan, P. (2016). On the Nature of Collaborations in Agile Software Engineering Course Projects. *International Journal of Quality Assurance in Engineering and Technology Education*, *5*(2), 42–59. doi:10.4018/IJQAETE.2016040104

Karaman, O., Celik, C., & Urkmez, A. S. (2016). Self-Assembled Biomimetic Scaffolds for Bone Tissue Engineering. In M. Bououdina (Ed.), *Emerging Research on Bioinspired Materials Engineering* (pp. 104–132). Hershey, PA: IGI Global. doi:10.4018/978-1-4666-9811-6.ch004

Karkalos, N. E., Markopoulos, A. P., & Dossis, M. F. (2017). Optimal Model Parameters of Inverse Kinematics Solution of a 3R Robotic Manipulator Using ANN Models. *International Journal of Manufacturing, Materials, and Mechanical Engineering*, *7*(3), 20–40. doi:10.4018/IJMMME.2017070102

Kesimal, A., Karaman, K., Cihangir, F., & Ercikdi, B. (2018). Excavatability Assessment of Rock Masses for Geotechnical Studies. In N. Ceryan (Ed.), *Handbook of Research on Trends and Digital Advances in Engineering Geology* (pp. 231–256). Hershey, PA: IGI Global. doi:10.4018/978-1-5225-2709-1.ch006

Khanh, D. V., Vasant, P. M., Elamvazuthi, I., & Dieu, V. N. (2016). Multi-Objective Optimization of Two-Stage Thermo-Electric Cooler Using Differential Evolution: MO Optimization of TEC Using DE. In F. Miranda & C. Abreu (Eds.), *Handbook of Research on Computational Simulation and Modeling in Engineering* (pp. 139–170). Hershey, PA: IGI Global. doi:10.4018/978-1-4666-8823-0.ch004

Kim, D., Hassan, M. K., Chang, S., & Bigdeli, Y. (2016). Nonlinear Vibration Control of 3D Irregular Structures Subjected to Seismic Loads. In P. Samui (Ed.), *Handbook of Research on Advanced Computational Techniques for Simulation-Based Engineering* (pp. 103–119). Hershey, PA: IGI Global. doi:10.4018/978-1-4666-9479-8.ch003

Knoflacher, H. (2017). The Role of Engineers and Their Tools in the Transport Sector after Paradigm Change: From Assumptions and Extrapolations to Science. In H. Knoflacher & E. Ocalir-Akunal (Eds.), *Engineering Tools and Solutions for Sustainable Transportation Planning* (pp. 1–29). Hershey, PA: IGI Global. doi:10.4018/978-1-5225-2116-7.ch001

Kose, U. (2018). Towards an Intelligent Biomedical Engineering With Nature-Inspired Artificial Intelligence Techniques. In U. Kose, G. Guraksin, & O. Deperlioglu (Eds.), *Nature-Inspired Intelligent Techniques for Solving Biomedical Engineering Problems* (pp. 1–26). Hershey, PA: IGI Global. doi:10.4018/978-1-5225-4769-3.ch001

Kostić, S. (2018). A Review on Enhanced Stability Analyses of Soil Slopes Using Statistical Design. In N. Ceryan (Ed.), *Handbook of Research on Trends and Digital Advances in Engineering Geology* (pp. 446–481). Hershey, PA: IGI Global. doi:10.4018/978-1-5225-2709-1.ch013

Kumar, A., Patil, P. P., & Prajapati, Y. K. (2018). *Advanced Numerical Simulations in Mechanical Engineering*. Hershey, PA: IGI Global. doi:10.4018/978-1-5225-3722-9

Kumar, G. R., Rajyalakshmi, G., & Manupati, V. K. (2017). Surface Micro Patterning of Aluminium Reinforced Composite through Laser Peening. *International Journal of Manufacturing, Materials, and Mechanical Engineering, 7*(4), 15–27. doi:10.4018/IJMMME.2017100102

Kumari, N., & Kumar, K. (2018). Fabrication of Orthotic Calipers With Epoxy-Based Green Composite. In K. Kumar & J. Davim (Eds.), *Composites and Advanced Materials for Industrial Applications* (pp. 157–176). Hershey, PA: IGI Global. doi:10.4018/978-1-5225-5216-1.ch008

Kuppusamy, R. R. (2018). Development of Aerospace Composite Structures Through Vacuum-Enhanced Resin Transfer Moulding Technology (VERTMTy): Vacuum-Enhanced Resin Transfer Moulding. In K. Kumar & J. Davim (Eds.), *Composites and Advanced Materials for Industrial Applications* (pp. 99–111). Hershey, PA: IGI Global. doi:10.4018/978-1-5225-5216-1.ch005

Lemos, J. V. (2016). The Basis for Masonry Analysis with UDEC and 3DEC. In V. Sarhosis, K. Bagi, J. Lemos, & G. Milani (Eds.), *Computational Modeling of Masonry Structures Using the Discrete Element Method* (pp. 61–89). Hershey, PA: IGI Global. doi:10.4018/978-1-5225-0231-9.ch003

Loy, J., Howell, S., & Cooper, R. (2017). Engineering Teams: Supporting Diversity in Engineering Education. In M. Gray & K. Thomas (Eds.), *Strategies for Increasing Diversity in Engineering Majors and Careers* (pp. 106–129). Hershey, PA: IGI Global. doi:10.4018/978-1-5225-2212-6.ch006

Macher, G., Armengaud, E., Kreiner, C., Brenner, E., Schmittner, C., Ma, Z., ... Krammer, M. (2018). Integration of Security in the Development Lifecycle of Dependable Automotive CPS. In N. Druml, A. Genser, A. Krieg, M. Menghin, & A. Hoeller (Eds.), *Solutions for Cyber-Physical Systems Ubiquity* (pp. 383–423). Hershey, PA: IGI Global. doi:10.4018/978-1-5225-2845-6.ch015

Maghsoodlou, S., & Poreskandar, S. (2016). Controlling Electrospinning Jet Using Microscopic Model for Ideal Tissue Engineering Scaffolds. *International Journal of Chemoinformatics and Chemical Engineering*, *5*(2), 1–16. doi:10.4018/IJCCE.2016070101

Mahendramani, G., & Lakshmana Swamy, N. (2018). Effect of Weld Groove Area on Distortion of Butt Welded Joints in Submerged Arc Welding. *International Journal of Manufacturing, Materials, and Mechanical Engineering*, *8*(2), 33–44. doi:10.4018/IJMMME.2018040103

Maiti, S. (2016). Engineered Gellan Polysaccharides in the Design of Controlled Drug Delivery Systems. In M. Bououdina (Ed.), *Emerging Research on Bioinspired Materials Engineering* (pp. 266–293). Hershey, PA: IGI Global. doi:10.4018/978-1-4666-9811-6.ch010

Majumdar, J. D., Weisheit, A., & Manna, I. (2016). Laser Surface Processing for Tailoring of Properties by Optimization of Microstructure. In E. Akinlabi, R. Mahamood, & S. Akinlabi (Eds.), *Advanced Manufacturing Techniques Using Laser Material Processing* (pp. 121–171). Hershey, PA: IGI Global. doi:10.4018/978-1-5225-0329-3.ch006

Maldonado-Macías, A. A., García-Alcaraz, J. L., Hernández-Arellano, J. L., & Cortes-Robles, G. (2016). An Ergonomic Compatibility Perspective on the Selection of Advanced Manufacturing Technology: A Case Study for CNC Vertical Machining Centers. In G. Alor-Hernández, C. Sánchez-Ramírez, & J. García-Alcaraz (Eds.), *Handbook of Research on Managerial Strategies for Achieving Optimal Performance in Industrial Processes* (pp. 137–165). Hershey, PA: IGI Global. doi:10.4018/978-1-5225-0130-5.ch008

Mamaghani, I. H. (2016). Application of Discrete Finite Element Method for Analysis of Unreinforced Masonry Structures. In V. Sarhosis, K. Bagi, J. Lemos, & G. Milani (Eds.), *Computational Modeling of Masonry Structures Using the Discrete Element Method* (pp. 440–458). Hershey, PA: IGI Global. doi:10.4018/978-1-5225-0231-9.ch017

Mansor, M. R., Sapuan, S. M., Salim, M. A., Akop, M. Z., Musthafah, M. T., & Shaharuzaman, M. A. (2016). Concurrent Design of Green Composites. In D. Verma, S. Jain, X. Zhang, & P. Gope (Eds.), *Green Approaches to Biocomposite Materials Science and Engineering* (pp. 48–75). Hershey, PA: IGI Global. doi:10.4018/978-1-5225-0424-5.ch003

Mansouri, I., & Esmaeili, E. (2016). Nanotechnology Applications in the Construction Industry. In A. Khitab & W. Anwar (Eds.), *Advanced Research on Nanotechnology for Civil Engineering Applications* (pp. 111–140). Hershey, PA: IGI Global. doi:10.4018/978-1-5225-0344-6.ch004

Manzoor, A. (2016). MOOCs for Enhancing Engineering Education. In D. Fonseca & E. Redondo (Eds.), *Handbook of Research on Applied E-Learning in Engineering and Architecture Education* (pp. 204–223). Hershey, PA: IGI Global. doi:10.4018/978-1-4666-8803-2.ch010

Martin, A., Kalevaru, V. N., & Radnik, J. (2016). Palladium in Heterogeneous Oxidation Catalysis. In H. Al-Megren & T. Xiao (Eds.), *Petrochemical Catalyst Materials, Processes, and Emerging Technologies* (pp. 53–81). Hershey, PA: IGI Global. doi:10.4018/978-1-4666-9975-5.ch003

Melnyczuk, J. M., & Palchoudhury, S. (2016). Introduction to Bio-Inspired Hydrogel and Their Application: Hydrogels. In M. Bououdina (Ed.), *Emerging Research on Bioinspired Materials Engineering* (pp. 133–159). Hershey, PA: IGI Global. doi:10.4018/978-1-4666-9811-6.ch005

Mitra-Kirtley, S., Mullins, O. C., & Pomerantz, A. E. (2016). Sulfur and Nitrogen Chemical Speciation in Crude Oils and Related Carbonaceous Materials. In T. Saleh (Ed.), *Applying Nanotechnology to the Desulfurization Process in Petroleum Engineering* (pp. 53–83). Hershey, PA: IGI Global. doi:10.4018/978-1-4666-9545-0.ch002

Moalosi, R., Uziak, J., & Oladiran, M. T. (2016). Using Blended Learning Approach to Deliver Courses in An Engineering Programme. *International Journal of Quality Assurance in Engineering and Technology Education, 5*(1), 23–39. doi:10.4018/IJQAETE.2016010103

Mohammadzadeh, S., & Kim, Y. (2017). Nonlinear System Identification of Smart Buildings. In P. Samui, S. Chakraborty, & D. Kim (Eds.), *Modeling and Simulation Techniques in Structural Engineering* (pp. 328–347). Hershey, PA: IGI Global. doi:10.4018/978-1-5225-0588-4.ch011

Mohanty, I., & Bhattacherjee, D. (2016). Artificial Neural Network and Its Application in Steel Industry. In S. Datta & J. Davim (Eds.), *Computational Approaches to Materials Design: Theoretical and Practical Aspects* (pp. 267–300). Hershey, PA: IGI Global. doi:10.4018/978-1-5225-0290-6.ch010

Mohebkhah, A., & Sarhosis, V. (2016). Discrete Element Modeling of Masonry-Infilled Frames. In V. Sarhosis, K. Bagi, J. Lemos, & G. Milani (Eds.), *Computational Modeling of Masonry Structures Using the Discrete Element Method* (pp. 200–234). Hershey, PA: IGI Global. doi:10.4018/978-1-5225-0231-9.ch009

Molina, G. J., Aktaruzzaman, F., Soloiu, V., & Rahman, M. (2017). Design and Testing of a Jet-Impingement Instrument to Study Surface-Modification Effects by Nanofluids. *International Journal of Surface Engineering and Interdisciplinary Materials Science*, *5*(2), 43–61. doi:10.4018/IJSEIMS.2017070104

Montalvan-Sorrosa, D., de los Cobos-Vasconcelos, D., & Gonzalez-Sanchez, A. (2016). Nanotechnology Applied to the Biodesulfurization of Fossil Fuels and Spent Caustic Streams. In T. Saleh (Ed.), *Applying Nanotechnology to the Desulfurization Process in Petroleum Engineering* (pp. 378–389). Hershey, PA: IGI Global. doi:10.4018/978-1-4666-9545-0.ch012

Montillet, J., Yu, K., Bonenberg, L. K., & Roberts, G. W. (2016). Optimization Algorithms in Local and Global Positioning. In P. Vasant, G. Weber, & V. Dieu (Eds.), *Handbook of Research on Modern Optimization Algorithms and Applications in Engineering and Economics* (pp. 1–53). Hershey, PA: IGI Global. doi:10.4018/978-1-4666-9644-0.ch001

Moreira, F., & Ferreira, M. J. (2016). Teaching and Learning Requirements Engineering Based on Mobile Devices and Cloud: A Case Study. In D. Fonseca & E. Redondo (Eds.), *Handbook of Research on Applied E-Learning in Engineering and Architecture Education* (pp. 237–262). Hershey, PA: IGI Global. doi:10.4018/978-1-4666-8803-2.ch012

Mukherjee, A., Saeed, R. A., Dutta, S., & Naskar, M. K. (2017). Fault Tracking Framework for Software-Defined Networking (SDN). In C. Singhal & S. De (Eds.), *Resource Allocation in Next-Generation Broadband Wireless Access Networks* (pp. 247–272). Hershey, PA: IGI Global. doi:10.4018/978-1-5225-2023-8.ch011

Mukhopadhyay, A., Barman, T. K., & Sahoo, P. (2018). Electroless Nickel Coatings for High Temperature Applications. In K. Kumar & J. Davim (Eds.), *Composites and Advanced Materials for Industrial Applications* (pp. 297–331). Hershey, PA: IGI Global. doi:10.4018/978-1-5225-5216-1.ch013

Náprstek, J., & Fischer, C. (2017). Dynamic Stability and Post-Critical Processes of Slender Auto-Parametric Systems. In V. Plevris, G. Kremmyda, & Y. Fahjan (Eds.), *Performance-Based Seismic Design of Concrete Structures and Infrastructures* (pp. 128–171). Hershey, PA: IGI Global. doi:10.4018/978-1-5225-2089-4.ch006

Nautiyal, L., Shivach, P., & Ram, M. (2018). Optimal Designs by Means of Genetic Algorithms. In M. Ram & J. Davim (Eds.), *Soft Computing Techniques and Applications in Mechanical Engineering* (pp. 151–161). Hershey, PA: IGI Global. doi:10.4018/978-1-5225-3035-0.ch007

Nazir, R. (2017). Advanced Nanomaterials for Water Engineering and Treatment: Nano-Metal Oxides and Their Nanocomposites. In T. Saleh (Ed.), *Advanced Nanomaterials for Water Engineering, Treatment, and Hydraulics* (pp. 84–126). Hershey, PA: IGI Global. doi:10.4018/978-1-5225-2136-5.ch005

Nogueira, A. F., Ribeiro, J. C., Fernández de Vega, F., & Zenha-Rela, M. A. (2018). Evolutionary Approaches to Test Data Generation for Object-Oriented Software: Overview of Techniques and Tools. In M. Khosrow-Pour, D.B.A. (Ed.), Incorporating Nature-Inspired Paradigms in Computational Applications (pp. 162-194). Hershey, PA: IGI Global. doi:10.4018/978-1-5225-5020-4.ch006

Nunes, J. F., Moreira, P. M., & Tavares, J. M. (2016). Human Motion Analysis and Simulation Tools: A Survey. In F. Miranda & C. Abreu (Eds.), *Handbook of Research on Computational Simulation and Modeling in Engineering* (pp. 359–388). Hershey, PA: IGI Global. doi:10.4018/978-1-4666-8823-0.ch012

Ogunlaja, A. S., & Tshentu, Z. R. (2016). Molecularly Imprinted Polymer Nanofibers for Adsorptive Desulfurization. In T. Saleh (Ed.), *Applying Nanotechnology to the Desulfurization Process in Petroleum Engineering* (pp. 281–336). Hershey, PA: IGI Global. doi:10.4018/978-1-4666-9545-0.ch010

Ong, P., & Kohshelan, S. (2016). Performances of Adaptive Cuckoo Search Algorithm in Engineering Optimization. In P. Vasant, G. Weber, & V. Dieu (Eds.), *Handbook of Research on Modern Optimization Algorithms and Applications in Engineering and Economics* (pp. 676–699). Hershey, PA: IGI Global. doi:10.4018/978-1-4666-9644-0.ch026

Osho, M. B. (2018). Industrial Enzyme Technology: Potential Applications. In S. Bharati & P. Chaurasia (Eds.), *Research Advancements in Pharmaceutical, Nutritional, and Industrial Enzymology* (pp. 375–394). Hershey, PA: IGI Global. doi:10.4018/978-1-5225-5237-6.ch017

Padmaja, P., & Marutheswar, G. (2017). Certain Investigation on Secured Data Transmission in Wireless Sensor Networks. *International Journal of Mobile Computing and Multimedia Communications*, *8*(1), 48–61. doi:10.4018/IJMCMC.2017010104

Paixão, S. M., Silva, T. P., Arez, B. F., & Alves, L. (2016). Advances in the Reduction of the Costs Inherent to Fossil Fuels' Biodesulfurization towards Its Potential Industrial Application. In T. Saleh (Ed.), *Applying Nanotechnology to the Desulfurization Process in Petroleum Engineering* (pp. 390–425). Hershey, PA: IGI Global. doi:10.4018/978-1-4666-9545-0.ch013

Palmer, S., & Hall, W. (2017). An Evaluation of Group Work in First-Year Engineering Design Education. In R. Tucker (Ed.), *Collaboration and Student Engagement in Design Education* (pp. 145–168). Hershey, PA: IGI Global. doi:10.4018/978-1-5225-0726-0.ch007

Panneer, R. (2017). Effect of Composition of Fibers on Properties of Hybrid Composites. *International Journal of Manufacturing, Materials, and Mechanical Engineering*, *7*(4), 28–43. doi:10.4018/IJMMME.2017100103

Parker, J. (2016). Hubble's Expanding Universe: A Model for Quality in Technology Infused engineering and Technology Education. *International Journal of Quality Assurance in Engineering and Technology Education*, *5*(2), 16–29. doi:10.4018/IJQAETE.2016040102

Paul, S., & Roy, P. (2018). Optimal Design of Power System Stabilizer Using a Novel Evolutionary Algorithm. *International Journal of Energy Optimization and Engineering*, *7*(3), 24–46. doi:10.4018/IJEOE.2018070102

Pavaloiu, A. (2018). Artificial Intelligence Ethics in Biomedical-Engineering-Oriented Problems. In U. Kose, G. Guraksin, & O. Deperlioglu (Eds.), *Nature-Inspired Intelligent Techniques for Solving Biomedical Engineering Problems* (pp. 219–231). Hershey, PA: IGI Global. doi:10.4018/978-1-5225-4769-3.ch010

Peña, F. (2016). A Semi-Discrete Approach for the Numerical Simulation of Freestanding Blocks. In V. Sarhosis, K. Bagi, J. Lemos, & G. Milani (Eds.), *Computational Modeling of Masonry Structures Using the Discrete Element Method* (pp. 416–439). Hershey, PA: IGI Global. doi:10.4018/978-1-5225-0231-9.ch016

Penchovsky, R., & Traykovska, M. (2016). Synthetic Approaches to Biology: Engineering Gene Control Circuits, Synthesizing, and Editing Genomes. In M. Bououdina (Ed.), *Emerging Research on Bioinspired Materials Engineering* (pp. 323–351). Hershey, PA: IGI Global. doi:10.4018/978-1-4666-9811-6.ch012

Pieroni, A., & Iazeolla, G. (2016). Engineering QoS and Energy Saving in the Delivery of ICT Services. In P. Vasant & N. Voropai (Eds.), *Sustaining Power Resources through Energy Optimization and Engineering* (pp. 208–226). Hershey, PA: IGI Global. doi:10.4018/978-1-4666-9755-3.ch009

Pioro, I., Mahdi, M., & Popov, R. (2017). Application of Supercritical Pressures in Power Engineering. In L. Chen & Y. Iwamoto (Eds.), *Advanced Applications of Supercritical Fluids in Energy Systems* (pp. 404–457). Hershey, PA: IGI Global. doi:10.4018/978-1-5225-2047-4.ch013

Plaksina, T., & Gildin, E. (2017). Rigorous Integrated Evolutionary Workflow for Optimal Exploitation of Unconventional Gas Assets. *International Journal of Energy Optimization and Engineering*, *6*(1), 101–122. doi:10.4018/IJEOE.2017010106

Puppala, A. J., Bheemasetti, T. V., Zou, H., Yu, X., Pedarla, A., & Cai, G. (2016). Spatial Variability Analysis of Soil Properties using Geostatistics. In P. Samui (Ed.), *Handbook of Research on Advanced Computational Techniques for Simulation-Based Engineering* (pp. 195–226). Hershey, PA: IGI Global. doi:10.4018/978-1-4666-9479-8.ch008

Ramdani, N., & Azibi, M. (2018). Polymer Composite Materials for Microelectronics Packaging Applications: Composites for Microelectronics Packaging. In K. Kumar & J. Davim (Eds.), *Composites and Advanced Materials for Industrial Applications* (pp. 177–211). Hershey, PA: IGI Global. doi:10.4018/978-1-5225-5216-1.ch009

Ramesh, M., Garg, R., & Subrahmanyam, G. V. (2017). Investigation of Influence of Quenching and Annealing on the Plane Fracture Toughness and Brittle to Ductile Transition Temperature of the Zinc Coated Structural Steel Materials. *International Journal of Surface Engineering and Interdisciplinary Materials Science*, *5*(2), 33–42. doi:10.4018/IJSEIMS.2017070103

Razavi, A. M., & Ahmad, R. (2016). Agile Software Development Challenges in Implementation and Adoption: Focusing on Large and Distributed Settings – Past Experiences, Emergent Topics. In I. Ghani, D. Jawawi, S. Dorairaj, & A. Sidky (Eds.), *Emerging Innovations in Agile Software Development* (pp. 175–207). Hershey, PA: IGI Global. doi:10.4018/978-1-4666-9858-1.ch010

Reccia, E., Cecchi, A., & Milani, G. (2016). FEM/DEM Approach for the Analysis of Masonry Arch Bridges. In V. Sarhosis, K. Bagi, J. Lemos, & G. Milani (Eds.), *Computational Modeling of Masonry Structures Using the Discrete Element Method* (pp. 367–392). Hershey, PA: IGI Global. doi:10.4018/978-1-5225-0231-9.ch014

Ro, H. K., & McIntosh, K. (2016). Constructing Conducive Environment for Women of Color in Engineering Undergraduate Education. In U. Thomas & J. Drake (Eds.), *Critical Research on Sexism and Racism in STEM Fields* (pp. 23–48). Hershey, PA: IGI Global. doi:10.4018/978-1-5225-0174-9.ch002

Rodulfo-Baechler, S. M. (2016). Dual Role of Perovskite Hollow Fiber Membrane in the Methane Oxidation Reactions. In H. Al-Megren & T. Xiao (Eds.), *Petrochemical Catalyst Materials, Processes, and Emerging Technologies* (pp. 385–430). Hershey, PA: IGI Global. doi:10.4018/978-1-4666-9975-5.ch014

Rudolf, S., Biryuk, V. V., & Volov, V. (2018). Vortex Effect, Vortex Power: Technology of Vortex Power Engineering. In V. Kharchenko & P. Vasant (Eds.), *Handbook of Research on Renewable Energy and Electric Resources for Sustainable Rural Development* (pp. 500–533). Hershey, PA: IGI Global. doi:10.4018/978-1-5225-3867-7.ch021

Sah, A., Bhadula, S. J., Dumka, A., & Rawat, S. (2018). A Software Engineering Perspective for Development of Enterprise Applications. In A. Elçi (Ed.), *Handbook of Research on Contemporary Perspectives on Web-Based Systems* (pp. 1–23). Hershey, PA: IGI Global. doi:10.4018/978-1-5225-5384-7.ch001

Sahoo, P., & Roy, S. (2017). Tribological Behavior of Electroless Ni-P, Ni-P-W and Ni-P-Cu Coatings: A Comparison. *International Journal of Surface Engineering and Interdisciplinary Materials Science*, *5*(1), 1–15. doi:10.4018/IJSEIMS.2017010101

Sahoo, S. (2018). Laminated Composite Hypar Shells as Roofing Units: Static and Dynamic Behavior. In K. Kumar & J. Davim (Eds.), *Composites and Advanced Materials for Industrial Applications* (pp. 249–269). Hershey, PA: IGI Global. doi:10.4018/978-1-5225-5216-1.ch011

Sahu, H., & Hungyo, M. (2018). Introduction to SDN and NFV. In A. Dumka (Ed.), *Innovations in Software-Defined Networking and Network Functions Virtualization* (pp. 1–25). Hershey, PA: IGI Global. doi:10.4018/978-1-5225-3640-6.ch001

Saikia, P., Bharadwaj, S. K., & Miah, A. T. (2016). Peroxovanadates and Its Bio-Mimicking Relation with Vanadium Haloperoxidases. In M. Bououdina (Ed.), *Emerging Research on Bioinspired Materials Engineering* (pp. 197–219). Hershey, PA: IGI Global. doi:10.4018/978-1-4666-9811-6.ch007

Saladino, R., Botta, G., & Crucianelli, M. (2016). Advances in Nanotechnology Transition Metal Catalysts in Oxidative Desulfurization (ODS) Processes: Nanotechnology Applied to ODS Processing. In T. Saleh (Ed.), *Applying Nanotechnology to the Desulfurization Process in Petroleum Engineering* (pp. 180–215). Hershey, PA: IGI Global. doi:10.4018/978-1-4666-9545-0.ch006

Saleh, T. A., Danmaliki, G. I., & Shuaib, T. D. (2016). Nanocomposites and Hybrid Materials for Adsorptive Desulfurization. In T. Saleh (Ed.), *Applying Nanotechnology to the Desulfurization Process in Petroleum Engineering* (pp. 129–153). Hershey, PA: IGI Global. doi:10.4018/978-1-4666-9545-0.ch004

Saleh, T. A., Shuaib, T. D., Danmaliki, G. I., & Al-Daous, M. A. (2016). Carbon-Based Nanomaterials for Desulfurization: Classification, Preparation, and Evaluation. In T. Saleh (Ed.), *Applying Nanotechnology to the Desulfurization Process in Petroleum Engineering* (pp. 154–179). Hershey, PA: IGI Global. doi:10.4018/978-1-4666-9545-0.ch005

Salem, A. M., & Shmelova, T. (2018). Intelligent Expert Decision Support Systems: Methodologies, Applications, and Challenges. In T. Shmelova, Y. Sikirda, N. Rizun, A. Salem, & Y. Kovalyov (Eds.), *Socio-Technical Decision Support in Air Navigation Systems: Emerging Research and Opportunities* (pp. 215–242). Hershey, PA: IGI Global. doi:10.4018/978-1-5225-3108-1.ch007

Samal, M. (2017). FE Analysis and Experimental Investigation of Cracked and Un-Cracked Thin-Walled Tubular Components to Evaluate Mechanical and Fracture Properties. In P. Samui, S. Chakraborty, & D. Kim (Eds.), *Modeling and Simulation Techniques in Structural Engineering* (pp. 266–293). Hershey, PA: IGI Global. doi:10.4018/978-1-5225-0588-4.ch009

Samal, M., & Balakrishnan, K. (2017). Experiments on a Ring Tension Setup and FE Analysis to Evaluate Transverse Mechanical Properties of Tubular Components. In P. Samui, S. Chakraborty, & D. Kim (Eds.), *Modeling and Simulation Techniques in Structural Engineering* (pp. 91–115). Hershey, PA: IGI Global. doi:10.4018/978-1-5225-0588-4.ch004

Santhanakumar, M., Adalarasan, R., & Rajmohan, M. (2016). An Investigation in Abrasive Waterjet Cutting of Al6061/SiC/Al2O3 Composite Using Principal Component Based Response Surface Methodology. *International Journal of Manufacturing, Materials, and Mechanical Engineering*, *6*(4), 30–47. doi:10.4018/IJMMME.2016100103

Sareen, N., & Bhattacharya, S. (2016). Cleaner Energy Fuels: Hydrodesulfurization and Beyond. In T. Saleh (Ed.), *Applying Nanotechnology to the Desulfurization Process in Petroleum Engineering* (pp. 84–128). Hershey, PA: IGI Global. doi:10.4018/978-1-4666-9545-0.ch003

Sarhosis, V. (2016). Micro-Modeling Options for Masonry. In V. Sarhosis, K. Bagi, J. Lemos, & G. Milani (Eds.), *Computational Modeling of Masonry Structures Using the Discrete Element Method* (pp. 28–60). Hershey, PA: IGI Global. doi:10.4018/978-1-5225-0231-9.ch002

Sarhosis, V., Oliveira, D. V., & Lourenco, P. B. (2016). On the Mechanical Behavior of Masonry. In V. Sarhosis, K. Bagi, J. Lemos, & G. Milani (Eds.), *Computational Modeling of Masonry Structures Using the Discrete Element Method* (pp. 1–27). Hershey, PA: IGI Global. doi:10.4018/978-1-5225-0231-9.ch001

Satyam, N. (2016). Liquefaction Modelling of Granular Soils using Discrete Element Method. In P. Samui (Ed.), *Handbook of Research on Advanced Computational Techniques for Simulation-Based Engineering* (pp. 381–441). Hershey, PA: IGI Global. doi:10.4018/978-1-4666-9479-8.ch015

Sawant, S. (2018). Deep Learning and Biomedical Engineering. In U. Kose, G. Guraksin, & O. Deperlioglu (Eds.), *Nature-Inspired Intelligent Techniques for Solving Biomedical Engineering Problems* (pp. 283–296). Hershey, PA: IGI Global. doi:10.4018/978-1-5225-4769-3.ch014

Sezgin, H., & Berkalp, O. B. (2018). Textile-Reinforced Composites for the Automotive Industry. In K. Kumar & J. Davim (Eds.), *Composites and Advanced Materials for Industrial Applications* (pp. 129–156). Hershey, PA: IGI Global. doi:10.4018/978-1-5225-5216-1.ch007

Shah, M. Z., Gazder, U., Bhatti, M. S., & Hussain, M. (2018). Comparative Performance Evaluation of Effects of Modifier in Asphaltic Concrete Mix. *International Journal of Strategic Engineering*, *1*(2), 13–25. doi:10.4018/IJoSE.2018070102

Shah, V. S., Shah, H. R., & Samui, P. (2016). Application of Meta-Models (MPMR and ELM) for Determining OMC, MDD and Soaked CBR Value of Soil. In S. Bhattacharyya, P. Banerjee, D. Majumdar, & P. Dutta (Eds.), *Handbook of Research on Advanced Hybrid Intelligent Techniques and Applications* (pp. 454–482). Hershey, PA: IGI Global. doi:10.4018/978-1-4666-9474-3.ch015

Sharma, N., & Kumar, K. (2018). Fabrication of Porous NiTi Alloy Using Organic Binders. In K. Kumar & J. Davim (Eds.), *Composites and Advanced Materials for Industrial Applications* (pp. 38–62). Hershey, PA: IGI Global. doi:10.4018/978-1-5225-5216-1.ch003

Sharma, T. K. (2016). Application of Shuffled Frog Leaping Algorithm in Software Project Scheduling. In P. Saxena, D. Singh, & M. Pant (Eds.), *Problem Solving and Uncertainty Modeling through Optimization and Soft Computing Applications* (pp. 225–238). Hershey, PA: IGI Global. doi:10.4018/978-1-4666-9885-7.ch011

Shivach, P., Nautiyal, L., & Ram, M. (2018). Applying Multi-Objective Optimization Algorithms to Mechanical Engineering. In M. Ram & J. Davim (Eds.), *Soft Computing Techniques and Applications in Mechanical Engineering* (pp. 287–301). Hershey, PA: IGI Global. doi:10.4018/978-1-5225-3035-0.ch014

Shmelova, T. (2018). Stochastic Methods for Estimation and Problem Solving in Engineering: Stochastic Methods of Decision Making in Aviation. In S. Kadry (Ed.), *Stochastic Methods for Estimation and Problem Solving in Engineering* (pp. 139–160). Hershey, PA: IGI Global. doi:10.4018/978-1-5225-5045-7.ch006

Shukla, R., Anapagaddi, R., Singh, A. K., Allen, J. K., Panchal, J. H., & Mistree, F. (2016). Integrated Computational Materials Engineering for Determining the Set Points of Unit Operations for Production of a Steel Product Mix. In S. Datta & J. Davim (Eds.), *Computational Approaches to Materials Design: Theoretical and Practical Aspects* (pp. 163–191). Hershey, PA: IGI Global. doi:10.4018/978-1-5225-0290-6.ch006

Siero González, L. R., & Romo Vázquez, A. (2017). Didactic Sequences Teaching Mathematics for Engineers With Focus on Differential Equations. In M. Ramírez-Montoya (Ed.), *Handbook of Research on Driving STEM Learning With Educational Technologies* (pp. 129–151). Hershey, PA: IGI Global. doi:10.4018/978-1-5225-2026-9.ch007

Singh, R., & Dutta, S. (2018). Visible Light Active Nanocomposites for Photocatalytic Applications. In K. Kumar & J. Davim (Eds.), *Composites and Advanced Materials for Industrial Applications* (pp. 270–296). Hershey, PA: IGI Global. doi:10.4018/978-1-5225-5216-1.ch012

Singh, R., & Lou, H. H. (2016). Safety and Efficiency Enhancement in LNG Terminals. In H. Al-Megren & T. Xiao (Eds.), *Petrochemical Catalyst Materials, Processes, and Emerging Technologies* (pp. 164–176). Hershey, PA: IGI Global. doi:10.4018/978-1-4666-9975-5.ch007

Sözbilir, H., Özkaymak, Ç., Uzel, B., & Sümer, Ö. (2018). Criteria for Surface Rupture Microzonation of Active Faults for Earthquake Hazards in Urban Areas. In N. Ceryan (Ed.), *Handbook of Research on Trends and Digital Advances in Engineering Geology* (pp. 187–230). Hershey, PA: IGI Global. doi:10.4018/978-1-5225-2709-1.ch005

Stanciu, I. (2018). Stochastic Methods in Microsystems Engineering. In S. Kadry (Ed.), *Stochastic Methods for Estimation and Problem Solving in Engineering* (pp. 161–176). Hershey, PA: IGI Global. doi:10.4018/978-1-5225-5045-7.ch007

Strebkov, D., Nekrasov, A., Trubnikov, V., & Nekrasov, A. (2018). Single-Wire Resonant Electric Power Systems for Renewable-Based Electric Grid. In V. Kharchenko & P. Vasant (Eds.), *Handbook of Research on Renewable Energy and Electric Resources for Sustainable Rural Development* (pp. 449–474). Hershey, PA: IGI Global. doi:10.4018/978-1-5225-3867-7.ch019

Subburaman, D., Jagan, J., Dalkiliç, Y., & Samui, P. (2016). Reliability Analysis of Slope Using MPMR, GRNN and GPR. In F. Miranda & C. Abreu (Eds.), *Handbook of Research on Computational Simulation and Modeling in Engineering* (pp. 208–224). Hershey, PA: IGI Global. doi:10.4018/978-1-4666-8823-0.ch007

Sun, J., Wan, S., Lin, J., & Wang, Y. (2016). Advances in Catalytic Conversion of Syngas to Ethanol and Higher Alcohols. In H. Al-Megren & T. Xiao (Eds.), *Petrochemical Catalyst Materials, Processes, and Emerging Technologies* (pp. 177–215). Hershey, PA: IGI Global. doi:10.4018/978-1-4666-9975-5.ch008

Tüdeş, Ş., Kumlu, K. B., & Ceryan, S. (2018). Integration Between Urban Planning and Natural Hazards For Resilient City. In N. Ceryan (Ed.), *Handbook of Research on Trends and Digital Advances in Engineering Geology* (pp. 591–630). Hershey, PA: IGI Global. doi:10.4018/978-1-5225-2709-1.ch017

Tyukhov, I., Rezk, H., & Vasant, P. (2016). Modern Optimization Algorithms and Applications in Solar Photovoltaic Engineering. In P. Vasant & N. Voropai (Eds.), *Sustaining Power Resources through Energy Optimization and Engineering* (pp. 390–445). Hershey, PA: IGI Global. doi:10.4018/978-1-4666-9755-3.ch016

Ulamis, K. (2018). Soil Liquefaction Assessment by Anisotropic Cyclic Triaxial Test. In N. Ceryan (Ed.), *Handbook of Research on Trends and Digital Advances in Engineering Geology* (pp. 631–664). Hershey, PA: IGI Global. doi:10.4018/978-1-5225-2709-1.ch018

Umar, M. A., Tenuche, S. S., Yusuf, S. A., Abdulsalami, A. O., & Kufena, A. M. (2016). Usability Engineering in Agile Software Development Processes. In I. Ghani, D. Jawawi, S. Dorairaj, & A. Sidky (Eds.), *Emerging Innovations in Agile Software Development* (pp. 208–221). Hershey, PA: IGI Global. doi:10.4018/978-1-4666-9858-1.ch011

Üzüm, O., & Çakır, Ö. A. (2016). A Bio-Inspired Phenomena in Cementitious Materials: Self-Healing. In M. Bououdina (Ed.), *Emerging Research on Bioinspired Materials Engineering* (pp. 220–246). Hershey, PA: IGI Global. doi:10.4018/978-1-4666-9811-6.ch008

Valente, M., & Milani, G. (2017). Seismic Assessment and Retrofitting of an Under-Designed RC Frame Through a Displacement-Based Approach. In V. Plevris, G. Kremmyda, & Y. Fahjan (Eds.), *Performance-Based Seismic Design of Concrete Structures and Infrastructures* (pp. 36–58). Hershey, PA: IGI Global. doi:10.4018/978-1-5225-2089-4.ch002

Vasant, P. (2018). A General Medical Diagnosis System Formed by Artificial Neural Networks and Swarm Intelligence Techniques. In U. Kose, G. Guraksin, & O. Deperlioglu (Eds.), *Nature-Inspired Intelligent Techniques for Solving Biomedical Engineering Problems* (pp. 130–145). Hershey, PA: IGI Global. doi:10.4018/978-1-5225-4769-3.ch006

Vergara, D., Lorenzo, M., & Rubio, M. (2016). On the Use of Virtual Environments in Engineering Education. *International Journal of Quality Assurance in Engineering and Technology Education*, *5*(2), 30–41. doi:10.4018/IJQAETE.2016040103

Verrollot, J., Tolonen, A., Harkonen, J., & Haapasalo, H. J. (2018). Challenges and Enablers for Rapid Product Development. *International Journal of Applied Industrial Engineering*, *5*(1), 25–49. doi:10.4018/IJAIE.2018010102

Wagner, C., & Ryan, C. (2016). Physical and Digital Integration Strategies of Electronic Device Supply Chains and Their Applicability to ETO Supply Chains. In R. Addo-Tenkorang, J. Kantola, P. Helo, & A. Shamsuzzoha (Eds.), *Supply Chain Strategies and the Engineer-to-Order Approach* (pp. 224–245). Hershey, PA: IGI Global. doi:10.4018/978-1-5225-0021-6.ch011

Wang, Z., Wu, P., Lan, L., & Ji, S. (2016). Preparation, Characterization and Desulfurization of the Supported Nickel Phosphide Catalysts. In H. Al-Megren & T. Xiao (Eds.), *Petrochemical Catalyst Materials, Processes, and Emerging Technologies* (pp. 431–458). Hershey, PA: IGI Global. doi:10.4018/978-1-4666-9975-5.ch015

Yardimci, A. G., & Karpuz, C. (2018). Fuzzy Rock Mass Rating: Soft-Computing-Aided Preliminary Stability Analysis of Weak Rock Slopes. In N. Ceryan (Ed.), *Handbook of Research on Trends and Digital Advances in Engineering Geology* (pp. 97–131). Hershey, PA: IGI Global. doi:10.4018/978-1-5225-2709-1.ch003

Zhang, L., Ding, S., Sun, S., Han, B., Yu, X., & Ou, J. (2016). Nano-Scale Behavior and Nano-Modification of Cement and Concrete Materials. In A. Khitab & W. Anwar (Eds.), *Advanced Research on Nanotechnology for Civil Engineering Applications* (pp. 28–79). Hershey, PA: IGI Global. doi:10.4018/978-1-5225-0344-6.ch002

Zindani, D., & Kumar, K. (2018). Industrial Applications of Polymer Composite Materials. In K. Kumar & J. Davim (Eds.), *Composites and Advanced Materials for Industrial Applications* (pp. 1–15). Hershey, PA: IGI Global. doi:10.4018/978-1-5225-5216-1.ch001

Zindani, D., Maity, S. R., & Bhowmik, S. (2018). A Decision-Making Approach for Material Selection of Polymeric Composite Bumper Beam. In K. Kumar & J. Davim (Eds.), *Composites and Advanced Materials for Industrial Applications* (pp. 112–128). Hershey, PA: IGI Global. doi:10.4018/978-1-5225-5216-1.ch006

About the Contributors

Gabor Kecskemeti (M.Sc., University of Miskolc, 2004; Ph.D., University of Westminster, 2011) is a Lecturer within the Department of Computer Science at Liverpool John Moores University, UK. Between 2006-2016, he worked as a research fellow at the Laboratory of Parallel and Distributed Systems (LPDS) of MTA SZTAKI. He also works for the computer science doctoral school of the University of Miskolc, Hungary. In, 2013, he was a postdoctoral researcher at the University of Innsbruck, Austria. He was involved in several successful Grid and SOA research projects (e.g., ePerSpace, EDGeS, S-Cube) funded by the EU. In 2015 and early 2016, he was steering committee member and work package leader in the ENTICE project (focusing on cloud computing) which was financed by the EU's Horizon2020 framework programme. He was member/chair of the program committees of over 40 European conferences/workshops. He was guest editor for the Journal of Grid Computing for a special issue on Cloud federations and he also edited the book titled "Developing Interoperable and Federated Cloud Architecture". He has published over 70 scientific papers (incl. 18 journal articles and 4 edited volumes) about cloud and grid computing, particularly from the fields of simulating distributed systems and virtual appliance delivery in IaaS clouds.

* * *

Laura Belli is a Postdoctoral Research Associate at the Internet of Things (IoT) Lab, at the Department of Engineering and Architecture of the University of Parma, Italy. She received her Dr. Ing. (Laurea) degree in Computer Science from the University of Parma, Italy, in 2011. In 2016, she received her Ph.D. in Information Technologies at the Department of Information Engineering of the same university. Her research interests are Internet of Things, Pervasive Computing, Big Stream, Database Integration, Mobile Computing.

Luca Davoli is a Postdoctoral Research Associate at the Internet of Things (IoT) Lab, at the Department of Engineering and Architecture of the University of Parma, Italy. He received his Dr. Ing. (Laurea) degree in Computer Science from the University of Parma, Italy, in 2013. In 2017, he received his Ph.D. in Information Technologies at the Department of Information Engineering of the same university. His research interests are Internet of Things, Power Line Communications, Pervasive Computing, Big Stream, Mobile Computing and Software-Defined Networking.

Manoj Devare received BSc & MSc degree from North Maharashtra University and PhD in Computer Science from Bharati Vidyapeeth University, India. He is working as Associate Professor at Amity Institute of Information Technology, Amity University Mumbai. He has 14 years of teaching and research experience in Computer Science. His PhD thesis was based on the Congestion Controlling in Homogeneous and Heterogeneous Computer Networks. Dr. Manoj won the "Best Paper Award", in ICSCI 2008. He has served as Post Doctorate Fellow at Centre of Excellence on HPC, Uni. of Calabria, Italy under young researcher scheme. He has been developed Desktop Cloud system. His research deals with IoT, Cloud, Machine Learning and innovative applications of those technologies to scientific problems. He has 02 Patents pending; he edited 05 book chapters, 09 Int. Journal papers, 15 conference Papers. He has delivered 08 national and international keynote speeches. He is connected with review process of reputed international journal papers, edited chapters from the reputed journals like Elsevier's FGCS, Springer's review system, Symbiosis International Journal.

Gianluigi Ferrari (http://www.tlc.unipr.it/ferrari) received his "Laurea" and PhD degrees from the University of Parma, Italy, in 1998 and 2002, respectively. Since 2002, he has been with the University Parma, where he currently is an Associate Professor of Telecommunications (with National Scientific Qualification to the Role of Full Professor since 2013). He was a visiting researcher at USC (Los Angeles, CA, USA, 2000-2001), CMU (Pittsburgh, PA, USA, 2002-2004), KMITL (Bangkok, Thailand, 2007), and ULB (Brussels, Belgium, 2010). Since 2006, he has been the Coordinator of the Internet of Things (IoT) Lab (http://iotlab.unipr.it/) in the Department of Engineering and Architecture. In 2015, he has been nominated, by the Italian Ministry of Defense, as the only Italian representative (Technical Team Member) in the NATO Research Task Group (RTG) HFM-260 "Enhancing Warfighter Effectiveness with Wearable Bio Sensors and Physiologicol Models," in the period 2015-2018. As of September 2018, he has (published or in press) 116 papers in international journals, 29 book chapters, 151 papers international conference proceedings, and 14 patents. He is coauthor of 7 books, including "Ad Hoc Wireless Networks: A Communication-Theoretic Perspective" (Wiley: 2006-technical best seller). He single-edited the book "Sensor Networks: where Theory Meets Practice" (Springer: 2010). He is also co-author of the upcoming book "Internet of Things: Architectures, Protocols and Standards" (Wiley: 2018). Prof. Ferrari's research interest revolve around three main areas: advanced communication and networking; signal processing; IoT and smart systems. His research activity has been funded by international/national public and private bodies, and the amount of recovered research funding is in excess of 2.8 MEuro. Prof. Ferrari received best paper/technical awards at international conferences. He is currently member of the Editorial boards of a few international journals. He is an IEEE Senior Member. Since 2016, he is Co-founder, President and Chief Executive Officer of things2i s.r.l. (http://www.things2i.com/), a spin-off company of the University of Parma dedicated to Internet of Things and Smart Systems.

Naveen Chandra Gowda holds a B.E and M. Tech degree in Computer Science and Engineering. He has around 8 years of teaching experience, teaching various subjects like Data structures, Design and Analysis of Algorithms, System Software, Operating System, Computer Networks, Data Base Management System, Computer Graphics & Visualization, AdHoc Networks, Computer Network Security, etc. His area of research Cloud Security. He has published many papers in National and International journals and presented in national conferences. He is Life Member of ISTE, Member of CSI and ACM. He is currently working as Assistant Professor in School of Computing and Information Technology, REVA University, Bengaluru-64.

Sunilkumar S. Manvi received his B. E. Degree from Karnataka University, M. E. degree in Electronics from the University of Visweshwariah College of Engineering, Bangalore and Ph. D. degree in Electrical Communication Engineering, Indian Institute of Science, Bangalore, India. He has vast experience of more than 30 years in teaching in Electronics / Computer Science and Engineering. His research interests are: Software Agent based Network Management, Wireless Networks, Multimedia Networking, Underwater Networks, Wireless Network Security, Grid and Cloud computing, E-commerce, and Mobile computing. He has published around 160 papers in national and international conferences, 115 papers in national and international journals, and 15 publications/books/books.chapters. He is Fellow IETE (FIETE, India), Fellow IE (FIE, India), and senior member of IEEE(SMIEEE,USA). He received best research publication award from VGST Karnataka in 2014. He is a reviewer and programme committee member for many journals (published by

IEEE, Springer, Elsevier, etc) and international conferences, respectively. He has executed several research projects sponsored by government funding agencies. Recently he has been awarded with "Sathish Dhawan Young Engineers State Award" for Outstanding contribution in the field of Engineering Sciences. He is currently working as Dean, Faculty of Engineering and Technology, Director for School of Computing and Information Technology, REVA University, Bengluru-64.

Monica Mordonini is a researcher at the Department of Engineering and Architecture of the University of Parma. She received a Laurea degree in Electronics Engineering in 1994 (defending a thesis on the "Compression of images using massively parallel algorithms") and a Ph.D. in Information Technologies in 1998 (defending a thesis on the "Navigation of autonomous vehicles in partially known environments"), both from the University of Parma. Her research was conducted mainly in the field of Artificial Intelligence and in particular, she has studied techniques of analysis and processing of signals and images, with particular emphasis on computational aspects related to these topics and their applications in the field of the classification of human activity and the assistive domotics. More recently, the research has focused on issues of information and knowledge extraction from complex systems, applications of semantic web, analysis of social networks, sentiment analysis and opinion mining.

Shefali Naik is an Assistant Professor at School of Computer Studies, Ahmedabad University since 2000. She is teaching subjects related to Databases. Her area of research is distributed database transactions. Her book "Concepts of Database Management System" is published by Pearson Education. She has presented and published few papers in national and international conferences and journals. She did her PhD in Computer Science from Sardar Patel University.

Hoai Son Nguyen received the B.Eng., B.Eng. and Dr. Eng. degrees from the University of Tokyo, Japan, in 2001, 2003, and 2006 respectively. He is currently a lecturer of the Faculty of Information Technology at VNU-University of Engineering and Technology. His research interests are in the area of mobile wireless networks, overlay networks and ubiquitous computing and Internet of Things.

Bogdan Nicolae is a Computer Scientist at Argonne National Laboratory, USA. In the past, he held appointments at Huawei Research Germany and IBM Research Ireland. He specializes in scalable storage, data management and fault tolerance for large scale distributed systems, with a focus on high performance architectures cloud computing. He holds a PhD from University of Rennes 1, France and a Dipl. Eng. degree from Politehnica University Bucharest, Romania. He is interested by and authored numerous papers in the areas of scalable I/O, storage elasticity and virtualization, data and metadata decentralization and availability, multi-versioning, data-intensive and big data analytics, checkpoint-restart, live migration.

Kiran Pattanaik received Ph.D. in Engineering with Computer Science as major from Birla Institute of Technology, Mesra, Ranchi, India in the year 2010. Currently, he is working as Associate Professor at ABV-Indian Institute of Information Technology and Management Gwalior, MP, India. His research interests are Distributed Systems, Grid Computing, Mobile Computing, Multi-Agent Systems and Wireless Sensor Networks. He is a Senior Member of IEEE and reviewer for various key journals on the fields of distributed computing and networks.

Agostino Poggi is full professor of Computer Engineering at the Department of Engineering and Architecture of the University of Parma. His research focuses on agent, Web and object-oriented technologies and their use to develop distributed and complex systems. He is author of more than two hundreds of technical papers in international scientific journals, books and refereed conference proceedings, and his scientific contribution has been recognized through the "System Research Foundation Outstanding Scholarly Contribution Award" in 1988 and through the "Innovation System Award" in 2001. He is currently editor of the Software Practice & Experience Journal and in the editorial board of the following scientific journals: International Journal of Agent-Oriented Software Engineering, International Journal on Advances in Intelligent Systems, International Journal of Hybrid Intelligent Systems and International Journal of Multiagent and Grid Systems.

Mamata Rath, M.Tech, Ph.D (Comp.Sc), has twelve years of experience in teaching as well as in research and her research interests include Mobile Adhoc Networks, Internet of Things, Ubiquitous Computing, VANET, and Computer Security.

Pierre Riteau is a Senior Technical Lead at StackHPC. He is deeply involved in the OpenStack Blazar project, acting as Project Team Lead for the Stein and Train releases. Previously at University of Chicago, he was DevOps Lead of the Chameleon testbed, a configurable experimental environment for large-scale cloud research. Pierre Riteau holds a PhD in Computer Science from the University of Rennes 1, France.

Mahatim Singh received Master of Technology degree in Computer Science & Engineering from National Institute of Technology Jamshedpur, India in 2017. Currently, he is pursuing Doctor of Philosophy from the Department of Computer Science of Institute of Science, Banaras Hindu University Varanasi, India. He has research interest in Distributed systems, Mobile computing, Computer Vision, and Machine Learning.

Anshul Verma received Master of Technology and Ph.D., both degrees in Computer Science & Engineering from ABV-Indian Institute of Information Technology and Management Gwalior, India in 2011 and 2016 respectively. He has done Post-doctorate from Indian Institute of Technology Kharagpur, India in 2017. Currently, he is serving as Assistant Professor in Department of Computer Science of Institute of Science, Banaras Hindu University Varanasi, India. He has research interest in Mobile Ad-hoc networks, Distributed systems, Formal methods, Mobile computing, and Communication based transportation systems.

Zhuo Zhen is a Cloud Computing Software Developer at University of Chicago, where she develops and operates the national Chameleon testbed (www.chameleon-cloud.org) which supports research and innovation in cloud computing providing insight into tomorrow's technology. Dr. Zhen also collaborates with scientific application groups to build and evaluate innovative solutions.

Index

H

I

M

N

P

R

S

T

V

Printed in the United States
By Bookmasters